Exile and Return

SOCIETY FOR THE PROMOTION OF TRAVEL IN THE HOLY LAND

FOR, LO, THE WINTER IS PAST, THE RAIN IS OVER AND GONE; THE FLOWERS APPEAR ON THE EARTH; THE TIME OF THE SINGING OF BIRDS IS COME, AND THE VOICE OF THE TURTLE IS HEARD IN OUR LAND.

COME TO PALESTINE

Exile and Return

Predicaments of Palestinians and Jews

Edited by Ann M. Lesch and Ian S. Lustick

PENN

University of Pennsylvania Press

Philadelphia

Copyright © 2005 University of Pennsylvania Press
All rights reserved
Printed in the United States of America on acid-free paper

10 9 8 7 6 5 4 3 2 1

Published by
University of Pennsylvania Press
Philadelphia, Pennsylvania 19104–4112

Library of Congress Cataloging-in-Publication Data

Exile and return : predicaments of Palestinians and Jews / edited by Ann M. Lesch and Ian
S. Lustick.
    p. cm.
    Papers from two meetings at Asch Center, University of Pennsylvania, October 2002,
and at both Asch Center and Villanova University, June 2003.
    Includes bibliographical references and index.
    ISBN 0-8122-3874-5 (cloth : alk. paper)
    1. Arab-Israeli conflict—Refugees—Congresses.   2. Repatriation—Palestine—Congresses.
3. Exile (Punishment)—Israel—Congresses.   4. Refugees, Palestinian Arab—Legal status,
laws, etc.—Congresses.   5. Zionism—Congresses.   6. Palestine—Emigration and
immigration—Congresses.   I. Lesch, Ann Mosely.   II. Lustick, Ian, 1949–

DS119.6.E95   2005
956.9405'4'086914—dc22   2004063822

Frontispiece: Poster, circa 1927–29, by Zeev Raban of the Bezalel School in Jerusalem to
promote tourism in Palestine.

Contents

Part IV. Property Issues for Arab and Jewish Migrants and Refugees

Part V. The Refugee Issue in Context

Preface

The idea for this volume came when Ian S. Lustick initiated a conversation with Ann M. Lesch in the spring of 2001. Although the failure of the Camp David summit, followed by the violence of the al-Aqsa intifada, had dashed hopes for any quick progress toward an Israeli-Palestinian peace agreement, we agreed on two things: that the two sides were actually very close to an agreement on the basis of two states separated by a boundary close to the Green Line, and that the problem of the Palestinian refugees would constitute the most important obstacle to the consummation of a peace agreement when serious negotiations eventually resumed. In light of these judgments, we decided that, just as imaginative scholarly research had made important contributions to the development and diffusion of the principle of the two-state solution, the necessity for evacuation of settlements, and the possible shape of a compromise on Jerusalem, so too could well-informed and imaginative scholarship contribute to building a new intellectual infrastructure for approaching the refugee question. Rather than seeking to create a blueprint to resolve the question of Palestinian return, we sought to reexamine the basic concept of return in the context of a discussion—and reconceptualization—of exile, rights, and return, as those ideas arose within the Jewish-Zionist discourse over the return of Jews to the Land of Israel after centuries of life in the diaspora and within the Palestinian Arab discourse over the return of Palestinian refugees and their descendants to the Palestine from which they have largely been excluded since 1948. We sought to examine these concepts from multiple Jewish/Israeli and Palestinian perspectives, drawing on decades of new archival research on the origins and dynamics of the Palestinian refugee problem and on the development of competing understandings within Israel of Zionist imperatives. We charged the participants in this project not to accept any assumptions about the process or to embrace the idea of parallels between the experiences of the two peoples. The only requirement was that participants accept the need for new thinking and for doing so in a collective context that would yet permit a wide diversity of views.

Our efforts led to a grant from the US Institute of Peace, managed by the Solomon Asch Center for Study of Ethnopolitical Conflict. With this support we were able to bring together a small, carefully selected group of scholars to consider these issues in depth. The group met twice, initially at the Asch Center on the University of Pennsylvania campus in October 2002 and then in June 2003 at both the Asch Center and Villanova University. We are very grateful to the Asch Center in particular for hosting and help-ing to organize these conferences, for providing their facilities, and for additional financial support necessary to complete the project. A special word of thanks is due to Roy J. Eidelson, Executive Director of the Center, and to his staffers, Diane Kagoyire and Sahar Ghazanfar, who devoted many hours to this project. A word of appreciation is also due to the Middle East Center at the University of Pennsylvania, and its Director, Robert Vitalis, for providing assistance necessary to produce the index for this vol-ume. Erica Ginsburg, Ellie Goldberg, and Peter Agree at the University of Pennsylvania Press were effective and enthusiastic collaborators whose careful attention to detail and matters of schedule helped bring this vol-ume to timely completion. Sarah F. Salwen also made important contribu-tions to the editorial process. We would also like to thank Stephan Stohler, Hilary Lustick, and Gus Hartman for their administrative and research assistance, as well as Steven Riskin and Judy Barsalou at the United States Institute of Peace for their steady support and guidance. Finally we wish to thank all the scholars who participated, as contributors or discussants, in the two conferences. In addition to the authors of the chapters in this volume, participants included Beshara Doumani of the University of Cali-fornia, Berkeley, Adina Friedman of George Mason University, and Susan Slyomovics of the Massachusetts Institute of Technology. We greatly appre-ciate the openness, insights, and enthusiasm displayed by all participants during extended discussions of topics as sensitive as they are important.

We hope this volume will encourage others to think deeply, compassion-ately, and imaginatively about approaches to the refugee problem that can transcend sterile discussions of legal and logistical technicalities and offer alternatives to concepts and slogans more significant for their ideological than for their practical or political meaning.

Introduction

Chapter 1
The Failure of Oslo and the Abiding Question of the Refugees

Ian S. Lustick and Ann M. Lesch

The Oslo process failed to bring peace between Israelis and Palestinians. That much is clear. The bloody years that ensued following the collapse of the Camp David II summit in the summer of 2000 have reminded everyone of what the costs of failure are. A vigorous debate has developed over exactly why that effort failed, and there seems to be plenty of blame to go around: stinginess, presumptiveness, and ineptitude on the Israeli side; lack of imagination and inflexibility on the Palestinian side; and poor planning and execution on the American side.[1] But the dramatic failure of the summit also demonstrated just how close it is possible to get to a workable compromise between the demands of the Israeli state and Palestinian nationalism. Most observers agree that follow-up discussions between Israelis and Palestinians, culminating in the Taba talks of December and January, brought the two sides excruciatingly close to agreement on the terms of a treaty. Indeed, the Geneva initiative, signed in 2003 by Labor and Meretz leaders and ranking Palestinian officials, closely follows the Taba ideas and the "Clinton parameters" of January 2001 and stands as a remarkable testimony to the continued possibility of a negotiated solution.

It is significant to note that both at Taba and in the Geneva negotiations the most sensitive issues were those pertaining to the problem of the Palestinian refugees and issues linked to that problem. The problem has cast its shadow over all efforts to imagine or implement a comprehensive settlement to the Israeli-Palestinian conflict, and over the years much has been written on the subject. Scholars have documented and evaluated the extent of the problem and discussed efforts to ameliorate the plight of the refugees.[2] Legal scholars have asked about the implications of international law for its analysis and treatment.[3] Analysts of Arab-Israeli political and military relations have investigated the role of the refugees and the refugee issue in subsequent conflicts.[4] Others have focused on the suffering of refugees and their yearning to return;[5] and the predicament of refugees who remained inside the borders of Israel but without rights to return to their villages.[6] Sociological and political studies of the political behavior and attitudes of refugee populations in various Arab countries are also available.[7] In addition, considerable efforts have been devoted to imagining what specific kinds of schemes for the solution to the problem might be feasible.[8] Most recently, real breakthroughs have been made via surveys of Palestinian refugee attitudes;[9] and careful archival assessments of lost property and confiscation issues.[10] This research has helped establish the resiliency of Palestinian refugee aspirations and the scale and complexity of the compensation issue, while highlighting often-ignored intricacies, variation, and nuances in their demands.

However, with some exceptions,[11] there is a striking absence of scholarly work that poses the question of the past and future of Palestinian "exiles" in ways that are consistent with the perceived vital interests and essential categories of thought of Palestinian Arabs and Israeli Jews. Accordingly, there is a high scholarly and public policy priority on the development of formulas, categories, and approaches to questions pertaining to refugee return that can be used by Palestinian as well as Israeli leaders to convince their peoples that the agreement being sought will destroy neither the state that Israeli Jews have built nor the deep yearnings for vindication or return that lie at the emotional core of the Palestinian struggle. The project that produced this volume is an attempt to lay the intellectual infrastructure for such efforts. We have sought new ways of framing and conceptualizing the key issues—morally and politically—so as to make the many detailed and clever options for calibrating the implementation of refugee return relevant to those who would seek to sign a comprehensive political agreement.

Over the last two decades, crucial resources for moving forward in this area have been produced as a result of the indefatigable efforts of scholars afforded access to Israeli state and army archives. The result of this work, along with the appearance of uncensored memoirs by leading participants in the 1948 war, such as the late Prime Minister Yitzhak Rabin,[12] has been a much more sophisticated and detailed understanding of the events of that year. Complementing and mostly validating findings of a few earlier researchers,[13] these scholars document the predominant role played by violence, force, and intimidation on the part of Jewish forces in the transformation of more than 700,000 Palestinian Arabs into Palestinian Arab refugees.[14] Segev and Morris also emphasize the subsequent and systematic enforcement of Israel's immediate decision to bar the return of refugees to their homes.[15]

In very direct ways, this research made itself felt at Camp David and in other Israeli-Palestinian negotiations. On the Palestinian side, it may have helped reinforce the memories of refugees and the commitments of their descendants to the principle of return, narrowing the maneuverability available to Palestinian leaders seeking a "practical" two-state solution focused on the West Bank and Gaza. On the Israeli side, it meant that Palestinian positions on this issue could not convincingly be rebuffed by reference to the claims, now widely acknowledged to be without foundation, that in 1948 Israel's primary policy was to try to persuade Arabs to stay, that force was not a significant factor in the production of the mass exodus, and that Arab leaders bore the main responsibility for the tragedy as a result of radio broadcasts in which they, supposedly, ordered the Palestinians to flee.

The result of this increase in the quality of generally available historical knowledge has contributed toward moving discussion of the refugee question into new areas. At Taba and at Geneva, the sides went beyond arguing about legal issues or the number of refugees who should or could return and under what circumstances. They also discussed questions of culpability, public acceptance of moral responsibility, and the possibility that truth or apology could play a role that might enable an agreement less just than might otherwise be the case. In addition to negotiating over specific arrangements for limited implementation of Palestinian refugee return, the sides explicitly argued about alternative wordings for the public statement that Israel would make characterizing the origins of the refugee problem and either its regret, its pain, its responsibility (shared or otherwise), or its apology.[16]

It is often suggested that any consideration of the Palestinian Arab refugee question must be accompanied (and "balanced") by consideration of the fate of Jews who left Arab countries, often as a result of persecution, following the creation of the State of Israel. We do consider the fate of Jews in Arab countries and the related status of these Israeli Mizrahim (Easterners, as they generally now prefer to be named) an important issue. But instead of relying on this comparison as a means of establishing a principle of equivalence, symmetry, or balance (an objective we reject if pursued for its own sake), we offer a fresh perspective—one that we believe has a much better chance of serving as a basis for reciprocal appreciation of the imperatives and outlooks of the two sides.

Rights of Return and the Mutuality of Terror

It is not an exaggeration to describe Jewish Israelis as terrified at the prospect of a return of Palestinian refugees to Israel. What for Palestinians is an elementally just request, that they be allowed to return to homes and communities from which they have been excluded for over fifty-five years, is a nightmare for Israeli Jews. The Israeli imagination of Palestinian return is dominated by images of an uncontrolled and open-ended process leading to the demographic, cultural, and political submergence of Israel as a

Jewish state and, ultimately, the disappearance of the Land of Israel as a place where a Jewish society and polity could thrive.

It is one of the innumerable ironies of the Israeli-Palestinian conflict that the terror of Israeli Jews at the effect that a mass immigration of self-styled returnees would have on their country is strikingly similar to the fear that animated Palestinian opposition to the Zionist movement's project in the late nineteenth and early twentieth century. Palestinian Arabs opposed the central demand of Zionism, for unlimited immigration of Jews, because they imagined that such a mass immigration of self-styled returnees would transform the country unacceptably, making it virtually uninhabitable as a space for the development of an independent Palestinian society and polity. And just as most Zionist representatives in the pre-1948 period rejected the dire warnings of Palestinian leaders as self-serving and hysterical portrayals of a future that would instead be marked by coexistence between Jews and Arabs, so too do Palestinians now reject as hysterical and self-serving the expressed fears of Israelis that the return of Palestinian refugees would destroy Israel or end opportunities for Jews to live happily in the country.

In the pre-1948 period, Palestinians heard Zionist reassurances about the prosperity they would enjoy as a result of Jewish immigration and statehood as absurd or disingenuous. Now Israeli Jews hear Palestinian reassurances—about the manageable impact of implementing the right of Palestinian Arab return—in exactly the same way. In short, the historical experiences of Israeli Jews and Palestinian Arabs provide each people with emotional, psychological, and analytic access to each other's most hopeful and most fearful states of mind. By thinking carefully about itself, each side can understand the other better. For each side knows exactly what it is like to see one's own return as unthreatening and the other's return as terrifyingly threatening. For example, Israelis need look no further than their own fears about the implications of Palestinian return to lands inside Israel to appreciate the intensity of the fears and resentments aroused among Palestinians at what Israeli settlers in the West Bank and Gaza have seen as their return to those portions of the ancient Jewish homeland.

For the project that resulted in the chapters of this volume, it is important to note that drawing analogies between the two peoples' experience does not serve as a technique for discovering or proving moral or political equivalency or for erasing or obscuring the enormous differences in the experiences, motivations, and programs of action of the two peoples. But as the issue of the Palestinian refugees emerged in the wake of the failure at Camp David in 2000 as perhaps the single most difficult issue preventing a peace agreement between the two sides, it was clear that new thinking on the issue was desperately required—thinking that would go beyond detailed, important, but ultimately technical formulas for lotteries and fast-versus slow-track applications for immigration permits. In this context, the idea of comparing rights and practices of return in Zionism and Palestinian nationalism presented itself as a general framework for posing and developing fresh approaches to political, psychological, moral, and economic aspects of the problem.

It is significant that the contributions to this volume do not rehash familiar debates about refugee return as it may relate to legal questions of the texts of United Nations resolutions or of applicable international law. Nor are these studies focused on exactly what happened in 1948—such as how many Arabs were expelled by force and how many by intimidation; how many left out of panic and how many in response to Arab leaders' calls to evacuate prior to an Arab conquest of the country. Instead, our emphasis is on new ideas and new ways of framing the problem. This shift in focus is especially noticeable in a corresponding redirection of attention from theoretical questions of right to practical questions about return—the requisites and implications of agreements on and implemented policies of actual migration to Israel/Palestine.

A number of factors lay behind this shift by scholars engaged both professionally and personally in the Palestinian-Israeli struggle. First, as noted above, almost two decades of scholarship based on gradually released Israeli government archives have allowed anyone who wants to do so to separate propaganda and myth from empirically sustainable claims regarding who did what to whom, why, and how during the period Palestinians call al-Nakba (the catastrophe) and Israelis have traditionally called the War of Independence. Another reason for a shift away from this sort of debate is one particular crucial finding of this body of scholarship, namely, that the refugee problem per se was not caused by either mass expulsion or mass flight. Expulsion or mass flight would certainly have produced and did produce displacement. But the long-term mass refugee problem could only have been created by the Israeli government's decision to promulgate a draconian ban on return against all those deemed to have been displaced (including Arabs remaining within Israel but displaced from their homes during the fighting). This ban was enforced immediately, systematically, and coercively.[17] On this point there is no controversy. Regardless of whether Palestinian refugees were granted citizenship by their "host" countries (as in Jordan) or whether their lives were severely circumscribed (as in Lebanon), it is this initial, immediate, and continuing Israeli policy of exclusion from their country of origin and from their property that gives rise to the problem—not an injustice felt to have occurred in 1948 which can be contemplated but neither mitigated nor reversed, but a continuing sense of enforced injustice that still could be mitigated. It is this continuing source of distress and dissatisfaction that must be the primary object of discussion if progress on this problem is to be made, even as the events, rights, and wrongs, of the 1948 war itself, the displacement of refugees associated with it, and the opening of the gates to unfettered Jewish immigration are neither forgotten nor ignored.

The impetus to search carefully in the experiences of the two peoples for useful techniques to mitigate the Palestinian sense of injustice and the Israeli Jewish sense of fear arises in part from a realization of how careful consideration of analogous elements in the relationship helps to remove one of the most intractable aspects of the problem—the demand by Palestinians that Israelis not only allow the return of Palestinian refugees but that Israel recognize and accept the Palestinian right of return. In this context, it is crucial to understand how powerfully the claim to a "right" to do anything, or avoid doing something, can be heard by those to whom that claim is directed as a demand to accept as a duty discretion to exercise that right by those who claim it. For example, we may claim to have a right to exclusive use or disposition of a piece of property, and we are likely to advance that claim without believing that we have the physical wherewithal to prevent others from using their strength to take the property that we say is ours. But our claim to a right is precisely our claim that others should experience an obligation or duty not to use their strength to take what we say is rightfully ours if we insist on exercising that right.

Early Zionist immigrants to Palestine and Zionist spokesmen explaining their program to various international investigating commissions and panels advanced a variety of formulas for justifying unlimited Jewish immigration into the country and the creation of a Jewish homeland there, or a state. These justifications were appeals to values that, if accepted by non-Jews either in or outside of Palestine, would produce in them a sense of duty not to try to prevent the building of a Jewish national home in Palestine. They ranged from appeals to biblical or divine authority, the principle of first possession (Jews having preceded Arabs historically as inhabitants of the land), the labor of Jewish pioneers as generating rights to Jewish ownership and rule of the country, the extraordinary and even desperate need of the Jews for a refuge compared in their view with the less pressing political requirements of the local Arab population, the economic benefits for the Arabs of Palestine that were said would be associated with the success of Zionism, and legal arguments associated with European promulgation of the Balfour Declaration or the League of Nations Mandate for Palestine.

Despite these various appeals the Zionist movement was well aware that it had virtually no prospect of convincing Arabs in the country that Jews had a right to return there and that, concomitantly, Palestine's Arabs had a duty to allow them to do so. Instead, the mainstream of the movement, including both the Revisionists led by Vladimir Jabotinsky and the Labor Zionists led by David Ben-Gurion, adopted the strategy made famous by Jabotinsky's theory of the iron wall. This approach accepted the fact that the Arabs of Palestine not only would not, but could not, be expected to accept the right of Jews to return to the Land of Israel. According to Jabotinsky, the country's Arab inhabitants "cling to Palestine, at least with the same instinctive love and natural jealousy displayed by the Aztecs to their Mexico or the Sioux to their prairies." For Palestinian Arabs, he argued, the Jews were naturally and even correctly regarded as "alien settlers." Zionist "colonization," he continued, "is self-explanatory and what it implies is fully understood by every sensible Jew and Arab. There can be only one purpose in colonization. For the country's Arabs, that purpose is essentially unacceptable. This is a natural reaction and nothing will change it."[18]

Unable to hope for instilling a sense of the rightness of the Zionist cause in the minds of Palestinian Arabs, and with it a felt obligation to allow Zionism to succeed, both Jabotinsky and Ben-Gurion adopted a strategy of using force to establish the Jewish national home. Their intent was to erase Arab hopes for ending or reversing the project, leading Arabs, eventually, to agree to accept a Jewish state's existence out of necessity, rather than out of obligation or right.

To a large extent, this strategy has succeeded. Most Palestinians are ready to accept Israel within definite boundaries, not because they believe in the right to return of Jews to "their land" but because they have determined that continuing the struggle to eradicate Zionism is either unachievable or too costly. It is in this context that one can appreciate the asymmetry of demands by Palestinians that Israeli Jews accept the right of Palestinian return, why Israelis have difficulty distinguishing between acceptance of the right and the expectation that it will not be fully implemented, and why Israeli representatives may be much more willing to negotiate practical arrangements for solving the refugee problem that entail some partial return than they are willing to accept the principle of the right of return. For such acceptance would mean, or is likely to seem to mean, acceptance of a Jewish duty to allow Palestinian refugees to move into the State of Israel. However just one may feel this demand to be, it does go further in what it requires at a psychological level than the Israeli demand that Arabs accommodate themselves to the practical reality of Jewish return to at least part of Palestine, rather than a demand that Palestinian Arabs accept as just and valid the Jewish right of return, namely, the ideological principle at the basis of Zionism.

These considerations may help to explain what the chapters in this volume do not focus on—restatements of the elemental justice associated with one side's demands, or the irrationality, danger, or injustice associated with the other. Instead, they address topics connected directly to the practical, complex, and often messy realities associated with the actual "return" of Jews to contemporary Israel and with the prospective "return" of Palestinians to Israel or Palestine.

Organization of the Volume

The volume is divided into five dialogic clusters—dialogic because the essays in each cluster represent in part the outcome of actual dialogue within the group of scholars assembled for this project and because in the terms of their analyses the essays in each group problematize, build upon, or contend with one another.

Part I, entitled "Collective Memories and Actual Choices," includes three essays. Laleh Khalili focuses on the use of collective memory among Palestinian refugees in Lebanon to build national identity. She argues that the social and political marginalization of Palestinian refugees, as well as their exclusion from the decision-making process that will determine their fate, have led them increasingly to assert their right to return and reaffirm their historical roots in and memory of Palestine, largely through grass-roots commemorative practices such as writing ethnographies of villages and creating memory museums. Asserting their membership in a village community that is part of the larger Palestinian nation underscores their demand to influence the nation's—as well as their own—fate. Khalili concludes that these commemorative practices indicate that refugees' desire to return remains strong, without determining absolutely what their choices would be if they were presented with actual options involving compensation, relocation, or return. Elie Podeh treats collective memory as well, but by examining how Israeli and Palestinian textbooks contribute to forging collective memories integral to processes of nation-building. Podeh observes that recent Israeli textbooks are less biased than earlier ones, in his view, but still extol the heroic Jewish pioneer and emphasize Jewish victimization while only partially conceding Israeli responsibility for creating the Palestinian refugee problem and staunchly negating any Palestinian right of return. Palestinian textbooks are also nationalistic, emphasizing Palestinian victimization and the right of return and ignoring Jewish rights. Textbooks thereby reinforce dichotomized national positions rather than open up debate on issues of responsibility and mutual rights. Sari Hanafi's contribution provides a counterpoint to these treatments of collective memory by focusing on the practical imperatives of life that, he argues, will actually determine choices about return if options of one kind or another are offered to the Palestinian refugees. He distinguishes between the "sociology of return" and the "right of return" in his assessment of the possibility that substantial numbers would return to the Palestinian territories or to Israel in the event of a peace accord. Formidable barriers to contact between Palestinians inside and outside have weakened the ability of Palestinians to maintain transnational family relations and economic ties. Thus, despite refugees' emotional commitment to return and despite the positive impact from returnees' investments in the 1990s, Hanafi finds a differentiated refugee community, holding varying preferences. Accordingly, individual decisions to return will be based on complex calculations concerning economic and political prospects in their host countries outside Palestine; the relative attractiveness of return from varying social, economic, and political perspectives; and the degree of ongoing ties they maintain with relatives at home.

The two essays in Part II, entitled "Truth and Political Consequences," engage practical political aspects of large moral questions attached to the refugee issue—questions of truth-telling and historical responsibility. Elazar Barkan examines the growing international demand that governments acknowledge the historical injustices that they have perpetrated against other peoples and provide some sort of restitution to those past victims. Despite the weakness of the international legal framework to support refugees' right to return and despite the few historical cases in which refugees were repatriated or compensated, he views it as important for victims to receive some form of acknowledgment and compensation for their refugeehood. Barkan seeks to shift the debate from the level of legal rights, which he views as unproductive and polarizing, to one of moral obligations and political pragmatism, enabling Israel to recognize its role in creating the refugee problem and its obligations to be a lead partner in its solution. Ian S. Lustick then asks how negotiators might formulate a mutually acceptable narrative statement in which a portion of responsibility for the refugee problem would be allocated to a portion of Israeli actions and policies in 1948 and in which Israel would not only express regret but also commit significant resources to resolving the problem. He examines the negotiations over such a text that took place between West Germany and Israel prior to the reparations agreement between those two countries. He notes that although the West German statement of responsibility for the Holocaust accepted neither responsibility nor guilt, and although it characterized German behavior during World War II in terms exceedingly favorable to German national sentiments, it did contain "just enough truth" to make diplomatic relations and a generous program of financial assistance politically acceptable to the Israeli government. Lustick suggests that a comparable formula is possible in the Palestinian refugee case, one that would enable both parties to move toward closure on this divisive issue.

In Part III, "Practical Consequences of Exile and Return," Amal Jamal, Ann M. Lesch, and Ze'ev (Vladimir) Khanin analyze the predicaments and achievements of three groups moving, or seeking to move, between states of exile and states of return. Amal Jamal focuses on the Palestinians who are internally displaced persons (IDPs) inside Israel and who contitute a quarter of the Palestinian citizens of Israel. Most had fled their homes during the 1948 war but were not allowed to return; others became IDPs when Israel expropriated their land or, in the 1960s, categorized many villages as "illegal." When IDPs' efforts to use the Israeli courts and political system to solve their problem failed, they sought to globalize awareness of their situation by appeals to UN bodies. Moreover, they mobilized locally through educational programs and well-publicized visits to the sites of their original villages. Since allowing IDPs to go home would not endanger Israeli security or alter its demographic balance, Jamal concludes that the government's failure to resolve their problem challenges the idea that Israeli opposition to the Palestinian right of return is based essentially on security and on demographic fears. Ann M. Lesch examines the difficulties faced by even those Palestinian refugees who formed prosperous and seemingly stable communities in the diaspora. Focusing on Kuwait, she demonstrates how Palestinians remained outsiders, encountering discrimination in jobs, education, and legal status, and always at risk of expulsion. For Lesch, this lack of security in exile means that statehood, provisions for permanent residency in Arab states, or recognition of the legal right to return are essential for creating a moral and political balance in the region. Ze'ev Khanin traces the complex trajectory of immigrants to Israel, including a majority of Jewish "returnees," from the former Soviet Union in the 1970s and 1990s. Now constituting 15 percent of the Israeli population, these new Israelis differ among themselves on the role of religion in politics, the value of Hebrew versus Russian culture, the importance of Israel's retaining its Jewish majority, and the modes of resolving Israel's conflicts with the Palestinians and the Arab world. Khanin concludes that these cleavages reflect perspectives they held before immigration but are also affected by their encounter with the realities on the ground in Israel, a sometimes painful encounter, given their previous romanticized views of the homeland.

Part IV, "Property Issues for Arab and Jewish Migrants and Refugees," features essays by Michael R. Fischbach, Yehouda Shenhav, and Salim Tamari. Michael R. Fischbach compares two sets of property losses: Palestinian refugees' claims to property in Israel and Jewish immigrants' claims to property left behind and confiscated in Arab countries. Emphasizing that the origins of these claims are quite different, he shows how each displacement and each set of claims has shaped the discourse and political culture of the respective protagonists in the Israeli-Palestinian conflict. Though not linked in their origins, both sets of claims will likely need to be addressed in a final negotiated settlement, according to Fischbach.

A crucial element leading to the political connection between these problems is that Israel has linked the issues of compensating Palestinian refugees, or allowing some of them to return, to the issue of compensating the Mizrahim—a group that Yehouda Shenhav sometimes describes as "Arab Jews." Shenhav rejects the assertion of a parallel between the two cases, viewing that as an effort by Israel to use the concept of "population exchange" in order to abdicate its moral and political responsibilities toward the Palestinian refugees. Similarly, Salim Tamari criticizes claims of a parallel between the two cases. He focuses on the mechanisms by which

Palestinians might be compensated for their property, irrespective of whether they actually repatriate. He proposes a multipronged solution that would include payments to the Palestinian state; restitution of still-standing property to its owners without dispossessing current occupiers, who would gain long-term leases; and package deals for small-property holders and landless refugees. Tamari argues that it is in the interest of Israel to achieve closure on the core refugee issue, as that is the only way for Israel to end the conflict and gain acceptance as a legitimate state in the region.

In Part V, "The Refugee Issue in Context," Nadim N. Rouhana, Ilan Pappé, and Gershon Shafir each lay out broad reconceptualizations of the relationship between the refugee issue and the Israeli-Palestinian conflict as a whole. Rouhana addresses the failure of both sides to imagine the other's place in the identity space that it constructs in its homeland. He argues that resistance to resolution is inherent in the facts that the conflict is over both symbolic and territorial space and that there is a severe power imbalance between the two sides. Moreover, differences over the right of return reflect the two sides' sense of an irreconcilable past and their divergent visions of the future. Therefore, while a limited peace settlement is imaginable, based on the two-state formula, a process leading to a fundamental reconciliation can only end the existential conflict through addressing core issues of historical truth and responsibility and securing justice through restructuring the social and political relationship between the two parties. Ilan Pappé similarly questions negotiators' focus on solving the post-1967 conflict without addressing its core, arising from the 1948 war and the refugee problem. He also seeks a reconciliation process focused on fairness and justice, not only a division of land along the 1967 lines. International truth commissions and educational programs, permitting both communities recognize each other as communities of suffering, might supplement material programs for compensation and repatriation. Ultimately, in Pappé's view, both parties need to overcome their nationalism and ethnocentrism in order to reach a true reconciliation. Gershon Shafir, however, maintains that it is possible—indeed, necessary—to address simultaneously the issues of post-1967 land and the refugees. Despite the rigid and narrow Palestinian and Israeli images of the "Other," it is essential to move beyond a zero-sum perspective. Israeli withdrawal to the 1967 lines would end its colonialist approach of linking settlement and the establishing of sovereign borders, and an Israeli apology for its part in creating the refugee problem would alleviate some of the Palestinian sense of grievance, particularly in the context of a truth commission, a program for partial repatriation, and compensation. Despite their differences, all three authors seek to formulate complementary moral epistemologies and mutually respectful historical narratives, viewing those steps as essential in resolving the core issues epitomized by the refugee problem and the issue of the right of return.

Conclusion

No claim is advanced in this volume that is accepted in detail by all of the authors except the implicit but important claims that the Palestinian refugee problem is of crucial importance, that understanding of it can be deepened by comparison with other cases, and that absent serious and systematic consideration, no amount of hand waving or sloganeering will make it disappear. Beyond these principles, the essays, in their detailed treatment of specific topics, combine in complex ways to suggest the following guidelines for subsequent scholarship and for policy makers.

Whatever practical arrangements are orchestrated and implemented to satisfy the material requirements of Palestinian refugees, these practical arrangements themselves will not be sufficient to achieve the kind of end-of-conflict status so desired in Israel unless attention is also paid to mitigating the pain of felt injustice and its relationship to peacemaking.

Both for Zionism and for Palestinian nationalism, the ideological fires and formulas that created and sustained the movements through periods of their greatest struggles, including unlimited and eternal rights of return, will have unintended but powerful and negative implications if used unquestioningly to guide the shape of a final, peaceful, and stable peace between the two peoples.

Once the problem is broken into its parts, at the level of real people, and removed from the domain of rhetoric and ideology, there are practical and sensible solutions to specific challenges and injustices encountered by those who have suffered and still suffer from displacement and enforced exclusion.

It is our hope that this volume will make a significant contribution to the work of all those seeking to achieve a lasting, stable, and just peace between two peoples who, loving one land, have wrestled too long with each other.

Notes

1. In the summer of 2001, detailed articles arguing this point were published: Robert Malley and Hussein Agha, "The Truth About Camp David," *New York Review of Books*, August 9, 2001; and Deborah Sontag, "Quest for Mideast Peace: How and Why It Failed," *New York Times*, July 26, 2001. For the argument that the Palestinians were virtually entirely to blame for the failure, see Robert Satloff, "The Times Tries to Rewrite History: Times Bomb," *The New Republic*, August 13, 2001.

2. Don Peretz, *Israel and the Palestinian Arabs* (Washington, D.C.: Middle East Institute, 1958); Sami Hadawi, *Palestinian Rights and Losses in 1948: A Comprehensive Study* (London: Saqi Books, 1988); Atif A. Kubursi, "Palestinian Losses in 1948: Calculating Refugee Compensation 2001," Information Brief no. 81, 3, Centre for Pol-

icy Analysis on Palestine, August 2001; Benjamin N. Schiff, *Refugees unto the Third Generation: U.N. Aid to Palestinians* (Syracuse: Syracuse University Press, 1995).

3. Ruth Lapidoth, "The Right of Return in International Law, with Special Reference to the Palestinian Refugees," *Israel Yearbook on Human Rights* 16 (1986): 103–25; John Quigley, "Displaced Palestinians and a Right of Return," *Harvard International Law Journal* 39 (winter 1998): 171–229; Lex Takkenberg, *The Status of Palestinian Refugees in International Law* (New York: Oxford University Press, 1998).

4. Avi Plascov, *The Palestinian Refugees in Jordan 1948–1957* (London: Frank Cass, 1981); Benny Morris, *Israel's Border Wars: 1949–1956: Arab Infiltration, Israeli Retaliation, and the Countdown to the Suez War* (Oxford: Clarendon Press, 1993); Yezid Y. Sayigh, *Armed Struggle and the Search for State: The Palestinian National Movement, 1949–1993* (Oxford: Oxford University Press, 1997).

5. Rosemary Sayigh, *Palestinians: From Peasants to Revolutionaries* (London: Zed, 1979); Shafeeq N. Ghabra, *Palestinians in Kuwait: The Family and the Politics of Survival* (Boulder, Colo.: Westview, 1987); Julie Peteet, "From Refugees to Minority: Palestinians in Post-War Lebanon," *Middle East Report*, no. 200 (July-September 1996): 27–29; Elia Zureik, "The Trek Back Home: Palestinians Returning Home and Their Problem of Adaptation," in Are Hovdenak et al., *Constructing Order: Palestinian Adaptation to Refugee Life* (Oslo: Fafo Institute for Applied Social Science, 1997).

6. Majid Al-Haj, "Adjustment Patterns of the Arab Internal Refugees in Israel," *International Migration* 24:3 (September 1988): 651–74; Danny Rubinstein, *The People of Nowhere: The Palestinian Vision of Home* (New York: Times Books, 1991).

7. Ghabra, *Palestinians in Kuwait*; Laurie A. Brand , *The Palestinians in the Arab World: Institution Building and the Search for a* State (New York: Columbia University Press, 1988); Khalil Nakhleh and Elia Zureik, eds., *The Sociology of the Palestinians* (New York: St. Martin's Press, 1980).

8. Donna E. Arzt, *Refugees into Citizens: Palestinians and the End of the Arab-Israeli Conflict* (Syracuse, N.Y.: Syracuse University Press, 1997); Rex Brynen, *A Very Political Economy: Peacebuilding and Foreign Aid in the West Bank and Gaza* (Washington, D.C.: United States Institute of Peace Press, 2000); S. Gazit, *The Palestinian Refugee Problem, Final Status Issue 2* (Tel Aviv: Jaffee Center for Strategic Studies, Tel Aviv University, 1995); Don Peretz, *Palestinians, Refugees, and the Middle East Peace Process* (Washington, D.C.: United States Institute of Peace, 1993).

9. Khalil Shikaki, "Results of Palestinian Survey Research Unit's Refugees' Polls in the West Bank/Gaza Strip, Jordan and Lebanon on Refugees' Preferences and Behavior in a Palestinian-Israeli Permanent Refugee Agreement" (press release, July 18, 2003); idem, "The Right of Return," *Wall Street Journal*, July 30, 2003..

10. Michael R. Fischbach, *Records of Dispossession: Palestinian Refugee Property and the Arab-Israeli Conflict* (New York: Columbia University Press, 2003).

11. N. N. Rouhana and H. C. Kelman, "Promoting Joint Thinking in International Conflicts: An Israeli-Palestinian Continuing Workshop," *Journal of Social Issues* 50 (1994): 157–78.

12. Yitzhak Rabin, *The Rabin Memoirs* (Boston: Little, Brown, 1979).

13. Rony Gabbay, *A Political Study of the Arab-Jewish Conflict: The Arab Refugee Problem, a Case Study* (Genève: Librairie Droz, 1959); Nafez Nazzal, *The Palestinian Exodus from Galilee, 1948* (Beirut: Institute for Palestine Studies, 1978); Erskine Childers, "The Other Exodus," *The* Spectator (May 12, 1961).

14. Benny Morris, *The Birth of the Palestinian Refugee Problem, 1947–1949* (Cambridge: Cambridge University Press, 1987); idem, *1948 and After: Israel and the Palestinians* (Oxford: Clarendon, 1990); Ilan Pappé, *The Making of the Arab-Israeli Conflict, 1947–51* (London: I.B. Tauris, 1994); Nur Masalha, *Expulsion of the Palestinians:Tthe*

Concept of "Transfer" in Zionist Political Thought, 1882–1948 (Washington, D.C.: Institute for Palestine Studies, 1992); Michael Palumbo, *The Palestinian Catastrophe: The 1948 Expulsion of a People from Their Homeland* (London: Faber and Faber, 1987).

15. Tom Segev, *1949: The First Israelis* (New York: The Free Press, 1986); Benny Morris, "The Causes and Character of the Arab Exodus from Palestine: The Israeli Defense Forces Intelligence Branch Analysis of June 1948," *Middle East Studies* 22 (1986): 5–19; idem, *Israel's Border Wars, 1949–1956: Arab Infiltration, Israeli Retaliation, and the Countdown to the Suez War* (Oxford: Clarendon, 1993).

16. The Geneva initiative was touted by its Israeli signatories as having addressed all the issues in detail, including those never before resolved explicitly in an Israeli-Palestinian agreement. Instructively, there was one topic that was put aside, even though it was discussed in detail at Taba and acknowledged there and by the Clinton parameters as a key element in an eventual agreement. This was the question of agreeing on a common narrative or a statement or statements about what actually happened in 1948 or about culpability, sorrow, or regret. Although Palestinians made demands in this area, they accepted Israeli arguments that, for the purposes of the initiative, inclusion of this issue would be politically inexpedient.

17. Morris, *Israel's Border Wars.*

18. *Passages translated from the original Russian as published in "O zheleznoi stene" (On the iron wall) in Razsviet* (Berlin, 1923). For details, see Ian Lustick, "To Build and to Be Built By: Israel and the Hidden Logic of the Iron Wall," *Israel Studies* 1:1 (summer 1996): 196–223.

Part I
Collective Memories and
Actual Choices

Chapter 2
Commemorating Contested Lands

Laleh Khalili

In recent debates about the Palestinian refugees' right of return, when the focus of the debate has turned to what the refugees really want, the responses have varied widely between those that claim that all refugees want to—and can—return[1] and those that—on the basis of surveys—claim that only a very small percentage of the refugees will have any interest in returning to their villages within the borders of Israel.[2] In this essay, I argue that we do not know with any certainty what the specific demands of Palestinian refugees as a community are, but that grassroots perpetuation of memories of pre-1948 villages and the inextricability of right of return from these memories indicate the persistence of the refugees' claims to these lost villages.

Our lack of knowledge about Palestinian refugees' demands is partially due to the absence of survey data for large numbers of refugees.[3] More important, the information vacuum extends to the refugees themselves, who do not know what possible, practical, and achievable alternatives for their future exist. Without the refugees' direct participation in concrete negotiation processes out of which acceptable alternatives can emerge, speculative polls and surveys of their attitudes will not necessarily reflect their demands or choices. In the absence of concrete information about the views of Palestinian refugees vis-à-vis the right of return, I argue that a close reading of their political practices and performances will reveal that the refugees insist on preserving a package of rights (from the very possibility of return to their village to compensation or recognition of the injustice done to them) bundled under the term the "right of return." Dogged insistence on this bundle of rights is a way in which Palestinian refugees prevent their options from becoming entirely circumscribed by much more powerful actors. Furthermore, insistence on the right of return also means that they insist on belonging to a larger Palestinian polity.

Among the refugee practices that frequently affirm the right of return are those popular commemorations that celebrate life in Palestine before the Nakba. Scholars have long studied memory and commemoration as a domain of political contestation, a claim to moral accounting and a critique of injustice.[4] Examining Palestinian commemorations is important, because memorializing practices have emerged at a time when most refugees feel a great deal of anxiety about their fate and relationship with a putative Palestinian state. Since the advent of the Oslo accords, diasporan Palestinians have increasingly found themselves excluded from the decision-making processes that directly and drastically affect their lives. Their commemorative practices—which invoke the village in family histories, popular ethnographies of lost villages, camp institutions, and commemorative narratives—engage these exclusions. By reviving memories of their villages as Palestinian places and as constituent parts of the Palestinian identity, the refugees are demanding a recognition of their membership in the Palestinian polity. Furthermore, the fact that their commemorations sometimes—though not always—occur without institutional support indicates that the right of return is a salient focus of grassroots politics for the Palestinians.

The reassertion of the memory of the pre-1948 land at this juncture performs a series of functions for the refugees. First, it reaffirms their membership in the Palestinian polity through emphasizing the refugees' connections with the Palestinian land and their possession of documentary and commemorative claims to it. Second, through their extensive linkage of commemorative tropes to the right of return, these practices indicate the political content of the commemorative practices. Finally, these practices indicate the grassroots origins of attempts at refugee mobilization around the right of return, as most of their practices are not materially supported by the political organizations, even if the forms of commemoration are borrowed from the political organizations.

To elucidate the relationship between refugees' memory and the right of return, I choose to examine their commemorations. In contrast to most studies analyzing legal or political solutions to the problems of Palestinian refugees, I foreground the refugees' narratives and practices in the camps of Lebanon, which I have observed and recorded during extensive personal interviews and field research in Lebanon (when I lived and worked in the Burj al-Barajna refugee camp).[5] I combine these with an examination of memoirs, autobiographies, factional publications, and literary works of fiction. I first provide the historical and social background for the current condition and predicaments of Palestinian refugees in Lebanon. Next, I discuss the institutional and official practices of commemoration and the ways in which these practices have been appropriated, adapted, and transformed by refugees themselves. I then explore the village books, folk ethnographic museums, camp institutions, and narratives that commemorate the lost village. I conclude by examining the relationship between commemoration and refugees' attitudes toward the right of return. I hope to show that the commemorative practices are forward-looking political acts intended by the refugees as claims to the right of return and a demand for the participation in the political processes that define and implement this right.

Palestinians in Lebanon: Historical Background

In 1948, some 726,000 Palestinians fled or were expelled from Palestine, around 110,000 of whom eventually settled in Lebanon.[6] The number of Palestinian refugees now registered with the United Nations Relief and Works Agency (UNRWA) in Lebanon stands just under 400,000; however, in 2002, unofficial sources placed the total number of refugees in all of Lebanon around 250,000, with around 150,000 refugees remaining in the camps, and with the difference made up by Palestinian residents of Lebanon working in the Gulf or Europe. As Rosemary Sayigh points out, the Lebanese government estimates the number of refugees in Lebanon to be as high as or even higher than 400,000, in order to receive higher resettlement compensations from international or Israeli bodies in any future negotiations.[7]

Many of the refugees who became camp residents in Lebanon were originally rural laborers, smallholders, or village artisans. Their uprooting and resettlement resulted in simultaneous, radical, and traumatic processes of urbanization,[8] proletarianization, and loss of whatever political rights they may have held in Palestine. Life in the camps itself was lived with considerable hardship in tents that flooded easily, with no running water or sewerage system, and under the malign gaze of the Lebanese security apparatus.

TABLE 2.1. Population of Official Camps in Lebanon

Ain al-Hilwa	44,953
Al-Bass	9,986
Biddawi	16,038
Burj al-Barajna	20,182
Burj al-Shamali	18,471
Dbayeh	4,202
Mar Elias	1,413
Miyya-Miyya	5,008
Nahr al-Barid	30,620
Rashidiyya	25,263
Shatila	12,130
Wavell (Jalil)	7,492
Registered refugees from the destroyed Dikwana (Tal al-Za'tar) and Nabatiyya camps	16,011
TOTAL	211,769

Source: UNRWA, June 30, 2003.

It was only in the late 1950s that the tents gradually gave way to cement-block houses with corrugated tin roofs, and only in the 1970s did the camps receive electricity, sewerage, and water services. Throughout this period, the Lebanese security services severely monitored all residents' activities. The daily harassment of Palestinians and prevention of their free movement[9] were accompanied by imprisonment, torture,[10] and deportation of Palestinian men[11] and, in a few instances, even execution of a number of youths thought to be politically active.[12]

The emergence and consolidation of the national movement in the refugee camps of Lebanon were the results of protracted political and military maneuvering of the armed groups against the Lebanese state,[13] which at the time was more or less dominated by Maronite Christian parties who were less sympathetic[14] to Palestinians than the majority Muslim population of Lebanon.[15] Thus, with the Cairo accords of 1969, camp residents gained control over the administration of the camps and, after the expulsion of Palestinian political leaders from Jordan in 1970–71, Beirut and especially the Palestinian refugee camps in Lebanon became foci of the Palestine Liberation Organization (PLO) state-building activities and the location for factional political mobilization. After 1969, the camps established Popular Committees, which took over the task of camp administration; the various factions all had representatives on the committee, thus enacting a quasi-representative pluralism in the camps.

The Lebanese civil war terminated the substantial gains in living standards in the camps. Between 1975 and 1991, Palestinians suffered successive massacres,[16] destruction of their camps,[17] internecine warfare,[18] sieges,[19] and ongoing harassment and arrests by Lebanese, Israeli, and Syrian security forces. Though the level of violence against Palestinians has dropped substantially since the end of the civil war, the deteriorating socioeconomic conditions of the Palestinians in Lebanon in the post-Oslo period attest to their increasing marginalization. With an ever-diminishing budget, the UNRWA offices in Lebanon attempt to provide hundreds of thousands of refugees with free education until the age of sixteen, inexpensive health care until the age of sixty, and assistance in housing construction and repair in the camps. The individual camps do not have access to telephone lines, and electric supplies to the camps are highly erratic, especially during the winter, when daily power outages of at least four hours are typical. The camp water supplies, especially in and around Beirut, are polluted and non-potable. Under Lebanese law, Palestinians are unable to find employment in more than seventy occupations,[20] cannot own or inherit property,[21] cannot petition to gain Lebanese citizenship[22] and, in fact, may have their citizenships revoked,[23] have to endure a difficult process to obtain housing repair or construction permits,[24] cannot establish NGOs solely dedicated to Palestinians,[25] and have to pay a substantial fee to attend Lebanese universities.[26]

With the 1982 evacuation of the PLO leadership from Lebanon, the Palestinian community in Lebanon has found itself increasingly wrenched apart and disassociated from the Palestinian national community and isolated from its nominal leadership's decision-making processes. The Oslo accords have deepened this sense of isolation, as most refugees outside the occupied territories feel their right to return traded for Palestinian statehood (however provisional and uncertain). Additionally, with the establishment of the proto-state of Palestine in the West Bank and Gaza, most humanitarian aid from donor nations and organizations was rerouted to the occupied territories, encouraging competition between the diaspora and home communities for scarce funds.[27] Occasional debates about mass *tawtin* (resettlement) meet with vehement refusal from the Lebanese public. Since the declaration of a general amnesty at the end of the Lebanese civil war, various confessional groups have found it easier to apportion blame for the civil war and for any political domestic disturbances on Palestinians, casting them as provocateurs or a proverbial "fifth column." Labor strikes, attacks against American fast-food restaurants, and assassination attempts against political figures are all blamed on Palestinians, even if those responsible are themselves Lebanese.[28] As Peteet notes, the "Palestinian presence, perceived as a problem, can and does serve as a common denominator in unifying often disparate elements of the Lebanese polity."[29] In fact, the nationalist Lebanese discourse requires the social exclusion of Palestinians as a prerequisite for sectarian reconciliation. Ironically, a number of political organizations in Lebanon tout the right of return as non-negotiable, not necessarily out of any particular political principle but because enforcing the right of return would entail the removal of Palestinian refugees from Lebanon.

Palestinian refugees are under a great deal of pressure to conform to the demands of more powerful actors. Israel, most Western powers, and the mainstream Palestinian Authority officialdom want them to accept resettlement in Lebanon or a third country. Policy guidelines of successive Likud regimes in Israel even preclude the possibility of refugees settling in the occupied territories.[30] Clause 7 of the Geneva Accord—an agreement reached between PA officials and left-wing members of the Israeli Labor Party (who are not in power)—leaves the possibility of refugee return to their villages (now in Israel) at "the sovereign discretion of Israel."[31] Rejectionist factions, nationalist NGOs, and nearly all Lebanese vehemently demand that the refugees reject resettlement anywhere outside Palestine.[32] The refugees themselves have no desire necessarily to settle amid the Lebanese, with whom they share such a painful history of conflict; yet they have no sense of alternative possibilities available to them, and no guarantee that their leadership will acknowledge their rights and support their demands. In this atmosphere of uncertainty, Palestinian refugees in Lebanon have invoked memories of the past in order to lay claim to their political rights. Though the refugees have borrowed familiar ritual forms from political institutions, they have nevertheless appropriated these commemorative practices to voice their demand for return.

Official and Institutional Commemorative Practices

States expend resources on national(ist) commemoration through monuments, ceremonies, and pedagogic texts such as tourist brochures, political pamphlets, television programs, and school textbooks. Between the late 1960s and 1982, the PLO established proto-state institutions in Beirut that aimed to administer the affairs of Palestinians in exile while struggling for the establishment of a Palestinian state in some part of Mandate Palestine. During this period, the PLO's parastatal institutions perpetuated commemorative practices by filling calendars with commemorated days and ceremonies and, less frequently, commissioning monuments to massacres and national martyrs. Interestingly, commemoration of life in the villages was maintained at a highly abstract level, even by those Palestinian factions that ostensibly spoke for the workers and peasants.

Throughout this period, the publications of various Palestinian political organizations were far more interested in the geostrategic aspects of the Israel/Palestine conflict and the cold war than they were in the local histories of the villages left behind by the refugees. For example, *Al-Hadaf,* the organ of the Popular Front for the Liberation of Palestine (PFLP), wrote more extensively about U.S. imperialism, Israeli relations with the Shah's Iran, and apartheid South Africa than about the histories and lives of Palestinian people. If village lives were referred to at all, it was in abstract theoretical essays about precapitalist modes of production or in articles about the lives of Vietnamese peasants. Fatah's *Filastin al-Thawra* was more attentive to Palestinian history, but this history was abstract, documentary, and elite-centered. While a handful of memoirs of the 1948 exodus appeared in scholarly journals published by the PLO Research Center (then in Beirut), these were mostly written by urban and urbane Palestinians then living in Arab or European capitals. When, in the late 1990s, the Arab Resource Center for Popular Arts (ARCPA) interviewed elderly Palestinians in the camps, the elders would greet the interviewers with "It's good that you're doing this. The political organizations and leaders before you should have paid some attention. [B]ut if you are doing it, well, bravo."[33]

The lack of interest in the more textured, and perhaps fractious, histories of smaller locales went hand in hand with the imperatives of the nationalist movement, which demanded a more homogeneous and harmonious history. Scholars performing oral history research during this period remember being refused institutional support[34] and recall that various Palestinian national research institutions and even PLO activists "weren't convinced that [oral history] research could help the national struggle, or the aims of their *tanzim.*"[35] The absence of finely textured and complex local histories, however, did not prevent the proto-state Palestinian political institutions from commemorating the lost villages in iconized images, detailed maps of Palestine, and commemoration-rich calendars. Posters and postcards published by the PLO, especially during the 1970s, brim with references to oranges, harvests of wheat and olives, keys to lost houses, stone dwellings, and the local costumes of men and women.[36] Many of these references were adopted from the literary works of nationalist writers (such as Ghassan Kanafani) who were sensitive to the cultural signifiers of Palestinian village life and eager to record it.

Immediately following the evacuation of the PLO from Lebanon, factional publications (whose headquarters had moved to Tunis, Cyprus, or Damascus) feverishly commemorated the cities and villages of pre-1948 Palestine. Among these were the PLO Research Center's series of books on the elite histories of Palestinian cities and larger villages. Factional articles reflected the political divisions within the PLO. Rejectionist organizations such as the Fatah-Revolutionary Council, PFLP-General Command, and even PFLP, whose goal more or less was still a larger Palestinian state that overlay the state of Israel, commemorated the places that fell on the map of this imaginary nation-state. In contrast, Fatah organs reduced these types of commemoration in line with the shift in policy that began to imagine the Palestinian state as territorialized in the occupied territories.

With the beginning of the intifada and the PLO's acceptance of Israel's existence in 1988, PLO organs ceased their commemoration of villages and cities. As Arafat took a conciliatory approach toward Israel, references to places inside the Green Line disappeared from PLO periodicals, and commemoration took a backseat to the realities of popular struggle in the occupied territories. In response, the rejectionist factions increased their commemorative articles and ceremonies. After the Oslo negotiations and the intensification of diaspora anxieties about their fate, commemoration of Palestinian villages in rejectionist organs became ubiquitous and multifaceted (though there were still no oral histories to speak of). While, for example, commemoration of Land Day was underplayed in the PLO periodicals during this period, rejectionist factions held festivals and political gatherings to faithfully commemorate it.[37]

The rise of Islamism has also been reflected in the memorialization of land. The Islamist organs, much like the nationalist ones in their heyday, have resorted to abstract justifications of the importance of land rather than concrete histories and claims by those Palestinians who inhabited those lands. Divine edict is invoked as legitimation for Islamist claims to land, and the land itself is considered sanctified and blessed by God, thus obliging the believers to ensure its maintenance in pious hands.[38] Commemorative Islamist practices have focused on Muslim-Crusader struggles for land and histories so remote as to be easily maintained within the realm of the ideologically abstract and thus uncompromised by historical and social complexities.

The post-1982 contraction in number and extravagance of factional commemorative practices reflects the dwindling resources of the factions that do the commemorating. Before 1982, commemorative practices were held at frequent intervals, but today, events supported and funded by factions are few and far between. NGOs, with funding from international and local sources, tend to hold such commemorative events, but the role of these events is more ceremonial than pedagogic, to the extent that most young men and women I questioned could not tell me what the commemorated Land Day signified. Nonetheless, the evacuation of historical details from these commemorative practices makes the factional ceremonies surrounding them no less emotionally charged.

Grassroots Commemorative Practices

Many commemorative practices of Palestinian refugees in the camps of Lebanon adopt the familiar forms institutionalized by Palestinian factions or NGOs. However, ceremonial or narrative forms are appropriated, localized, and transformed, such that the meanings conveyed by the commemoration are not the same (or exactly the same) as what was originally intended by the proto-state and parastatal organizations. This popularization of commemorative practices is significant in that it challenges solely state-based theories of commemoration.

Institutionalized and proto-state commemorative practices of Palestinians focus on the nation and the "imagined community"[39] as a whole, but grassroots practices of commemoration in the camps emphasize the local and the regional, concrete village connections, and corporeal places of origin. Since these commemorative efforts emerge in the context of an ongoing struggle over the definition of the nation's boundaries ("Is the diaspora to be included in the nascent Palestinian nation-state?"), constant reaffirmation of the refugees' belonging to a national locale legitimizes their membership in the national polity. The timing of the revival of village memories is significant. As lines of fracture and disagreements over the refugees' future emerge in the cross-border Palestinian polity, attachments to both subnational (such as village, camp, and kinship networks) and supranational identities (such as Islamist ideologies) grow.[40] The emergence of the village as the primary marker of identity becomes an important signifier of political position within national debates. In a way, the commemoration reaffirms what Boyarin has called (in reference to Zionism) the "collective claims to a land title grounded in suffering ancestry."[41]

Village attachments are consciously cultivated and touted, and their utility as mobilizing tools are well known: individual commemorators and the authors of the village books are aware that their commemoration can act as a pedagogic tool "to inform and clarify to Western understanding what happened to the Palestinian in 1948 and why [the refugees'] current state of exile is so unjust and intolerable."[42] It has long become a performative trope of Palestinian commemoration that grandparents pass the stories and memories of their childhood down to the future generations. However, these days, foreign researchers, journalists, activists, and electronic media belonging to local and regional actors are far more important catalysts for such narrative commemoration. Although members of the younger generation are learning about the memories of previous generations through third parties rather than at the foot of their grandparents, their engagement and curiosity about memory as a central element of a reconfigured nationalism is noteworthy. In the following sections, I will discuss forms of commemoration that fall outside the domain of jurisdiction of factions and NGOs and will discuss their audiences and their relevance.

Villages Mapped upon the Camps

One of the most significant ways in which village life is commemorated is in the geography of the camps. The cramped spaces of most Palestinian camps in Lebanon have undergone significant changes in cartographic notation. When the camps were originally established, their residents gathered in groupings that replicated village and family ties in Palestine. Over time, as the tents slowly gave way to cement-block dwellings, the quarters of the camps retained their village names.[43] With the consolidation of factional control in the camps during the 1970s, the camp quarters' designations changed, reflecting the locales of political factions.[44] After the exodus of Palestinian political leadership from Lebanon in 1982, the camps' geographic designation reverted to the familiar village names, indicating both the durability of the original village connections and conscious renaming efforts by camp residents.[45]

Institutionally, village ties continue to form the basis of social relations in the camp and even allow for various forms of social mobilization. For example, the importance of village notables in social relations of the camp has persisted through the substantial social transformations during the Thawra (revolutionary) era. The role of village notables as arbitrators and local headmen was preserved (especially by Fatah), where they acted as intermediaries between factions and provided a coping mechanism against the excesses of armed youths.[46] After the Thawra period and in the deteriorating social and economic circumstances following 1982, camp residents organized village committees to mitigate the absence of social security. These organizations preserve pre-1948 village ties, do not play a direct political role (thus staving off potential competition from the factions), and provide their members with assistance and resources necessary for funerals, weddings, educational aid, and collection and documentation of village books and maps.[47] Therefore, village connections are not only invoked in the quotidian aspects of life in the camps; they also play a significant role in the social mobilization of the community.

Commemorative Names and Symbols

Names and symbols play a significant role in Palestinian commemorative practices. Many Palestinian daughters are named after lost villages, thus embodying villages, regions, and cities.[48] Self-naming also incorporates Palestinian place names, especially in the Internet and e-mail monikers that Palestinian youths choose for themselves. The descendants of the generations that left their villages in Palestine in 1948 choose to name themselves after these lost—and, in many instances, destroyed—villages: SAFFURIE-H2001@aaa.com commemorates the village of Saffuriya in the Galilee, whereas WALID_FARA@aaa.com combines the real name of a young man and the name of his grandfather's village in Safad province.[49] The number 48 appears repeatedly in e-mail addresses and Instant Messenger (IM) names, denoting and commemorating the year of exile with each evocation. Though many of the youths are only vaguely aware of the detailed histories of their dispossession in 1948, their invocation of pre-1948 place names reveals how these places are being constituted as part of their identity.

Among the commemorative symbols, the key to one's lost—and, most likely, destroyed—house has deep resonance in the refugee community. I was told by an elderly man, "Do you think I wanted to leave? I locked the door and brought the key, thinking I was going to go back a few days later." The key has become such an important commemorative symbol that even those families that no longer have their own key (as it may have passed down to another sibling or been lost in the multiple displacements of the civil war) have mass-produced copies of a large key displayed in prominent places on walls, often next to a reproduction of the Dome of the Rock. The key appears again and again in handmade and printed posters produced by camp children and teachers and, more than any other symbol, refers to the desire to return to Palestine. Since it indicates the ability to reopen closed doors, it suggests return to lost villages and, as such, explicitly makes a claim on the future. The key appears not only as a house decoration but is also worn around the necks of demonstrators, is pictured on right-of-return posters, is digitized in cyber-circulars, and is the very first thing that is shown to a foreign interviewer looking for pre-1948 life stories. When children in after-school programs are asked to draw images of their lives, they often incorporate the key into their drawings. While NGOs and factions have been crucial in the iconization of the key, its ability to have such a hold on popular imagination is due to the fact that it embodies the memory of the past, the expectation of return, and the tangibility of the right to reclaim one's original dwelling.

Memory Museums

Popular efforts to document Palestinian village life have often been undertaken by Palestinian teachers who have extended their pedagogic efforts into the realm of memory museums and memory texts. Mahmud Dakwar's ethnographic museum (a small room in his house filled with hundreds of objects) near Burj al-Shamali camp in Tyre "presents in the name of Palestine, and not under the title of a person, or a party or an organization"[50] a collection of everyday artifacts used by Palestinian villagers in Galilee before their diaspora. He started the museum in 1991 with his own money and collected hundreds of different objects used daily by Palestinian villagers. For Dakwar, one can only belong to a nation if one preserves the objects that embody its heritage and history. He says: "I am not a man of weapons and guns. . . . I understand the homeland through the logic of culture and civilization."[51] Dakwar's equation between armed struggle and preservation of cultural heritage points to the claim-making content of commemoration. Dakwar emphasizes the absence of an attachment between himself and any political faction and laments the lack of interest by political organizations in the kind of work he undertakes. He is aware of the political implications and importance of his own work; that he is well known in the Palestinian community of Tyre and his museum is visited, particularly by camp youth, also speaks to the revived grassroots interest in the social histories of the 1948 generation.

Village Books

Among the most significant grassroots commemorative efforts by Palestinian refugees in Lebanon has been the publication of local village books. Following the examples of the Birzeit University[52] and the Dar al-Shajara series[53] (the latter of which is published in Damascus[54] and is thus easily available to the Palestinians in the Lebanese camps), descendants of the generation of 1948 have begun writing and self-publishing popular historical ethnographies of lost villages. These books—on Dayr Al-Qassi, 'Alma, Al-Damun, and Kwaykat, among others—are often published with the author's savings, sold in the camp grocery stores (or are distributed by him to his network of friends and kin), and are spoken about by the descendants of the inhabitants of those villages.

The noninstitutional and personally financed efforts at publishing village books arose only after the Palestinian community in Lebanon was left after 1982 with a fractious political leadership that was further delegitimized in the refugees' eyes by its participation in the Oslo process. The weakening of this leadership allowed for emergence of critical voices that had previously been suppressed in the interest of national unity. For example, Faisal Jallul's *A Critique of Palestinian Armed Resistance* was penned in the late 1970s, but did not find a publisher in Lebanon until 1994.[55] Oral histories that had not received institutional support—and even faced skepticism from the cadres of political factions during the Thawra era—began to flourish only after the leadership left Lebanon. During this same period, noninstitutional village books penned by refugees in Lebanon began to emerge.

These self-published village books generally contain physical and geographic descriptions of the village (often taken from Walid Khalidi's *All That Remains*)[56] as well as detailed listings of the families or heads of households who lived in the village before 1948, including their properties and professions. These books additionally describe village folk customs, clothes, and sayings, reproduce pre-1948 documents (e.g., identity cards, title deeds), and create "memory maps" of the village or region. Most significant, the books contain advocacy for the refugees. Their readers cross generations. The elderly read the books as a way of jogging their memories about their home villages, while the youth pore over the pictures and the names of families to trace past relations of current camp neighbors and friends and look wistfully at the details of village crafts, agriculture, and businesses.

Keen documentation of ephemeral oral histories is a prime motivation for writing the books. As Ibrahim Uthman, author of *Dayr al-Qassi*, states, the dying-off of the old generation compelled him to gather the minutiae of its history before it was lost. Uthman felt he was in a race against time, as "some [of the elders] passed away a few days after the interview and others died before I had a chance to reach them."[57] Authors voice their concern that the material remembered will be lost if it is not written down and are assiduous about the accuracy of the details that they record on paper.[58] The intent of compiling these detailed books is not simply to salvage the past for the sake of study or research; the authors of these books explicitly declare their primary motive to be leaving behind a legacy for future generations. This material matters, they claim, not only as historical documents, but as the possible bases for legal claims. Uthman speaks about leaving aside fifty copies of the book for his descendants, while 'Abd al-Majid al-Ali, author of *Kwaykat*, claims that he writes "so that the generations wouldn't forget this village and our heritage, our customs, and our habits and our sayings, and the methods of farming and construction and commerce and everything else."[59]

The impetus for writing is a sense of accelerating loss—not only of the land itself but of its memory—brought about by the further dispersion of the communities that originated in those villages. But the trigger for the writing of these books is often an external political event: Ahmad Atiya,

one of the authors of *'Alma*, decided to write in order to protest "resettlement" options being discussed in the late 1990s.[60] Al-Ali mentions his visit
to Kwaykat in the late 1970s as the impetus for writing the book some
twenty-five years later: "We went to visit our village, which is now [partially]
occupied and [partially] destroyed. We saw the graves in the graveyard, covered with wild thorns and trees. We saw the destroyed houses, and I went
to where our old house stood, which my father had built with his own
hands, and there I saw the millstone. And the house and the mill around
it were all broken up. I have included its picture in the book. So, after
twenty-five years had passed, I decided to go back to these memories and
write and record them. I decided to write a book on the heritage of our
village, Kwaykat. And that is how it was. So I gathered information that I
did not have from the elderly."[61]

For al-Ali, it is the sight of his destroyed village and the luxurious Jewish
settlement nearby that some quarter of a century later impels him to write
the history of the village. It is the perception of how things are now that
motivates the authors to record and document how things were then. The
commemorative practices, more than an act of salvage ethnography, are
acts of political advocacy.[62] Al-Ali's book includes photographs of massacres
not of Kwaykat, but of Dayr Yasin, thus emphasizing the national(ist) basis
of the writing. The book also contains photographs of border meetings
between Palestinians in Lebanon and their relatives in Israel after the
Israeli evacuation of southern Lebanon. The inclusion of these photographs reaffirms what one author calls the "unity" of the peoples across
borders. The authors of the 'Alma volume end their book by declaring that
documentation of the history of the defeated is itself a necessary step in the
"war against the colonizers." Uthman writes in *Dayr al-Qassi* that history
and blood will defeat "the sword" and thus the history of every tree needs
to be documented.[63] Husayn Ali Lubani, author of *Damun*, includes a six-
page passage on the right of return, where he declares that the "refugee
problem is at the core of the Palestinian cause"[64] and that, by recording
the history of ownership of lands by the inhabitants of Damun, he is in
effect reaffirming their claim to the lost village. He is also providing documentation that he hopes can be used in any future judicial contest over
land ownership.

Commemorative Narratives

Memories of Palestine as it was before 1948 have become such a significant
element in the collective narrative of loss and exile in the community in
Lebanon that when I, in the course of a life-story interview, asked a twenty-
year-old Palestinian woman what her worst memory (*zakira*) was, she said,
"the Nakba, of course."[65] The naturalization of memories of exile across
generations, however those memories are transmitted, is significant: for the

younger generations who do not personally remember the Nakba, its memory is nevertheless a signpost to the future, a part of their identity as Palestinians, and an important element of their claim to right of return.

As I mentioned, in the absence of refugee participation in negotiations about their fate, they insist on packing a bundle of rights in the "right of return." This bundle includes, but is not limited to, a combination of the following possibilities: Israel's recognition of its culpability in the 1948 eviction of Palestinians from their villages; Israel's recognition of the right of return; compensation for lost properties; return to the former villages (with or without Israeli citizenship); citizenship of a future binational state; and settling in the putative Palestinian state. The narratives that commemorate the past point to these options.

When I asked Abu Sa'id, a thirty-six-year-old who had spent his life shuttling between a job in Saudi Arabia and his family in the Burj al-Barajna camp in Beirut, what he imagined Palestine to look like, he responded: "Palestine is like paradise. First, it makes me feel secure and comfortable. But I also imagine it another way: it is all green, and there are rivers and trees, and it has a beautiful nature."[66]

For Abu Sa'id, the ability to labor on the land, to cultivate its trees and partake of its rivers were inseparable from the sense of security and comfort that the instability and impermanence of his refugee life had denied him. The image of a land full of rivers and trees, and the Edenic (past and future) utopia were as much a comment on the political economy of his life as about aesthetic deprivations. Further conversation revealed that for him, the sense of security could be achieved if and when he could settle alongside other Palestinians unthreatened by impermanence.

A Palestinian woman in her early forties told me that she had an image of her old village, Tarshiha, that had been formed from conversations with and stories told by her family. When she was offered a videotape of the village as it is today, she was at first apprehensive about what she would see. She was aware that the video image might subvert her idealistic vision of Palestine; nonetheless, she wanted to see it, because it was, after all, Tarshiha. She said, "In the end, of course, I saw it. The film was not long and didn't really show much of Tarshiha. But I wasn't disappointed." For her, Tarshiha was where she ("or if not me, my sons, and if not them, their children") could eventually live. Aware of different political solutions, she thought that only a binational state would redeem her memories of Tarshiha.[67]

Some refugees could not imagine living alongside Jews or as Jewish citizens. Their vision of an Edenic past systematically destroyed by colonization precluded the possibility of coexistence. Umm Walid described Palestine: "I am sure it's a beautiful country. . . . My grandmother on my mother's side always talked about Palestine. A lot of old women talked about Palestine and always said it had the most beautiful villages and countryside." When I asked her if she wanted to return, she replied, "Of course," but after a momentary hesitation, she added, "I would rather stay here in the camp. I can't live under a Jewish government."[68]

Others, however, saw living alongside Jews as a continuation of a prewar history of coexistence, if not friendship. Umm Jamal spoke about the commercial relations between the two communities: "We were living with the Jews and they bought things from us, and we lived next to each other peacefully. But then the Jews from the outside came and started attacking the people in the village. In our region, there were lots of Jews, but there were more Arabs. But they were organized, and we were divided. Maybe among the Jews there were people who would have wanted to live with us, but the more of them that came from outside, that changed."[69]

Several older women recounted how they took their children to Jewish doctors who lived in nearby settlements. One even mentioned having heard rumors of a love affair between a Palestinian man and a Jewish woman. Clear distinctions were made between the Jews who used to live there and those who arrived later, closer to the 1948 war.

Interestingly, a number of the Palestinian refugees I interviewed had visited their Galilee villages. During the Israeli occupation of Lebanon, several had obtained permits from the South Lebanese Army (or the Lahad Army, as they called it) and from the Israeli state, and had traveled through the border zones to meet with relatives whom they had not seen in decades. Among the stories they recounted (often with a sense of wonderment at the ease of the interaction) was their first encounter with Jewish Israelis, where the interaction was often made even more memorable by the Arab provenance of their Sephardic interlocutors' mastery of an Arabic dialect. Umm Mahmud recounted her experience visiting her uncle's village along with her eldest son, Mahmud:

There were all these Jews from Yemen and Lebanon and Morocco and Russia, so many of them. They would ask me, "Do you like Israel?" and one of them, a Yemeni woman, asked me the same question. I said, "What Israel are you talking about? No, I like Palestine!" She was shocked and said, "No, there is no Palestine." Mahmud said to her, "Do you like Yemen?" And she said, "Yes, I like it; it is my *balad* [country]." And I said, "I like Palestine, too. It is *my balad.*" After that, we went and visited them, and they were so kind. She was a neighbor to my stepdaughter. And I told her that even if we spend a 100 years outside, we will go back to Palestine. And we will live separately, if we have to, but we will go back and we will even live next to them. Given the chance, we will go and live next to them. But their government is convincing the world that we are terrorists, but all we really want is to live there. I am an old woman, and I will probably die. So maybe my son will return, and if not him, then maybe his son.[70]

Though those who had visited Israel and returned were a small percentage of the overall camp population, their anecdotes illustrated their effort to show the human side of Jewish Israelis and perhaps even to find a commonality with those who spoke Arabic or originated from Arab nations. When Umm Mahmud was recounting her story, a younger Palestinian woman was present in the room. When Umm Mahmud said: "Given the chance, we will go and live next to them," the younger woman was incredulous, not toward the notion of return, but regarding the possibility of coexistence. She voiced her protest, and Umm Mahmud and her son Ahmad (who was also present) shook their heads. Ahmad, who is in his early forties and had not visited Israel, supported his mother's assertion: "You will see. They even speak Arabic. They are just like us!"

Significantly, the content of the refugees' memory images and narratives often pointedly includes signposts to the future and to the range of options that are possible under the right of return. The refugees with whom I spoke struggle on a daily basis against exclusion from the Palestinian polity and abandonment by the world and the international community. In facing contradictory pressures from all quarters about their fate, they insist on the right of return, where the phrase bundles a range of meanings and possibilities. For them, until they are allowed a forum in which they can participate with the full knowledge of and the ability to choose from a set of just, concrete, and acceptable solutions, remembering their villages in Palestine is a way to declare their belonging to the Palestinian nation and to contest the circumscription of their options.

Conclusion: Remembering and Returning

It has sometimes been said that when Palestinian refugees in the diaspora are asked whether they want to return to (some version of) Palestine, they inevitably give a rote affirmative response in order to adhere to the official narrative of national unity. It is also implied that this rote response is given as a result of elite manipulation and that, in fact, the refugees may not want any further upheavals. Here I have challenged several aspects of this argument: that the affirmative response is rote; that it indicates a desire to maintain narratives of national unity; and that ordinary refugees are easily manipulated by an intransigent and uncompromising elite. I have done so by examining the ways in which Palestinian refugees in Lebanon commemorate their lost villages using various media and the reflexive transmission of these narratives across generations.

In the contest over the character and content of the Palestinian polity, many 1948 Palestinian refugees feel that their right of return will be bargained away in return for the establishment of a Palestinian state in the Palestinian lands occupied by Israel in 1967. The "1948 for 1967" bargain is considered highly problematic within the Palestinian diaspora, as it demands an arbitrary and unjust breaking apart of a polity that has been unified—however fractiously—in its identity, institutions, and organizations. This division would be nothing short of a cataclysmic schism that explicitly requires the forced exclusion of one segment of this polity from the decision-making processes that will affect its fate most decisively and possibly disastrously. The intensification of the commemorative practices in the last few years shows conscious efforts at grassroots mobilization by refugees in Lebanon against such political exclusion. Those I interviewed and interacted with all displayed a profound and multifaceted understanding of their predicament and were also intensely aware of their marginalization as refugees within the larger Palestinian polity. As one refugee said, "None of the leaders ever asks the refugees what *they* want."[71] The refugees in Lebanon have never been asked their opinions directly, nor have they been informed of their options honestly. It is disingenuous to say that because a Palestinian refugee in Lebanon may accept a possible resettlement in Lebanon or elsewhere as an option of last resort, he or she has no desire to return. As Peteet has pointed out, though Palestinians in Lebanon would gladly accept improvements in their living conditions and even tactically acquire Lebanese citizenship should such an option present itself, they are deeply aware of their moral claims to a Palestinian nationality, and they continue to demand participation in whatever decision-making processes concern their fate.[72] This awareness is why the ties to the land are constantly renewed, symbolically and commemoratively: commemorative practices do not simply look back nostalgically to the past but also chart a way for the future.

The demands for the right of return and political participation not only emerge out of the economic deprivations of life in Lebanon—which is perhaps the most hostile host environment for Palestinian refugees among the Arab countries—but also out of a history of political mobilization and struggle centered in and around their camps. Since narratives of dispossession and return have become the cornerstone of Palestinian diasporic identity, asking Palestinians to abdicate their right of return without being offered any viable and respectable alternatives or even the possibility of participating in the political decision-making process is akin to demanding that they not only abandon their claims to their past and their cultural and historical inheritance, but also relinquish their fundamental right to determine their own fate as members of a political community and accede to a permanently inferior status as second-class residents of foreign nations. Thus, the refugees' commemorative practices encourage mobilization around the right of return, form the basis of struggle for inclusion, reaffirm that, despite efforts to marginalize them, the Palestinian refugees in Lebanon still demand to be part of the larger Palestinian polity, and ultimately voice the refugees' demand to be heard.

Notes

1. Salman Abu-Sitta, *The End of the Palestinian-Israeli Conflice: From Refugees to Citizens at Home* (London: Palestinian Land Society and Palestinian Return Center, 2001).

2. Palestinian Centre for Policy and Survey Research (PCPSR). "Press Release on Refugee Views on the Settlement of the Refugee Issue, Ramallah, 18 July 2003," in documents and source material of *Journal of Palestine Studies* 33:1 (2003):160–62; Khalil Shikaki, "Results of Palestinian Survey Research Unit's Refugees' Polls in the West Bank/Gaza Strip, Jordan and Lebanon on Refugees' Preferences and Behavior in a Palestinian-Israeli Permanent Refugee Agreement" (press release, July 18, 2003); for a critique, see Salman Abu-Sitta, "The Right of Return: Inalienable and Sacred," *Al-Ahram Weekly* 14–20 (August 2003).

3. Although Shikaki interviewed "4,500 refugee families in the West Bank, Gaza, Lebanon and Jordan" ("Results of Palestinian Survey"), further, more extensive research is required to find the specific demands of larger percentages of each refugee community, the members of which now collectively number over four million. The Shikaki interview was based on the Taba talks of 2001, and as such do not include a full range of possible options. On July 22, 2003, nearly a hundred refugee organizations and NGOs in Lebanon denounced Shikaki's survey, as no local organization was aware of its implementation in Lebanon.

4. Ted Swedenburg, *Memories of Revolt: The 1936–1939 Rebellion and the Palestinian National Past* (Minneapolis: University of Minnesota Press, 1995); Raymond Williams, *The Country and the City* (London: Hogarth, 1985); Richard Werbner, ed., *Memory and the Postcolony: African Anthropology and the Critique of Power* (London: Zed, 1998); Yael Zerubavel, *Recovered Roots: Collective Memory and the Making of Israeli National Tradition* (Chicago: University of Chicago Press, 1995).

5. In this essay, I distinguish between ordinary camp residents, who have little access to political or economic resources and are unprotected by any state or parastatal apparatus, and those Palestinians who by virtue of their political position, social class, or possession of European or North American passports have social mobility, university education, the ability to support their families, and even a choice of places to live around the globe.

6. Benny Morris, *The Birth of the Palestinian Refugee Problem Revisited* (Cambridge: Cambridge University Press, 2004); and Rosemary Sayigh, *Too Many Enemies: The Palestinian Experience in Lebanon* (London: Zed, 1994), 17.

7. Rosemary Sayigh, "Palestinian Refugees in Lebanon: Implantation, Transfer or Return?" *Middle East Policy* 8:1 (2001): 101.

8. Even in instances where the refugee camps were located in more rural areas, the high congestion of inhabitants in the camp created a quasi-urban spatial and social context.

9. Yezid Y. Sayigh, *Armed Struggle and the Search for State: The Palestinian National Movement, 1949–1993* (Oxford: Oxford University Press, 1997), 41; Abu Iyad with Eric Rouleau, *My Home, My Land: A Narrative of the Palestinian Struggle* (New York: Times Books, 1981), 38–39.

10. Faisal Jallul, *Naqd al-silah al-Filastini; Burj al-Barajna: Ahlan wa thawratan wa mukhayyaman* (Critique of Palestinian armed resistance; Burj al-Barajna: Its people, revolution and refugee camp) (Beirut: Dar al-Jadid, 1994), 35.

11. Shafiq Al-Hut, *'Ashrun 'aman fi Munazzamat al-Tahrir al-Filastiniyya 1964–1984* (Twenty years in the Palestine Liberation Organization 1964–1984) (Beirut: Dar al-Istiqlal, 1986), 52.

12. R. Sayigh, *Too Many Enemies*, 68.

13. Rex Brynen, *Sanctuary and Survival: The PLO in Lebanon* (Boulder, Colo.: Westview, 1990), 37–52.

14. On the Maronite community's ambivalence and later hostility toward Palestinians, see Walid Phares, *Lebanese Christian Nationalism: The Rise and Fall of an Ethnic Resistance* (Boulder, Colo.: Lynne Rienner, 1995); Walid Khalidi, *Conflict and Violence*

in Lebanon: Confrontation in the Middle East (Cambridge, Mass.: Center for International Affairs, Harvard University, 1979), 113; and Michael Hudson, "Palestinians and Lebanon: The Common Story" (paper presented at the Palestinians in Lebanon conference organized by the Centre for Lebanese Studies and the Refugee Studies Programme, Queen Elizabeth House, Oxford, 1996), 9.

15. "The concurrent halos of martyrdom and championship [of the Palestinian cause] surrounding the Palestinian revolution exerted a powerful fascination over the Moslem masses and radicals of Lebanon" (Khalidi, *Conflict and Violence in Lebanon*, 80).

16. The most notable massacres occurred in 1976 in the Tal al-Za'tar camp with Syrian collusion and in 1982 in Sabra and Shatila with Israeli cooperation.

17. In addition to Tal al-Za'tar in 1975–76, Dbayeh and Jisr al-Basha camps and the mixed-nationality slums of Karantina were razed by the Lebanese Phalange Party. Nabatiyya and Ain al-Hilwa were totally destroyed by IDF bombing during the 1982 Israeli invasion of Lebanon (Ain al-Hilwa was subsequently rebuilt), and all southern and Beirut camps suffered massive damage during 1982 and subsequent years.

18. The 1983 battles between Syria-supported factions and Fatah splinter groups on the one side and Fatah on the other side are of special note.

19. Tal al-Za'tar camp suffered a long siege in 1975–76 before it fell to the Phalange. Rashidiyya, Burj al-Barajna, and Shatila all suffered several sieges by Syria-supported Amal during the War of the Camps (1985–88).

20. The Republic of Lebanon Ministry of Labour Decision No. 621/1 stipulates that most professional and managerial positions (including occupations in the service industry), small-business ownership, and engineering and teaching professions are open only to Lebanese. Additionally, even illegal day jobs in the construction sector are becoming increasingly scarce as Palestinian workers face competition from lower-wage Syrian migrant laborers.

21. Property Law No. 296, published on April 5, 2001, is specifically designed to disinherit Palestinians (rather than other aliens residing in Lebanon) from properties they own. The Palestinians' usual protectors and allies in the Parliament (the Hezbollah as well as the Progressive Socialist Party) have been remarkably silent on this issue.

22. In 1994, a deal between Nabih Berri (leader of the Shi'a Amal Party) and Sunni political notables facilitated the naturalization of around 15,000–20,000 Palestinians (Julie Peteet, "From Refugees to Minority: Palestinians in Post-War Lebanon," *Middle East Report* 26:3 [1996]: 29), some of whom were Shi'a and all others Sunni; they mostly belonged to seven villages in Galilee near the border between Israel and Lebanon and to which Lebanon lays historical claims. The naturalization of Shi'a Palestinians was part of confessional/demographic maneuvering by the political leaders rather than a sign of humanitarian concern for the plight of Palestinians.

23. A recent court ruling in Lebanon has declared illegal the 1994 deal described above, and the Lebanese government has seized on this ruling in order to declare a review of the naturalization of Palestinians.

24. The Lebanese state has varying housing policies vis-à-vis Palestinians in different locations. Whereas reconstruction in the southern camps is usually allowed pending UNRWA approval and processing, all repairs and reconstruction of camp housing in and around Beirut camps are prohibited.

25. All NGOs have to be registered with the Lebanese government and meet state-set quotas on hiring and serving Lebanese citizens.

26. These fees are now 700,000 Lebanese liras (approximately $500), which is

beyond what most camp students or their families can afford. Since the imposition of these fees, many Palestinian students have dropped out of universities or have put their university plans on hold.

27. Ramsay Short, "Struggling to Create a Future for Women," *Daily Star*, March 18, 2003.

28. Jaber Suleiman, "The Current Political, Organizational, and Security Situation in the Palestinian Refugee Camps of Lebanon," *Journal of Palestine Studies* 29:1 (1999): 72.

29. Peteet, "From Refugees to Minority," 27. The scapegoating of Palestinians in Lebanon, is very similar to European anti-Semitism, especially in the interwar years, where the Jews as a category of people were blamed for all manner of political and social malaise.

30. Dore Gold, adviser and spokesman for successive Likud governments, has, for example, stated that preservation of Israel's "demographic security" would require prevention of "a situation where the Palestinian Authority floods Judea and Samaria with [returning] refugees" (Rex Brynen, "Imagining a Solution: Final Status Arrangements and Palestinian Refugees in Lebanon," *Journal of Palestine Studies* 26:2 [1997]: 46).

31. The Geneva Accord (GA), *Journal of Palestine Studies* 33:2 (2004): 96.

32. For example, in the shadow of the Geneva Accords, the Palestinian Religious Scholars Association has issued a decree forbidding any Muslim from signing an agreement that forgoes the right of return for all refugees to their original homes inside Israel (see *Jerusalem Post*, December 2, 2003)..

33. Arab Resource Center for Popular Arts (ARCPA), "'This Illiterate Woman . . . She Talked to Us': Participants' Responses to ARCPA's 1948 Uprooting Oral History Project," *Al-Jana* (May 1998): 43.

34. "Before the invasion of 1982, I and a number of comrades tried our hardest to convince leading academic institutions, any of which would have been able to start collecting oral history testimonies, even if only from certain camps or in a limited number. However, our attempts . . . failed" (Bayan Al-Hout, "Oral History: Continuous, Permanent Connection," *Al-Jana* [May 1998]: 11).

35. Rosemary Sayigh, "Oral History for Palestinians: The Beginning of a Discipline," *Al-Jana* (May 1998): 6.

36. Ted Swedenburg, "The Palestinian Peasant as National Signifier," *Anthropological Quarterly* 63 (1990): 18–30.

37. To protest Israeli state's seizures of lands owned by its Palestinian citizens, Palestinians in Nazareth and several other villages in Israel held a demonstration on March 30, 1976. Israeli police opened fire on the demonstrators, and six Palestinians were killed and more than fifty were injured. The day became an important Palestinian commemorative day. See Faisal Darraj, "'An 'Alaqat al-Ardh wa al-Watan wa al-Zakira" (On the relations between land, homeland, and memory), *Al-Hadaf* 1183 (April 3, 1994): 8–9; Rashid Quwaidar, "Yawm al ardh: Min tadmir al-mujtama' al-Filastini . . . ila I'ada bana' al-huwiyya al-wataniyya wa al-qawmiyya" (Land Day: From the destruction of Palestinian society . . . to the reestablishment of national and pan-Arab identity), *Al-Hurriyya* 801 (April 9, 2000).

38. See, for example, Salah Al-Khalidi, "Al-ardh al-Muqaddasa fi al-Qur'an" (The Holy Land in the Qur'an), *Filistin al-Muslima* (July 1993): 44–45.

39. Benedict Anderson, *Imagined Communities: Reflections on the Origin and Spread of Nationalism* (London: Verso, 1991).

40. Randa Farah, "Reconstruction of Palestinian Identities in al-Baq'a Camp," in *Palestine, palestiniens: Territoire national, espaces communautaires*, Riccardo Bocco, Blandine Destremau, and Jean Honnoyer, eds. (Amman: CERMOC, 1997), 262.

41. Jonathan Boyarin, *Palestine and Jewish History: Criticism at the Borders of Ethnography* (Minneapolis: University of Minnesota Press, 1996), 8.

42. Kirsten Scheid, "'This Illiterate Woman . . . She Talked to Us': A Summary and Evaluation," *Al-Jana* (May 1998): 52.

43. Hallah Ghazzawi, "La Mémoire du village et la préservation de l'identité palestinienne," in Abdulaziz et al., *Palestine: Mémoire et territoires* (Paris: École des Hautes Études en Sciences Sociales, 1989), 36.

44. R. Sayigh, *Too Many Enemies*, 92.

45. Rebecca Roberts, "Bourj al-Barahneh: The Significance of Village Origin in a Palestinian Refugee Camp," master's thesis, University of Durham, 1999.

46. R. Sayigh, *Too Many Enemies*, 98–99.

47. Suleiman, "The Current Political, Organizational, and Security Situation," 75. Suleiman names the following villages as having spawned committees: al-Nahr, Dayr al-Qasi, 'Alma, Suhmata, Qaditha, al-Suwayalat, and Bassa. I am aware of the Tarshiha and Kwaykat committees, among others.

48. Susan Slyomovics, *The Objects of Memory: Arab and Jew Narrate the Palestinian Village* (Philadelphia: University of Pennsylvania Press, 1998), 201–3.

49. In the interest of anonymity of my interlocutors, I have slightly modified some Internet monikers.

50. Jabir Abu Hawash, "Majmu'a Mahmud Dakwar turathiyya: Mathaf ithnugrafi lil-zakira al-Filastiniyya" (Mahmud Dakwar's heritage collection: An ethnographic museum commemorating Palestine), *Al-Jana* 5 (1997): 15.

51. Ibid.

52. Between 1987 and 1997, the Centre for Documentation and Research at Birzeit University published two series of village books. The first series consisted of books on Majdu 'Asqlan (1986), Maslamah (1986), 'Ayn Hawd (1987), Deir Yassin (1987), Faluja (1987), 'Inaba (1987), Al-Lajjoun (1987), Al-Koofkh (1987), Abu-Kishk (1990), Miska (1991), Kufr Saba (1991), Lifta (1991), and Kufr Bir'im (1991). The second series covered Qaqoun (1994), 'Imwas (1994), Zir'een (1994), Lubya (1994), Abu Shusha (1995), Tiret-Haifa (1995), Beit Jibreen (1995), and Dawaymeh (1997) (ARCPA, bibliography, *Al-Jana* [2002]: 68).

53. This series includes books on Tabariyya (1998), Tantura (1998), Tirat-Haifa (1998), Lubya (1998), Balad al-Shaykh (2001), and Kufr Qana (2001) (ARCPA, bibliography, 68–69).

54. There are other village books published mostly in the occupied territories by independent scholars and researchers, but these are not easily available in Lebanon. See ARCPA bibliography.

55. Jallul, *Naqd al-silah al-Filastini*.

56. Walid Khalidi, ed., *All That Remains: The Palestinian Villages Occupied and Destroyed by Israel in 1948* (Washington, D.C.: Institute for Palestine Studies, 1991).

57. Reem Haddad, "Labor of Love Produces History of Lost Village," *Daily Star*, May 10, 2001.

58. This kind of obsessive attention to the accuracy of facts is a common characteristics of narratives by the dispossessed and defeated. Hilary Mantel writes about the nineteenth-century slave narratives in the United States: "The Abolitionist preference was for facts, facts, facts: not for fantasy, which can be forged. Slave writers were urged to be specific, to skewer names and dates and places, as protection against the owners' frequent allegation that slave narratives were the product of white Northern do-gooders with too little information and too much imagination" ("The Shape of Absence," *London Review of Books* 24:15 [2002]).

59. Interview with author, March 9, 2002.

60. Ahmad and Hasan Atiya, *'Alma: Zaytuna bilad Safad* ('Alma: The olive tree of Safad province) (Beirut: n.p., 1998), 10.

61. Interview with author, March 9, 2002.

62. James Clifford, "On Ethnographic Allegory," in *Writing Culture: The Poetics and Politics of Ethnography*, James Clifford and George E. Marcus, eds. (Berkeley: University of California Press, 1986), 112–13.

63. Ibrahim Khalil Uthman, *Dayr al-Qassi: Zanbaqa al-Jalil al-awsat al-gharbi* (Dayr al-Qasi: The lily of midwest Galilee) (Beirut: n.p., 2000), 218.

64. Husayn Ali Lubani (al-Damuni), *Al-Damun: Qariya Filastiniyya fi al-bal* (Damun: A Palestinian village in the mind) (Beirut: Dar al-Arabi, 1999), 255.

65. Other researchers have also found that many Palestinians in Lebanon tell their life stories as a metonym of the larger Palestinian refugee community's story. Scheid writes that it "is a standard trait of oral testimony, to feature an 'I' that refers neither to an individual with a destiny (as in a novel) nor to an individual with acute observation skills (as in an ethnography), but rather who has taken it upon him or herself to represent through participation an entire group, to personify a society" (Scheid, " 'This Illiterate Woman,' " 52).

66. Interview with author, Burj al-Barajna camp, February 10, 2002.

67. Interview with author, Beirut, January 15, 2002.

68. Interview with author, Burj al-Barajna, January 19, 2002.

69. Interview with author, March 4, 2002.

70. Interview with author, Burj al-Barajna, February 6, 2002.

71. Abdelma'ta Husayn, February 14, 2003.

72. Peteet, "From Refugees to Minority," 30.

Chapter 3
The Right of Return versus the Law of Return: Contrasting Historical Narratives in Israeli and Palestinian School Textbooks

Elie Podeh

"The temptation is often overwhelmingly strong to tell it, not as it really was, but as we would wish it to have been."[1] When he wrote that in the mid-1970s, Bernard Lewis was alluding to a truism that had eluded many: that in search of buttressing their legitimacy, elites have often invented or shaped history according to their desires and beliefs. Further research, however, has made it clear that any historical narrative is a contested terrain, even among historians.[2] Naturally, this relativism has affected the way in which history has been analyzed, told, and received; yet research shows that in their quest for legitimacy and identity, elites have continued assiduously and eagerly to tell history as they wish it to have been.

History, Memory, and Textbooks

Forging the nation's collective memory is an integral part of the nation-building. The powerful link between history and memory is especially salient in the educational system, which is responsible for implanting knowledge and values in young people. The successful completion of this task, it is assumed, will turn them into loyal citizens and will help instill a shared identity.

Historians and sociologists generally fail to note the political and social links between school textbooks and collective memory. Scholars dealing with the tools used by the state to create its own collective memory—such as historiography, literature, cinema, and national commemorations—tend to overlook the role of textbooks. At the same time, scholars of textbook research barely analyze them in the context of the attempts to build a collective memory, usually ignoring the social environment that helps shape textbook content as well.[3]

Since in many Western democracies and certainly in nondemocratic societies, the state controls the educational apparatus, it can shape the nation's collective memory by determining what is to be included and what is to be excluded from the curricula and from textbooks. Such a course of action opens the way for the manipulation of the past in order to mold the present and the future.[4] In this respect, the school system and its textbooks become yet another arm of the state, agents of memory whose aim is to ensure the transmission of certain "approved knowledge" to the younger generation. Textbooks thus function as a sort of "supreme historical court" whose task is to decipher "from all the accumulated 'pieces of the past' the 'true' collective memories which are appropriate for inclusion in the canonical national historical narrative."[5] In constructing the collective memory, textbooks play a dual role: they provide a sense of continuity between the past and the present, transmitting accepted historical narratives; and they alter, or rewrite, the past to suit contemporary needs.[6]

The manipulation of the past often entails the use of stereotypes and prejudice in describing the Other.[7] Carried to the extreme, stereotyping and prejudice foster delegitimization—the "categorization of groups into extreme negative social categories which are excluded from human groups that are considered as acting within the limits of acceptable norms and/or values."[8] Common means used for delegitimization, according to Daniel Bar-Tal, are dehumanization, out-casting, trait characterization, use of political labels, and group comparison.[9]

It is common knowledge that textbooks in social sciences and humanities do not merely convey an objective body of information. Textbooks, according to Howard Mehlinger, are the modern version of village storytellers, since they "are responsible for conveying to youth what adults believe they should know about their own culture as well as that of other societies." In his opinion, none of the socialization instruments can be compared with textbooks "in their capacity to convey a uniform, approved, even official version of what youth should believe."[10] Though textbooks pretend to teach neutral, legitimate knowledge, they are often used as ideological tools to promote a certain belief system and legitimize an established political and social order. In other words, the selection and organization of knowledge for schools is an ideological process that serves the interests of particular classes and social groups.[11]

It is difficult to establish the exact role played by textbooks in comparison with other socialization instruments. The growing exposure of the younger generation to electronic media undoubtedly has diminished the centrality of the textbook as an instrument of education. Still, scholars tend to agree that textbooks have remained crucial. In his analysis of European history textbooks in the last hundred years, Wolfgang Jacobmeyer concluded that "our modern societies have developed history textbooks as the most remarkable medium for the transmission of history, outnumbering press, radio, and TV."[12] Philip Altbach, too, observed that "in an age of computers and satellite communications, the most powerful and pervasive educational technology is the textbook."[13] A recent study concluded that, although some 85 percent of students' knowledge came from outside school, "dependence on textbooks in some form or other was likely to remain an important element in the learning of history, geography and social studies."[14]

Another major problem inherent in the study of textbooks is that, although they constitute the core of the school curriculum, it cannot be assumed that what is included in the text is actually taught or learned. According to Michael Apple, students respond to the text in three different ways: in the first, dominant way, the student accepts the messages contained in the text at face value. In the second, negotiated way, the reader may dispute a certain claim but accept the overall interpretation of the text. In the third way, the student rejects the dominant interpretation of the text.[15] While these observations are illuminating, it may be assumed that most students lack sufficient historical knowledge to prompt them to contest existing narratives. It is likely, therefore, that most students, especially in nondemocratic societies, belong to the dominant or negotiated categories.

Furthermore, textbooks carry the authority of print. Written texts, according to David Olson, "are devices which separate speech from speaker, and that separation in itself makes the words impersonal, objective and above criticism." In his opinion, textbooks resemble religious rituals, since both "are devices for putting ideas and beliefs above criticism."[16] When the message originates in the textbook, which teachers and parents themselves consult, students attach greater authority to them. Moreover, since textbooks often constitute the ultimate reference source for the student (as well as for the teacher, in certain cases), it is likely that beliefs implanted through them will "persist for a lifetime."[17] A recent study found that when pressed, students chose the textbook as the most accurate of reference sources because "its apparent objective, encyclopedic nature fit more readily with their view of history and because many of their classroom activities involved searching for facts."[18]

The role ascribed to the textbook of legitimizing an established political and social order is particularly relevant to textbooks in the field of history. Since each generation makes a considerable effort to transmit its traditions and belief system to the next generation, history textbooks have traditionally been "geared to the teaching of the national past and to generating an identification with it."[19] Ever since the rise of the nation-state in Europe in the nineteenth century, history textbooks have been used by states as instruments for glorifying the nation, consolidating its national identity, and justifying particular forms of social and political systems.[20] Many studies in the West have demonstrated that ethnocentric views and myths, stereotypes and prejudices often pervade history textbooks.[21]

Israel is no exception. The Israeli education system and its textbooks, side by side with such factors as Zionist historiography, children's books, and the media, have functioned as "memory agents," helping to mold the nation's collective memory.[22] In addition to history textbooks, civics, local geography (called *moledet*), literature, and even Bible lessons constituted important channels for strengthening the students' attachment to the homeland.

The case of the Palestinians is more complex. Until the formation of the Palestinian Ministry of Education in 1994, following the Oslo agreements, Israel was in charge of the educational system in the West Bank and the Gaza Strip, using censored Egyptian (Gaza Strip) and Jordanian (West Bank) textbooks. Thus, although historiography and literature have always been instrumental in shaping Palestinian identity, the educational system and its textbooks could not play a comparable role. Only in the 1994/95 school year, with the publication of the first set of new textbooks, did Palestinian textbooks begin to play an important role in the formation of a shared Palestinian collective memory. This memory was primarily shaped by history and national education (*al-tarbiya al-wataniyya*) textbooks as well textbooks used for geography and Islamic education.

My aim is to unveil the way in which Israelis and Palestinians use school textbooks to advance a certain narrative of their right of return to their respective homelands. In Israel, this right was translated into a law in 1950 (*hoq ha-shvut*, in Hebrew), while within the Palestinian community this right remains an unfulfilled aspiration (*haqq al-'awda*, in Arabic). Since this question is closely connected with the story of the refugee problem, this chapter will also analyze the historical narrative of the refugee problem, as portrayed by each party in its textbooks. The main argument of this chapter is that the Israeli and Palestinian education systems offer dichotomous historical narratives of their right of return. Surprisingly, however, the meaning of these narratives is not dissimilar, as both parties perceive the other's narrative as menacing to its very existence. Hence, it is suggested that each party should offer a narrative that in no way threatens—or implies to threaten—the other's existence.

In order to maintain some consistency in analysis, a methodology based on the following criteria has been used:[23]

1. *Categories of Analysis.* How is the Other described—in terms of religion or ethnicity, as part of the larger Arab nation, or according to specific nationality?
2. *Stereotypical Content.* Is the other nation, group, or individual described in positive, neutral, or negative terms? Special emphasis is attached

to the use of delegitimizing and dehumanizing terms (for example, terrorists, thieves, Nazis).

3. *Role Performance.* Is the Other presented in a conflictual or a peaceful context? In what role is the Other described? Is it a positive or a negative role?

4. *Intentions, Blame, and Lessons to Be Learned.* How are the aims or the intentions of the Other described? Whose fault is the conflict? Who is to blame for the perpetuation of the conflict? Are there any lessons to be learned about the Other from certain historical episodes?

5. *Data Accuracy.* To what extent is the material presented in the textbooks accurate? This is a complex issue, as any historical narrative, including the selection of facts, is subjective. Moreover, some of the information known in the present was unknown at the time of writing the textbook. It is necessary, therefore, to compare the textbook's presentation with existing historiography.

6. *Linguistic Usage and Tone.* To what extent is the material presented in a rational tone or in an emotional tone? Does the author express biased opinions or is his or her presentation neutral? Does the author conceal his or her presence in the text? Does the presentation reflect a patronizing or superior attitude?

7. *Bias by Omission and Self-Censorship.* Have important details been omitted or censored from the text? What kind of information has the author sought to hide from the student and for what reasons? Is the omission or censorship done in a subtle and sophisticated or blatant way?

8. Bias by Proportion or Disproportion. Are certain topics presented in a disproportional way? For example, is too much information provided on wars, conflicts, and acts of aggression rather than on peaceful initiatives?

The Israeli Narrative

Israeli school textbooks convey the common Jewish contention that exile was forced on the Jews and that the emergence of the modern Jewish national movement in the nineteenth century was, in addition to several immediate reasons, a culmination of two thousand years of yearning for Zion. Therefore, the return of the Jews to Eretz Israel (the Land of Israel) is depicted as "inevitable" and "long-anticipated."[24] The process of Jewish immigration (called ascendance, or aliyah) is described in detail in each history textbook as a heroic chapter of Zionism.[25]

While the issues of exile and immigration form important parts of the narrative in history textbooks, the Jewish Law of Return (*hoq ha-shvut*) is studied briefly in civics textbooks. In addition to the text of the law (enacted in 1950), the junior high civics textbook explains that it is "unique" to the Israeli state, deriving from the Israeli Declaration of Independence.[26] Under a chapter entitled "The State of Israel: The State of the Jewish People," the high school civics textbook also makes a connection between the law and the declaration. The narrative explains that its first article ("every Jew has the right to immigrate to the [Israeli] State") "expresses the yearning of the Jews throughout the centuries to return to their homeland." In addition, the textbook quotes a member of one of the religious parties in the Knesset, during the debate over the law, to the effect that a Jew who desires to return to Israel "is not an immigrant but a repatriate."[27] In both textbooks, the discussion of the citizenship law (enacted in 1952), which deals with the question of the rights of non-Jewish citizens, immediately follows the discussion of *hoq ha-shvut*. In such a way, the narrative attempts to bridge the latent gap between Israel as a Jewish and a democratic state.

The description of the Jewish Law of Return is not depicted as menacing to the Palestinians, the other party in the conflict. Yet the legal affirmation to every Jew to immigrate to the state, along with the undefined nature of the state's boundaries, means that Jews are allowed to "return" to any part of the land controlled by the Israeli government, including the territories occupied in 1967. This is not just a theoretical issue, as many Jewish immigrants have settled in those territories. Therefore from the point of view of Palestinians, who view the occupied territories as the core of their future state, the Jewish Law of Return is perceived as menacing to their own future. Moreover, Palestinian citizens of Israel view the law as constricting their rights within Israel, and Palestinian refugees consider that the law complicates the realization of their own claim to the right to return to their historical homeland.

Six history textbooks address the 1948 refugee problem in the context of the Arab-Israeli conflict: three for junior high school and three for high school. The educational system has maintained a certain measure of pluralism by authorizing several textbooks from which teachers or schools may select.[28] These textbooks are part of a new wave, which differs substantially from the writings of earlier generations in terms of methodology and content. Moreover, these textbooks contain fewer biases and stereotypes than the previous textbooks with regard to the depiction of Arabs.[29] A thorough analysis of the extant textbooks reveals the following observations:

1. All textbooks make use of the New Historians' most recent academic studies, particularly Benny Morris's study on the refugee problem (although they do not necessarily attribute the historical narrative to him).[30] Indeed, in contrast to previous textbooks, all current textbooks admit that in certain places and at certain times, the Israel Defense Forces (IDF) did expel Palestinians. However, they emphasize—as does Morris—that there was no Israeli master plan for expel-

ling the Palestinians. In adopting Morris's thesis, one textbook rejects previous Israeli and Arab explanations: the Israeli assertion that Arab leaders encouraged the Palestinians to depart and the Arab claim that the displacement of the Palestinians resulted from a well-planned Zionist scheme. As for the number of the refugees, all textbooks cite Israeli, Palestinian, and United Nations (UN) figures, while usually giving more credence to UN estimates.

2. In terms of space, the description of the refugee problem seems fair and reasonable.[31] But when one takes into account the lengthy narrative of the 1948 war, the discussion of the refugee problem—which is one of the most important consequences of the war from a historical perspective—seems lacking. Moreover, the fact that in certain textbooks the discussion of this topic has been separated from the discussion of the war and removed to another chapter that deals with the Palestinian problem means that the refugee issue may not be taught at all.[32] In addition, several textbooks contain a map that illustrates the directions in which Palestinians fled.[33] Some present a photo of the refugees,[34] and, in certain cases, the student is asked a question about the refugee problem.[35]

3. Predictably, all the textbooks present the refugee problem from a Zionist perspective, but some also attempt to present it from the Other's point of view. The 1948 war, which from an Israeli perspective is the War of Liberation or Independence, is also described in most of them as the Disaster (Nakba) of the Palestinians. Sometimes students are even asked to explain the reasons and meaning for the contrasting names of the war.[36]

4. Only three textbooks mention the Palestinian right of return. In all of them, the discussion is highly negative. Inbar writes that Israel always refused to allow the return of Palestinians, as this step would lead Israel to suffer a "demographic calamity." Barnavie and Naveh write that it became clear after the war that Israel would not allow the return of the refugees. Its leaders thought it was unreasonable "to demand from Israel to let unconditionally to its territory hostile masses of refugees while [at the same time] the Arabs [were] demanding the destruction of the 'Zionist entity'." Finally, Domke writes that in the aftermath of the war, the Palestinians hoped that the Arab states would facilitate their return, but this thinking changed with the establishment of the Palestine Liberation Organization (PLO).[37] All the textbooks blame the Arab states for the refugees' miserable plight in the refugee camps and elsewhere.

5. All the textbooks ignore the issue of the Palestinian refugees who resulted from the 1967 war.

In sum, the Israeli education system recently adopted a rather pluralistic attitude, which allows the teacher (or the school) to choose one of several authorized history textbooks. This pluralism is less reflected in civics text-books. In comparison with many other countries in which each subject matter has only one textbook, Israel has made noticeable progress. How-ever, there are only minor variations among the various historical narra-tives. This means that the margins of consensus or the desired collective memory are narrow and largely fixed. Reflecting the new historiography, the textbooks admit that Israel was responsible for some acts of expul-sion—a narrative that was unthinkable in previous generations.[38] Yet the issue of a Palestinian return is still taboo. Some textbooks ignore the issue altogether whereas others see it as an illegitimate claim, a Trojan horse that would allow the Palestinians to annihilate the Israeli state from within. The absence of any discussion of the 1967 refugees is not surprising, since the discussion of that is reminiscent of the biased narratives in the older text-books.[39]

The Palestinian Narrative

From 1967 and until the founding of the Palestinian Ministry of Education in 1994, the educational system in the occupied territories operated according to the Egyptian (Gaza Strip) and Jordanian (West Bank) curric-ula and textbooks. These texts were carefully scrutinized by the Israeli Civil Administration, and all parts considered offensive to Israel, Zionism, and Judaism were systematically deleted. Predictably, these textbooks accentu-ated Arab—and, in certain cases, Egyptian and Jordanian—national iden-tity while marginalizing or ignoring Palestinian national identity.[40]

With the transfer of authority in the sphere of education to the Palestin-ians, new Palestinian textbooks started to be published, even before the publication of a written curriculum. During the late 1990s, six experimen-tal textbooks were published in the field of national education. In early 2000, another fourteen textbooks were published for elementary grades in the fields of national education, language, geography, and Islamic educa-tion. During 2000, more than fifty textbooks were published in various fields for grades one, two, six, seven, and eleven. Meanwhile, Egyptian and Jordanian textbooks continued to be used in those grades and fields for which the Palestinian Authority has not yet provided textbooks.[41] Each grade uses only one source; there is no alternative textbook or narrative.

The first Palestinian textbooks referred only briefly to the refugee prob-lem, surprisingly ignoring the issue of the right of return. Post-1948 history was given in a factual manner in a national education textbook for the fifth grade, in which it was written that the post-1948 period was characterized by: "1) flight [*tasharud*] of many of the Palestinians who found refuge in Arab countries such as Syria, Lebanon, Jordan, and Egypt. 2) Many Pales-tinians lost their lands and as a result were compelled to learn new voca-tions. 3) The Palestinians were concerned to preserve their cultural existence [*kiyyanhum al-hidari*] through building Palestinian national, popular, and social institutions."[42] It can only be speculated that the need to produce several Palestinian textbooks as quickly as possible led to this general, and rather skimpy, way in which the historical narrative was presented to students.

The Palestinian textbooks produced in 2000–2002 treated the subject in a more comprehensive way. In contrast to the Israeli textbooks, which refer to the issue only in their history textbooks, the refugee problem is discussed in different Palestinian textbooks: national education, language, demography, and Islamic education. The Palestinian textbooks do not mention the Jewish right of return. The general impression, however, in reading the Palestinian textbooks, is that the whole issue of Jewish immigration into Palestine is considered illegal or illegitimate. With regard to the Palestinian refugee problem and right of return, a close scrutiny of the texts leads to the following conclusions:

1. The texts emphasize the victimization of the Palestinians during and after the 1948 war. They say that 479 villages out of 807 came under Israeli occupation and that more than 370 were destroyed between 1948 and 1950. In some cases, Jewish settlements were established on the sites of demolished Palestinian villages. Most often, the student is given several assignments in this connection, such as recounting the names of and collecting information on the destroyed villages. The cited number of refugees is "more than three-quarters of a million," a figure close to UN estimates. This number, according to the narrative, tripled from 1950 to 1994.[43]

2. Most texts emphasize that Israelis (euphemistically called "Jewish throngs" or "Zionist terrorist organizations") deliberately expelled the Palestinians from their land and that they faced repeated massacres, such as Deir Yassin, and other acts of extermination. This kind of narrative pervades not only national education textbooks but also geography, literary, and Islamic texts.[44]

3. On the other hand, several textbooks, mainly in geography, refer to "the war" as a primary reason for Palestinian emigration.[45] One textbook cites five reasons for the emigration, in which political motivation—that is, "compulsory emigration"—is listed only in fifth place.[46]

4. In contrast to Israeli textbooks, Palestinian textbooks refer to their right of return in three different textbooks. An Islamic education textbook asserts: "All Palestinians wait for the return of every Palestinian to his city or village from which he was made to emigrate."[47] A national education textbook for the second grade states that the camp is "a place established for the Palestinian refugees who had been forced to depart from their cities and villages in Palestine and who are determined to return to them."[48] Finally, a textbook for

teaching Arabic presents the text of a poem called "We Shall Return," which forms the basis for several questions and assignments for students.[49]

5. In contrast to Israeli textbooks, Palestinian textbooks do briefly mention the 1967 refugees. A book on demography states that this war led to "the second Palestinian compulsory emigration in which the number of emigrants from the West Bank exceeded 350,000."[50]

Conclusion

An analysis of the way in which the right of return or the Law of Return and the refugee problem are depicted in Israeli and Palestinian school textbooks reveals a gap, though it is less significant than one would initially have expected. The greatest gap is with regard to the textbooks' content: current Israeli books reflect the present state of historiography in the field, including the findings of Israeli New Historians. The Palestinian narrative, on the other hand, still fully adheres to the old Palestinian assertion that Israel's policy is solely responsible for the displacement of the Palestinians. Fouad Moughrabi claims that "objective non-Arab and non-Zionist scholars or even Israeli scholars associated with the 'new historians' revisionist interpretations of 1948" do not contest this narrative.[51] This argument is misleading, since most of the New Historians do not claim that Israel deliberately expelled all Palestinians but instead that there were certain cases of expulsion. Apart from this one-sided Palestinian perception of the refugee problem, the narrative truly and accurately reflects the Palestinian sense of victimization as a result of the war.

A more complicated reality emerges with regard to the depiction of the Palestinian right of return and the Jewish Law of Return. Israeli textbooks attempt to bridge the latent contradiction between Israel as a Jewish state (a product of *hoq ha-shvut*), and Israel as democratic state by emphasizing that non-Jewish citizens are entitled by law to equal rights. Palestinian textbooks altogether ignore the whole issue of the Jewish right of return. Though such an evasion by itself is not necessarily lamentable, the fact that the Palestinian narrative on the whole negates Jewish claims to Palestine is problematic. On the other hand, the Palestinian right of return is often discussed in the written text, maps, illustrations, and student class activities. Another important point is that the Jewish Law of Return in Israeli textbooks refers only to the boundaries of Israel, while Palestinian textbooks assert their right of return to the whole of Palestine or to the original places from where the Palestinians fled. From a Jewish point of view, such a narrative has threatening implications. The important point is, however, that since Israel's boundaries have not as yet been conclusively established, the Israeli narrative may be perceived as menacing by Palestinians, just as the Palestinian narrative may be perceived as menacing by Jews. In this respect, therefore, a similarity exists between the way Palestinians depict the right of return and Israelis depict the Law of Return.

Three reasons may account for the gap between the Israeli and Palestinian narratives. First, the current Palestinian textbooks—the first generation of educational textbooks—reflect the elite's attempt to mold a shared identity and collective memory for an integrated Palestinian society. It has been proved that textbooks during this stage tend to display a more nationalistic attitude. In contrast, since the current Israeli textbooks constitute the third generation of textbooks since the foundation of the state in 1948, Israeli textbooks have gone through a process of at least partial de-mythologization. The first- and second-generation textbooks were replete with myths, inaccuracies, and biases toward Arabs. With regard to the refugee problem, for example, they consistently denied any Israeli involvement in acts of expulsion.[52] It was only in the mid-1990s, as a result of the peace process and the appearance of the new historiography, that Israelis were willing to confront their past more openly—a process reflected in the historical narrative of the third-generation textbooks.[53] In other words, current Palestinian textbooks should not be compared with current Israeli textbooks but with Israel's first-generation textbooks. Thus, a significant asymmetry exists between the Israeli and Palestinian textbooks in terms of their stage of development, which is displayed by their divergent narratives.

Second, most of the Palestinian textbooks had been written during the second intifada, which began in late 2000, a period of struggle against continuing Israeli rule. It is reasonable to assume that during such a violent, turbulent period, textbooks would reflect a more hard-line approach than during a peaceful period.

Third, one must assume that a certain gap between Israeli and Palestinian narratives will always exist. Although a recent study concludes that "finding a solution acceptable to both sides for the right of return issue is widely acknowledged [by Israelis] as a key condition for any potential Israeli-Palestinian permanent agreement,"[54] it seems that Israeli and Palestinian perspectives on that issue remain widely divergent.

Is it possible to reconcile Israeli and Palestinian historical narratives? "The more we become aware of our cognitive differences as members of different thought communities," wrote Eviatar Zerubavel, "the less likely we are to follow the common ethnocentric tendency to regard the particular way in which we ourselves happen to process the world in our minds as based on some absolute standard of 'logic' or 'reason.'"[55] Thus, the awareness that the Israelis and the Palestinians constitute different thought communities with disparate historical narrative is an essential first prerequisite for any reconciliation.

Curiously, Israeli and Palestinian memories have one thing in common: a strong sense of historical victimization. As long as these memories continue to shape and dominate Israeli and Palestinian discourses, it will be difficult to reconcile their memories.[56] To build a climate of reconciliation, it is necessary to delete all biases, stereotypes, and inaccuracies concerning the Other from textbooks. Israel has partially achieved this target after fifty years of statehood, and still some claim that this process has been either premature or incomplete. The paradox is that, in order to build a climate of peace, Palestinians are required to skip over several stages in the development of their education, which, as we have seen in other countries, are necessary for the process of state- and nation-building. It seems, however, that Palestinians cannot enjoy the luxury of gradual development.

Moreover, if one is to make a comparison between Israel's legal institutionalization of its Law of Return and the Palestinian demand for similar recognition, one could argue that this right should be implemented within the state's boundaries. A peaceful solution based on the 1967 borders and the removal of Israeli settlements from the occupied territories will necessarily limit implementation of the Israeli law to the land inside these boundaries and hence remove the Palestinian fear that implementation of the Jewish Law of Return will complete their dispossession from their ancestral homeland. If the Palestinian desire to realize their right of return were to be portrayed as limited to the boundaries of the future Palestinian state, it would duly serve to alleviate the Israeli fear of this concept. In fact, it would be a solution that many Israelis would find realistic and workable.

TABLE 3.1. The Right of Return versus the Law of Return: A Comparison of Israeli and Palestinian Narratives

	Israeli Textbooks	*Palestinian Textbooks*
Israeli Law of Return (*hoq ha-shvut*)	Factual depiction; return only to the boundaries of Israel. Since these are not fixed, the message is implicitly menacing to the Palestinians.	No reference, but implicit, repeated negation of the right of Israel to exist.
Palestinian right of return (*haqq al-'awda*)	Negative references in several history textbooks.	References in written texts and pictures to Palestinian right of return to the whole of Palestine.
Palestinian exodus	Older textbooks' narrative contained conventional old Zionist historiography, but current textbooks carry narrative largely based on the New Historians.	Narrative largely based on old, mythical Palestinian historiography.

Notes

1. Bernard Lewis, *History: Remembered, Recovered, Invented* (Princeton, N.J.: Princeton University Press, 1975), 53. The theoretical section of this chapter is largely based on my *The Arab-Israeli Conflict in Israeli History Textbooks, 1948–2000* (Westport, Conn.: Bergin and Garvey, 2002), chap. 1.

2. See, in particular, David Lowenthal, *The Past Is a Foreign Country* (Cambridge: Cambridge University Press, 1985).

3. For an exception to this generalization, see Hanna Schissler, "Perceptions of the Other and the Discovery of the Self," in *Perceptions of History: International Textbook Research on Britain, Germany and the United States,* Volker R. Berghahn and Hanna Schissler, eds. (Oxford: Berg, 1987), 26. My generalization certainly applies to textbook research on Israel.

4. Michael G. Kammen, *Mystic Chords of Memory: The Transformation of Tradition in American Culture* (New York: Knopf, 1991), 3. See also Benedict Anderson, *Imagined Communities,* revised ed. (London: Verso, 1991), 201; Amos Funkenstein, "Collective Memory and Historical Consciousness," *History and Memory* 1 (1989): 8.

5. This was written in relation to Zionist historiography, but I think it applies as well to history textbooks; see Baruch Kimmerling, "Academic History Caught in the Cross-Fire: The Case of Israeli-Jewish Historiography," *History and Memory* 6 (1995), 57.

6. Nachman Ben-Yehuda, *The Masada Myth: Collective Memory and Mythmaking in Israel* (Madison: University of Wisconsin Press, 1995), 273–74. See also, in this connection, Yael Zerubavel, *Recovered Roots: Collective Memory and the Making of Israeli National Tradition* (Chicago: University of Chicago Press, 1995), 4; Anthony Smith, *The Ethnic Origins of Nations* (Oxford: Verso, 1987), 206.

7. On stereotypes, see Schissler, "Limitations and Priorities for International Social Studies Textbook Research," *International Journal of Social Education* 4 (1989–90); 86. Elsewhere, Schissler asserts that stereotypes protect the members of the group from "cognitive chaos"; see Berghahn and Schissler, *Perceptions of History,* 14–15. On prejudice, see Gordon W. Allport, *The Nature of Prejudice* (New York: Addison and Wesley, 1954), 6.

8. Daniel Bar-Tal, "Delegitimization: The Extreme Case of Stereotyping and Prejudice," in *Stereotyping and Prejudice: Changing Conceptions,* Daniel Bar-Tal et al., eds. (New York: Springer-Verlag, 1989), 170.

9. Ibid., 172–73.

10. Howard D. Mehlinger, "International Textbook Revision: Examples from the United States," *Internationale Schulbuchforschung* 7 (1985): 287. See also Michael W. Apple, *Official Knowledge: Democratic Education in a Conservative Age* (New York: Routledge, 1993), 1–14, 44–63.

11. Michael W. Apple, *The Politics of the Textbook* (London: Routledge, 1991), 10; K. Wain, "Different Perspectives on Evaluating Textbooks," in *History and Social Studies: Methodologies of Textbook Analysis,* Hilary Bourdillon, ed. (Amsterdam: Swets and Zeitlinger, 1992), 39.

12. Wolfgang Jacobmeyer, *International Textbook Research* (Göteborg: Göteborg University Press, 1990), 8.

13. Philip G. Altbach, "Textbooks in Comparative Context," in *Educational Technology: Its Creation, Development and Cross-Cultural Transfer,* R. Murray Thomas and Victor N. Kobayashi, eds. (Oxford: Pergamon, 1987), 159.

14. Based on research in England; see John Slater, "Methodologies of Textbook Analysis," in *International Yearbook of History Education,* Alaric Dickinson et al., eds.

(London: Woburn, 1995), 1: 180. Another study, by Rahima C. Wade, shows that "students engage in textbook-related activities 70%–95% of the time they spend in classrooms"; see "Content Analysis of Social Studies Textbooks: A Review of Ten Years of Research," *Theory and Research in Social Education* 21 (1993): 232. See also Shevach Eden, "A Comparative Examination of History Textbooks in Israel and Germany" (Hebrew), *Kivunim* (1986): 201.

15. Apple, *Official Knowledge*, 61.

16. David R. Olson, "On the Language and Authority of Textbooks," in *Language, Authority and Criticism: Readings on the School Textbook*, Suzanne De Castelle, Allan Luke, and Carmen Luke, eds. (London: Falmer, 1989), 241.

17. Elizabeth Dean, Paul Hartmann, and May Katzen, *History in Black and White: An Analysis of South African School History Textbooks* (Paris: Unesco, 1983), 102.

18. Jane Brophy and Bruce Van Sledright, *Teaching and Learning History* (New York: Teachers College Press, 1997), 20.

19. Berghahn and Schissler, *Perception of History*, 1.

20. Jacobmeyer, *International Textbook Research*, 4–5; Berghahn and Schissler, *Perceptions of History*, 2; Dean et al., *History in Black and White*, 13.

21. See, e.g., Michael Apple, *Ideology and Curriculum*, (Boston: Routledge, 1979), 85.

22. Anita Shapira, *New Jews, Old Jews* (Hebrew) (Tel Aviv: Am Oved, 1997) (Hebrew); Ya'akov Barnai, *Historiography and Nationalism: Trends in the Study of Israel and the Jewish Community, 634–1881* (Hebrew) (Jerusalem: Magnes, 1995); Yaffah Berlovitz, *Inventing a Country, Inventing a People: The Literary and Cultural Infrastructure of the First Aliyah* (Hebrew); (Tel Aviv: Hakibbutz Hameuhad, 1996) (Hebrew); Adir Cohen, *The Ugly Face in the Mirror: The Arab-Israeli Conflict in Hebrew Children's* (Hebrew) *Books* (Tel Aviv: Reshafim, 1985).

23. This methodology is largely based on Falk Pingel, *UNESCO Guidebook on Textbook Research and Textbook Revision* (Hannover: Verlag, Hahnsche Buchhandlung, 1999).

24. For examples, see *From Conservatism to Progress*, history for eighth grade (Jerusalem: Ministry of Education, 1998), 238–46; Eliezer Domke, ed., *The World and the Jews in Recent Generations, 1870–1920*, a textbook for high school (Jerusalem: Zalman Shazar Institute, 1998), 126–30; Moshe Bar-Hillel, *Change and Progress in Israel and the Nations in the Contemporary Age, 1870–1920* (Petach Tiqva: Lilach, 1998), 184–93.

25. Each history textbook deals extensively with the five waves of Jewish immigration to Eretz Israel since the late nineteenth century.

26. *A Journey to the Israeli Democracy: A Civics Textbook*, for state and state-religious schools (Jerusalem: Ministry of Education, 1994), 86–87.

27. *Being Citizens in Israel: A Jewish and Democratic State*, a high school civics textbook for state and state-religious schools (Jerusalem: Ministry of Education, 2000), 44–45. For a more elaborate discussion of the law, see a civics textbook intended for junior high students, which has not yet been approved by the Ministry of Education: David Shahar, *The State of Israel* (Rehovot: Idan, 2002), 92–95.

28. Of the six textbooks, Inbar's was not officially authorized by the Ministry of Education but is widely used in schools; Ya'akobi's textbook was abolished. The Education Committee of the Knesset decided to withhold the use of this textbook because it lacked "important chapters in the history of the Holocaust, Zionism and the State of Israel." See *Haaretz*, November 21–22, 2000. Still, I have decided to include these textbooks in my study.

29. See Podeh, *The Arab-Israeli Conflict in Israeli History Textbooks, 1948–2000*, for a comprehensive examination of the three "generations" of textbooks.

30. Benny Morris, *The Birth of the Palestinian Refugee Problem* (Cambridge: Cambridge University Press, 1988).

31. Tabibyan: 17 sentences; Naveh: 14; Ya'akobi: 10; Naveh and Barnavie: 130; Inbar: 110; Domke: 19.

32. Shula Inbar, *Revival and State in Israel and the Nations in the New Age, 1945–1970,* 69–75; Eliezer Domke, ed., *The World and the Jews in Recent Generations, 1920–1970* (Jerusalem: Zalman Shazar Institute, 1999), 220. This is important because the 1948 war is a subject taught by every history teacher, while the issue of the Palestinian problem is more voluntary. In any case, such separation between the 1948 war and the refugee problem is methodologically flawed.

33. Danny Ya'akobi, *A World of Changes* (Jerusalem: Ministry of Education and Culture, 1999), 162; Inbar, *Revival and State,* 74 (the author titled it "the map of the flight [*briha*] of the Arabs of Israel").

34. Ktzia'a Tabibyan, *A Journey to the Past: From the Middle Ages to Modern Times* (Jerusalem: Ministry of Education and Culture and the Center for Educational Technology, 1999), 293 (the caption reads "Arab Refugees 1948"); Eliezes Domke, The World and the Jews in Recent Generations, 1920–1970, 219 (the caption reads "A Convoy of Arab Refugees, 1948"); Elie Barnavie and Eyal Naveh gave a vivid picture of the refugee reality. They wrote under the photo: "Many of the Palestinian refugees found shelter in the refugee camps, which turned within years into permanent lodging. The Palestinian problem festered in the poverty, inactivity and frustration that beset the refugees in their miserable camps" (*Modern Times, 1920–2000,* History for High School (Tel Aviv: Tel Aviv Books, 1999), 238.

35. Domke, *The World and the Jews in Recent Generations, 1920–1970,* 244; Ya'akobi, *A World of Changes,* 163; Eyal Naveh, *The Twentieth Century: On the Verge of Tomorrow,* History for ninth grade (Tel Avis: Tel Aviv Books), 1994, 147; Tabibyan, *A Journey to the Past,* 294.

36. Tabibyan, *A Journey to the Past,* 293–94; Naveh, *The Twentieth Century,* 147; Naveh, *Teacher's Guide,* 108; Domke, *The World and the Jews in Recent Generations, 1920–1970,* 219; Barnavie and Naveh, *Modern Times,* 239.

37. Inbar, *Revival and State,* 74; Barnavie and Naveh, *Modern Times,* 239; Domke, *The World and the Jews in Recent Generations, 1920–1970,* 220.

38. For the treatment of Palestinian refugees in Israeli textbooks, see Podeh, "History and Memory in the Israeli Educational System: The Portrayal of the Arab-Israeli Conflict in History Textbooks (1948–2000)," *History and Memory* 12:1 (spring/summer 2000): 65–100.

39. The reason for the appearance of an old narrative in new history textbooks with regard to the 1967 war (in contrast to the 1948 war) presumably relates to the absence of new historiography on the 1967 war and the absence of any public dialogue on this issue. Only recently a new book, based on archival sources, has been published: Michael Oren, *Six Days of War: June 1967 and the Making of the Modern Middle East* (Oxford: Oxford University Press, 2002).

40. On the development of education in Mandatory Palestine and afterward, see Nathan J. Brown, "Education as a Site of Contestation: Democracy, Nationalism and the Palestinian Curriculum," unpublished draft; and Fouad Moughrabi, "The Politics of Palestinian Textbooks," *Journal of Palestine Studies* 31:1 (autumn 2001): 6.

41. This brief summary is based on Arnon Groiss, ed., *Jews, Israel and Peace in Palestinian School Textbooks: A Survey of the Textbooks Published by the Palestinian National Authority in the Years 2000–2001* (Jerusalem: Center for Monitoring the Impact of Peace, 2001), 9. See also Moughrabi, "The Politics of Palestinian Textbooks," 6–7, and "Analysis and Evaluation of the New Palestinian Curriculum," Israel/Palestine Center for Research and Information (IPCRI), March 2003.

42. *Palestinian National Education,* fifth grade (1998), 36.

43. *Palestinian National Education,* seventh grade (2001), 54–57; *The Palestinian Society: Demographic Education,* eleventh grade (2001), 34. In the latter textbook, students are given the following assignment: "Let us be helped by our acquaintances and relatives in order to get acquainted with the Palestinian towns from which some of us have been made to emigrate, and let us talk about them in class to our colleagues" (37).

44. *Palestinian National Education,* seventh grade (2001), 20–21, 54–57; sixth grade (2000), 13, 16; *Our Beautiful Language,* seventh grade, part 1, 94–95; *The Palestinian Society: Demographic Education,* eleventh grade (2000), 21, 34; *Geography of Palestine,* seventh grade (2001), 43–44; *Islamic Culture,* twelfth grade (1998), 247–48.

45. *Principles in Human Geography,* sixth grade (2000), 22, 33.

46. *Geography in Palestine,* sixth grade (2001), 36. The first four reasons relate to natural, social, and economic reasons for the emigration. The text here does not refer directly to Israel but states obliquely that the Palestinians "faced compulsory emigration following the wars of 1948 and 1967."

47. *Islamic Education,* sixth grade, part 1 (2000), 69.

48. *Palestinian National Education,* second grade (2001), 36.

49. *Our Beautiful Language,* seventh grade, part 1 (2001), 40–42.

50. *The Palestinian Society: Demographic Education,* eleventh grade (2000), 21, 34.

51. Moughrabi, "The Politics of Palestinian Textbooks," 8.

52. See Podeh, *The Arab-Israeli Conflict in Israeli History Textbooks,* 105–10.

53. The appearance of the third-generation textbooks aroused a heated public debate. It focused on how the 1948 war was depicted in the textbooks, but in fact related to the whole issue of how Israeli society should teach its past. For a comprehensive analysis of the various attitudes in this debate, see Eyal Naveh and Esther Yogev, *Histories: Toward a Dialogue with the Israeli Past* (Hebrew) (Tel Aviv: Bavel, 2002). In November 2000, the Knesset's Education Committee recommended abolishing Ya'akobi's textbook. Although this decision was thought to foreshadow a new trend taken by the new minister of education, Limor Livnat, to reverse the adoption of third-generation textbooks, in fact additional steps against other third-generation textbooks did not follow. It seems, therefore, that Ya'akobi's textbook was abolished mainly because of serious pedagogic flaws. This does not negate the possibility that Israeli fourth-generation textbooks might adopt certain elements of the older narrative, though I believe that the chances for such a development are slim.

54. Dan Zakay, Yechiel Klar, and Keren Sharvit, "Jewish Israelis on the Right of Return," *Palestine-Israel Journal* 9:2 (2002): 61.

55. Eviatar Zerubavel, *Social Mindscapes: An Invitation to Cognitive Sociology* (Cambridge, Mass.: Harvard University Press, 1997), 10.

56. For the same problem prevalent in the Irish conflict, see Margaret Mac Curtain, "Reconciliation of Memories," in *Reconciling Memories,* Alan D. Falconer and Joseph Liechty, eds. (Dublin: Columba Press, 1998), 99–107.

Chapter 4
Social Capital and Refugee Repatriation: A Study of Economic and Social Transnational Kinship Networks in Palestine/Israel

Sari Hanafi

The experience of the repatriation of refugees in many places in the world shows that there is likely to be very little international assistance for whatever process of Palestinian refugee repatriation occurs. Social capital, rather than external assistance, has played and will play a central role in supporting returnees, especially at the beginning of their return. This chapter examines the social capital from which eventual Palestinian returnees might benefit. It emphasizes the types of economic and social transnational kinship networks to which individuals have access and the processes by which inclusion in (or exclusion from) them is sustained. This is based on a survey conducted by the Palestinian Diaspora and Refugee Center (Shaml) between January and October 2003.[1] A total of 560 open questionnaires were completed by refugees living outside Palestine and by refugees living in the Palestinian territories and Israel. Other surveys, such as those conducted by the Norwegian Institute for Applied Social Science (Fafo) in Jordan and Lebanon and by the Palestinian Center for Policy and Survey Research (PSR) are used for comparison.[2]

This chapter highlights the role of kinship networks and economic ties linking Palestinians inside and outside the Palestinian territories. Unlike others who study the absorption of refugees, focusing on the contribution of the state and the international community to facilitating return, I am more interested in examining sociological factors that can encourage return or adaptation to the new economic environment. Therefore, I focus on the objective factors that influence the decision to return, such as economic and social kinship networks, entrepreneurship, and migration culture, as opposed to emotionally based attitudes that reflect refugees' political position but not necessarily their actual intention to return.

What pattern of return will take place and what will be the profile of the returnees? Will a mass of refugees rush in simultaneously, or will there be a trickle of fragmented groups? What is the motivation for return: pure nationalism and the desire to stabilize identity(ies) after the experience of exile, or some additional motivation? If Israel accepts the principle of the right of return, would return be voluntary or coerced? What constitutes return "in safety and dignity"? Should refugees be required to return if they cannot go back to their areas of origin but must settle in another part of the country? These are some of the questions that this chapter attempts to address.

I adopt two approaches. First, the *development approach* studies all the returnees who choose to go home (or to the Palestinian political entity) by supporting themselves financially, either independently or through the help of the extended family, with little intervention from the public authority. This category includes Palestinian refugees who fall within the framework of family reunification, refugees and displaced persons who are able to integrate easily because of their socioeconomic profile, and those who can be considered economic migrants.

The second approach, which I refer to as the *democratic approach*, studies the refugees who come home on the basis of a formal economic and social plan for their absorption in their place of return. In both approaches, "return" includes legal refugees with a fragile status (having only travel documents), diasporic refugees (having passports issued by one of the host countries), and economic migrants.

Examining return migration from the perspective of network analysis will be fruitful for the objectives of this study. I rely on studies that consider a wide spectrum of factors affecting the possibilities and potentialities of return, including the role of kin networks, refugee dispersion patterns, and pre- and post-return economic and social profiles. Other factors to be considered include the desires of individual refugees to return to the (or a) homeland and the likely ways in which return will be implemented (be it immediate or over an extended period of time).

For this study, I formulated four assumptions. The first assumption is that economic action is embedded in social structure. For this reason, it is very important to study social networks. What is this embeddedness? How do we understand the economic behavior of Palestinian returnees and local entrepreneurs, at present and in the cases of either return or the intensification of transnational movement? To understand the types of economic behavior exemplified by Palestinian entrepreneurs, one has to take into consideration the literature on economic sociology, especially Karl Polanyi and Marc Granovetter's concept of embeddedness.[3] Embeddedness refers to the fact that diverse economic transactions are inserted into overarching social and political structures that affect their outcomes. Thus, we cannot understand Palestinian economic transactions without referring to the social and legal status of the Palestinian communities.

The second assumption concerns the privileging of family ties. As mentioned, I attempt to identify the different levels of social structures into which the individual migrant is inserted: friendship networks, extended family, village ties, national ties. Concerning the decision to migrate and the system of support for the future absorption of Palestinian refugees, I consider the nuclear and extended family as major players in such decisions. Therefore, one objective of the fieldwork was to identify the different types of family ties: strong, weak, or torn.

The third assumption deals with a pattern of return that is not only definitive but also transnational. This means that the refugees/returnees would maintain their social, economic, and political lives in both the country of return and the country in which they lived and might be citizens of both countries.

The last assumption is political. The concept of two nation-states remains popular with the majority of Palestinians and Israelis. This means maintaining a system of apartheid in which the question of Jewish hegemony in the Israeli state will not change anytime soon. However, what is still at issue is the type of nation-states that Israelis and Palestinians will develop. If Israel accepts the Palestinian right of return, this will make the return of the Palestinian refugees subject to sociological and economic considerations; if not, quotas will influence tremendously the choices made by refugees concerning their future place of residence.

Palestinian return migration is likely to be complex. This complexity is not different from other return migration experiences in which international factors influence and even shape refugees' movement. Refugee movement must be understood in the larger context of globalization and international migration. There are 170 million international migrants who reside outside their countries of birth. During the cold war, the international community viewed resettlement as the preferred option; repatriation was incompatible with foreign policy objectives, as refugees were pawns in the superpowers' proxy wars, as in the case of the Afghani refugees. Now, however, resettlement is less possible because of the rise of anti-immigration sentiments in Europe, Australia, and elsewhere.

Concerning return migration, as data from the UN High Commissioner for Refugees (UNHCR) demonstrate, the number of refugees returning to their countries of origin (once return is possible) is far less than the number who choose resettlement in the host country or settlement in a third-party state. According to UNHCR statistics for 2002, only 21 percent of refugees exercised the right of return (2,252,804 returnees). That year was exceptional, as Afghanis constituted more than 80 percent of the returnees: of the 3,828,852 Afghan refugees, 47 percent returned, mainly from

Pakistan, Iran, and Tajikistan. In many places, statistics on return hide a lot of problems, particularly as internal displacement is as, or more, severe a problem.

The small number of refugees who return is due to several factors, chiefly the structure of the global labor market. The Bosnian case provides some hints: even before the ink was dry on the 1995 Dayton peace agreement, a vigorous debate was under way about return. The controversy intensified in 1996, when it became clear that large-scale, voluntary returns were not likely to take place quickly.[4] From the recent debates inside the UNHCR, one can question whether the return option is most popular and preferable for the concerned refugees.[5] While repatriation was downplayed during the ideological confrontation of the cold war, it emerged with renewed vigor in the 1990s.

Moreover, protracted refugee status creates new ties in host countries. Rural people become urban, and women are empowered in many receiving countries. The lesson for the Palestinian case is that one should partially disconnect the question of the right of return from the sociology of return. Rosemary Sayigh noted that the return of Palestinians has been subject not only to push factors from the host country but also to a collective desire for return on the part of the refugees. Daniel Warner, however, disputes the latter interpretation, challenging the "idealized" and "nostalgic" image of voluntary repatriation.[6] Over time, he argues, dispersal distorts the meaning of community and with it the memory of the homeland.[7] Similarly, many specialists in forced migration studies criticize the UNHCR's trend to favor repatriation and to force refugees to go home.

Factors Influencing the Movement of the Refugees

Many factors influence a refugee's decision of whether to return or to choose another option. Understanding likely patterns and pressures regarding Palestinian return cannot be achieved by focusing on macro processes of globalization or the operation of global markets according to neoclassical principles but must be achieved by a sociological understanding of the political, social, and cultural attributes of the Palestinian people.

I focus on some elements related mainly to the economic sociology of the Palestinian refugees (and the Palestinians abroad in general) in the host country and in the country of return (the Palestinian territories or Israel). Focusing on these elements, however, does not mean that they are the only important factors. For instance, geographical factors influence refugees' decisions. Here I must highlight the importance of Salman Abu-Sitta in opening the debate concerning geographic absorption in Israel.[8] He demonstrates that 68 percent of Israeli Jews now live in 8 percent of Israel and that the areas in and around former Palestinian villages remain empty and could absorb returning refugees. For him, this empty rural area corresponds to the peasant heritage of the majority of Palestinian refugees. However, it is important to ask if, after fifty-five years, these refugees, the majority of whom now dwell in cities, can still be considered peasants. Moreover, according to the PSR survey in 2003 in the Palestinian territories, the houses of half of these refugees were destroyed and 40 percent declared themselves unwilling to return if the family home no longer exists.

The ability to absorb refugees geographically is not a decisive factor in return scenarios. Irish Americans did not return to Ireland following the end of British colonialism, few Armenians returned to Armenia after its independence, and only a small number of Lebanese returned to their country of origin after the civil war. In all these cases, there was not only ample capacity but also the political will for reabsorption.

Another important factor, which demands attention but is outside the scope of this study, is the comparison between the social welfare systems in the host countries and the return areas. For instance, in comparison with Israel, the Palestinian territories and Jordan have inadequate health, social welfare, and educational services. This would encourage Palestinians to return to Israel rather than to the Palestinian territories.

Finally, the possibility of the return of the Palestinian refugees is still closely connected to three elements: the right of return, the urban situation of the refugee camps, and the position of the Arab host countries. The three scenarios elaborated in the conclusion are conditioned by these elements. It is worth mentioning that many studies show that refugees have a low expectation of a political solution that would allow most refugees to return. A PSR survey in 2003 found that half accepted the idea that, once a Palestinian state is established, the refugee issue will be postponed to the indefinite future. A survey conducted in 1993, a decade earlier, already revealed a significant trend indicating a readiness to find a realistic solution. That study's in-depth interviews in two refugee camps near Nablus found that a quarter would accept compensation and nearly half would return home to live under Israeli rule.[9]

Social Capital: The Density of Transnational Social Kinship Ties

Because the extended family network has been an important safety net for migrants, I focus on bonding, a form of social capital that involves ties to people who are similar in terms of their demographic characteristics, such as family members. I examine how transnational kinship networks are affected by the occupation and national borders that structure, extend, and deepen the rupture of Palestinian society. How should the strength of a tie be measured? Do close relationships link similar people? Do weaker ties link more dissimilar people? Indeed, some forms of social capital can be used to hinder rather than help a return migrant, such as when group membership norms confer obligations to share rather than accumulate wealth or when they deny members access to services.[10]

Connectedness between different members is based on a wide array of choices by individuals and families. The measurement of this feeling of connection is certainly subjective, but Shaml's survey chose a set of structural factors that may shape and ultimately limit these choices. The border predicament, the frequency of visits, phone calls, and the use of cyberspace are indicators of the (non)connectedness of the family network. They shape the relations among family members and thus influence decisions about return.

Transnationality

The Shaml survey confirmed a certain degree of transnationality among Palestinians (more among those in the Palestinian territories than in Israel). This suggests that there will be a transnational pattern of return migration in the future, much more than a definitive return, and that the kinship network can be used to facilitate this movement.

Among those living in the Palestinian territories, 40 percent of their close relatives (defined as parents, spouse, children, or siblings) live abroad and only a quarter of those are able to visit Palestine/Israel. In contrast, among Palestinians in Israel, only 15 percent of their close relatives live abroad, of whom 13 percent can travel to Palestine/Israel. Concerning second-degree relatives (defined as matrimonial and patrimonial aunts and uncles and their families), 76 percent of Palestinians living in the territories have second-degree relatives abroad, half of whom are able to visit Palestine/Israel; more than 79 percent of them are refugees. Social and economic ties are diminished, as only 15 percent of Palestinians living in the territories have received aid from their relatives abroad, compared to a mere 8 percent for those who live in Israel. There are also very few economic projects between the Palestinians abroad and those who are in Israel. The survey found that those who have property in Palestine tend to meet more often. It seems that the presence of property encourages them to maintain contact with their families, at least in order to discuss this important business issue.

Relations with more distant relatives are very weak. The overwhelming majority declared that they had no economic ties at all; only 25 percent had some form of ties. This is not unusual, but it means that the importance of the *hamula* (clan) level is fading, perhaps because of the rapid urbanization of Palestinian society as well as extended periods of separation.

The place of birth plays a major role in the degree of connection to the people who still live there. For example, 79 percent of those born in Jordan retained ties with their close relatives in Jordan, even though they no longer lived there. However, for those who returned to the Palestinian territories, their relations with Jordan diminish with the passage of time. This is probably due to the fact that they are unable to cross the border to visit one another.

Transnationality is also expressed by the interests of individuals who own property in host countries. When asked about what they intend to do with property in the host country when they return, the overwhelming majority of the refugees living outside the Palestinian territories stated that they would keep their property and rent it. This demonstrates that the refugees do not want to sever all their ties with their countries of refuge.

Solidarity and Connectedness

Palestinians in the territories retain many more transnational kinship ties than those in Israel. Nonetheless, the duration of the exodus, now over fifty-five years—and the impact of the borders have hindered the maintenance of ties between relatives.

The hypothesis that the closest ties are with family members and not with friends is confirmed by the fact that, when asked about their closest ties, only 5 percent of Palestinians living on the West Bank mentioned friends and 8 percent mentioned both family and friends. However, Palestinians who recently returned to the territories stress relations with friends, probably because these returnees do not have family in the Palestinian territories or because the long absence from these territories has made the ties diminish.

Visits with Relatives.   According to Shaml's survey, Palestinian men interviewed in Palestine/Israel lost contact with a third of their close relatives; they meet mainly every two years. In contrast, women lost less contact: 29 percent for the Palestinian territories and 14 percent in Israel. Women maintain more frequent contact with their parents than do men, whereas men have more ties with their sisters and daughters. Thus, women are the core of the Palestinian family. They are the clearinghouse for the economic and social ties inside the fragmented transnational Palestinian family.[11] The gender-constructed reality of ties is very important for return migration, as it concerns a vulnerable refugee population and a society in which women are the most vulnerable because of early marriage and a high proportion of widowed, divorced, and single middle-aged and elderly women.[12] This could lead to a propensity for more families who have ties to Palestine/Israel through maternal relatives to return than those who have ties through paternal relatives.

Thus, the decision to return will be shaped by the kind of relatives with whom the refugees have ties. Proximity of age plays a major role in social connectivity but less in terms of economic ties. This is partly because the generational gap between children and daughters and their parents and elderly siblings has widened rapidly, especially when people have transnational experience. This was obvious from Shaml's survey: some young people who had grown up in the United States expressed a cultural conflict with their relatives who did not have the same transnational experience.

The geographical location of the interviewees is very relevant. In the Gaza Strip, 43 percent do not visit (or receive visits from) their close relatives living outside of the strip. This percentage increases for those living in camps, as their relatives are more likely to be refugees who live outside Palestine. In Israel, 82 percent of interviewees from big cities like Haifa have lost direct contacts with close relatives. Visits decrease as people age. Whereas the economic situation seems irrelevant to the frequency of visits, better-educated people seem to visit their close relatives more often. It seems that education brings more possibility to travel and meet with transnational relatives.

The border is a major cause of the lack of physical meetings; approximately 56 percent of those whose relatives cannot visit Palestine/Israel have lost contact with those relatives. The geographical location of the relatives also affects meetings: Palestinian refugees in Jordan and Egypt are more likely than those who live in the Gulf to maintain contact, but even then, they meet about once every two years. It is practically impossible to meet relatives in Lebanon and Iraq. It is important to note that Palestinians living in Europe and the United States are able to meet with their Palestinian relatives in Palestine/Israel more easily than those living in Arab countries. This is likely due to the fact that travel between Arab countries and Palestine/Israel is difficult and even impossible in some cases.

Moreover, the second intifada sharply affects the ability of Palestinians living in the Palestinian territories to have physical contact with one another and with those living abroad. The situation is especially acute in Gaza, where Israel has imposed total closure.

Telephonic contact.   The use of the phone does not compensate for the absence of direct meetings. There are few phone calls between people who do not exchange visits. Generally, most speak on the phone once every two months, primarily to sons and daughters dwelling abroad. Calls abroad from Israel (or vice versa) are very rare, except for Um al Fahm, where that seems to be an act of solidarity with relatives in the West Bank and Jordan. In the Palestinian territories, men and women maintain phone contact with their relatives abroad at the same rate, but in Israel females use the phone less frequently. Overall, those who are less educated tend to use the phone less often. Conversations by phone with close relatives living abroad are more important with Europe and the United States than with the Gulf, Egypt, and Jordan. This could be explained by the cost of the communication; it is cheaper to call from the United States or Europe. Communication with Lebanon is very rare, as it is impossible to phone from Lebanon (and from Syria) to Israel/Palestine. One female interviewee declared that she used to give money to cover the equivalent of twelve phone cards a year to her sick and poor uncle living in Jordan so that he could call the family in Palestine.

E-mail communication among immediate family members in Palestine/Israel is infrequent; only one-third of close relatives are connected by e-mail with those who live in the Palestinian territories, mostly those under forty years old. In Palestine, women use e-mail less often than men, whereas in Israel it is the reverse. Several modes of communication, such as Internet chatting, Sort Messenger Service (SMS), and sending photos through the Internet are used to connect people beyond the borders.

Marriage Patterns.   Endogamous marriage—marriage within the same lineage, sect, community, group, village, or neighborhood—is an important indicator of connectedness. Marriage between first cousins and blood-related kin is the most common form of endogamy in the Arab world.[13] Many studies show the persistence of a high rate of endogamy in the Palestinian family. The Fafo study states: "The family, and in particular the parents, play an important role in the process of finding an appropriate marriage partner in Palestinian society."[14] Fafo researchers found that only 36.6 percent (for women born between 1940 and 1949) and 43 percent (for women born between 1960 and 1969) married outside of relatives or the *hamula.* Marriages are often arranged, as is the case in most of the Arab world.

The Shaml survey and Riina Isotalo's work show that endogamous practices exist even at the transnational level, but much less so than when the relative lives in the same country.[15] This allows many unexpected groups to join the family. The small number of transnational endogamous marriages can be explained by its high cost; in contrast, local endogamous marriages are economical since dowries are smaller.[16]

Economic Assistance.   Social capital refers to the capacity of the individual to command scarce resources through adhesion to networks and broader social structures. These resources include economic favors, such as the reduction of price, credit without interest, and information on business conditions. People, especially migrants, need not only jobs but also companionship, emotional support, help with everyday problems, care when ill, and other forms of social support.

This study distinguishes between two forms of help: non-mutual and reciprocal. According to exchange theory, the network is much stronger when help is non-mutual because "in the hiatus between giving and the reciprocation of an item, obligation, trust and cooperation are created and extended among exchangers."[17]

Solidarity between Palestinians in the Palestinian territories and abroad is important. One-third receive financial and nonfinancial help that began before the start of the current intifada and is therefore not related to the increased economic hardship experienced during the intifada. This help is mainly among parents, children, and siblings. It includes small gifts and the occasional major gift, such as the cost of education or health treatment. While payment for health treatment is extended to all relatives, payment for education is given only to the male members. Religious holidays, such as the Eid and Christmas, are also occasions when gifts are given.

Face-to-face contact is very important for economic transactions and especially for receiving and giving help. A Fafo study shows that the family living in the Palestinian territories relies on members abroad but that the lack of physical communication hinders transactions.[18] The Shaml study found that half of the transfers do not go through banks but rather are transmitted during familial visits. The study also found that money is brought as presents.

This is a radical change from the 1970s and 1980s, when most financial help was transferred through persons. Few Palestinians in Israel receive help from their relatives abroad, probably because of their good economic situation and the weakness of transnational social ties.

The survey found very few cases of reciprocal help on the transnational level. Help not only entered the Palestinian territories but was also sent from the territories to close relatives living abroad. However, this is not necessarily reciprocal or economically based assistance, as in the case of parents who give financial help to their daughters living abroad.

Economic ties based on partnership are very problematic in the current situation. However, there is some financial help for small entrepreneurs who are setting up their businesses. It seems that help in Palestine/Israel has an altruistic motivation, namely, transferring resources because of general moral imperatives or solidarity with in-group needs and goals, much more than instrumental motivations due to reciprocity or enforceable trust based on the expectation of commensurate returns by beneficiaries or based on the expectation of higher community status and commensurate returns by beneficiaries subject to collective sanctions.[19] This will have an important impact on facilitating the establishment of eventual returnees back home, especially in the initial period.

In brief, the outcome of Shaml's survey shows less social connectedness and solidarity than expected in Palestine/Israel and especially in Israel. This will make the use of kinship ties to assist return less important than generally assumed for a nation whose source of cohesion is its ongoing plight. The negative impact of borders and Israeli colonial practices on Palestinians' local and international ties is huge.

Fractured Nuclear Family

Recent field research presents a profile of fractured networks inside the nuclear family in the Palestinian territories, but not in Israel.[20] Mothers and children may reside in one country, husbands and fathers may live and work in another, and grandparents and more distant relatives may live elsewhere. The fractured family experience could indicate that return will not necessarily involve the whole family, especially in the first years. Males tend to decide whether to relocate to Palestine/Israel or choose another migration place for the whole or a fragment of a family, based on several factors, including market structures. In particular, the person who has found suitable employment brings the family to join him or her and makes the decisions concerning the family's mobility. The decision to migrate is also based on the availability of affordable educational opportunities for the children.

Mode of Entrepreneurship Favorable to Return

If some returnees will consume from the resources of the place to which they return, others will bring capital and expertise sufficient to generate improvements to the country's economy. Some studies have demonstrated that the capital influx and investment that accompany the return of professionals generate investment. This type of investment is significantly different from the classical model of remittances studied in the Arab world, which were dominated by limited economic benefits and negative effects of migration, weak investment of remittances in productive activities, and inflation provoked by the transfer of currency.[21]

Contrary to studies that view returnees as a future burden on Palestinian society[22] and that studied the absorptive capacity for Palestinian refugees from a narrow and short-term economic perspective, other studies have shown great potential benefit from the absorption of returnees, considering the new dynamics and positive externalities that might be established by their return.[23] The Oslo transition period generated a high rate of growth in the Palestinian territories. The Gross Domestic Product and Gross National Product were greater before the intifada than in the neighboring countries, with the exception of Israel. If this level is regained, the Palestinian territories will attract refugees at least from Jordan and Egypt, especially if family members contribute in the initial stage. Some Palestinians might move from the Gaza Strip to the West Bank, where income levels are higher. This also applies to Israel, where future government policy will determine whether Palestinian workers, engineers, and information technology professionals can assume or resume residence there.

The decision to move persons or capital is subject to a complex set of factors related to both host and return country, and also to other geographical areas, especially in the era of globalization. I refuse to assume a straightforward relationship between transnationalism and global capitalism, as advocated by Basch and others.[24] What I will show here is that the potential return of refugees (especially entrepreneurs and professionals) is more structurally constrained than a model of pure economic choice geared to optimal benefit would indicate. The recycling of de-territorialized Palestinian capital reveals fault lines in the international global market rather than the beneficial workings of globalization. For instance, the geographical de-localization of Palestinian economic transactions can best be understood as improving the fragile legal status of the refugees, regardless of their wealth. As such, most of their investments reflect an economy of survival more than the exercise of real political and economic power in the economy of globalization and the world system. As Grillo, Riccio, and Salih argue, "[e]conomic dislocation in both developing and industrialized nations has increased migration, but made it difficult for migrants to construct secure cultural, social and economic bases within their new settings."[25] Thus, transnationalism, as in the case of the Senegalese communities in Italy, does not exhibit a straightforward relation to global capital. The experience of Palestinians recruited through the UN Development Program's TOKTEN[26] program indicates that many people came to Palestine because of their precarious situation in their host country. Accordingly, their return expresses a model in which a constrained people seek to improve their flexibility, rather than one of people who have a straightforward choice between the country of residence and the country of origin.

I will present two interconnected arguments. First, the nature of the investment and the motivations for it are driven by noneconomic factors more than by economic ones; second, the familial mode of entrepreneurship predominates in the Palestinian territories and Israel. These two points indicate that the Palestinian economy in Palestine/Israel will be strongly affected by certain forms of refugee repatriation to these places.

Diaspora Investment

During the Oslo transitional period, local and international economic links were reestablished after a long period of conflict and separation. Already partially tied to their native community, the Palestinian diaspora contributed to the reshaping and the emergence of new transnational economic networks. The proportion of the investments of the Palestinian diaspora in the Palestinian territories to the volume of the Palestinian capital abroad was modest, although it was vital for the Palestinian economy. As an indicator, according to the Palestinian economist Fadl Naqib, from 1993 to 1999 the average investment growth was 12.3 percent.[27]

To give an idea of the size of the diaspora's contribution during a "normal" time (that is, before the intifada), one of my previous studies showed that the diaspora's contribution in investments and philanthropic activities could be valued at $408.006 million in 1996 (of which 74 percent was investment) and $410.211 million in 1997 (of which 76 percent was investment).[28] This represented one of the main resources available to the Palestinian society and economy. Indeed, compared with international aid to the territories, it constituted 74 percent of this assistance ($549.414 million) in 1996 and 95 percent in 1997 ($432.259 million).[29] (See table 4.1.) However, this contribution remained insufficient for a young entity ravaged by thirty years of de-development and was well below the capacity of the Palestinian diasporic business people.[30] In fact, these investments did not necessarily come from wealthy people but from Palestinian middle classes, especially in the Gulf, because of the familial nature of entrepreneurship in the Palestinian territories.

The impact of these contributions by the diaspora has been both quantitative and qualitative. A holding company permits strategic and long-term investment and the creation of substantial projects that are beyond the capacity of one entrepreneur. It is a new model introduced into a country dominated by family-based, small or medium firms. Infusing vitality into the Palestinian economy at this early stage is crucial to any future prospect of stability and sustainable development. This not only relieves the economic, social, and political tensions that are now a fact of daily life but also initiates a catalytic process of capital accumulation in a low-resource-based economy that consumes imports at a very high rate.

Nonetheless, the involvement by the Palestinian diaspora in the territories' economy has limits at present and in the future. This is partly because of the nature of the Palestinian diaspora's niches, which are mainly trade and construction. These two niches do not constitute value-added to local expertise. This has encouraged the diaspora to separate know-how and capital. Those who had capital did team up with those who have expertise externally in order to start businesses in the territories or Israel. The creation of holding companies resolved this structural problem. In the Oslo period, many Palestinian citizens of Israel who lacked the access and relationships to invest in the territories invested through such companies.

Concerning the motivation for investment, Palestinian diaspora busi-

TABLE 4.1. Financial Contributions of the Palestinian Diaspora (US$ millions)

Total Contribution	1996	1997
Total Investment	303.8	311.1
Philanthropic and Familial Aid	104.206	99.111
Total Contribution of the Diaspora	408.006	410.211
Donors' Foreign Aid	549.414	432.259

Diverse sources. See Hanafi, "Contribution de la diaspora palestinienne," *Maghreb-Machrek* 161 (November 1998).

nesspeople declared that they did not expect to achieve profits quickly. According to my preliminary survey, they noted that any other region in the Middle East would be a wiser location for investment, particularly in the industrial sector. Most decisions in favor of investment in Palestine were made for social rather than strictly economic reasons. Such economic behavior cannot be explained simply by portraying members of the Palestinian diaspora as particularly "patriotic." Thus, the Palestinian investor is neither purely a *homo economicus* nor a *homo patrioticus*.

Transnational Familial Entrepreneurship

The mode of entrepreneurship is a concept that allows us to understand how capital and the know-how necessary for launching development are acquired, as well as the sustainability of any business. Entrepreneurship does not mean a fixed behavior or a kind of economic mentality but rather a dynamic concept. Entrepreneurship concerns not only businesspeople but also entrepreneurs in general, including the self-employed and the employer.[31] According to this meaning, Palestinians in the diaspora (whether refugees or not) are somewhat entrepreneurial. Twenty percent of the labor force is self-employed or an employer.[32] This percentage becomes 15 percent in the Palestinian territories, according to Palestinian Central Bureau of Statistics.[33]

My fieldwork concerning the modes of entrepreneurship in Palestine/Israel and the diaspora indicates two types of Palestinian entrepreneurship: individualist and communitarian, both operating on a transnational level. Businesspeople diversify their business in different fields and also across many geographical areas, using mainly capital transfers and not physical relocation.

This diversification is not generally due to de-localization of business toward new markets or new methods of production designed to benefit from the economic environment in the host countries but is instead a strategy involving diversifying economic activity in new geographical areas and new sectors to ensure the security of the capital in case one economic sector in a country should encounter difficulties. The insecurity of Palestinian diasporic economic activity can be perceived as stemming from the generalized anxiety of a population characterized by a permanent liminality and a psychology of transition and impermanence.

The nature of sectoral diversification and choice of place of investment by Palestinian entrepreneurs does not depend solely on the economic rational model based on a complex calculation of factors related to the size of markets, labor costs, technological performance, and the presence of infrastructures to facilitate investment. Palestinian economic diversification is dependent on the vagaries of social and political criteria such as the impact of the Oslo peace process, the juridical status of the investor in the host and investment countries, mobility, access, and difficulties in obtaining visas. As a result of such factors in the Gulf States, for example, Palestinians were unable to convert and recycle the capital they acquired during the golden age in the Gulf when they migrated to North America after the Gulf crisis in 1990–91.

Kinship networks between the Palestinian diaspora and its gravitational center have assumed critical importance in diaspora economies, although the trend is not necessarily self-evident. In the Gulf countries, political instability and limited conditions for investment in the region have increased the value of economic kinship networks, while in other countries of the Palestinian diaspora individualist entrepreneurship has assumed a greater role.[34] While ethnic and kinship networks are not specifically necessary for the success of the investment and recycling of capital in the new receiving countries, the situation in the Palestinian territories may tend more toward entrepreneur-family rather than entrepreneur-individual relationships. Many interviewees indicated the importance of role models (other successful entrepreneurs) in their social networks. Many family stories show that people engaged in micro- or macro-enterprise creation have close relatives who operate businesses.

I found that transnational networks are not the expression of global capital but rather constitute strategies for survival. In many transnational experiences around the world, such as the Chinese in the United States,[35] the quest to accumulate capital and social prestige in the global arena emphasizes and is regulated by practices favoring flexibility, mobility, and repositioning in relation to markets, governments, and cultural regimes. In the Palestinian case, this acquisition of capital reflects a struggle for economic survival. While a New York businessman may not need to expend more than a second of his time on a million-dollar transaction thanks to the time-space compression enabled by new information technologies,[36] a Palestinian transnational refugee in many countries in the Middle East will likely need to spend days to make a much more modest transfer, rendering the transaction cost much higher.

Shaml's survey in 2003 focused on forty entrepreneurs, mostly in Ramallah. The results show the economic importance of Palestinian refugees: half of the entrepreneurs are refugees although few live in camps. The Oslo process seems to have generated around 40 percent of the entrepreneurial activities. The capital mobilized mostly came from inheritance or family aid. Very few cases indicate the use of bank credit. This was due mainly to the conservative policy of the banks in the territories, but it is also because using the familial partnership privileges a mode of trust that reduces the cost of the economic transactions. The familial partnership before Oslo tended to involve the family living in the territories more than those of the diaspora (the transnational family). The peace process created connections between the West Bank and Gaza and encouraged many partnerships. The sites of these partnerships went beyond the territories: a quarter of the entrepreneurs interviewed had investments abroad. The number of social familial ties that entrepreneurs maintain seemed more important than other socioeconomic categories in the Shaml survey. Telephone and travel encourage such connections. However, ties with distant relatives (aunts, uncles, and their offspring) are weak. Some entrepreneurs use their relatives abroad to facilitate export and import, especially if those relatives live in Jordan. This seems important, as the major constraint on developing businesses in Palestine is the Israeli occupation, travel restrictions, and closure.

The mobilization of the family to support the business does not mean that this fits a model of "ethnic" business. Many entrepreneurs are reluctant to employ people from their village of origin. They are afraid that their enterprise will become a welfare hotel, with relatives expecting handouts without having to work.[37]

Migration Culture

According to human capital theory, migration occurs if the discounted expected returns in a potential destination country minus the migration costs are larger than the discounted expected returns in the current country of residence. However, this theory has been challenged by analyses that focus on the importance of migrant networks for the migration decision. Shaml's survey covered both lifetime migration and circular/temporary migration within Palestine/Israel and internationally.

Not surprisingly, Palestinians in the territories were much more mobile than Palestinians inside Israel but less mobile than refugees living outside. This indicates that many migration movements were caused by political troubles and border restrictions. Some 60 percent of respondents had moved at least once, with three the average number of moves and the Gulf countries the favorite destination abroad. For Palestinians in the territories, the most important reasons to move are work, education, marriage, and improvement of housing, especially for refugees who wish to leave the camps and move to the cities. For Palestinians in Israel, marriage is an important reason, followed by work and then education. In over 90 percent of the cases, women follow the men in marriage-related moves. The same pattern is detected in family reunification: 77 percent of the cases in the territories involve women following their male relatives.

Although the Oslo peace process decreased the tendency to move, it created opportunities for people to move within the Palestinian territories. In fact, 94 percent of the moves during this period involved people moving within the territories, particularly on the part of the best-educated people. A Fafo survey in Jordan in 1996 found that half the adults had moved at least once, although not necessarily outside of Jordan.[38]

The tendency to migrate seems to have increased during the second intifada, with some leaving the territories because of the security and economic situation. Some 100,000 Palestinians are thought to have left the
West Bank for Jordan and the West since late 2000, marking a significant
increase in migration rates.[39] From 1967 to 1993, the annual migration rate
was 0.5–2 percent, or 5,000–15,000 from the West Bank, and 3,000–7,000
from the Gaza Strip.[40] It is very hard to find current statistics on migration,
as people feel ashamed to leave during the national struggle. However, a
World Bank report referred to poll data in which "2% of respondents said
that family members had gone abroad for extended periods."[41] People who
leave are likely to be well educated and not from the working class.

I therefore conclude that two main categories of people are likely to
migrate to Palestine/Israel. First, those without kinship ties in this country:
their "home"-coming is subject to the political push factor from the host
country; their legal status in the host country; sociological and economic
push factors from the host country; and sociological and economic pull
factors to Palestine/Israel. The second category is people who have access
to social capital through kinship ties with these areas, who are influenced
by the same push and pull factors but can also use their social capital to
encourage and facilitate their return.

Social capital, however, will also motivate Palestinian refugees' propensity to move to Palestine/Israel. Taking into consideration the fact that
many Palestinians from both categories also have connections with Canada
and the United States (according to a Fafo survey), the possibility of migrat-
ing there is significant. Canada or the United States (and Europe and Australia) will be favored for kinship reasons and because of their educational
systems. Around a third of those interviewed in the Gulf from 1990 to 1995
went to Canada and the United States to benefit from their educational
systems.

Scenarios of Refugee Movement

The most striking finding is the huge difference between the Palestinians
in the Palestinian territories and those in Israel concerning the impact of
many factors that will shape the eventual movement of Palestinian refugees. Concerning transnational kinship ties, Palestinians in the territories
retain many more ties than those in Israel. The duration of the exodus,
which is now over fifty-five years, and the impact of the borders have hindered ties among relatives. Arabs used to say *al bo'd Jafa* ("distance dries up
the relationship"). Reality is not far from this. The Israeli system of bio-
politics, with its surveillance and control, has created a huge distance
between the two sides.

Palestinian sociologist Aziz Haidar observed that after the 1967 war,
encounters were problematic between Palestinian refugees living in the

newly occupied West Bank and Gaza Strip and their relatives living within the 1948 borders. While their first meeting, after many years of separation, was warm, people quickly realized the differences between themselves.[42] Occupation, surveillance, and control had created a new Palestinian world inside Israel. In addition to the impact of the political system, a social-class issue should be addressed. The Palestinians inside Israel had become much wealthier than their relatives who were living as refugees in the West Bank and Gaza Strip. Haidar notes that the visits stopped quickly. One interviewee, a member of the Israeli Communist Party who lives in Haifa, told me that he became upset whenever he accompanied Palestinians to see their former homes in Wadi Salib and other parts of Haifa and therefore stopped doing so.

The current Israeli politics of space also hinders connections between Palestinians living in the West Bank and Gaza Strip in the name of humiliation and collective punishment. The long-term result is significant in creating borders in the minds of people. The story of Barta'a is revealing. In 1949, Israel[43] divided Barta'a into two sections, separated along the armistice line. Although Barta'a was composed mainly of one family, its ties were torn apart. From 1949 to 1967, both Israel and Jordan hindered such meetings.[44] The villagers only managed to hold funerals and weddings, organized along the border to allow both sides to participate. In 1967, the village reunified informally when Israel occupied the West Bank, but initially warm meetings quickly faded as cultural, economic, and political differences between the torn families became apparent.[45] While West Bank Barta'a was a bastion of the two intifadas, those on the Israeli side voted in 1995 for the Labor Party.[46] There have been very few marriages between their residents, due to the separation between the two sides, although some men from the West Bank side chose wives from the Israeli side in order to obtain Israeli IDs and thereby access to jobs in Israel. In other words, endogamous marriages were motivated by economic interest. Currently, the construction of the separation wall will isolate the two sides of the village from each other. Nonetheless, Israeli Barta'a residents do not want to shift their village to the Palestinian Authority's control. Although they assist their West Bank relatives—for example, when the Israeli army demolishes their homes—this solidarity resembles Palestinian Americans' support for the Palestine cause or American Jews' financial support for Israel.

From the vantage point of transnational kinship economic ties, the familial mode of entrepreneurship in the Palestinian territories and, to a lesser extent, in Israel will encourage many Palestinian refugees with entrepreneurial skills to return. I expect this category to exercise their return in a transnational mode, keeping their ties to both the place of return and the previous host country.

This study has clarified that return is determined by factors that go beyond the mere right of return. But the right of return is the key for any solution, as it will open up various choices available to the Palestinian refugees after more than half a century of exile.[47] Shaml's fieldwork and my studies in thirteen countries of the Palestinian diaspora from 1990 to 1995 did not uncover a homogeneous population of five million refugees, all of whom would exercise their right of return; rather, they found a far smaller number ready to return. For example, among the Palestinians in Lebanon, Fafo's survey in 2002 found only 1.2 percent who were originally from the Palestinian territories, whereas nearly all came from the parts of historical Palestine that are now inside Israel. In fact, 40 percent came from places that are now completely Jewish, such as Safad and Tiberias, or have a large Jewish majority, such as Acre and Haifa; only 10 percent came from Arab cities, notably Nazareth. Although two out of five Palestinians in Lebanon were born in Palestine, very few have maintained ties with Palestinians inside Israel.[48]

It is difficult to imagine a single scenario, due to the uncertainties of the results of negotiations and possible reactions on the part of Arab states.[49] Those uncertainties would cause the eventual number of returnees to vary tremendously. Based on a wide spectrum of factors influencing the realization of return, but without taking into account patriotism as a push factor for return, I can propose three scenarios for eventual refugee movement. They differ in regard to the possibility of exercising the right of return and the extent of improvement in the refugee camp conditions. As this work is in progress, and as I am still finalizing modulations of the return, I will present rough estimations of the potential movement of the refugees.

First Scenario: Application of the Right of Return Coupled with No Improvement in Camp Conditions

This scenario takes into account many surveys that question people about their willingness to return to their homes in 1948 or in the Palestinian territories. My estimate is not based on their declarations but on the interpretation and contextualization of such declarations. For the migration movement outside the Palestinian territories, a "generous" quota would be provided for the Palestinian refugees by third countries, a small percentage of refugee camp dwellers will choose to settle near their relatives abroad (of the Palestinian territories), and a still smaller percentage of the refugees outside of the camps. The percentage in both cases is small if we take into account the fractured nature of the Palestinian family. This means that the head of the family lives temporarily in the new location until finding a proper job and becoming relatively settled. The camps will not be improved. It is to be expected that 15 percent of camp dwellers in the Palestinian territories will leave the camps: around ninety thousand will leave to live in Palestinian cities, while the rest will stay in the camps or return home or to a third country.

This scenario also takes into account the high percentage of Palestinian refugees in the Palestinian territories who have relatives abroad. As the number of Palestinian refugees and displaced abroad who are originally from the West Bank and Gaza Strip is around one million, again taking into account the fractured nature of the Palestinian family, I expect that 20 percent of them would settle in the Palestinian territories. This is the equivalent of 200,000 potential newcomers.

The number of Palestinians in Arab countries, according to an estimate of PCBS, is around 4,017,000, of whom 402,000 are in Lebanon[50] and 525,000 in Western countries. Since the situation of the Palestinians in Lebanon is critical, I expect around half of them (mainly camp dwellers) to come to the Palestinian territories or Israel, even if they have no kinship ties; thus, around 150,000 will come. I expect the Palestinian refugees resident in other Arab countries (subtracting 30 percent of the Palestinians in Jordan and Egypt, as they are originally from the West Bank and Gaza) to come for different socioeconomic reasons—push factors from the host countries, pull factors for Israel or the Palestinian territories. If I talk about 15 percent, we will have 390,000. For people resident in Western countries, I expect 3 percent to return (15,000). Thus, around 500,000 will be distributed: two-thirds in the Palestinian territories and one-third inside Israel.

Second Scenario: A Restricted Right of Return with Improved Refugee Camp Conditions

Under this scenario, the urban rehabilitation of the camps is undertaken. The major problems are infrastructure and housing rather than health and educational services, which are currently provided at a relatively acceptable level by UNRWA (UN Relief and Works Agency). A key aspect of improving the camps is organizational and does not require vast financial resources; this particularly involves enhancing the representation of the camps in the local municipalities. These problems are also less serious in the West Bank than in Gaza, as the camp dwellers in the former constitute 6.4 percent of the population while in Gaza the figure is 31.1 percent.

The movement of refugees is predicted as follows: I predict the return to Israel would be much less than in the first scenario: around 10 percent, or 145,000 refugees. I also expect that 3 percent of refugee camp dwellers would choose to settle in a third country in order to be near their relatives (18,000) and 2 percent of the refugees would move out of the camps (17,000). A small portion would leave the camps for social reasons as even after the physical and practical improvement of the camps, their social and political stigma will remain for a long time. I expect 5 percent to leave the camps (30,000). As with the first scenario, I expect 20 percent of the Palestinians originally from the West Bank and Gaza who live abroad to settle in the Palestinian territories, that is, 200,000 potential newcomers. As with the first scenario, 500,000 could come from abroad and this would be shared: two-thirds in the Palestinian territories and one-third inside Israel.

Third Scenario: No Application of the Right of Return, with Varying Situations in Refugee Camps

Almost 20 percent of the West Bank and Gaza camp dwellers used to work in Israel before the second intifada. This work could be resumed, but people will experience a high degree of alienation as a result of working in one place and living in another. The movement of refugees is predicted as follows: I predict only a few individual returns to Israel through intermarriage (fewer than 10,000 coming from West Bank and Gaza and 20,000 coming from the diaspora). I also expect 10 percent of refugee camp dwellers to choose to settle in a third country near their relatives (60,000) and 3 percent of the refugees living outside the camps (25,000) to settle in a third country. As with the first and second scenarios, I expect 20 percent of the Palestinian refugees who live abroad and are originally from the West Bank and Gaza to settle in the Palestinian territories: this will create 200,000 potential newcomers. As with the first and second scenarios, 600,000 might come from abroad and, as they cannot go to Israel, those will dwell in the Palestinian territories.

The movement of Palestinian refugees will accordingly follow the logic of table 4.2. Certainly, those who are willing to return may be more numerous if we introduce other factors such as patriotism, or a strong push factor from the host countries, such as expulsion of refugees.

Conclusion

The potential returnees do not constitute a homogeneous group; on the contrary, they represent diverse social, cultural, political, and economic

TABLE 4.2. Scenarios Taking into Account Only the Socioeconomic Factors

	Return from Palestinian Territories to Israel	Return of refugees from abroad to Israel	Emigration from Palestinian Territories to Western countries	Leaving the camps	Coming from abroad to Palestinian Territories
First scenario	200,000	200,000	47,000	90,000	500,000
Second scenario	150,000	150,000	35,000	30,000	500,000
Third scenario	10,000	20,000	85,000	30,000–90,000	600,000

strata of the refugee and diaspora population, varying from illiterate laborers to highly educated professionals and entrepreneurs. It is hard to predict with precision the percentage of each of the socioeconomic categories and whether the returnees would opt for permanent family return; individual return, without the entire nuclear family; flexible return with transnational behavior (that is, being in two places and always keeping the possibility of moving); investment without moving; or providing expertise through short stays in the Palestinian territories. But it is likely that a combination of patterns will emerge that will benefit the Palestinian economy, because the mode of entrepreneurship is familial and kinship ties remain strong between those in the West Bank and Gaza Strip and those living abroad. However, the possibility of investing in the Palestinian economy in Israel is less probable, as there is no autonomous Palestinian economy there. Returning Palestinians will not feel loyal to the Israeli system if it maintains its Jewish character and kinship ties are weak.

The Palestinian economic elite abroad will invest via capital and physical return, as it will seek to enhance its social standing in its country or village of origin, even if the situation remains nonconducive to investment and economic rationalities are not ensured. I have seen similar behavior in other post-conflict and transitional countries (Hungary, Rumania, Armenia, and Bosnia), where the diaspora elite plays a role in the political arena. Extrapolating from the rate of investment and from family and other philanthropic activities of the Palestinian diaspora, I expect that the contribution would be at least half a billion U.S. dollars per year over the ten-year period following the independence of the Palestinian state.

As there will be two concurrent movements—one of the mass of returnees and one of select people, graduates and professionals as well as entrepreneurs—four conclusions can be drawn. First, researchers underestimate the importance of education and know-how among refugees. Many statistical indicators show that a quarter of the Palestinian refugees in the Arab host countries are entrepreneurs, according to the definition of the ILO (self-employed and employers). Thus, I expect that a quarter of the returnees will be able to integrate into the new Palestinian market. The return, in any case, cannot be viewed as purely a burden on the Palestinian economy. To the contrary, it could generate economic growth, thanks to the human and financial capital that the refugees will bring with them.

Second, the Palestinian state will have the right to adopt a policy of selectivity, as many countries in post-conflict areas have done. Historically, the policy of selecting the (return) migrants has been applied by all countries that received a mass return of their nationals or a like influx from another country. Even when the return is partially ideological, as with Israeli aliyah, selectivity was always the rule and has been kept firmly under Israeli government control. As Eliezer Kaplan, Israeli finance minister in 1949, said: "We need workers and fighters."[51]

Third, if the Arab states do not compel Palestinian refugees to leave, I expect that an initial pioneer group will return. Then, once they give a good report about their situation to their relatives and social networks, these will be encouraged to come.

Finally, I expect the return of retired people, especially from the Gulf and western countries, to the Palestinian territories and Israel. This form of lengthy "tourism" will benefit the Palestinian economy, and these people will not need direct state assistance.

As this study is one of the first on the sociology of return, I hope it will open this field to more investigations and studies, based essentially on the comparison with other refugee situations around the world.

Notes

Although Sari Hanafi is director of the Palestinian Diaspora and Refugee Center, Shaml, this work reflects his views only. He expresses his gratitude to Ann Lesch for her editing of this chapter. He thanks the many researchers who critiqued the first draft, including Roula ElRifai, Pamela Scholey, Riina Isotalo, and Cedric Parizot.

1. All percentages mentioned in this article come from Shaml's survey, unless otherwise stated. The Shaml survey was funded by International Development Research Center. The author thanks those who participated in the fieldwork, particularly Shereen Araj. The survey in Israel was conducted in cooperation with the Mada Center in Haifa.

2. PSR's survey was conducted between January 16 and February 5, 2003, targeting 1,498 Palestinian refugee households distributed among 150 localities in the West Bank and Gaza Strip. The Fafo survey is about the living conditions of Palestinian refugees in Lebanon and Jordan. In Lebanon, it covers a sample of four thousand households resident in refugee camps and relatively homogeneous refugee areas (Ole Fr. Ugland, ed., *Difficult Past, Uncertain Future: Living Conditions Among Palestinian Refugees in Camps and Gatherings in Lebanon*, Fafo report 409 [2003]). In Jordan, the survey employed two methods: a survey of stratified probability sample of about 3,100 households selected from twelve camps; and thirteen focus groups. The primary purpose of the focus-group discussions was to learn how camp dwellers perceive economic hardship, unemployment, and work opportunities (Marwan Khawaja and Åge A. Tiltnes, eds., *On the Margins: Migration and Living Conditions of Palestinian Camp Refugees in Jordan* [Oslo: Fafo, 2002]).

3. Karl Polanyi, "The Economy as Instituted Process," in *The Great Transformation* (Boston: Beacon, 1957); Marc Granovetter and Richard Swedberg, *The Sociology of Economic Life* (Boulder, Colo.: Westview, 1995).

4. UNHCR, *Les Réfugiés dans le monde: Cinquante ans d'action humanitaire* (Paris: Edition Autrement, 2000), 168.

5. The UNHCR was criticized for acquiescing in the coerced return of refugees to Rwanda in 1996, a violation of the duty under international law not to return a refugee to a place where he might experience persecution (Arthur Helton, *The Price of Indifference: Refugees and Humanitarian Action in the New Century* [New York: Oxford University Press, 2002], 22). East Timor may be an exception, as nearly all the refugees returned home after a political settlement was reached.

6. R. Sayigh, *Palestinians: From Peasants to Revolutionaries* (London: Zed, 1979);

Daniel Warner, "Voluntary Repatriation and the Meaning of Returning Home: A Critique of Liberal Mathematics," *Journal of Refugee Studies* 7:2–3 (1994): 160.

7. Elia Zureik, "The Trek Back Home: Palestinians Returning Home and Their Problem of Adaptation," in Are Hovdenak et al., *Constructing Order: Palestinian Adaptation to Refugee Life* (Oslo: Fafo Institute for Applied Social Science, 1997), 80.

8. Salman Abu-Sitta, *The End of the Palestinian-Israeli Conflict: From Refugees to Citizens at Home* (London: Palestinian Land Society and Palestinian Return Center, 2001).

9. Najeh Jarrar, *Palestinian Refugee Camps in the West Bank: Attitudes Towards Repatriation and Integration* (Ramallah: Palestinian Diaspora and Refugee Center, Shaml, 2003). Jarrar's study covers two refugee camps, Fari'a and Balata. Two methods were used to collect information: a survey questionnaire and in-depth interviews. The first method used a random sample of 5 percent of the total house units in the two camps; 58 house units from Fari'a camp out of 374, and 86 house units from Balata camp out of 801. This sample was drawn from the list of housing units available from the UNRWA director's office in each camp.

10. Alejandro Portes, "Social Capital: Its Origins and Applications in Contemporary Sociology," *Annual Review of Sociology* 24 (1998): 1–24.

11. However, this positive image of the status of the women that confirms the Islamic and Arabic value placed on *silate al arham* (maintaining the ties with the relatives) and *a'rd* (honor) should not blind us to the effects of a patriarchal society in which men are still favored in education and receive the most significant gifts from their families.

12. Rita Giacaman and Penny Johnson, eds., *Inside Palestinian Households: Initial Analysis of a Community-Based Household Survey*, vol. 1 (Birzeit: Birzeit University, 2002), 9.

13. Ladislav Holy, *Kinship, Honour and Solidarity: Cousin Marriage in the Middle East* (Manchester: Manchester University Press, 1989).

14. Jon Pedersen et al., eds., *Growing Fast: The Palestinian Population in the West Bank and Gaza Strip* (Oslo: Fafo, 2001), 80–84.

15. Riina Isotalo, "Gendering the Palestinian Return Migration: Migrants from the Gulf and Marriage as a Transnational Practise," paper presented at the Third Mediterranean Social and Political Research Meeting, Florence, Mediterranean Programme, Robert Schuman Centre for Advanced Studies, European University Institute, March 20–24, 2002; idem, "Yesterday's Outsiders, Today's Returnees: Transnational Processes and Cultural Encounters in the West Bank," in *Under the Olive Tree. Reconsidering Mediterranean Politics and Culture*, A. Linjakumpu and K. Virtanen, eds. (Tampere: European Science Foundation and Tampere Peace Research Institute, 1997).

16. Laurie Blome Jacobsen and Mary Deeb, "Social Network," in *Difficult Past, Uncertain Future*, Ugland, ed.

17. Edwina Uehara, "Dual Exchange Theory, Social Networks, and Informal Social Support," *American Journal of Sociology* 96 (1990): 524, cited by Jacobsen and Deeb, "Social Network," 223.

18. Pal Sletten and Jon Pedersen, *Coping with Conflict: Palestinian Communities Two Years into the Intifada* (Oslo: Fafo, 2003), 47.

19. Alejandro Portes, *Latin Journey: Cuban and Mexican Immigrants to the U.S.* (Berkeley: University of California Press, 1985).

20. Sari Hanafi, *Hona wa honaq: Nahwa tahlil lil 'alaqa bin al-shatat al-falastini wa al markaz* (Here and there: Toward an analysis of the relationship between the Palestinian diaspora and the center) (Ramallah: Muwatin; Jerusalem: Institute of Jerusalem Studies, 2001); Isotalo, "Gendering the Palestinian Return Migration";

B'tselem and Ha'Moded, *Families Torn Apart: Separaton of Palestinian Families in the Occupied Territories* (Center for the Defense of the Individual, July 1999).

21. Sari Hanafi, "Penser le rapport diaspora, centre. La contribution de la diaspora palestinienne à l'économie des territoires," in Hachan Hassan-Yari, ed., *Le processus de paix au Moyen-Orient* (Paris: Hartmattan, 2000); Saad al Din and Abdel Fadil, *Intiqal al 'amalah al 'arabiyya* (The movement of Arab labor) (Beirut: Center of Arab Unity Studies, 1983); Nader Fergany, *Sa'yan wara' al rizq* (Striving for subsistence) (Beirut: Centre d'Etudes de l'Unité Arabe, 1988).

22. See, for example, the European Union report: Tsardanidis Charalambos and Asteris Huliaras, *Prospects for Absorption of Returning Refugees in the West Bank and the Gaza Strip,* Institute of International Economic Relations (unpublished report, December 1999).

23. Nicholas Van Hear, *Reintegration of the Palestinian* Refugees, monograph no. 6 (Ramallah: Shaml Publications, 1996).

24. L. Basch, Nina Glick Schiller, and Cristina Szanton Blanc, *Nations Unbound: Transnational Projects, Postcolonial Predicaments, and Deterritorialized Nation-States* (New York: Gordon and Breach, 1994), 22. See the critique by Ralph Grillo, Bruno Riccio, and Ruba Salih, introduction to *Here or There? Contrasting Experiences of Transnationalism: Moroccans and Senegalese in Italy* (Sussex: University of Sussex Press, 2000), 19.

25. Grillo et al., *Here or There,* 19.

26. Transfer of Knowledge Through Expatriate Nationals (TOKTEN) is an interesting mechanism for tapping into national expatriate human resources and mobilizing them to undertake short-term consultancy work in their countries of origin. The UN Development Program, which founded it, demonstrated that specialists (who had migrated to other countries and achieved professional success abroad) were enthusiastic about providing short-term technical assistance to their country of origin.

27. Fadl Naqib, "Absorption of the Palestinian Refugee: Economic Aspects" (unpublished paper, PRC, Ramallah, 2003), 45.

28. Sari Hanafi, "Contribution de la diaspora palestinienne à l'économie des territoires investissement et philanthropie," in *Maghreb-Machrek* 161 (November 1998). The Palestinian economy and economic development are now so uneven that generalizations based on central data are extremely hazardous. To trace investments from the host countries into the homeland, six hundred 600 interviews with Palestinian business people (mainly from Jordan, the United Arab Emirates, Egypt, Syria, Israel, Lebanon, Saudi Arabia, the United States, Canada, Chile, the United Kingdom, and Australia) were conducted during 1995–97.

29. Ministry of Planning and International Cooperation (MOPIC), Aid Coordination Department. *MOPIC's 1997 Fourth Quarterly Monitoring Report of Donor Assistance* (Ramallah, 1998) (www.pna.net).

30. Sara Roy, *The Gaza Strip: The Political Economy of De-development* (Washington, D.C.: Institute of Palestine Studies, 1995).

31. ILO (International Labor Organization), "Resolution concerning the Measurement of Underemployment and Inadequate Employment Situations," Sixteenth International Conference of Labor Statistics (Geneva: ILO, 1998).

32. Khawaja and Tiltnes, *On the Margins,* 99.

33. Hussein Al-Rimmawi and Hana Bukhari, *Population Characteristics of the Population Refugee Camps, Ramallah: PCBS and Dissemination and Analysis of Census Findings* (Arabic), Analytical Report Series no. 3 (2002), 54.

34. Hanafi, "Penser le raprt diaspora," 2000.

35. Ohayo Ong, *Flexible Citizenship: The Cultural Logic of Transnationality* (Durham, N.C.: Duke University Press, 1999), 6.

36. David Harvey, *The Condition of Postmodernity* (London: Blackwell, 1990).

37. Clifford Geertz, *Peddlers and Princes* (Chicago: University of Chicago Press, 1993).

38. Khawaja and Tiltnes, *On the Margins*, 28–29.

39. Sletten and Pedersen, *Coping with Conflict*, 31.

40. ICBS, *Statistical Abstract of Israel* (Jerusalem: Central Bureau of Statistics, 2003), 760.

41. World Bank, *Fifteen Months—Intifada, Closure, and Palestinian Economy* (Jerusalem: World Bank, 2002), 35.

42. Personal communication with the author.

43. After the Rhodes agreement with Jordan in 1949, Jordan handed over to Israel many villages in the triangle area, including half of the village of Barta'a.

44. Ziad Mohammed Daoud Kabha, *Barta'a: The Divided* Heart (Ramallah: Edition of Ziad Mohammed Daoud Kabha, 2003), 69.

45. Mary Totary, "The Political Attitude in a Divided Village," in *The Case of Western Barta'a/Eastern Barta'a* (Haifa: Galilee Center for Social Research, 1999), 13.

46. This contrasted with Arab voting in general: 51 percent supported Arab parties, whereas those parties obtained only 17 percentof the vote in Barta'a (ibid., 18).

47. I believe that the right of return is the key to any durable solution to the Palestinian-Israeli conflict, including the end of the occupation and the resolution of the land issue, because the right of return requires Israelis to acknowledge their moral responsibility and to be accountable for the birth of the Palestinian refugee problem and the colonial practices deployed during the war of 1948.

48. Marwan Khawaja, "Population," in *Difficult Past, Uncertain Future*, Ugland, ed.

49. Palestinians residing in Lebanon may not be able to determine their intention to return if the Lebanese position remains unclear. Will the Palestinians be thrown across the border, as occurred in Libya, or will they be given the right to choose?

50. This figure is too high for Palestinians actually resident in Lebanon. This includes the Palestinians who have Lebanese travel documents or passports. I think the number cannot exceed 300,000.

51. Quoted in Tom Segev, *1949: The First Israelis* (New York: The Free Press, 1986), 117.

Part II
Truth and Political Consequences

Chapter 5
Considerations Toward Accepting Historical Responsibility

Elazar Barkan

Morality as Realpolitik

The demand that nations act morally and acknowledge their own gross historical injustices is a novel phenomenon. Traditionally, realpolitik was the stronghold of international diplomacy. National security and economic interests excluded other considerations. But beginning at the end of World War II, and quickening since the end of the cold war, questions of morality and justice have received growing attention as political issues. As such, the need for restitution to past victims has become a major part of national politics and international diplomacy.

The pace of transition since 1989 in the international arena has been dramatic. This change includes the horrendous wars in Africa and Yugoslavia as well as the liberation of Eastern Europe and South Africa and the return to democracy in many Latin American countries. Nonetheless, even the positive shifts from a totalitarian regime or a dictatorship have been a painful experience for many countries. In several of these transitions, instead of revenge against the perpetrators, truth and reconciliation committees—such as in South Africa and Latin America—have tried to weigh culpability and the need to punish the guilty against the need for national stability. Before the end of the cold war, the fear of the unknown, the risk of a full confrontation with the Soviet Union, and the memory of Vietnam shaped the West's lack of response to human catastrophes. After 1989 the United Nations, NATO, and individual countries struggled to define their own place in a world that was paying less attention to realpolitik and more to moral values, at least until September 11, 2001.

This new moral frame in the nineties confuses observers/critics and participants/politicians alike. Instead of containment and security, moral rhetoric as motivation began to shape politics. The lack of response to the

genocide in Rwanda was despicable for moral reasons—not because anyone's security (besides the victims') was hurt. Yet even following the second
Iraq war, there remained a need for a moral gloss. While under certain
circumstances it is possible to ignore moral context, in most instances
moral considerations are significant for political efficacy, especially in the
long run.

The dynamics of realpolitik and morality are central in the Palestinian
demand for the right of return as restitution. The concept of the right of
return has very different meanings for Palestinians and Israelis. This
demand has been a central piece of the Palestinian identity since 1967 but
has only been explicated since 1988, as discussed below. The demand for
repatriation and restitution serves for many Palestinians as both a concrete
political aspiration and a symbolic claim. For the Palestinians, the demand
is a manifestation of frustration informed by real hardships, including the
continuous suffering by the refugees under the Israeli occupation. For
most Israelis, it symbolizes a plan to destroy Israel. In the political rhetoric
of the region, it is an aspect of the plan to throw the Jews into the sea—
another tactic aimed at the same goal as that of Palestinian terrorism, to
bring an end to the Jewish state.

The conflicting views of what the right of return means provide much
heated public rhetoric. At the most abstract level, the "pro" or "anti" declarations by both groups map national commitments rather than positions
about a concrete political plan. Consider the opening salvo in the comments over the "road map" (summer 2003). The Israeli right-wing government, while formally endorsing a Palestinian state, took the formal step of
rejecting the Palestinian right of return to what is now Israel. The Palestinian prime minister at the time, Mahmoud Abbas (Abu Mazen), stated,
"This is one of Israel's dreams: [Our] giving up the right of return," and
added, "The right of return, or the issue of the refugees, is part of the final
status issues and we shouldn't be talking about it now."[1] Even more than
Jerusalem, conflict over the right of return has become the emblem of the
national conflict.

The demand for a right of return is relatively uncommon in international relations and is hardly ever implemented. Most frequently, it appears
in the Palestinian-Israeli context, but rarely if ever in any of the other
numerous cases involving tens of millions of refugees worldwide. There are
exceptions, such as in the Dayton peace agreement. Bosnia, however, is an
example of the violation of the repatriation across the ethnic divide.[2] In
this sense, the Palestinian campaign for the right of return has been gaining international legitimacy for a set of political demands that are widely
viewed as a right. Today the international discussion on the subject revolves
on some level around issues of feasibility and resources, while many of the
protagonists declaim principled demands and rejections of one another's
positions with little indication of a readiness for political compromise.

Among historical analogies for the Palestinian demand for the right of return, none is more conspicuous than Zionism. Both national movements sought to reverse exile, diasporic existence, and historical deprivation. Both employ the term "return" as a core national belief. This is clearly not the place to review the numerous similarities and differences between the two nations, but it is worth noting the obvious: both sides are locked in a struggle over distinct and interwoven rights of return. Indeed, although Palestinians have been repeatedly making this comparison, Israelis have refrained from doing so. I shall come back to the comparison in the conclusion.

The novelty of amending historical injustices for moral reasons means that much in this area lacks precedent. Reparations have never been paid voluntarily in the past. The new regime of guilt-informed reparation is a post–World War II phenomenon. It ranged from German reparations to Jews and others, to various other compensation and affirmative-action programs that went further than mere social welfare. Previously, victors' justice enforced reparations, but victims who did not win a war or a conflict did not receive compensation. Apologies are another aspect of this new phenomenon. Despite the critique that the economic and power disparities increase with globalism, never in the past have victims received as much attention as they do today.

The newness of the phenomenon under discussion produces the first dilemma of this chapter. Historians can only work by studying the past, yet much of the way the past is treated by contemporary society is new. The past therefore may be only a partial or even inaccurate descriptor of the way we treat the past currently. Yet the historian is limited to comparing actual precedents. I am mindful that many of the interesting developments regarding responsibility and restitution of past injustices involve novel actions and interpretation of approaches to history. With the limitation of contextualizing the right of return in analogous previous events, this chapter attempts to explore the politics of restitution as a frame for accepting historical responsibility and amending the past.

The Meanings of "Right"

The following discussion is meant to critically explore the rhetoric of "right" as it is specifically employed in this dispute within the relevant historical contexts and analogies. The notion of right has multiple meanings, and it is crucial to remind ourselves that the claim of right, while it might have the appearance of empowerment, often turns out to be of little practical value. In the Palestinian case, the claim of right might have become an ideological credo turned into a political stumbling block. While relinquishing this claim would be denounced by believers, it is worthwhile to think about the possibility, since the analysis might suggest alternative ways to address the issue.

Rights are not born equal. Although there is a long list of international rights, the conventional division between political and civil rights, on the one hand, and economic, social, and cultural rights, on the other, is useful if only to remind us about the contentious nature of the second category. One only has to think of the "right to the highest attainable standard of health" in light of the health of the poor from the U.S. through much of the Third World, to the catastrophes in Africa, to recognize that those billions of people benefit very little from the classification of their suffering and needs as rights. The nature of economic and social rights is that these are always questions of distribution of resources. The notion of a standard as a right is so vague that often the measly resources available for alleviation of suffering are directed to the formulations of rights and conventions by a multitude of officials who produce papers and reports that directly provide the illusion of attention and the reality of neglect. On the other hand, there are cases where the rhetoric of rights leads to policies that improve the state of the poor. This is most evident in Europe, and one might ask whether the will to achieve these social welfare goals—for example, in the case of the limited help to refugees—would not have been achieved without the rhetoric of rights. Those who are involved in the protection of these rights are all well intentioned; the structure, however, created commotion and no action. Indeed, the case that this industry of social and economic rights is counterproductive needs to be addressed.

The Palestinian refugee question falls into the debate of rights because supporters have formulated it as such. Rights first and foremost raise the bar for what is at stake. At least rhetorically, it removes the debate onto a higher moral plateau. Are there any duties that are imposed as a result of the existence of these rights? Who has these duties, and what specifically do these contain? Is the discussion of rights merely an excuse to do little until these rights are fulfilled to attend to the deprivation of the refugees? This is not meant as a moral or a political discussion, and I do not think that there is one preferred solution to the dispute. My discussion is structured comparatively around the question of what is realistic and necessary in the Israeli-Palestinian case, based on the supposition that any workable agreed-upon solution between the sides is preferable to the conflict.

There is significant disconnect between the principled discussion over the right of return and a pragmatic political solution. Much of the public discourse on the subject amounts to declarations of doctrines. Most commentators and politicians demand or reject the principle of return with little discussion of the particulars. In contrast, there have been several attempts to move in the direction of bringing an end to the conflict by envisioning the parameters for an agreed-upon solution. In addition to scholars who study the refugee issue, several prominent Palestinians and

Israelis have issued statements that outline principled compromised solutions. These pronouncements share recognition that the urgent need to resolve the conflict limits the scope of action regarding the refugees to a symbolic action vis-à-vis the right of return. This results from the view that the ongoing conflict inflicts greater suffering on both sides and that the aspiration to resolve the suffering of refugees should not prove a cause of greater anguish and an obstacle to a political solution.

The difficult problem that informs the contributors to this volume is both intellectual and political: What actions can be taken in order to facilitate greater recognition, to amend the violation of human rights, and enhance their protection? And what mechanisms and strategies could be developed for the advancement of Palestinian claims? I will try to address these questions within the local and the global context.

The Palestinian View of the Right of Return

Over the past ten days, while Palestinian and Israeli negotiators have been sequestered at Camp David, Palestinians from all political factions have taken to the streets calling upon the Palestinian leadership and the international community to uphold refugee rights, foremost being the right of return. . . .

While a durable solution for Palestinian refugees—and the Arab-Israeli conflict in general—must be based on international law, press reports have suggested that what is being pushed by Israel, and through American bridging proposals, is an arrangement based on subjective political factors—namely, Israel's refusal to allow refugees to return.[3]

This in a nutshell is the prevalent Palestinian position. The interests of the refugees are presented as a violated right of return that ought to be resolved according to international law and, if unresolved, should prevent a resolution of the Israeli-Palestinian conflict. The opposition presented is between politics based on lack of transparency ("sequestered at Camp David") and public democratic action ("Palestinians from all political factions have taken to the streets"), and between objective considerations ("international law") and Israeli intransigence ("on subjective political factors"). Similarly, the rhetoric employed by the Council for Palestinian Restitution and Repatriation (CPRR)[4] appealed to the moral sensibility of the democratic world: "This is a matter that should go to the conscience of the world—and the democratic world especially." The plea by Haidar Abdel Shafi was directed first to the Palestinian Authority, and then "to all the parties who are involved in peace, especially the United States government and the world democracies in general."

Palestinians perceive themselves as victims of a long process that started with the British and continued with Israel in 1947–49, a process that denied their national existence. Al-Nakba has become the most important experience in the Palestinian identity. The Palestinian refugees of 1948 did not resettle in Arab countries but instead remain in refugee camps. The popular Palestinian view is that maintaining the status of refugees was a national act of rejecting exile, a political national stand, not a result of rebuff and denial of rights by the host Arab governments. In this view, the Palestinians view themselves as having full agency in maintaining their national identity, but not in the victimizations and catastrophes that inflicted their history.

What constitutes the right of return? There is no formal Palestinian position on the subject. For some, the right is mostly moral, abstract, a matter of recognition, not physical property. Indeed, in 1992, Rashid Khalidi, in search of historical analogies, settled on the Jewish claims of return as the cornerstone of his analysis. He imagined that the implementation of the right of return could be achieved primarily symbolically and "carefully." The demand for the right of return has a history of its own. Although the public impression is that the right of return was always an intense Palestinian aspiration, Khalidi reminds us that the right of return became a formulation of the Palestinian suffering relatively recently. Some among Arab countries have contemplated and demanded the right of return as part of an agreement with Israel since 1949, yet the Palestinian representatives, who initially were self-appointed and were followed by the Palestine Liberation Organization (PLO), have subsumed the right of return under the demand for the total liberation of Palestine.

Thus, after 1967, when the PLO become the preeminent representative of the Palestinians in place of the Arab countries, the right of return became a central component of the charter, but as a consequence of conquering Israel and not of an agreement with it. It was only in 1974, following the 1973 war, that new Palestinian National Council (PNC) resolutions stipulated implicitly a Palestinian entity in part, rather than the whole, of Palestine.[5] This implied compromise, or at least envisioned a coexistence with Israel. The charter explicated the right of return as a prominent demand for the first time. These new formulations were challenged and overshadowed by militant language that was part of the rejectionist front, which continuously played a central role in Palestinian politics. For the following twenty years, the language of the charter became the focus of the internal Palestinian struggle and the dispute with Israel. Khalidi views the emergence of the demand for the right of return as a form of compromise, of giving up the demand for the exclusive control of Palestine.

It took another fourteen years, until 1988, before the PLO grounded its demands in "international legitimacy" and in resolutions 181 and 194. Resolution 194 came to be interpreted to mean restitution and reparation for the refugees. These claims, however, remained abstract. There has not been any formal Palestinian position of what constitutes the right of return. Thus, it is a subject of projections and conflicting interpretation.

Since 2000, some voices have suggested a limited implementation of the right of return, but the popular Palestinian view merges all Palestinian sorrow into the debate over the right of return. The predicament of some five million refugees, anchored in the memory of massacres, is viewed as the touchstone of the Palestinian nation. "[As] all Palestinians come together annually to commemorate those who died [they remember] the UN resolution that dealt with the urgent refugee crisis, General Assembly resolution 194 of 1948, has yet to be implemented: Israel refuses to do so. Every Palestinian refugee today knows this resolution, calling for the return to their homes of those who wish to do so, as well as compensation."[6] Though it was only relatively late (1988) that the right of return based on Resolution 194 became a focus for the Palestinian demands and justification, it has become eternal in public opinion. The Palestinian public discourse avoids formulating an official explicit substantive statement of the right of return and rejects any concession regarding an absolute full right of return. The constructions are subjective and a matter of manipulations. These conflicting interpretations are subject to political squabbling within and between Palestinians and Israelis. Khalidi is correct to underscore that by accepting the UN resolutions, the Palestinians accepted implicitly the stipulation in 194 "to live at peace with their neighbors" as a prerequisite of an agreement. That means a willingness to give up the conflict after a resolution is achieved. This interpretation contrasts with the Israeli perspective, which views terror and Hamas fundamentalism as proof that the Palestinians do not foreground the "peaceful" component of Resolution 194. A Hamas statement following a suicide bombing that "these attacks will continue in all the territories of 1948 and 1967, and we will not stop attacking the Zionist Jewish people as long as any of them remain in our land"[7] is in line with popular notions of complete return to the homes left behind. This confusion between a right of return that is limited in scope, but is undefined, and an actual rejection of Israel's existence, remains prudent at the popular level. This suggests to Israelis that the right of return as a focus of Palestinian aspiration is a focus that has changed little from the height of the ideology of the rejectionist camp.

The public demonstrations by Palestinians to pressure Palestinian negotiators and leaders to adhere to the more expansive interpretation of the right of return during Camp David II reflect the demand as a symbol of Palestinian nationalism. From an implicit secondary issue, it has become central to the Palestinian national identity. The reluctance of the Palestinian Authority to outline the content of the demand leaves it in the hands of nongovernmental individuals and organizations. These include the whole spectrum from Sari Nusseibeh to Hamas.[8] Sari Nusseibeh's original declaration in 2001 provided the opening for the debate among Palestinians. The declaration stated that, in a two-state solution, Palestinian refugees would return only to the State of Palestine. His joint declaration with Ami Ayalon followed. A controversy ensued, and Palestinian leaders such as Abu

Mazen (before becoming prime minister) rephrased their own position ("If you acknowledge the principle, we will give you the number now"). Palestinian Minister for Information Yasser Abed Rabbo, on several occasions, also reframed the right of return as a negotiable demand.[9] These statements were rejected by several Palestinian organizations—including those representing refugee issues—such as the Department of Refugee Affairs of the Palestine Liberation Organization, the Popular Refugee Committees, the Palestinian Return Centre, and the al-Awda network. They called for the resignations of the compromising officials and branded Nusseibeh a traitor.

In October 2003, the Geneva initiative was signed by distinguished Palestinians and Israeli leaders; the Israelis were mostly from the opposition, but several of the Palestinians held formal positions, were connected to Fatah, and were said to have received Arafat's blessing for the agreement. The initiative discussed in detail the solution to the refugee question, which included a very limited number of Palestinians returning to Israel, at its own discretion. This elicited a strong Palestinian response among refugee advocates, similar to that discussed above. The difference this time was the significant support that the accord had in mainstream Palestinian political discourse. At the time this chapter is being written, it is hard to judge where these discussions will go.

The Israeli Perspective

Israeli Jewish nationalism is precisely that: Israeli and Jewish. The demand to allow one to three million Palestinians to settle within Israel, which is a frequent interpretation of the right of return, is viewed by Israelis as a plan to deny and erase this right of Israeli nationalism. Many critics of Israel would embrace such an outcome. Israel itself struggles domestically with notions of "who is a Jew" as it works out the relation between being a democracy and a Jewish state. The demand to transform the internal balance of power and transform the nature of Israel from a Jewish state to a state of its citizens, which explicitly means the demand for human-rights equality for Arabs in Israel, is viewed as a slogan to erase Jewish nationalism.

The dispute within Israel over the Palestinian right of return overlaps with the debate on the Jewish character of the state. Those who reject the Jewish character of Israel are also the most vocal supporters of the expansive interpretation of the right of return for Palestinians. Mainstream Israelis deem both demands to constitute a two-pronged attack on their national identity. The vast majority of Jewish Israelis believe that there is a national consensus of rejecting the right of return and that the demand is a nonstarter in negotiation, but rather is meant to scuttle a settlement. The second intifada and the various pronouncements by Palestinians of intentions, beliefs, and plans to eliminate Israel combine with terror to ensure that many left-wing Israelis also subscribe to that view. There are exceptions to this Israeli consensus, but I doubt that they translate into even small percentages of the Israeli public.

The publication of the Geneva accord created intense public discussion in Israel, unprecedented since the beginning of the intifada. The focus was on whether the Palestinians have given up the right of return. It is, of course, an unofficial document, and thus before it is incorporated into any agreement, we must expect that it would be revised. Therefore its import here is the immediate response it elicited, which was to reawaken substantial support for peace and withdrawal from the territories among many who would reject it as long as the right of return remained a risk. As a factor in shaping Israeli public opinion, the right of return has become more important than any other issue, including Jerusalem.

The political dismissal of the right of return is accompanied by interpretations that aim to invalidate the claim and minimize its implication. For example, one question relates to international standards. Should international standards that evolved after the 1940s (such as the 1951 and 1967 conventions relating to the status of refugees) apply retroactively? Even if the right of return were to be accepted, at the very minimum they assert that international law lacks reference to descendants of immigrants, that is, the status of refugee is not inherited. Furthermore, they claim that it excludes all those who acquired other nationalities in the meantime.[10] With that in mind, the Israeli contention is that the number of entitled refugees would diminish dramatically. Another objection emphasizes that international conventions regarding refugees, such as the 1966 covenant, address the rights of individual refugees, not those of the collective. Moreover, the 1949 Geneva convention for the protection of victims of war does not recognize the right of return. Moving from the general to the particular, Israel's position is that Resolution 194 itself does not establish a right of return as such. Instead it is viewed as a framework for a peace agreement. Most important from the Israeli perspective is that the Arab countries rejected the resolution in the original vote and continued to reject it up to the 1960s.[11] Whatever one may think of UN General Assembly resolutions, Israel has long viewed that body as an anti-Israeli forum and has rejected many other General Assembly resolutions. It is probably more than of passing interest that Resolution 194 includes another aspirational provision, namely, the part that Jerusalem should "be accorded special and separate treatment from the rest of Palestine and should be placed under effective United Nations control." The nature of General Assembly resolutions is that, with changing circumstances, the new resolutions supersede previous ones. Israel points to 242 and 338 as the basis for an agreement, neither of which mentions 194 or the right of return, and in contrast to 194, these resolutions were accepted by both sides.

Historical Analogies

What historical analogies could one explore to ground the question of the right of return? Since the 1990s, Palestinians have described the refugee question as arising from an attempt at "ethnic cleansing." Israel rejects the term. Perhaps less controversial is the need to have historical analogies. Even the Jewish claim that the Holocaust is unique has come under criticism, and with time it is less likely to sustain its sui generis status. The reason has perhaps less to do with the particulars of the justification and more with the audience's unwillingness to accept this order of priorities: a hierarchy of suffering. Historical debates have to be comparative, because we can only understand through comparison and within this context. Ranking of affliction may work for a domestic audience, but outsiders have less patience for the details and are more concerned with ascertaining that their own pain is not forgotten in the process. In searching for comparative historical cases to the Palestinian refugees, the first task is to determine productive analogies. Part of the historical analysis is to contextualize the issue. The analysis can help construct a narrative that narrows the conflict between the sides.

In evaluating the historical context, we ought to observe that history itself has changed significantly in the last generation. Both historians and the public recognize the duality of history: it is both malleable and real. While conflicting perspectives offer us different histories, history is neither infinitely flexible nor a fairy tale, and it is the belief in the realism of history that lends it significance. Here is the tension. History is crucial as a manifestation of our identity because it is "real": it defines and describes what and who we are; yet through changing the account, we can affect our identity by legitimizing a new narrative. This new story line functions at several levels and is aimed at distinct audiences: the home crowd, the international community, and our rivals or enemies. The narrative becomes a manifestation of the competition for resources. The narrative becomes the national struggle, and the "historical context" of the Israeli-Palestinian struggle is multiple and political, but is constrained, at least in principle, by the "realism" of history.

How are we to respond to historical injustices? Even if Israelis and Palestinians agreed on the history of the Palestinian refugees—that is, what happened when, and even why—what would be the moral and political analogies that can help as precedents to provide a solution? Jeremy Waldron has attempted perhaps as systematically as anyone to theorize from philosophical and legal perspectives about repairing historical injustices.[12] His conclusion is that while it is "a difficult business," it is "almost always undertaken by people of good will." The parties don't even begin a conversation unless need and goodwill combine. But goodwill does not take us very far. The tension in efforts to amend the past is between "the simple conviction that, if something was wrongly taken, it must be right to give it back" and abstractions such as "entitlements that fade with time, counterfactuals that are impossible to verify, injustices that are overtaken by circumstances." In other words, the challenge is to imagine the past prevailing in the present situation without playing out all the possible scenarios in the meantime. To imagine the counterfactuals is obviously impossible. We cannot do it on the personal level, let alone the national. The longer the passage of time, the more fictional such a time machine becomes. Waldron opts for a narrow interpretation of repair: "The fallacy" to his mind, "lies in thinking that the directness" of outrage can be translated "into simple and straightforward certainty about what is to be done once such injustices have occurred."[13]

Because Waldron is very guarded in transforming historical claims into contemporary situations, his critique of Hume's position ("let bygones . . .") provides the strongest case for reparation in general and as a frame for a discussion of the right of return. Waldron suggests that we view the historical wrong as a case of continuous, not past, wrong. Instead of "regarding the expropriation" of lands "as an isolated act of injustice that took place at a certain time now relegated firmly to the past, we may think of it as a persisting injustice. The injustice persists, and it is perpetuated by the legal system, as long as the land that was expropriated is not returned to those from whom it was taken." In the Palestinian case, as in many others, a broader question arises: What is the political or other impact for a group that survives over several generations in the context of claims about injustice? To put it differently, when does the injustice become an identity, not primarily a deprivation? Few peoples have longer experiences of injustice than do the Jews. The distinction between injustice as deprivation (a cause for scarcity) and as an identity is significant for the task of determining alternative forms available to amend the injustice. Beyond the general issue of historical injustices, another pertinent context is the history of refugees.

Addressing Refugee Situations

Although the refugees have always suffered, attempts to alleviate that suffering emerge only in the second half of the twentieth century. As such, the international regime for the protection of refugees is a relatively recent phenomenon. There are close to twenty million refugees today under the mandate of the UN High Commissioner for Refugees (UNHCR), and a similar order of internally displaced persons (IDPs), who are not counted as refugees but share most attributes and suffering of full-fledged refugees and escape beyond recognized international borders.[14] The number of twenty million does not include the Palestinians, who are under the umbrella of the UN Relief and Works Agency (UNRWA). The international attention to refugees began in earnest only after World War II, in tandem with the formation of the UN. The International Refugee Organization (IRO) became one of several international efforts that attempted to address the increasing tidal wave of refugees.[15] The Geneva convention (1949) and the 1951 convention relating to the status of refugees were early attempts to respond to the immeasurable suffering of the immediate postwar period. This is not the place to describe the history of high ideals and the deplorable commitment of the international community response to refugees globally, but perhaps it is worth reminding ourselves that the term "refugee" only refers to a person who is displaced across borders, not within a country. For the international community to develop protective guidelines for IDPs took much longer and only succeeded in the 1990s.[16] Clearly, there is much more compassion and concern for refugees than there is international legal framework or political will. While the glorious days of the early protection of refugees recently celebrated fifty years, the challenges have only increased and are further from a solution in a world where many more people are moved across borders with great ease.

During the twentieth century, there have been nearly 200 million refugees worldwide. Among the predicaments bedeviling the refugees is the dispute over the number of refugees, a subject of continuous political quarrel. Refugee crises often take place in the midst of political anarchy, which aggravates the suffering. Even refugee crises that are spared explicit competition over resources are often subject to a dispute regarding the number of refugees. How many refugees were expelled, had to run away, chose to leave, or died? Such disputes arise not only with regard to cases such as the Armenian genocide, where everything revolves around the enormity of the tragedy measured to a great extent by the number of victims, but also more recent cases, such as the Hutu expulsion in Rwanda and other civil wars in Africa.[17] The purpose of international refugee law is to provide rehabilitation and protection from prosecution, not repatriation. The evolving customary law, as well as voluntary repatriation, primarily has individuals, not groups or nations, as its subjects of protection.[18]

What could we learn from the scores of instances of population displacements and ethnic cleansing as precedents for amending the deprivation of the Palestinian refugees? It is a challenge for historians to construct a convincing historical analogy. While all analogies are a partial match and consequently critics often choose the more convenient cases for their own position, imperfect analogies are still enlightening.

The worst global refugee crisis took place in the aftermath of World War II. For the current discussion, these cases were the most pertinent, both for geopolitical and chronological reasons. That postwar interethnic violence points to population transfers, forcible expulsions, and partitions as the prevalent policies.[19] Expulsions in Europe and in the Indian subcontinent included, in each region, ten million to twenty million refugees. In India, the disagreements are whether the number of refugees in the nine months after August 1947 is closer to ten million or eighteen million Hindus, Sikhs, and Muslims who were expelled and forced to flee. The disagreements over the number of dead are comparable: from under 200,000 to more than a million and a half.[20] Since then, numerous other wars have created multiple crises of refugees worldwide, the extent of which remains subject to significant discrepancies. These disagreements are the norm rather than the exception.

The ethnic cleansings at the end of World War II were criticized by few at the time but, from a historical distance and high moral ground, are clearly indefensible. It is also crucial to remember that given the ethnic xenophobia, which served as the excuse for the violence of the war, many accepted the expulsions as necessary and, one would dare say, morally right in order to avoid future ethnic feuds. This is a sorrowful historical reminder, but one that is indispensable if we are to understand the political context of what, under other circumstances, would constitute a crime.

The national subjective perspective remains constitutive of national memory even in cases where goodwill and political resolution have led to joint efforts between the sides to resolve historical disputes. The writing of a joint narrative at times can bridge some of the differences but can rarely resolve them. The Czech-German historical commission during the nineties tried to adjudicate the conflicting claims between the Germans who had claimed that more than a quarter of a million died in the expulsions and the Czech number of fifteen thousand to thirty thousand, which included in the Czech narrative several thousands who committed suicide. The commission of historical research stated that the Czech version was closer to the truth. In the spirit of compromise—and as a matter of accurate historical record—it emphasized that the precise number would never be known.

Compare the example of the demands of the Sudeten Germans with the Palestinian demands. From the Czech and Israeli perspective, in each case an ethnic group that had lived in the country for hundreds of years participated in and supported an external country in attacking their own state/ territory. (Neither the Sudeten Germans nor the Palestinians see it this way.) After the defeat of the aggressor, the irredentist ethnic minority was exiled (fully in the Sudeten, partially in Israel). In time, the Sudeten refugees settled and integrated in Germany, where they found refuge. While some Palestinians have settled individually in Arab countries, the Palestinian nation did not: many remain in the refugee camps, and the experience of exile has become the dominating national experience. In this sense, the historical deprivation might be analogous, but the contemporary situation remains acute for the Palestinians but not for the Sudeten Germans. Fifty years later, while both groups maintain their grievance, the Sudeten refugees are a minor political issue, and their demands, while problematic, are not threatening to the Czech Republic. Nonetheless, the Sudeten demands excite the national sentiments of the Czechs and are a potential (and occasionally manifested) trouble spot in German-Czech relations. With the growing attention to German suffering during and after World War II in Germany, the exiled German refugees (*Volksdeutsche*) may receive more attention. This would include the exiled Germans from Poland and other places, in addition to the Sudeten Germans. The Sudeten Germans demand minority status in the Czech Republic, including language rights. The question of amends to the Sudeten has never become a viable political option in the Czech Republic, although Václav Havel and occasional other voices did recognize the obligations of the Czech Republic to acknowledge the expulsion as a wrong. The numerous cases of ethnic cleansing in the East Central European borderlands, particularly after World War II, suggest that politicians should be careful in opening this Pandora's box.[21]

The historical precedents for repatriation are grim. Most refugees are never repatriated or compensated. This was the case with the post–World War II refugees. Yet there are exceptions. Most recently, the largest numbers of repatriated refugees were Afghanis. Since the Taliban were overthrown, nearly two million Afghanis returned, primarily from Pakistan and Iran.[22] It is more than of passing interest to note in this context how few resources were allocated for the returned refugees or to the country to assist in the repatriation: a mere $200 million, despite all the international attention! Very few Afghanis who lived in the West were willing, even with cash incentives, to be repatriated. (Similar cash incentives for Iranian and Iraqi refugees resulted in a comparable lukewarm reception.) Three decades ago, nine million refugees were repatriated to Bangladesh.[23] In most other cases, the numbers are far smaller. In the 1980s, for example, the UNHCR facilitated voluntary repatriation, such as 32,000 Ethiopian refugees from Djibouti (1983–84), 27,000 Ugandan refugees from Zaire and nearly 6,000 Ugandans from the Sudan, 12,000 refugees of various nationalities from Spain, and an unspecified number of Laotian refugees from Thailand.[24] More recently, there have been numerous cases of attempted repatriation, including: East Timorese and Burmese, two of the ethnicities that the Indonesian government attempted to repatriate while encountering ethno-political opposition; Sri Lankan refugees from India; and Kenyans from Ethiopia.[25] In most of these cases, repatriation involves a single ethnic or national group. The more pertinent examples are cases of repatriation across the ethnic divide.

The 1990s witnessed horrendous mass expulsions in Yugoslavia and Rwanda. The public was transfixed by an ethnic cleansing in the former Yugoslavia, which displaced more than two million Serbs, Croats, and Bosnian Muslims and later Kosovars and Macedonians. Rwanda received belated and brief attention, but numerous other cases never entered the public consciousness. Attention to refugees, beyond the time of the immediate catastrophe, is rare. Chechnya is the only Russian region that has received any international attention; the Caucasus and the Muslim republics in the former Soviet Union, and certainly most places in Africa, are mostly ignored. Similarly, refugees in various Chinese provinces—except Tibet, which receives a headline at times—never exist for the world.[26] Perhaps more surprising is the fact that the British government contemplated ethnic transfer in Northern Ireland even as recently as 1972.

Perhaps Bosnia in particular, and the former Yugoslavia in general, are the most prominent examples of the challenges facing refugee policies regarding the right of return. This is one of the few cases where the right of return across the ethnic divide was explicitly established in an international agreement. The Dayton peace agreement included explicit provisions for the voluntary return of refugees or alternative compensation. Indeed, Secretary of State Warren Christopher avowed at the time that "refugees and displaced persons will have the right to return home or to obtain just compensation."[27] Yet those who returned did so to areas dominated by their own ethnicity, while only a few thousand returned to areas ruled by other ethnicities. Most were afraid, unwilling, or could not return. Few received any compensation or help in the form of redress.[28] The focus on the right of return for all Bosnian refugees and displaced persons was complicated by the option of contemplating compensation as an alternative.[29] Even though the peace agreement included a mechanism to implement repatriation, little came of it. Repatriation faced opposition from all three ethnic minorities when it came to welcoming the refugees.[30]

Although the agreement and policies of return in Bosnia were formulated in the immediate aftermath of the war, choosing between repatriation and compensation collided with an overwhelming concern for ethnic integration. Maintaining future coexistence among the three ethnicities overshadowed any efforts to restore rights. In this, the Bosnian refugees resemble most other refugees in the world, even in cases where formal agreements are reached. Consequently, there is very little customary international law regarding compensation for refugees who are unwilling or unable to return for property they have left behind. Certainly, there is little precedent for placing the responsibility on the state of origin, if it is not part of a peace settlement. A survey of the rights of refugees to redress and of obligations to compensate refugees suggests that these might exist in theory, but implementation is rare and useful precedents are few. The vast majority of cases have been unsuccessful. If we look to the experience of tens of millions of refugees who are pushed from one territory to another, we quickly conclude that being a refugee is a miserable affair and that refugees rarely secure any rights, individual or communal.

Amending the Past

Notwithstanding the general political practice of attempting to resolve political disputes by looking to the future and minimizing the past, historical grievances continue to play a central role in certain conflicts and in general receive growing attention. In my book *The Guilt of Nations*,[31] I described numerous instances in which claims based upon historical injustices led to new political discourse. My conclusion from the global survey was that, notwithstanding good intentions, the amends are minimal and mostly symbolic.

The guiding principle for restitution and compensation is its symbolic nature, mostly in-kind or reparation. The obligations accepted in voluntary reparation should never inflict pain on current possessors or redistribute wealth but must make a meaningful difference for the victims. Since in most cases the victims are the poorer party among the two, this can work. For example, the German compensation to Jews, which began modestly and grew larger over time, was always meaningful economically, both to individual recipients and to Israel. Nor did the arrangement ever burden Germany in a way that changed German society or its economy in any meaningful way. Indeed, the situation has been worse when we look at the historical record of compensating refugees. However, when we look at that record, the most prominent cases in the twentieth century of population exchanges failed to implement corresponding restitution and compensation for the victims. These include the violent reciprocal expulsions between Greece and Bulgaria, Greece and Turkey; and India and Pakistan. Instead, in each case, the governments seized the immovable property left by the expellees but provided only limited relief to the incoming refugees.

One important generalization to be made from these and other cases is that the restitution process has a much more significant impact on the lives of the victims than on the perpetrators who consent to make the payments. Furthermore, restitution never approximates the actual inflicted damage. The indigenous peoples in various countries might dream but do not expect to have all their land back or to reverse the continent to its precolonial times. Yet even from the partial and limited restitution, they often benefit dramatically. The benefits of the restitution process are both economic and cultural. The victims are able to reduce their economic misery and are able to validate in their own eyes and the eyes of the world their culture and national identity. Yet even when such agreements are reached, there is a great internal opposition and claims that they have sold out. I propose that a study of these agreements may suggest a relevant comparison for formulating Palestinian policy.

Reparation Proposals

Resolution 194 established a three-member UN Conciliation Commission for Palestine (CCP), which led in 1951 to a proposed scheme of compensation to settle Arab refugees. Israel would compensate the Arabs for abandoned property with a global sum through a long payment plan that took into consideration its fragile economy at the time. Not least of the contested issues was the valuation of the lost property. Another was the Palestinian refusal to accept the ability of Israel to pay as one determinant of its liability, as well as Palestinian objections to settling on a global sum rather than for compensation to individuals. The Palestinian losses of property ranged between the low end as estimated by the CCP of 122 million British pounds (which would be about two billion U.S. dollars) to tens of billions today as demanded, for example, by the Arab League. These are possible considerations for an open discussion of what recognition of the right of return would entail.

The Israeli-Palestinian negotiation over the question of the right of return has moved between complete Israeli rejection to a grudging acceptance to admit 100,000 Palestinian refugees back into the country, within the context of family reunification, but without Israeli acceptance of responsibility for their original expulsion. Analogously, many Palestinians refuse to recognize any Arab role in creating and sustaining the refugee suffering or the exceptional circumstances that kept the issue politically alive longer than any refugee question post–World War II. In the 1950s, Israel preferred to deal with the refugees as a collective group right and was willing to pay a global sum as compensation for the property left behind by the refugees. The Palestinians rejected a global solution and demanded restitution and reparation as individual rights, available for each family separately. In the 1990s, the position was reversed, when Israel accepted individual reparation and family reunification, while the Palestinian demands became communal and national.

The dispute between Israel and the Palestinians over the right of return can benefit from historical and comparative analysis both of the legal and moral case. This analysis has only been sketched here and ought to confront the antagonists' perspectives. Much of what the literature offers is an argument in favor of one of the two positions. In contrast, I would argue that the frame of a joint narrative of the refugee displacement would lead to Israel's recognition of its role in creating the problem and its obligations to be a lead partner in its solution. Such a narrative would also help shift the debate on the right of return from declarations and condemnations to moral obligations and political pragmatism—perhaps something along the line of a shift from the right of return to the necessity for recognition and solution. While space precludes a full development of these points, the lack of such analysis is fertile ground for political extremism. In contrast, such historical analysis and political realism can advance the resolution of the overall conflict greatly. This opinion is apparently held by several central peacemakers in both Palestine and Israel. It is regrettable that those opinions are in the minority within each community.

Notes

1. James Bennet, "Israeli Cabinet Endorses American-Backed Peace Plan," *New York Times,* May 25, 2003; Khaled Abu Toameh, "Abbas Rejects Israel's Demand to Give Up Right of Return Now," *Jerusalem Post,* May 5, 2003.

2. Elazar Barkan, "Repatriating Refugees and Crossing the Ethnic Divide: A Comparative Perspective," paper delivered in Deadly Neighbors conference, Haifa University, November 2003.

3. *Camp David II, UN Resolution 194, and a Durable Solution for Palestinian Refugees* (Ramallah: Badil Resource Center, July 21, 2000).

4. Haidar Abdel Shafi, in a press conference in Washington in 2000, said that "the refugee issue is the heart and the core of the problem" (http://rightofreturn .org/frames.html).

5. Ghayth Armanazi, "The Rights of the Palestinians: The International Definition," *Journal of Palestine Studies (JPS)* 3:3 (1974): 88–96, describes the recent proliferation of references to Palestinian rights and the lack of definitions. Armanazi counted twenty UN resolutions in support of the right of return. Since then, the number has increased to ver a hundred.

6. Karma Nabulsi, "Right of Return," *The Guardian,* September 17, 2002.

7. James Rogers, "Why the Attacks Continue," BBC, May 19, 2003.

8. "Right of Return: Sari Nusseibeh Controversy," http://www.shaml.org/ ground/Nusseibeh. Recently, the Copenhagen Group (which consists of Israelis and Palestinians) issued a statement of compromise. Akiva Eldar, "People and Politics: Sharon's Bantustans Are Far from Copenhagen's Hope," *Haaretz,* May 13, 2003.

9. See Ian S. Lustick, "Negotiating Truth: The Holocaust, *Lehavdil,* and al-Nakba" (this volume) for treatment of the right of return by the Israeli and Palestinian representatives who signed the informal Geneva Accords.

10. Eliyahu Tal, "The Loopholes in 194," *Jerusalem Post,* November 29, 2002, quoting Ruth Lapidoth of the Hebrew University.

11. Efraim Karsh, *Fabricating Israeli History: "The New Historians,"* 2d rev. ed. (London: Frank Cass, 2000). Karsh is one of the staunchest supporters of the traditional Israeli position. Quoted by Tal, ibid.

12. Jeremy Waldron, "Redressing Historic Injustice," *University of Toronto Law Journal* (winter 2002), Lexis. Also "Superseding Historic Injustice," *Ethics* 103 (1992).

13. In "Redressing Historic Injustice," Waldron begins with Kant and the simple recognition that justice comes from a social contract. We need to "construct a common sense of justice" and set up a single system "despite (indeed, precisely because of) our disagreements over what an appropriate system" would be. Like Hobbes, Kant begins from the assumption that our agreements have to be made with those with whom we disagree. Justice has to adjudicate among those who agree to go beyond force and violence and exist alongside others whom they don't trust. This still "leaves open the question of what justice requires in relation to the historic injustice." Despite all the limitations of converting historical rights into contemporary parameters, Waldron assumes that we aspire to go beyond David Hume's view that over time, although possessions and right of property are largely arbitrary, any stable pattern of de facto possession is superior to continuous struggle. Hume focuses on the "peace dividend," whereby everyone would benefit, and thus leaves aside historical injustices. In Waldron's view, Hume's perspective leans too much to the position of "let bygones be bygones," which in effect will encourage a cynical future of violence and dispossession. This leaves the principle of when hegemony

should be accepted, or honored, unresolved, yet alerts us to the predicament of choosing between two conflicting ills.

If realpolitik often advocates precisely this Humean position, and has been the convention among international relations theorists for years, there has also been a countertrend in the last fifty years. Primarily since the Second World War, with few precedents, we see a slowly developing norm that pays attention to historical violations and the consequences that those events have in our present day.

Waldron extrapolates from the theory to a real-world situation by exploring the Maori in New Zealand. He concludes that the "best hope of reparation is to make some sort of adjustment in the present circumstances of those descended from the persons who suffered injustice." Time, as Waldron reminds us, is of the essence (à la Hume?). The passage of time shapes the type of feasible and just adjustments. The single most significant change that ought to change the perception of injustice for Waldron is population change. In New Zealand, that means that since the 1860s, the "population has increased many-fold, and most of the descendants of the colonists, unlike their ancestors, have nowhere else to go." Quite apart from anything else, the historical changes mean that the costs of respecting earlier entitlements are much greater now than they were at the time that the injustice took place.

Waldron formulates a narrow test for the return, primarily one that is tied to the personal identity and organizational structure of the victims, not to the wider group identity. Thus in the Maori case that he examines, the traditional tribal identity has to be the beneficiary and specific descendants, not the Maoris in general, including those who do not identify with the traditional society. For Waldron, entitlements are sensitive to circumstances, which could be adjudicated only by contemporaries who are willing to supersede historic injustice, that is, "claims about justice and injustice must be responsive to changes in circumstances."

Waldron concludes that "claims about historic injustice predicated on the status quo ante may be superseded by our determination to distribute the resources of the world in a way that is fair to all of its existing inhabitants in their existing circumstances." This stipulation moves us from the ethical to the political, from abstract principles to political demands.

14. The formal numbers, according to the UNHCR, in 2002: Asia, 8,820,700; Europe, 4,855,400; Africa, 4,173,500; North America, 1,086,800; Latin America, 765,400; Oceania, 81,300. Total, 19,783,100. http://www.unhcr.ch/cgi-bin/texis/vtx/statistics. There were about eighteen million IDPs in the mid-1990s. Also, *Refugees and Others of Concern to UNHCR, 2000 Statistical Overview,* United Nations High Commissioner for Refugees (UNHCR), Geneva, June 2002.

15. In 1921, Fridtjof Nansen was appointed the first refugee High Commissioner of the League of Nations. Little took place in the face of the Nazis, and only during and after the war, new institutional arrangements came into place. The IRO (1946–52) in part replaced the United Nations Relief and Rehabilitation Administration and the Intergovernmental Committee on Refugees. Its functions were taken over by the office of the United Nations High Commissioner for Refugees (1951).

16. United Nations Office for the Coordination of Humanitarian Affairs, Ocha-Online Guiding Principles on Internal Displacement.

17. Africa hardly ever receives international attention, and thus ethnic cleansing is rarely noticed. Millions of deaths were directly or indirectly the result of civil wars, from Congo to Sierra Leone and from Ivory Coast to Liberia and Sudan. Even in relatively post-conflict situations, ethnic cleansing is mostly ignored. One example is of the Ethiopian expulsion of Eritreans (C. Calhoun, "Ethiopia's Ethnic Cleansing," *Dissent* [winter 1999]: 47–51). Somini Sengupta, "Ivory Coast Haven Turns Hostile for Liberians," *New York Times,* January 21, 2003. Millions of IDPs and refu-

gees are never even reported. An analysis of the multiplicity of ethnocide in Europe might be instructive in understanding the African situation. Alfred J. Reiber, "Repressive Population Transfers in Central, Eastern and South-Eastern Europe: A Historical Overview," *Journal of Communist Studies and Transition Politics* 16:1–2 (2000): 1–27, emphasis on the multinational unstable nature of the empires in the region.

18. Cf. Elia Zureik, "Palestinian Refugees and Peace," *JPS* 24:1 (1994): 5–17.

19. Robert K. Schaeffer, *Warpaths: The Politics of Partition* (New York: Hill and Wang, 1990); idem, *Severed States: Dilemmas of Democracy in a Divided World* (Lanham, Md.: Rowman and Littlefield, 1999); Andrew Bell-Fialkoff, *Ethnic Cleansing* (New York: St. Martin's, 1996).

20. On Europe, Joseph Rothschild, *East Central Europe Between the Two World Wars* (Seattle: University of Washington Press, 1990); Eugene M. Kulischer, *Europe on the Move: War and Population Changes 1917–1947* (New York: Columbia University Press, 1948); Norman M. Naimark, *Fires of Hatred: Ethnic Cleansing in Twentieth-Century Europe* (Cambridge, Mass.: Harvard University Press, 2000); Timothy Snyder, " 'To Resolve the Ukrainian Problem Once and for All': The Ethnic Cleansing of Ukrainians in Poland, 1943–1947," *Journal of Cold War Studies* 1:2 (1999): 86–120. Ethnic cleansing continued during the cold war: Tomasz D.I. Kamusella, "Ethnic Cleansing in Silesia 1950–89 and the Nationalizing Policies of Poland and Germany," *Patterns of Prejudice* 33:2 (1999): 51–73. Jews, too, were expelled from Poland in waves. On India, Kavita Daiya, "Migration, Gender, Refugees, and South Asia: On International Migration and Its Implications for the Study of Cultural Geographies," University of Chicago, http://regionalworlds.uchicago.edu/bibliographicessayson migrat.pedf. Jennifer Jackson Preece, "Ethnic Cleansing as an Instrument of Nation-State Creation: Changing State Practices and Evolving Legal Norms," *Human Rights Quarterly* 20:4 (1998): 817–42.

21. The ethnic cleansing of Germans from Eastern Europe after 1945 received extensive and, recently, growing attention. Less so was the fate of Jews who returned to Poland right after the war but were forced out, mostly immediately and the rest later in several small waves. Ethnic Germans who remained in Poland were also discriminated against, and they left before the end of the cold war.

22. The numbers are hard to verify. It has been established that tens of thousands in Pakistan defrauded the UN by crossing the border numerous times, receiving several assistance packages. Christina Lamb, *Sunday Telegraph*, November 10, 2002.

23. Chris Kraul, "Flood of Afghan Returnees Continues," *Los Angeles Times*, December 30, 2002. The large number of refugees of various ethnicities has left many victims whose identity is not recognized. See, for example, the largely unknown case of the Bihari: Sumit Sen, "Stateless Refugees and the Right to Return: The Bihari Refugees of South Asia," part 1, *International Journal of Refugee Law* 11:4 (1999): 625–45; and part 2, 12:1 (2000): 41–70. Another group that struggles to receive international attention in its struggle to return to a country from which it was exiled by the ruling majority are "tens of thousands of ethnic Nepalese settlers who the Bhutanese government forced out" in 1990. Since then, the Nepali-speaking population in Bhutan (about a third of the children) has been further marginalized. " 'Ethnic Cleansing' the Bhutan Way," *Bangkok Post*, April 9, 2000; "Whither Nepal?" *The Statesman* (India), September 11, 2001.

24. Luke T. Lee, "The Right to Compensation: Refugees and Countries of Asylum," *The American Journal International Law*, 80 (July 1986): 532–67.

25. "Three-Year Repatriation Goal Urged for Burmese Refugees," *Bangkok Post*, December 13, 2001; "Xanana Seeks Speedy Repatriation of East Timorese Refu-

gees," *Jakarta Post*, November 27, 2001; "India: No Repatriation of Sri Lankan Refugees since March '95," *The Hindu*, June 24, 2000.

26. J. Birch, "Ethnic Cleansing in the Caucasus," *Nationalism & Ethnic Politics* 1:4 (1996): 90–107; Brian Glyn Williams, "The Hidden Ethnic Cleansing of Muslims in the Soviet Union: The Exile and Repatriation of the Crimean Tatars," *Journal of Contemporary History* 37:3 (2002): 323–47. The relatively small number of repatriated Tatars were harassed by Russians and Ukrainians. Terry Martin, "The Origins of Soviet Ethnic Cleansing," *Journal of Modern History* 70:4 (1998): 813–61. Damien McElroy, "Uighurs Warn of Return to Terror," *The Scotsman*, May 31, 2000. North Korean refugees are another unacknowledged group in China who face the danger of forced repatriation.

27. Warren Christopher, statement at the opening of the Balkan proximity peace talks (November 1, 1995), in Warren Christopher, *In the Stream of History: Shaping Foreign Policy for a New Era* (Stanford, Calif.: Stanford University Press, 1998), 362.

28. Marcus Cox, "The Right to Return Home: International Intervention and Ethnic Cleansing in Bosnia and Herzegovina," *International & Comparative Law Quarterly* 47 (1998): 599, 611.

29. Eric Rosand, "The Right to Compensation in Bosnia: An Unfulfilled Promise and a Challenge to International Law," *Cornell International Law Journal* 33 (2000): 113–58.

30. Other ethnic cleansing in Yugoslavia included the "cleansing" of Magyars in Yugoslavia's Vojvodina region, which has been largely ignored and is a good example for the diminished ethnic plurality in the region since 1918 (Andrew Ludanyi, "The Fate of Magyars in Yugoslavia: Genocide, Ethnocide or Ethnic Cleansing?" *Canadian Review of Studies in Nationalism* 28:1–2 [2001]: 127–41). More than four years into the peace process, very few minorities returned to their homes in Bosnia, despite the attention of the international community. The objectives of the ethnic cleansing, despite the defeat of the Serbians, have largely succeeded. Catherine Phuong, "'Freely to Return': Reversing Ethnic Cleansing in Bosnia-Herzegovina," *Journal of Refugee Studies* 13:2 (2000): 165–83.

31. Elazar Barkan, *The Guilt of Nations: Restitution and Negotiating Historical Injustices* (New York: Norton, 2000).

Chapter 6
Negotiating Truth: The Holocaust, *Lehavdil,* and al-Nakba

Ian S. Lustick

In the debates and recriminations that followed the collapse of the Israeli-Palestinian negotiations at Camp David in the summer of 2000 and the inconclusive follow-up discussions at Taba, attention was directed primarily to issues concerning leadership, settlements, withdrawals, the disposition of Yerushalayim/al-Quds, and Palestinian demands for the return of refugees. Mostly ignored, however, was one particular demand made by the Palestinian side regarding the refugees. Although most commentators have focused on the demand for return itself and the complex set of options that might be used to parse, distribute, and effectively limit that right, it is worth exploring the implications of the separate demand that Israel formally acknowledge its moral responsibility for the creation of the Palestinian refugee problem in 1948.

Somewhat surprisingly, it appears that the Barak government was prepared to issue a statement announcing Israel's regret for the suffering entailed, and perhaps acknowledging a share of responsibility for the tragedy. On the other hand, Israel would not agree to accept "moral or legal responsibility for the creation of the refugee problem."[1] Israel, according to David Schenker, in an article published during the Camp David summit itself, rejected Palestinian demands for "formal Israeli apology and admission of responsibility for the refugee crisis" out of a belief that to do so "would leave the Jewish state exposed to future financial and emigration claims."[2]

What is interesting about this rationale is that the Palestinian claims were not rejected because they were deemed to be false. Nor were they rejected because it was considered that to accept them, acknowledge responsibility, and offer an apology would not have contributed toward peace and reconciliation. On the contrary, in official Israeli arguments that too many economic and legal liabilities would arise from offering such public and official statements, one hears an implicit acceptance of the justice and appropriateness, if not the practicality, of the Palestinian demand. In this light, it is unsurprising that in the follow-up negotiations at Taba in the fall of 2000, attention was focused directly on the practical means for addressing the refugee problem, including the kind of language that would be included in an Israeli declaration regarding the events of 1948.[3]

The main purpose of this chapter is to highlight the political significance of these discussions by considering the negotiations between Israel, the World Jewish Congress, and the Federal Republic of Germany in 1951, prior to the beginning of German reparations payments and prior to the onset of diplomatic relations between Israel and West Germany. After saying *lehavdil*,[4] we may yet see in the agony of Jews, wrestling with the challenge of settling for infinitely less than the justice and retribution for which they yearned, an instructive "limiting case" for analyzing the distress of the Palestinians, a people called upon to abandon their struggle for justice, who seek public acknowledgment by Israel of the evil inflicted on them as an element in a comprehensive peace package. We may also learn from the artful avoidances and measured doses of truth contained in Konrad Adenauer's speech before the Bundestag in September 1951. From that carefully orchestrated speech, we can learn something about how necessary, but in all likelihood how limited and symbolic, will be the Israeli proclamation enabling a practical solution to the Palestinian refugee problem and the end of the Arab-Israeli conflict. Such an analysis and such comparisons are similar to those used by Israel's first foreign minister, Moshe Sharett. In 1952, he suggested "transferring some of the money [from German reparations] to the Palestinian refugees, in order to rectify what has been called the small injustice (the Palestinian tragedy), caused by the more terrible one (the Holocaust)."[5]

Germans, Jews, and the Holocaust: Finding Just Enough Truth

As early as 1945, Weizmann and others had considered the possibility of obtaining substantial financial support for the building of the Jewish state and its economic consolidation by demanding compensation for the property of murdered European Jews. Just one month after the end of World War II, Weizmann sent the four powers occupying Germany a demand for title to what he estimated to be $8 billion worth of property whose owners had died in the Holocaust.[6] The Allies did respond to this overture, though only in the amount of $25 million, to be allocated to many Jewish relief organizations. Of more significance than the amount of the demand and Weizmann's failure was that it was not directed toward the Germans, but toward the Allied powers occupying Germany. Thus, there was no question of receiving property directly from the German state, nation, or collectivity and therefore no issue, at that point, of whether acceptance of economic support from Germany was morally acceptable.

In the late 1940s and early 1950s, the attitudes of many Israelis were hysterically anti-German. The dominant view in Israel was categorical rejection of any contact with Germany or Germans and a strong tendency to view the Germany of Chancellor Adenauer, who himself had been anti-Nazi, as no more acceptable a point of contact for Jews than the Nazi regime.[7] As Tom Segev reports, "[T]he foreign ministry stamped on every Israeli passport in English, a notification that the document was not valid in Germany. The Government Press Office announced that Israelis who settled in Germany permanently would not be allowed to return."[8] As future prime minister, then head of the opposition, Menachem Begin asserted during the 1951/52 Knesset debate on reparations (more than six years after the end of the Third Reich): "From a Jewish point of view, there is not a single German who is not a Nazi, nor is there a single German who is not a murderer."[9] Even future prime minister Golda Meyerson (Meir), who opposed Begin by supporting reparations negotiations with Germany, told the Knesset at that time, "As far as I am concerned, there is one rule regarding the German people. Every German, whether in the East or the West, is guilty in my eyes."[10]

But despite overwhelming Jewish disgust with and hatred toward Germany and Germans, an agreement, based on direct negotiations, was reached between the Israeli and German governments over how a small measure of justice for survivors of the Holocaust and for the Jewish people as a whole might be achieved through reparations payments that would, inter alia, be explicitly devoted to the absorption of new Jewish immigrants in Israel.

A crucial element in moving Israeli leaders toward direct negotiations with Germany was the severity of Israel's economic circumstances. Felix Shinnar was co-head of the Israeli delegation to the 1952 Wassenaar conference, where Israel and Germany hammered out the details of what became the Luxembourg agreement on reparations. According to Shinnar, the main stimulus for Israel's willingness to become involved in such negotiations was "definitely economic."[11] David Horowitz, another lead negotiator who at the time served as director general of the Israeli Ministry of Finance, later portrayed Israel in the early 1950s as in "desperate economic straits. We looked into the face of possible collapse. Foreign exchange reserves were practically exhausted. Every ship was important, for the reserve of bread in the country [1950–51] was sufficient for one week only."[12] Indeed, by some basic measures it would appear that although Germany was devastated by the effects of the war, in the early 1950s economic conditions were worse in Israel than in Germany. In 1950/51, the average German diet included 340 percent more meat and poultry than the average diet of Israelis, 187 percent more milk, 176 percent more fat, and 162 percent more sugar.[13]

Closed discussions within the Israeli foreign ministry in late 1949 and 1950 focused on the importance of using Germany's need for Israeli goodwill, while that need still existed, to gain access to substantial economic resources. The primary task was to find a diplomatic and public relations formula that would alleviate the moral distress of establishing relations with Germany and accepting German money. No Israeli leader argued that accepting reparations would close the moral account of the Jewish people with Germany.[14] What was argued was the practical importance of getting sizable German payments while they were available. Segev describes the attitude of Moshe Shapira, Minister of the Interior, Health, and Immigration, as representative: "[E]verything depended on how much money was at stake [for] it would be pointless to soil oneself with the taint of German contact for a pittance, but if the sum was substantial, it might well be worthwhile."[15]

Other arguments, including revenge and the achievement of a vicarious sort of victory over Germany, were also important. Defending the government's efforts to gain German reparations through direct contacts with Bonn, David Ben-Gurion, Golda Meir, and Pinchas Lavon emphasized the aspect of revenge and equity involved in forcing Germans to work for the rehabilitation of Jews and described the increased vitality of Israel that would result from the reparations as enhancing the "victory" of the Jewish people [who survived] over Hitler [who did not].[16] An element of particular importance in this debate was the emphasis of leading advocates of reparations on Israel's approaching the German government for reparations with "the consciousness that the German people in its entirety is responsible for the killing and plunder inflicted by the former regime on the House of Israel."[17] It was not that Israel could deal with Germany because a change of regime had replaced the Nazi enemy with a fundamentally different political or moral entity, but precisely because, despite the disappearance of the Nazi regime, there was moral continuity. In his major speech to the Knesset during the debate on reparations, Ben-Gurion declared that "the German people, all of whom are responsible for the destruction wrought by their government under Hitler, continue to benefit . . . Let not the murderers of our people be their inheritors as well!"[18]

However, to seal this connection between reparations and German collective responsibility, Israeli and non-Israeli Jewish leaders were not satisfied with their own public statements. They required some kind of public declaration of contrition that would express the German nation's acknowledgment of responsibility and sorrow for the suffering of the Jews at German hands as well as its condemnation of Nazi policies, but that would not require any explicit words of "forgiveness" on the Jewish side.[19]

In March 1951, Ben-Gurion's government delivered a note to the four occupying powers, demanding $1.5 billion as a German indemnity, making clear "that no amount of material compensation would ever expiate the Nazi crimes against the Jews."[20] All that resulted was a suggestion that Israel approach Germany directly. In fact, some exploratory contacts between Israeli and German representatives had already occurred. In this prenegotiation period, Israeli emissaries emphasized the critical importance—indeed, the necessity—for a solemn and official German statement of collective responsibility for the Holocaust if practical negotiations toward an actual reparations agreement were to begin.

The first Jewish representative to engage in these discussions was Noah Barou, chairman of the European Executive of the World Jewish Congress. When he met Adenauer's close confidant Herbert Blankenhorn early in 1950, Barou said that he placed two preconditions on the initiation of such negotiations. As his interviewer reports, "Barou emphasized two preconditions on Jewish contact with the Bonn regime: *A solemn public declaration by the Chancellor acknowledging Germany's national responsibility* for the horrible deeds committed against the Jews of Europe during the Second World War; and an expressed willingness to compensate Jewry for material losses."[21]

In March 1951, the two men met once again in London. Barou made Israel's position even clearer: "Before the start of any official negotiations between Federal Germany and the Jewish people, the *chancellor must declare in the Bundestag that the Federal Republic accepted responsibility* for what had been done to the Jewish people by the Nazis."[22] Similarly, when Horowitz met Adenauer in Paris in May 1951, he told the German chancellor that at Sharett's behest he was delivering a demand that Germany issue "'a guilt declaration'" before financial negotiations could begin.[23]

Although Adenauer claimed to have already condemned Nazi crimes on many occasions, he accepted the Israeli demand for a solemn expression of Germany's moral perspective on the Holocaust.[24] Negotiations then proceeded between the Adenauer government, on the one hand, and the government of Israel and the World Jewish Congress, on the other, over the wording of the declaration to be made by Adenauer on behalf of the German people—negotiations that lasted from July through September 1951. On September 27, 1951, Adenauer made the solemn speech before the Bundestag demanded by the Israelis and their non-Israeli Jewish associates.

Before that speech, however, in the summer of 1951, Israeli negotiators had pushed Adenauer to put in his speech references to the guilt of the German people, the existence of groups in Germany still actively anti-Semitic, the role of the German army in the Holocaust, and the innocence of the people killed by the Nazis. They also wanted an explicit reference to Israel. Adenauer did accept many adjustments in his original draft but refused to describe the German nation as "guilty of the extermination of the Jews." He refused to mention Israel by name, to include an explicit reference to the "innocence" of the victims, to acknowledge the role of the German army, or to agree that the entire German nation be said to be guilty of the crimes committed by the Nazis.[25]

Most of Adenauer's speech dealt with legal and educational principles honored in the Federal Republic, which had the purpose of combating anti-Semitism. In the end, the speech contained one and only one relevant paragraph—a set of formulations drafted, redrafted, and negotiated in exquisite and painful detail.[26] Although kept secret at the time, it is of fundamental importance that its wording had been negotiated, edited, and approved by the government of Israel and the World Jewish Congress before it was read out by Adenauer on the floor of the German parliament. The key paragraph of this oft-cited text pertained explicitly to the question of Germany's relationship to its Nazi past and to the Jewish people:

> The government of the Federal Republic and with it the great majority of the German people are aware of the immeasurable suffering that was brought upon the Jews in Germany and the occupied territories during the time of National Socialism. The overwhelming majority of the German people abominated the crimes committed against the Jews and did not participate in them. During the National Socialist time, there were many among the German people who showed their readiness to help their Jewish fellow citizens at their own peril—for religious reasons, from distress of conscience, out of shame at the disgrace of the German name. But unspeakable crimes have been committed in the name of the German people, calling for moral and material indemnity, both with regard to the individual harm done to the Jews and with regard to the Jewish property for which no legitimate individual claimants still exist.[27]

Although there was considerable opposition to the speech from right-of-center parties, Adenauer's delivery was followed by three minutes of silence with all members of the Bundestag standing.

In relation to what we now know and was widely believed then about the Holocaust and the involvement, support, or acquiescence of the majority of Germans in the war against the Jews, this statement would seem to offer very little in the way of acknowledged truth. As noted by Jeffrey Herf in his careful analysis, the paragraph sticks firmly to the passive voice. It begins by exculpating the majority of Germans. Indeed, two of its four sentences describe the opposition of the "overwhelming majority" of Germans to the Nazis' extermination policies and the efforts of "many" to protect Jews. Nor does the statement provide an enumeration of German crimes or include any specific indication of who the perpetrators were.[28] Contrary to the repeated demands of the Israeli negotiators, the statement did not include words that pointed clearly toward an admission of guilt or responsibility. Nor did it include the expression of sentiments of contrition or repentance. Nor did it contain an apology. The most that can be said about the paragraph is that some of these sentiments may be inferred from the description of "unspeakable crimes committed in the name of the German people, calling for moral and material indemnity."

But the sentence containing this formulation is worthy of particularly close consideration, especially the artful phrase: "in the name of the German people." It was a deft maneuver. Israel had demanded a declaration of guilt and acceptance of responsibility for the crimes committed by the German people under the previous regime. Instead, the German chancellor was admitting that some (unnamed) persons had committed crimes that had publicly been attached to the *name* of the German people, but not endorsed or committed by them. Implicitly, what the phrase further suggested was that it was only out of the German people's enormous sense of honor that they felt duty bound to pay "indemnity" for actions done, not by them, but in their name—as if a tire manufacturer, for example, might agree to compensate those who purchased faulty tires with the company's brand name on the tires, even if the tires were not admitted to have been produced by the company. As Herf puts it, "The phrase 'in the name of the German people' had the effect, and perhaps the intent as well, of distancing these acts from the Germans of the Nazi era."[29]

In retrospect, the only thing as remarkable as the pallor of Adenauer's carefully vetted and widely heralded public statement on the Holocaust was how little critical attention it received. For most Israelis who opposed negotiations with Germany, such a declaration was irrelevant no matter what its content—Germany and Germans would remain beyond the pale of acceptability and no reparations agreement could be tolerated. For most others, the fact of the declaration, rather than its relative lack of content, was treated (usually implicitly) as a sine qua non for accepting the distasteful process of entering into a reparations agreement with Germany. Alternatively, it was taken as the beginning of the process that would enable the Federal Republic to be accepted by the world community, whether Israel accepted the reparations idea or not.

In fact, one of the only detailed attacks on the actual text of the Adenauer declaration was made on the floor of the Knesset by Menachem Begin. It was based on a report that the Israeli government had, despite its feigned ignorance, known about and granted prior approval to the Adenauer statement. Begin's accusation is worth quoting at length:

A member of the Knesset has accused both Mr. Sharett, and yourself, Mr. Ben-Gurion, of having this statement in your possession before Mr. Adenauer revealed it to his Nazi advisors. If this is true, woe unto us! You read it; you accepted, as the basis of the negotiations with the Germans, the suggestion that the majority of the German people were revolted by these crimes and took no part in them. You accepted, as a basis of the negotiations, a statement according to which this money would be given to you for the spiritual cleansing of unending suffering. If you didn't read it, how could Mr. Sharett consider it as a basis for negotiation? And if you did read and approve it—then let the Jewish people know upon what sort of base the bridge between Hebrew Jerusalem and the Nazi Bonn government was erected. Adenauer's note has been read by millions of Germans, millions of Americans, millions of Frenchmen; it has penetrated the hearts of non-Jews. All the nations of the world knew that that was the basis upon which we were to receive the money, as a "payment for unending suffering." How they will bemoan us, how they will despise us! What have you made of us? . . . The nations will see only one thing: you sat down at the table with the murderers of your people, you acknowledged that they are capable of signing an agreement, that they are capable of keeping an agreement, that they are a nation, a nation among the family of nations.[30]

The Israeli government's immediate response to Adenauer's Bundestag statement (issued the day before it was actually delivered) began as follows: "First, the Government adheres steadfastly to the view that the entire German people bears responsibility for the mass murder of European Jewry."[31] Without mentioning that this view, and several softer formulations of it, had been rejected by Adenauer for inclusion in his declaration and indeed without mentioning that the government of Israel had ever been involved in negotiating, editing, or approving the German chancellor's words, the official statement continued with an acknowledgment "that the declaration was an attempt on the part of the Federal Government to solve the problem."[32] Thus it was accepted as satisfying Israel's demand for a public and solemn declaration of moral responsibility. Emphasizing that no German statement, "however sincere and repentant," could erase the crimes that had been committed, the Israeli government spokesman nevertheless commented that "it seems the German Federal Government unreservedly acknowledges that it has an obligation to make moral and material reparations." The spokesman went on to criticize East Germany for failing to do so.[33] Several days later, Foreign Minister Sharett emphasized the same idea, stating that nothing Germany could do could fully atone for the sufferings of the victims of the Holocaust. Yet, he added, "The Government of Israel regards it, nevertheless, as significant that the Government and Parliament of Western Germany . . . have issued an appeal to the German people to divest themselves of the accursed heritage of anti-Semitism and racial discrimination and declared their readiness to enter into negotiations with representatives of the Jewish people and the State of Israel."[34] On December 30, 1951, the Israeli cabinet decided to present the Knesset with its proposal to conduct direct negotiations for reparations with the German government.

The government's response to the Adenauer speech—formally repeating its views about full collective responsibility and guilt on the part of the German people, while accepting as operative a declaration that fell far short of that—enabled the process of negotiations to begin. The entire episode was a carefully choreographed performance of minimal substance and maximum form. As part of this performance, journalists, Jews supportive of negotiations with Germany over reparations, American officials, and indeed much subsequent scholarship hailed Adenauer's speech in terms considerably more dramatic than were warranted by the text itself.

For example, in October 1952, Noah Barou published a short article entitled "Origin of the German Agreement." To my knowledge, this has been the only substantial firsthand account published about the negotiations over the Adenauer declaration. Strikingly, Barou's point was not to criticize the statement for what it lacked, but to emphasize how unsatisfactory it had been when originally formulated by Adenauer! In sharp contrast to what clearly appears to have been the case, Barou described the diligence and effectiveness of Jewish negotiators and how cooperative and responsive had been their German counterparts.

The first draft of the German declaration dealing with German-Jewish relations was prepared by the Germans in July 1951 and had been studied by responsible Jewish leaders. This declaration dealt with all the problems raised by the World Jewish Congress in 1949. But it was couched in general terms; and since it was to serve as [the] basis for negotiations dealing with problems of restitution and reparation, with compensation and indemnification, it needed much adjustment and clarification. It took nearly two and a half months to achieve this, and it must be noted that in these difficult and delicate negotiations the German side showed considerable understanding and made great efforts to meet the justified Jewish demands.[35]

Nahum Goldmann, president of the World Jewish Congress and cochairman of the Jewish Agency for Palestine, who had played an important personal role in the negotiations over Adenauer's statement, commented on it by hailing Adenauer for "open[ing] the way to the only restitution, considering the nature of the crime, which it is still in human power to make. As such, the statement must be noted with satisfaction."[36] Looking back, Ben-Gurion later characterized "Adenauer's Germany" as having "recognized the moral responsibility of the entire German people for the crimes of the Nazis."[37] The American Jewish Committee commented that Adenauer's statement was "a significant first step toward Germany's assumption of its moral and legal responsibilities."[38] Leo Baeck, the famous German Jewish philosopher, praised Adenauer immediately following the speech as having "created the basis for frank and sincere discussions between Jews and Germans."[39]

The tendency to ignore the concessions made by Jewish negotiators and the unsatisfying substance of Adenauer's statement is just as apparent in much of the journalistic and scholarly analysis produced by Jewish and other supporters of the German-Israeli reparations agreement. Indeed, most press reaction in Britain and the United States was "extremely favorable."[40] The *New York Times* welcomed the speech as proof of "moral regeneration" and "the assumption of moral responsibility on the part of the Germans [reflecting a] realization that the Germans as a group incurred a dreadful burden of guilt."[41] The *Washington Post* described the speech as "the best thing that [has come] from Germany since before 1933."[42]

Subsequent scholarly work published by authors with close ties to leading Israeli, Zionist, and American Jewish institutions adhered to the same general line. In her study of the German-Israeli negotiations, Nana Sagi acknowledges the role that the Israeli government played in drafting the famous paragraph, but then characterizes its response to Adenauer's speech as "cautious but not hostile," as if the government's pose of having received a spontaneous expression of a German desire for atonement was genuine. Sagi calls the speech a "historic declaration . . . intended to help lay the foundation for a new Jewish attitude." Despite Adenauer's avoidance of the terms "guilt" and "responsibility," Sagi describes his speech as having met "the first . . . condition[s] presented to him by the State of Israel and the Jewish organizations: acceptance by the Federal Republic of responsibility for the crimes of the Third Reich."[43] Kurt Grossman, in a study sponsored by American Jewish organizations, noted the Israeli government's lukewarm response, while ignoring its role in editing and vetting the statement. Grossman's characterization of the speech in very positive terms was clearly meant to justify what he also characterized as the readiness of the majority of Israeli and non-Israeli Jews to strike a reparations deal with Germany, despite opposition from "extremist opinion."[44] In his volume on German reparations and the Jews, Ronald Zweig also avoided raising questions about the specific wording of Adenauer's statement, even while quoting it. Zweig described the German government as having "agreed to a public statement of responsibility to which the Jewish organizations and Israel could respond positively" and praised (not inaccurately) Adenauer's tact for helping "overcome the opposition of those in the Jewish world who rejected the very concept of dealing with the Germans."[45]

These works all reflected a general desire, if not to whitewash the German declaration, certainly to avoid critical analysis. The idea was to redirect attention to the reparations negotiations themselves. They thereby treated the Israeli-German or Jewish-German relationship as somehow having been qualitatively changed by the mostly unexamined paragraph. Nor did American politicians and officials anxious to find rationales for integrating the Federal Republic fully into the Western alliance have an interest in subjecting Adenauer's statement to critical evaluation. Indeed, American officials had a very specific interest in encouraging Israelis and Jews to deal directly with Germany, and then to move forward based on whatever statement they could get from Adenauer toward a reparations deal. John J. McCloy, the American High Commissioner for Germany, telegraphed Adenauer that he was "greatly moved" by the speech, and it is probably not a coincidence that the final phase of negotiations over the end of the American occupation of Germany began just days after Adenauer's speech.[46]

The United States, Israel, and the Rehabilitation of West Germany

McCloy was in overall command of the process of transforming West Germany from a defeated Nazi power to a full-fledged member of NATO, the Western European economic community, and the civilized world. He had been an architect of the Nuremberg trials. After they ended in October 1946, U.S. tribunals indicted 185 high-ranking Nazis, convicting approximately a hundred. Sentences gradually became lighter, and by 1949, when Military Governor General Lucius Clay was replaced by McCloy as High Commissioner, the atmosphere in both the United States and in Germany had become much less supportive of rigorous treatment of Nazi war criminals. When he assumed his post, McCloy found that he had inherited fifteen cases of Nazis sentenced to death but whose punishments had not been carried out. Following Adenauer's assumption of office as the first chancellor of the Federal Republic, McCloy and the American administration as a whole came under intense pressure from inside Germany to extend clemency to imprisoned Nazis, prevent further executions, and bring an end to tribunals altogether.

McCloy responded to these pressures in 1950 by setting up an appeals process based on individual interviews and a set of rules for clemency, including five days off per month for good behavior calculated retroactively, no matter what the gravity of the offender's crimes. These measures, including a generous posture by the interviewers and the redefinition of many offenses as "white collar" crimes, set the stage for the board of appeals to recommend that the sentences of seventy-seven of ninety-three defendants be reduced and almost half the outstanding death sentences be commuted. McCloy pondered the fate of these prisoners from August 1950 to January 1951, during which time the German demands for clemency intensified, including death threats against the High Commissioner and his family. On January 31, 1951, McCloy announced his decision. "He extended commutations, paroles, and reductions of sentences to 79 of the 89 war criminals still imprisoned . . . who came under his jurisdiction. He affirmed only five death sentences."[47] Germans responded not with relief and gratitude but with a five-month campaign to spare the lives of those still condemned to death, a campaign that continued until June, when the executions took place.

In his masterful study of McCloy and the new Germany, Thomas Alan Schwartz concludes that McCloy's decisions made a crucial contribution "to the German Schlusstrich mentality about the war" (drawing a line between past and present) and, indeed, "to the refusal of Germans to face the past."[48] According to Schwartz, it also "undoubtedly led [McCloy] to press the Germans even harder for a generous policy of *Wiedergutmachung*, or restitution, toward the Jews and the state of Israel."[49] But McCloy and the U.S. government also came under fire for exhibiting excessive leniency toward former Nazi officials and leading German industrialists. This was the context, during this very period in which Israel was requesting that the Allies approach Germany directly for restitution to Jewish victims of the Holocaust, that the decision was made to force Israel and the Jews to deal directly with Adenauer's Germany. The reason was clear. If Jews were ready to negotiate with the new Germany in the wake of McCloy's acts of clemency and the virtual ending of the denazification policy, what justification could others have for criticizing the United States for being soft on German war criminals? It is thus reasonable to say that the Israeli decision to enter direct talks with Germany played a crucial role in the rehabilitation of a not wholly denazified Germany. Indeed, this was the view of Hendrik van Dam, general secretary of the Central Council of Jews in Germany, who advocated negotiations with Germany quickly, while it was still a high American priority. "The U.S. has . . . an interest in seeing that restitution is implemented . . . [as] a certain alibi for American policy to abandon Denazification and to continue with collaboration. . . . Restitution, especially reparations for Israel, could conceivably constitute such a counterweight."[50]

Emotional Truth and Political Realities for Germans and Jews, Israelis and Palestinians

The idea that Jews were accepting a bribe to help Nazis escape punishment and cleanse the German people of the sins it was deemed to have committed was the fundamental basis for the eruption in Israel of vitriolic opposition to the reparations negotiations. Yosef Sprinzak, speaker of the Knesset, denounced the negotiations as "morally absurd."[51] *Maariv* and *Yediot Ahronot* newspapers, along with the communist *Kol Haam* and Revisionist *Herut*, were fiercely opposed. In an editorial entitled "Amalek," published a week after Adenauer's speech, the editor of *Maariv* wrote that "a true peace movement will arise in the world and it will ensure peace in Europe by eradicating Germany from the face of the earth."[52] Mapam mobilized former partisans and ghetto fighters to oppose the negotiations. In a newspaper poll, 80 percent of twelve thousand respondents registered their opposition. Responding to fierce rhetoric by Herut leader Begin, who declared that "Adenauer is a murderer. . . . All his assistants are murderers," an enraged crowd launched a violent assault on the Knesset—battling with police, overturning cars, shattering store windows. Stones, broken glass, and tear gas forced an end to Knesset deliberations. Hundreds were wounded; hundreds more were arrested.

To counter fierce criticism that no amount of money could represent adequate indemnification for millions of murdered Jews, Foreign Minister Sharett made much of his choice of *shilumim* (payments) rather than *pitzu-*

iim (compensation for injury) to describe the reparations.[53] Government ministers denounced Begin's march on the Knesset as a mob attack on Israeli democracy, helping to transform the raging controversy over accepting "blood money" into a contest over the rule of law in the Jewish state.

Ben-Gurion, the founding father of the State of Israel and still the charismatic leader of the new state, was, in the view of many, the only Israeli leader capable of carrying the day against such opposition. He did so by representing Adenauer as emblematic of a new Germany, even if a great deal of evidence to the contrary had to be ignored. However, Ben-Gurion's most important contribution to the debate, uttered in his concluding speech to the raucous parliamentary debate on the reparations negotiations, was not part of his attempt to rehabilitate Germany in the eyes of the Jewish people. Quite the opposite; it was his use of a biblical verse that resonated with the angry and vengeful spirit that predominated in Israel: "Let not the murderers of our people be their inheritors as well."[54]

To achieve a positive vote in the Knesset, Mapai insisted on party discipline. At the same time, it freed most of its parliamentarians from having to vote explicitly for reparations by contriving a resolution that did not endorse the reparations negotiations but left it up to the Knesset Foreign Affairs and Security Committee to do so.[55] Following positive action by this Knesset committee, formal negotiations were undertaken. These resulted in an agreement—the Luxembourg treaty—signed on September 10, 1952, by representatives of Israel, the Federal Republic of Germany, and the World Jewish Congress. It has been meticulously implemented, resulting in payments of as much as $50 billion in cash and in-kind to Israel and to individual survivors and their families.

Fundamental differences make it difficult to compare efforts of Germans and Jews, on the one hand, and Israelis and Palestinians, on the other, to achieve reconciliation based in part on truth, apology, or political or economic compensation. Certainly, the greater scale of horror in the German-Jewish case might easily lead to the conclusion that Jewish/Israeli-German reconciliation would be much harder to achieve than Israeli-Palestinian.

However, other factors work in the opposite direction. Compensation paid to Israel and to individual victims of Nazism had a largely positive, invigorating effect on the German economy and greatly improved its political and diplomatic posture. While peace with the Palestinians would most certainly improve Israel's economic prospects and its international standing, satisfying Palestinian political demands and demands for the return of refugees will pose threats to Israeli/Jewish demographic, political, and security interests that the German agreement with Israel did not pose for Germany.

The Nazi regime was destroyed in a war of its own making. Its successor acknowledges that regime was German, but traces no political, moral, or ideological ancestry to it. Governments in Israel arise as products of a regime that proudly represents itself as responsible for the Israeli victory in 1948 and therefore for the Palestinians' al-Nakba. Most Germans drew back from denying or defending the Nazi war against the Jews, and debates over "revisionist" interpretations of the Holocaust are marginal affairs compared with the widespread conception (that eventually formed) among Germans and others of the Holocaust as an icon for the greatest crime that could be committed by one people against another. In Israel revisionist histories have greatly increased Israeli appreciation of the suffering of Palestinians in 1948 and the injustice of acts of expulsion and of enforced exile that produced and have maintained that suffering. Still, these findings have not achieved the emotionally reassuring status (for Palestinians) of official truth in Israel, although they are much more widely accepted outside of Israel.

In these and other ways, it is apparent how different is the counterpart Palestinians find in contemporary Israeli governments from the Germans with whom Israeli Jews negotiated in the early 1950s. Yet the degree of these differences may be substantially exaggerated in our minds because of the tendency to forget how differently Germans of the early 1950s, including Adenauer and the officials of his government, saw Germans, Jews, and the Holocaust, from the way that (we believe) most Germans came, much later, to view German-Jewish relations and the crimes of the Nazi period. It is important to remember that the Jews of the early 1950s who participated in these negotiations were dealing with Germans in the first decade after the war, when the experience of the Third Reich and the cataclysmic consequences of its collapse were fresh in their minds. It was with their beliefs, preferences, sensitivities, prejudices, and espoused values that those Jews had to contend, not with the "politically correct" attitudes of subsequent generations of Germans, German officials, and German diplomats.

It is a key contention of this chapter that only by understanding the state of mind of Germans in the period of the reparations agreement can one appreciate the powerful constraints under which the Adenauer government operated in its efforts to find any workable agreement with Jews and with Israel. Moreover, it is only by appreciating the pervasive and sometimes obsessive German sentiments of victimization, self-regard, and, yes, anti-Semitism, that one can appreciate the challenge faced by Jewish negotiators seeking to justify any contact at all with Bonn, let alone talks to arrange an agreement that would help rehabilitate Germany as an accepted member of the civilized world, the NATO alliance, and the new, emerging community of Western Europe. In this context, an Israeli delegation representing a mildly apologetic, but still Zionist, government in Israel may not pose quite as different a challenge to Palestinian negotiators as that posed by Adenauer's government in its negotiations with the government of Ben-Gurion and Sharett.

Thus, impressions that most Israelis would be resistant to expressing sympathy or solicitude to the suffering of Palestinians or to recognizing the extent of their own country's responsibility for that suffering may seem less decisive in judgments about agreements that may be possible between Israel and the Palestinians, if the state of mind of Germans at the time of the reparations agreement with Israel is appreciated. There was intense opposition inside Germany, especially on the Right, but even within Adenauer's Christian Democratic Party, to an agreement involving admission of guilt or generous restitution to Jews.[56] Indeed, German public opinion appears to have been opposed to paying much of anything to the Jews, and Adenauer's negotiations with Germans appear to have been as difficult as his negotiations with the Jews.[57] By 1949, the Allies had executed more than four hundred Nazi war criminals (including those executed by the Soviets), but, as noted above, German demands for the commutation of remaining capital punishments, parole of scores of high-ranking Nazis still imprisoned, and an end to the threat of prosecution against tens of thousands of former Nazi officials were building in intensity. German public opinion was obsessed by the disappearance of hundreds of thousands of German prisoners of war and the plight of millions of German refugees and expellees from Eastern Europe. In November 1950, trying hard to reflect dominant feelings in Germany that Germans were as much the victims of Nazism as were the Jews, Adenauer continued to press demands for clemency, an end to the tribunals, and an end to denazification on the American authorities as one of the highest, if not the highest, priority of his newly formed government.

It is true that according to American public opinion surveys, 68 percent of Germans in 1951 supported "restitution for the Jews" and only 21 percent were opposed. On the other hand, these figures were registered *after* McCloy, the High Commissioner for Germany, decided to commute or reduce the sentences of the great majority of convicted war criminals. These figures should also be compared with the 90 percent of West German respondents who favored assistance to "refugees and expellees."[58] It should also be noted that, according to U.S. government surveys, 44 percent of the West German public thought "that some races are more fit to rule than others."[59] Surveys in West Germany conducted in 1952 showed "a deep cynicism toward the Nuremberg judgments, as well as majority support for the proposition that 'we should cease trying people now for crimes they committed many years ago.'"[60] In the cabinet discussion over the final draft of the reparations treaty, one minister objected that benefits were being given only to Jews, asking "what should be done about the other 'non-Aryans.'"[61] The final vote in the German parliament on the reparations treaty was 236 in favor, 35 opposed, and 86 abstentions.

Israelis, Palestinians, and al-Nakba: Finding Just Enough Truth

There is much to be learned from this episode for gaining a perspective on what is achievable, useful, or likely in the Israeli-Palestinian case. It bears repeating, however, that such learning in no way can be interpreted as suggesting that the Holocaust and al-Nakba were intrinsically similar events. The Holocaust was the result of a systematic, premeditated plan for genocide. The creation of the Palestinian refugee problem was attendant upon the expulsion of Palestinians from their homes and refusal to allow them to return. It was a tragic and unjust and opportunistically accelerated unfolding of the logic of circumstances, not a genocidal campaign.

Thus, nothing can erase the overwhelming difference in the character and extent of the crimes committed in the two cases under review. It must be emphasized, however, that this is why the comparison may be so valuable. If we can learn from such comparison, it must be precisely because of, not in spite of, this enormous difference. In effect, the reparations agreement, or at least the formulation used by Adenauer and agreed to by Israel as the symbolic statement that would make that agreement possible, serves as a limiting case. Given that it is virtually impossible to imagine a more horrible crime committed by one nation against another than that which Nazi Germany committed against the Jews, we may therefore infer that: if at least a workable form of reconciliation has been possible between Israel and Germany, it cannot be said to be impossible with regard to Israel and Palestine; and if official and symbolic acts as restrained, self-serving, and historically pallid as the formula read out by Adenauer could be adequate to the political task, it may not be necessary for a future Israeli government to explicitly and fully acknowledge the detailed injustice meted out to the Palestinians in order for its "ceremonial act" to play a crucial political and psychological role.

In July 2000, prior to his departure for the Camp David summit, Israeli prime minister Ehud Barak stipulated to his cabinet the four "red lines" that he would not cross during negotiations with the Palestinians. One of the four was: "No Israeli recognition of legal or moral responsibility for creating the refugee problem."[62] This formulation is interesting in several respects. First, it implies that there is an outstanding demand for an Israeli declaration on the events of 1948 from the Palestinian side that stands apart from their material or political requirements. Second, it does not explicitly rule out some kind of response to this demand, short of formally accepting "legal or moral responsibility." Third, it opens the door for formulas about what occurred in 1948 that would include shared Israeli responsibility, Israeli sorrow and compassion for the plight of Palestinian refugees, acknowledgment of mistakes made and false propaganda employed that increased the number of refugees and aggravated their emotional and psychological difficulties, and readiness on the part of Israel to contribute materially and politically to a comprehensive solution to the refugee question in all its parts. Such exquisite parsing of Barak's statement, to accentuate the opening it gave to negotiations despite the sparse and negative form it took, can be justified by considering the speech that

Barak gave before the Knesset on October 4, 1999, expressing "regret for the suffering caused for the Palestinian people."[63] It is also instructive to consider how another of the four red lines, "a united Jerusalem under Israeli sovereignty," could just weeks later be interpreted as consistent with Israeli proposals that envisioned an end to Israeli sovereignty claims over most of al-Quds.

Of interest as well is that when the Barak government actually moved toward the limit of its negotiating position in the late fall and early winter of 2000, the prime minister shifted the location of his "red line" with regard to the refugee question. In an address to Jewish groups in Chicago prior to the Taba negotiations, he listed five elements that any agreement would have to include. Number four was "no right of return for Palestinian refugees into Israel proper." Significant by its omission was any mention of Israel's unwillingness to offer a statement about the suffering of Palestinians or the contribution of Israel toward that suffering.[64] Again, in a formal statement released by the Barak government on January 21, 2001, regarding its position at Taba, the prime minister declared that "Israel will never allow the right of Palestinian refugees to return inside the State of Israel" but again did not list refusal to make a statement of responsibility for the refugee problem as part of the Israeli government's position.[65]

On the Palestinian side, traditional demands for the complete return of all refugees were advanced in response to initial bargaining positions by Barak regarding Israeli sovereignty over the Temple Mount and mere "administrative autonomy" arrangements for Palestinians in Arab neighborhoods of expanded East Jerusalem. But at Taba, these strong demands were effectively, if not formally, withdrawn as Israeli positions loosened— reflecting Palestinian focus on the importance of formal Israeli acknowledgment of the truth of Palestinian suffering as a consequence of Israel's creation, on the crucial need for unlimited immigration into the Palestinian state, and on a symbolic opportunity for return of some 1948 refugees to territory inside pre-1967 Israel.[66]

In the joint statement released by the Palestinian and Israeli delegations at the conclusion of the Taba negotiations, the refugee issue was included as one of the four crucial questions that had been addressed and with respect to which gaps still remained. Nevertheless, these gaps were said to have narrowed sufficiently to warrant the belief that "in a short period of time and given an intensive effort and the acknowledgment of the essential and urgent nature of reaching an agreement, it will be possible to bridge the differences remaining and attain a permanent settlement of peace."[67]

Despite the reports of various participants, no official record of what was or was not agreed upon at Taba has been released. However, in the summer of 2001, *Le Monde* published what appears to be an accurate record of the final positions of the two sides.[68] In many respects, they correspond to the "Clinton parameters"—thirteen guidelines or target formulations for the achievement of a lasting compromise that President Bill Clinton believed could actually be accepted by both Israel and the Palestinians.

Interestingly, although Clinton emphasized the need to compensate and resettle refugees and guarantee full rights to immigrate into the Palestinian state, he did not refer explicitly to any statement of responsibility, regret, or blame that Israel might make. The president did argue that "the end of the conflict must manifest itself with concrete acts that demonstrate a new attitude and a new approach by Palestinians and Israelis toward each other." He also emphasized the need to "find a truth we can share."[69] In his account of the Clinton parameters, former Israeli justice minister Yossi Beilin described the president's approach as including Israeli acknowledgment of the "suffering of the Palestinian refugees" without accepting "sole responsibility" for it.[70] According to Beilin, at Taba a great deal of progress was made on various aspects of the refugee question and, in particular, on the question of how Israel was to express its sentiments with respect to the "truth" that Israelis and Palestinians would share:

At Taba, agreements were reached concerning the nature of personal compensation, compensation for assets, options of rehabilitation and absorption in third countries, and compensation for the host countries. *Above all, we were very close to an agreement concerning the story of the creation of the refugee problem, which described the Israeli approach and the Palestinian approach to the issue, and their common denominator.* Specific sums of money were not agreed on, nor was the actual number of refugees which would be permitted to come to Israel. However, the distance under dispute between the parties was narrowed substantially, and the Palestinian side agreed that the number of refugees must be such that it would not damage Israel's character as a Jewish country.[71]

The passages published in *Le Monde* relevant to the question of the official position that Israel would take as part of the peace agreement are consistent with this formula of two juxtaposed and partially overlapping narratives. Both positions used very similar language to recognize the centrality and moral weight of the Palestinian refugee question. The Palestinian proposal has both sides acknowledging that "a just resolution of the refugee problem is necessary for achieving a just, comprehensive and lasting peace." The Israeli proposal labeled the refugee question as "central to Israeli-Palestinian relations" and described "its comprehensive and just resolution [as] essential to creating a lasting and morally scrupulous peace." But clear differences remained.

The Palestinian position was articulated under the heading of Moral Responsibility:

2. Israel recognizes its moral and legal responsibility for the forced displacement and dispossession of the Palestinian civilian population during the 1948 war and for preventing the refugees from returning

to their homes in accordance with United Nations General Assembly Resolution 194.
3. Israel shall bear responsibility for the resolution of the refugee problem.[72]

The Israeli delegation preferred to put forward their ideas on this subject under the heading of Narrative—emphasizing Israeli recognition of the suffering and tragedy of the Palestinian refugees, their right to compensation, dignity, and resettlement options, but acknowledging Israeli responsibility for their fate only as part of a wider array of forces and actors.

2. The State of Israel solemnly expresses its sorrow for the tragedy of the Palestinian refugees, their suffering and losses, and will be an active partner in ending this terrible chapter that was opened 53 years ago, contributing its part to the attainment of a comprehensive and fair solution to the Palestinian refugee problem.
3. For all those parties directly or indirectly responsible for the creation of the status of Palestinian refugees, as well as those for whom a just and stable peace in the region is an imperative, it is incumbent to take upon themselves responsibility to assist in resolving the Palestinian refugee problem of 1948.
4. Despite accepting the UNGAR [UN General Assembly Resolution] 181 of November 1947, the emergent State of Israel became embroiled in the war and bloodshed of 1948–49, that led to victims and suffering on both sides, including the displacement and dispossession of the Palestinian civilian population who became refugees. These refugees spent decades without dignity, citizenship and property ever since.

Clearly, progress was made. In the Multilateral Working Group on Refugees talks in Ottawa in May 1992, the head of the Palestinian delegation made a rather moderate demand on Israelis for "moral recognition of the immense injustice inflicted upon our people 44 years ago."[73] One member of that delegation, Rashid Khalidi, published a more detailed statement of his view, at that time, of the specific kind of Israeli response that would be required to move to a full and final resolution of the refugee question. Khalidi emphasized as "essential" that "the existential hurt that was done to the majority of the Palestinian people be acknowledged by those who caused that hurt, or their successors in power." He argued that this was all the more important precisely because "there can probably be no fundamental redress of that grievance."[74] Khalidi went on to stress the reeducation and socialization programs that would be needed in Israel, along with symbolic actions and an acceptance in principle of the Palestinian "right to return." Only then would truly generous reparations along with immigration opportunities into the West Bank/Gaza state, he argued, be acceptable as the basis for a final settlement.[75]

At Taba, however, the Palestinian side demanded less than Khalidi's formulation contained—just an Israeli acknowledgment of its "moral and legal responsibility" for the fate of the Palestinian refugees and its "responsibility for the resolution of the refugee problem." Significantly, the Palestinian formulation (as reported in *Le Monde*) does not include a demand that Israel accept the Palestinian "right of return." Nor does it insist on an Israeli formulation that explicitly places "sole" or even "central" or "primary" responsibility for the fate of the Palestinians or for the solution of the refugee problem on Israeli shoulders. This is particularly noteworthy in light of Beilin's choice of words—refusing an Israeli acceptance of sole responsibility, but not ruling out accepting partial responsibility.

Indeed, the Israeli position at Taba acknowledged, albeit indirectly and implicitly, that Israel was to some extent responsible and ready to contribute "its part" to the solution to the problem. The negotiators were willing to articulate a narrative of the events of 1948 that emphasized the direct and terrible consequences for Palestinians of the war surrounding Israel's establishment and omitting any reference to Arab leaders' orders leading to the departure of the refugees. This formulation represents a considerable amount of change if compared, for example, with the Israeli position as stated during the negotiations of the Multilateral Working Group on Refugees in 1992. In his opening remarks to that group, the head of Israel's delegation, Shlomo Ben-Ami, refused to acknowledge any responsibility by Israel for the "exodus" of the refugees. While alternating between blaming the Arabs for the problem or characterizing it as inevitable, Ben-Ami used only awkward and passive-voice phrasing to suggest the possibility of a link between Israeli triumph and Palestinian catastrophe and showed no interest in the notion of a narrative that could be shared:

The Arab exodus was initiated by the wealthy and the powerful Arab families who left the masses insecure and leaderless. The mass escape that ensued was inflamed by the horrors of war and by the hope of a speedy return to an Arab Palestine once the victorious Arab armies had completed their task. . . . It is a travesty of historical truth to present the Palestinian refugee problem as the result of mass expulsion. There is no denying, however, that once the Jews, who for thousands of years waited with humility for their redemption, made their reencounter with history as a sovereign nation, they had to assume the inherent immorality of war. The suffering of the civilian population will always be a burden on the conscience of any nation at war. . . . Clearly the Palestinians were a major victim of the Arab-Israeli conflict. The Palestinian refugee problem was born as the land was bisected by the sword, not by design, Jewish or Arab. It was largely the inevitable byproduct of Arab and Jewish fears and the protracted bitter fighting.[76]

Despite the evident change that occurred during the 1990s on this issue, there is no question that even at Taba, important gaps remained between the Israeli and Palestinian positions. The Israeli side was not willing to explicitly acknowledge legal, moral, or historical responsibility for the fate of the refugees or to assume sole responsibility for the solution of the refugee problem. This refusal is consistent with long-standing fears in Israel that any such declaration would expose Israel to virtually unlimited property, rights of return, and compensation claims.[77] Moreover, it chose to include reference to "all those parties . . . responsible for" the refugee problem, thereby implying that the Arab states and perhaps the Palestinians themselves played a role. The Israeli proposal also included explicit reference to Israel's initial acceptance of the 1947 United Nations partition plan and to the mutuality of suffering that resulted from the (implicitly alluded to) failure of the Arab side to accept it.

But in this back-and-forth, we can see the outlines of the kind of agreement eventually reached by the German and Israeli governments in 1951. Not only did the German government (of course, not a Nazi government) not accept responsibility (legal or moral), but it explicitly included claims that the "overwhelming majority of the German people abominated the crimes committed against the Jews" and that they "did not participate in them." Such "apologetics," including the recollection of "many among the German people who showed their readiness to help their Jewish fellow citizens," were swallowed by the Jewish/Israeli side, even though most historians would argue that a more truthful account would not have been so generous in its memory of German public opinion and civic virtue during the Third Reich. What Adenauer did say was that what happened to the Jews was awful ("unspeakable"), that his government and the people of Germany were aware that it was awful, and that it had been done "in the name" of the German people. That it had been done in the name of the German people is what, he declared, warranted the new Germany's commitment to a measure of indemnification (no claim was made of full expiation, restitution, or rights to Jewish forgiveness).

Based on the negotiations over the reparations agreement, successful via a much less than fully accurate embrace by the successor regime of what had actually occurred, and based on the progress made so far in negotiations between Israelis and Palestinians, it is not difficult to imagine a workable package of arrangements and declarations to enable a mostly internationally funded compensation, resettlement, and return arrangement to be agreed upon. The formulas utilized would allocate a portion of responsibility for the refugee problem to a portion of Israeli actions and policies in 1948, thereby justifying a significant but certainly not majority role for the commitment of Israeli resources. Israeli acknowledgment of and expressions of regret for injustices committed either "in connection with the establishment of the State," "as a consequence of the establishment of the State," or "in the name of the State of Israel or of Zionism" would not require Israelis to deny their own truths—of a heroic, necessary struggle for elementary Jewish rights of survival and self-determination.

Two elements are likely to be key: the political imperatives of consolidating statehood; and an expectation that no denial, by Palestinians, of the truth of what befell them would be required to achieve it. If Palestinians are to receive a real state, with unfettered access to it for refugees living outside of Palestine, Palestinian leaders will likely act just as did Ben-Gurion, Goldmann, and Sharett—avidly searching for formulas to make massive packages of aid for that state and its newly arriving citizens politically acceptable. And if Israel were ready to include within the curricula of its schools the type of information and explanation about Jewish-Arab relations in 1948 available in the *Tekuma* series of TV documentaries on the establishment of the state, it would be well on the road toward the kind of treatment of the Nazi era, from the victims' perspective, that has featured in German textbooks since the 1960s (a decade after Adenauer's speech to the Bundestag). That Israelis would be gradually socialized away from depending on narratives of national pride that require the denial of palpable Palestinian truths will become a factor of immeasurable importance in the subsequent normalization of ties between the two nations that claim the Land of Israel/Palestine.

Notes

1. Excerpts from address to the Knesset by Prime Minister Ehud Barak on the Camp David summit, July 10, 2000, http://www.mfa.gov.il/mfa/go.asp?MFAH 0hmf0.

2. David Schenker, "Is a Jerusalem Deal Enough for Peace?" *New York Post*, July 24, 2000.

3. See Akiva Eldar's extensive reporting on the Taba negotiations, *Haaretz*, February 14, 2002, http://www.peacenow.org/nia/news/haaretzspecial0202.html.

4. *Lehavdil*, meaning in Hebrew "to distinguish between," is a traditional Jewish formula for legitimizing a comparison that might be considered somehow sacrilegious or otherwise inappropriate. The meaning of the speech act is the communication that despite what may be learned from the comparison, one understands that the two entities or phenomena being compared are intrinsically different and have different meanings.

5. Ilan Pappé, *The Making of the Arab-Israeli Conflict: 1947–1951* (London: I.B. Tauris, 1994), 268. Ben-Gurion and Nahum Goldmann also expressed support for the idea of linking reparations to Jews from Germany to Israel's agreement to compensate Palestinian Arabs for their losses. See Michael R. Fischbach, *Records of Dispossession: Palestinian Refugee Property and the Arab-Israeli Conflict* (New York: Columbia University Press, 2003), 189.

6. Tom Segev, *The Seventh Million: The Israelis and the Holocaust* (New York: Hill and Wang, 1993), 197.

7. Jewish extremists tried to kill Adenauer in Paris in the fall of 1951 by sending him a package bomb, but it killed a policeman instead.

8. Segev, *Seventh Million*, 191.

9. January 7, 1952, *Major Knesset Debates, 1948–1981*, Netanel Lorch, ed. (Lanham, Md.: University Press of America, 1993), 3:723.

10. Golda Meyerson (Meir), *Major Knesset Debates*, 740.

11. Michael Brecher, "Images, Process and Feedback in Foreign Policy: Israel's Decisions on German Reparations," *American Political Science Review* 67:1 (March 1973): 83.

12. Ibid. See also Nana Sagi, *German Reparations: A History of the Negotiations* (Jerusalem: Magnes, 1980), 62–63.

13. Kurt R. Grossman, *Germany's Moral Debt: The German-Israel Agreement* (Washington, D.C.: Public Affairs Press, 1954), 10–14. Concerning the severity of Israel's economic crisis in the early 1950s as an impetus for negotiations with Germany, see Lily Gardner Feldman, *The Special Relationship between West Germany and Israel* (Boston: George Allen and Unwin), 67–70.

14. Segev, *Seventh Million*, 198.

15. Ibid., 200.

16. Pinchas Lavon, *Major Knesset Debates*, 738; Golda Meyerson (Meir), ibid., 740–42.

17. Statement by Foreign Minister Moshe Sharett in the Knesset, March 14, 1951, quoted in Brecher, "Images," 55.

18. Quoted in Brecher, "Images," 88.

19. Segev, Seventh *Million*, 201.

20. Nicholas Balabkins, *West German Reparations to Israel* (New Brunswick, N.J.: Rutgers University Press, 1971), 88.

21. Ibid., 86, emphasis added.

22. Sagi, *German Reparations*, 69; emphasis added.

23. Brecher, "Images," 88. See also Balabkins, *West German Reparations*, 90.

24. Segev, *Seventh Million*, 201. The World Jewish Congress was another key player in the initiation and negotiation of the reparations agreement. Its president, Nahum Goldmann, first met with Chancellor Konrad Adenauer on December 6, 1951. In indirect contacts prior to that meeting, Goldmann had made clear his refusal to meet with the German leader until the latter had "issued a declaration that would clarify the German obligation towards the Jews." Inge Deutschkron, *Bonn and Jerusalem: The Strange Coalition* (Philadelphia: Chilton, 1970), 46.

25. Segev, *Seventh Million*, 203–4; Sagi, *German Reparations*, 70.

26. It is worth noting that in some respects, it is reminiscent of another famous paragraph—the Balfour Declaration—whose text was the result of tortuous negotiations between the World Zionist Organization and the British cabinet. Leonard Stein, *The Balfour Declaration* (London: Vallentine Mitchell, 1961), appendix.

27. Segev, *Seventh Million*, 202.

28. Jeffrey Herf, *Divided Memory: The Nazi Past in the Two Germanys* (Cambridge, Mass.: Harvard University Press, 1997), 282. See also, for the paucity of Adenauer's comments on the Holocaust and his pattern of evasion of explicit references to Nazi crimes and German responsibility, Frank Stern, *The Whitewashing of the Yellow Badge: Antisemitism and Philosemitism in Postwar Germany* (Oxford: Pergamon, 1992), 342, and 350; and Robert G. Moeller, *War Stories: The Search for a Usable Past in the Federal Republic of Germany* (Berkeley: University of California Press, 2001), 25–26.

29. Herf, *Divided Memory*, 283.

30. Menachem Begin, *Major Knesset Debates*, 724–25.

31. Brecher, "Images," 93.

32. Sagi, *German Reparations*, 72. See also Gabriel Sheffer, *Moshe Sharett: Biography of a Political Moderate* (Oxford: Clarendon, 1996), 601.

33. *New York Times*, September 28, 1951, 8.

34. Ibid., September 30, 1951.

35. Noah Barou, "Origin of the German Agreement," *Congress Weekly* 7 (October 13, 1952): 19–24.

36. *New York Times*, September 29, 1951.

37. Moshe Pearlman, *Ben Gurion Looks Back* (New York: Simon and Schuster, 1965), 163.

38. *New York Times*, September 28, 1951, 8.

39. Paul Weymar, *Konrad Adenauer: The Authorized Biography* (London: Andre Deutsch, 1957), 72.

40. Sagi, *German Reparations*, 71.

41. *New York Times*, September 29, 1951.

42. As quoted in Thomas Alan Schwartz, *America's Germany: John J. McCloy and the Federal Republic of Germany* (Cambridge, Mass.: Harvard University Press, 1991), 179.

43. Sagi, *German Reparations*, 71.

44. Grossman, *Germany's Moral Debt*, 16.

45. Ronald W. Zweig, *German Reparations and the Jewish World: A History of the Claims Conference* (London: Frank Cass, 2001), 21–22. Sagi, Grossman, and Zweig are all scholars with close ties to publishing houses, institutes, and journals affiliated with mainstream, official Jewish and Zionist organizations.

46. Ibid., 178–80; and Weymar, *Konrad Adenauer*, 72.

47. Schwartz, *America's Germany*, 168.

48. Ibid., 175, 177–78.

49. Ibid., 177–78.

50. Quoted in Stern, *Whitewashing*, 351.

51. Segev, *Seventh Million*, 206.

52. Quoted in Ibid ., 207. "Amalek" is a reference to the tribe that attacked Israelite stragglers in the desert. In this biblical account, God commands the Israelites to "blot out the name of Amalek." They are commanded to kill all Amalekites. Leading anti-Semites are traditionally considered by Jews to be descendants of Amalek. Here the entire German nation is being referred to in that way.

53. Ibid., 196n. Semantics did appear to be particularly significant. While the Hebrew word *shilumim* was chosen to avoid the image that the payments were closing an account of guilt, the German word *Widergutmachung*, meaning to make something good again, was intended, for Germans, to convey the opposite.

54. Quoted in Brecher, "Images," 88.

55. Ibid., 221–23.

56. Moeller, *War Stories*, 26–27.

57. Deutschkron, *Bonn and Jerusalem*, 53.

58. Herf, *Divided Memory*, 295, 482.

59. Stern, *Whitewashing*, 353.

60. Schwartz, *America's Germany*, 175.

61. Ibid., 183.

62. http://www.mfa.gov.il/mfa/go.asp?MFAH0hli0.

63. Cited in "What's New about the Israeli Position on the Palestinian Refugee Question: Summary and Comments," Badil Resource Center, October 14, 1999, http://www.badil.org/Press/1999/press77–99.htm.

64. http://www.mfa.gov.il/mfa/go.asp?MFAH0iaa0.

65. http://www.us-israel.org/jsource/Peace/tabatalks.html.

66. Rashid Khalidi, "Attainable Justice," *International Journal* 53:2 (spring 1998): 233–52.

67. From the Israeli-Palestinian joint statement, http://www.mideastweb.org/Taba.htm.

68. In February 2002, a more complete version of the "Moratinos Document" (notes taken by the EU observer at Taba) was published and authenticated by Israeli and Palestinian delegates, http://www.acj.org/articles/article.php ?article_id = 41.

69. "Remarks by the President at Israel Policy Forum Gala," Waldorf-Astoria Hotel, New York, January 7, 2001. Distributed by the Office of International Information Programs, U.S. Department of State, http://usinfo.state.gov.

70. Yossi Beilin, "Solving the Palestinian Refugee Problem," December 31, 2001, http://bitterlemons.org/previous/bl311201ed5.html.

71. Ibid., emphasis added.

72. http://www.mideastweb.org/Taba.htm.

73. Remarks by Eli Sanbar, published in *Palestine-Israel Journal* 2:4 (autumn 1995): 125.

74. Rashid Khalidi, "The Palestinian Refugee Problem: A Possible Solution," *Palestine-Israel Journal* 2:4 (autumn 1995): 74.

75. Ibid., p. 76.

76. Reprinted in ibid.,115–16.

77. For example, the Israel Supreme Court and more than one Cabinet have agreed that the Ikrit and Baram refugees should be allowed to return to at least a portion of their lands. These Israeli Arab citizens were evacuated from their homes in 1948 with the explicit promise that they would be allowed to return. But they have still not been allowed to do so, reflecting a deep-seated and oft-expressed fear on the part of Israeli authorities that any return of any refugees to their 1948 villages based on acceptance of their right to do so will open a Pandora's box—an endless array of cases of internal and external refugees with comparable rights based on principles of equity and due process.

Part III
Practical Consequences of Exile and Return

Chapter 7

The Palestinian IDPs in Israel and the Predicament of Return: Between Imagining the Impossible and Enabling the Imaginative

Amal Jamal

The yearning for return has been the essence of the Palestinian national struggle since 1948. Although not all Palestinians live as refugees, the sufferings of the refugees motivated Palestinian nationalism. After the Oslo accords and the establishment of the Palestinian Authority on part of Palestinian soil, the issue of return has been eased as a central motivating factor in Palestinian nationalism. However, this particular curve in the long march for return has led to major disparities between those who still wanted to locate return at the center of the national struggle and those who viewed the process of state-building as an ultimate goal that should be sought first in the political circumstances of the Middle East in the 1990s. The Oslo accords led most Palestinian refugee communities to criticize their national leadership.[1] Palestinian intellectuals and refugee leaders began exploring new strategies that could relocate their right of return at center stage in Palestinian nationalism.[2] Not all refugee communities adopted the same strategy of struggle. According to their place of current residence, Palestinian refugees began mobilizing their ranks in order to block any peaceful settlement that did not ensure their right of return.[3]

Among the Palestinian refugee communities that mobilized against what has been seen as the capitulation of their right of return is the refugee community in Israel, which has been legally and symbolically depicted as the "present absentees."[4] This community was completely overlooked by Israeli-Palestinian negotiating teams. Palestinian scholars of the refugee problem have also overlooked this community.[5] Most studies of the refugee problem do not relate to the internally displaced Palestinians in Israel as part of the refugee community, even though this community views itself as such. As a result, the community, which had been relatively quiet, had begun to mobilize and adopt new strategies of protest.

The present absentees' struggle for return has long been an issue within Israel. However, the 1990s demonstrated that this community adopted new legal and political strategies based on the new opportunity structures opened with the Israeli-Palestinian peace process, changes within the Israeli legal and political systems, and the globalization of human-rights discourse, especially its endorsement by strong international organizations such as the United Nations, Amnesty International, and Human Rights Watch. The new strategies of struggle for return have uncovered the dilemmas the Palestinian IDP (internally displaced person) community faces. Israel created a legal, moral, and political chasm between the IDPs and the rest of the refugee community. Israeli citizenship was viewed as a strong, albeit not always effective, legal tool in the struggle for some citizens' rights within Israel. Israeli citizenship, however, also set limits on the ability of the IDPs to be part of the Palestinian refugee community and be represented by the leadership of the national movement in the negotiations with Israel. Joining the campaign of the refugee communities would have placed the IDPs in direct conflict with the Israeli state, which their leaders did not want to happen. On the other hand, accepting the Israeli framing of the refugee problem would have left the IDPs out of any Israeli-Palestinian settlement of the conflict. This situation led the IDP community to develop its own strategies of struggle, seeking to overcome the limitations of its dual positioning as Israeli and Palestinian.

The historical sociology of the IDPs and their accommodation tactics in Israel have been the subject of a growing number of studies.[6] Therefore, this chapter is largely confined to exploring the legal and political constitution of the present absentees as a social category in Israel and its current implications. It also examines IDPs' tactics to overcome Israeli policies of social categorization and identity construction that aimed at eradicating their struggle for return to their original places of habitation. In this context, this chapter sheds light on the dilemmas that Palestinian IDPs in Israel face as a result of their dual positioning as Palestinians and part of the refugee community, on the one hand, and as Israeli citizens, on the other. Recent developments in IDP theory provide the theoretical framework and the tools for this discussion.

Refugees, IDPs, and Return

The problem of IDPs has not been clearly addressed by international law and by international agencies.[7] Recent decades have witnessed a sharp rise in the number of IDPs throughout the world. The intensity of the phenomenon has brought many human-rights organizations to pay more attention to the crisis of internal displacement that affects more than 25 million people worldwide. The United Nations invested increasing energy in investigating the issue and published "Guiding Principles on Internal Displacement."[8] While not an international binding treaty, the principles draw attention to the moral and legal repercussions of the IDP problem and to the assistance needed to solve it. There is a debate over the traditional distinction made between IDPs and refugees.[9]

The guiding principles define IDPs as follows: "[I]nternally displaced persons are persons or groups of persons who have been forced or obliged to flee or to leave their homes or places of habitual residence, in particular as a result of or in order to avoid the effects of armed conflict, situations of generalized violence, violations of human rights or natural or human made disasters, and who have not crossed internationally recognized state border."[10]

This definition, accepted by the United Nations as well as independent human-rights agencies, emphasizes the territorial factor as the main differentiation between IDPs and refugees. The lack of any clear criterion to measure suffering makes it impossible to differentiate between refugees and IDPs based on psycho-social criteria. Nevertheless, the suffering of IDPs may be not less devastating than that of refugees. The emphasis put on the territorial dimension of refuge turns the host states of IDPs, whose governments dispossessed them in the first place, into the main agency responsible for their well-being. This raises questions that have to be addressed in any normative standards that guide the treatment of IDPs' problems.

In the case of refugees, as defined in international law, countries of refuge have no legal and political responsibility for their return to their original places of habitation, unless these countries were directly involved in the atrocities that caused people to become refugees. Countries of refuge extend humanitarian aid to refugees by the mere fact of enabling them to stay on their territory. Although these states have direct interests in the return of refugees to their original places of habitation, they do not always have the power to facilitate this goal. According to international law, international agencies such as the UN High Commissioner for Refugees (UNHCR) and the Red Cross are viewed as the main institutions for protecting refugee rights.[11] These international agencies cannot always provide refugees physical protection, but in most cases they manage to supply basic needs for survival until a solution to the refugee problem is reached.

As opposed to the clear guidelines for international agencies charged to address refugee issues, IDPs were assumed to be the responsibility of their homeland states. The absence of legal tools to promote the intervention of international agencies in situations of crisis that created IDPs was debated in the human-rights community. Roberta Cohen and Francis M. Deng state in their book on the IDP crisis: "It has become essential to develop a broadly recognized framework of normative standards and institutional arrangements to guide the actions both of governments and of international humanitarian and development agencies in dealing with crises of internal displacement."[12]

Cohen and Deng emphasize that the sovereignty of states has hindered the intervention of international agencies in crisis situations that created IDPs. In their view:

[T]he concept of sovereignty cannot be dissociated from responsibility: that is to say, a state should not be able to claim the prerogatives of sovereignty unless it carries out its internationally recognized responsibilities to its citizens, which consist of providing them with protection and life-supporting assistance. Failure to do so would legitimate the involvement of the international community in such protection and assistance. . . . When states whose populations are at risk deliberately obstruct or outright refuse access, they should expect calibrated actions that range from diplomatic demarches to political pressures, sanctions, or, as a last resort, military intervention.[13]

Examining the Palestinian IDPs' case in Israel will help demonstrate how homeland states develop policies toward their IDPs that render solving their problem—especially enabling their return to their original places of habitation—almost impossible. States in situations of conflict tend to view IDP problems as domestic issues and have no interest in external intervention. In most cases, states seek to dissolve their IDP problem and erase its traces as those may be the only evidence of their atrocities. These policies place IDPs in an impossible situation in which their well-being depends on the intentions of the same state that turned them into IDPs. In recent cases, such as Kosovo, the international community used force to return IDPs to their homes. However, this has been the rare exception. In many cases, IDPs have to face state policies alone and must develop their own strategies that facilitate their goal of returning to their original places of habitation. IDPs' strategies are not disconnected from international developments. But, as the case of Palestinian IDPs in Israel demonstrates, internally displaced people, like any other social movement, must rely on their own struggle for return. They reframe their situation, appropriate human and material resources, and utilize structures of opportunities to promote their interests, rendering the international community secondary to solving their problem. Since internationalizing their problem may lead to a direct clash with their state and thereby harm them, Palestinian IDPs in Israel muddle through, alternating among utilizing their citizenship, international organizations, and international law as appropriate to promote their interests.

The Political History of Displacement

Some Palestinians became IDPs along with the creation of the general Palestinian refugee problem. The New History of Israel, written mostly by Jewish historians, demonstrates clearly that Israel made tremendous efforts to minimize the number of Palestinians who would remain within its borders at the end of the war.[14] The official policy of the state between May and November 1948 was to push the Palestinian population outside the borders of the areas occupied by the Israeli army.[15] The Israeli government justified its policies toward Palestinian refugees by the state of war and sought to create new demographic facts on the ground that would facilitate the identity of the state as Jewish. As a result, hundreds of thousands of Palestinian refugees were forced to leave their homes and flee.[16] Most fled to areas beyond the reach of the Israeli army. In many cases, refugees who found refuge in neighboring villages inside Palestine were expelled for a second time when their area of shelter fell under the control of the Israeli army.[17]

The exact number of Palestinian IDPs is hard to determine. According to Majid Al-Haj, the vast majority were villagers from about 370 villages destroyed during and after the 1948 war.[18] Estimates from the early 1950s spoke about 31,000–50,000.[19] The National Committee for the Rights of the Internally Displaced in Israel claims that the UN Relief and Works Agency (UNRWA) late-1940s' registry report of 46,000 people is correct, stating that this number was verified by Israeli sociologist Sami Smooha, who concluded that 23.1 percent of the Arab population in Israel were either IDPs or their descendants.[20] Thus, 250,000 Palestinian citizens of Israel would be IDPs. However, Israeli historian Hillel Cohen, who conducted extensive historical research on the IDPs, claims that these numbers are exaggerated.[21] He estimates the IDPs at around 15 percent of the Arab population, or 150,000 people today. But Cohen does not include IDPs who descend from families in which only one parent is an IDP. If we follow the Israeli legal definition, that is, all those who were not in their homes according to the Absent Property Law and as a result lost their homes or their lands, IDPs exceed 250,000 today.[22]

Israeli policies of evacuation and deportation did not stop with the end of the 1948 war.[23] The number of Palestinians who were deported from their villages increased as a result of the Israeli army's efforts to establish its control over the areas occupied during the war that the UN partition plan did not assign to the Jewish state. This led to evacuating several villages that were located in "security zones" (for example, Ikrit and Bir'am) or in areas of Jewish settlement (for example, Al-Ghabsiya and al-Majdal).[24]

The number of IDPs further increased from 1948 to 1951 as a result of Israeli land policies in the triangle area. In the Rhodes talks between Israel and Jordan, the two states agreed to exchange territories for security reasons. The areas that Israel received from Jordan—the triangle area—were populated with 25,000 Palestinians and included 4,000–8,500 refugees.[25] Israel absorbed the original Palestinians inhabitants of these areas into the state while deporting the vast majority of the refugees. It did not allow the small number of refugees who remained to return to their original villages and prevented local inhabitants from regaining their private lands, which the Israeli army had captured prior to the cease-fire agreement with Jordan. All the lands located west of the cease-fire line that were captured by the Israeli army before the Rhodes talks were considered absentee property and transferred to the custodian of absentee property. Palestinians thereby lost thousands of acres of private land even though they became Israeli citizens.

Subsequently, Israel implemented an intensive policy of Arab land confiscation and expropriation that led to the expulsion of thousands of Palestinian citizens from their original places of habitation.[26] In the Negev, in particular, the state established seven permanent residential areas in which it sought to concentrate all the Bedouin, thereby damaging their historical bond to their ancestral land and harming their lifestyle.[27] This process of land transfer from Arab to Jewish hands increased the number of IDPs and led to the categorization of fifty-eight villages as "unrecognized" because they were not legalized by the state planning authorities in the 1960s.[28]

The Legal and Political De/Constitution of Social Categories

Beginning in May 1948, the Israeli government began to "normalize" the lives of its Jewish citizens by investing resources in new settlements and in employment.[29] Any barrier hindering these goals was viewed as illegitimate. The Palestinian Arabs who remained in Israel, especially the IDPs, were viewed as a major hindrance to maximizing state control over land resources. As a result, Arab citizens were framed in militaristic terms that justified illegal policies under the cover of security reasoning.[30] State institutions—executive, legislative, and legal—introduced policies, laws, and rulings that formed a sophisticated system of dispossession, subjugation, and control.[31] This chapter illuminates three dimensions of Israeli policies that are most relevant to the IDP problem, although it should be noted that these policies were applied to Arab society in general. These policies sought to dissolve the IDPs as a social category and eliminate their negative repercussions on internal stability as well as on the international appeal of Israel as a democratic state.

The Legal System

To understand one of the main difficulties that IDPs face, it is necessary to pay attention to the centrality of the law and the legal system as major factors in the construction of political identities with peculiar social meaning.[32] Processes of legislation and their application by court rulings demarcate the lines between different social categories and influence processes of identity de/construction.[33] This process has been of central importance to the construction of Israeli Jewish identity and as a result to the categorization of Arab Palestinians who remained within the borders of the Israeli control system.[34] The Knesset and court system were central players in defining not only the legal and political identity of the state but also the dominant cultural, ideological, and symbolic ethos. Moreover, they played the central role in defining the lines of inclusion and exclusion for social groups. Israeli legal institutions introduced two important policy guidelines. First, they distinguished between the legal and the social status of the IDPs. Second, they established a clear difference between place and space and exploited that to maximize the interests of the state.

One of the first policies was to construct IDPs as a special legal category that enabled the state to appropriate their resources as "absentees," while at the same time dissolving them as a social "status group" that could claim special treatment by the state. The legal mechanism was the Law of Absentee Property, enacted in 1950 by the Knesset. That law provided the legal grounds for confiscating properties from anyone identified as an absentee. This classification enabled as much property as possible to be transferred from Arab to Jewish (state) hands.[35] The definition of "absentee" was based on a peculiar understanding of the time scale and a manipulative interplay between place and space and the obscuring of spatial boundaries. Concerning timing, the law considered as absentees all who left their "ordinary place of residence in Palestine" after November 29, 1947, no matter whether they left for security reasons, business purposes, or health needs. The date chosen assumed that these people chose not to be part of Israel, as if they knew that a war would break out leading to the establishment of the State of Israel six months later. Furthermore, the law assumed that all those who left their homes after that date opposed the establishment of the Jewish state or plotted against its creation. The retroactive legal validity of the law, which was introduced two years after the establishment of the state, proves that it was intended to legalize measures that had been already taken.

On the second level, the interplay between place and space, section two of the definition of "absentee," considered those who were "in any part of Palestine outside the area of Israel" as absentees. Israel did not exist between November 29, 1947, and May 15, 1948. Therefore, the retrospective validity of the law for this period is empty of any real legal meaning. Section three referred to any person who "left his ordinary place of residence in Palestine" for a place outside Palestine or "for a place in Palestine held at the time by forces that sought to prevent the establishment of the State of Israel or that fought against its establishment" as absentee. The law differentiates between "ordinary place of residence" as a particular place and Palestine as a more general spatial area. By leaving their concrete place of ordinary residence, Palestinians were not entitled to their property any more, even if they remained within the areas of Palestine that became the "area of Israel." The political space of Palestine that became Israel was not respected as a source of legal standing and territorial identity. Instead, place, in its concrete material sense, was treated as the only factor legitimating the entitlement for property. This stood in direct opposition to the criteria applied to Jews, which were established in the Law of Return, passed by the Knesset in the same year. Israel sought to establish a new "ethnospace"[36] that enabled it to reorganize power relations based on new ethnonational hierarchies. Joseph Schechla claimed in that

[b]y this "legal" criterion, those persons who were away from their property in the general area of any form of war action—whether engaged in fighting or not—during the said period would have their properties confiscated, which the Jewish National Fund (JNF) then would administer for the benefit of Jewish immigrants. Any joint owner with another person falling under that category would similarly lose his/her property to Israel. While that applied in absentia to those refugees outside Jewish-occupied Palestine (whom the law termed "absentees"), it also provided for the legal dispossession of those who never left the borders of the newly created state, or those who were reabsorbed into Israel as a result of the armistice agreements and hence not counted as "international" refugees.[37]

The Law of Absentee Property thereby established a legal order that superseded the historical and cultural bond between Palestinians and their land, establishing a new order that legalized the appropriation of these lands by the state. The establishment of "absence" from a concrete place in a particular time period as the moral and legal foundation for losing rights over property is especially important to the IDP problem. It not only reformulates their bond with a specific place but also reconstructs their identity and de-territorializes it. The act of de-territorialization conducted by the Zionist ideology is similar to any other colonial movement that confiscates the unity and homogeneity of the historical continuity of the native peoples in their homeland.[38] The act of splitting the space and its reorganization as embedded in the two laws mentioned above mirror the contradictions of the Israeli colonial discourse.

IDPs reject the theory that connects absence and rights.[39] In their view, this connection raises questions in regard to Jewish claims for historical rights over Palestine. If the rights over a place are superseded by absence, then what are the moral and legal grounds on which Jews establish their right to the territory on which they live?

Citizenship and Dis/Closure

Arab Palestinians were incorporated into the Israeli political system as "regular" citizens, losing thereby their special historical, national, and cultural bonds with their homeland, which became Israel after 1948. They were treated as individual "newcomers" into the Israeli system. Their incorporation was limited to a particular understanding of citizenship, which is liberal-individualistic in nature, denying their communal or national identity as Palestinians. This treatment was part of the grand socio-political engineering project that the Israeli government enacted in order to dissolve the "Arab problem" inside Israel and prevent any external involvement in it. Arabs, who had lived on the land for thousands of years, became immigrants in their legal status, and Jews, who had just arrived into the country, became the masters of the land. This change in legal status was most apparent in the case of IDPs. Among the latter, some were granted citizenship, becoming "regular" citizens and losing thereby their status as refugees. Others were not granted citizenship, since they did not meet the conditions set in the Nationality Law (1952). These persons remained refugees without any special treatment until the law was amended in 1980.

Arabs were turned into newcomers by defining the main sources of entitlement to Israeli citizenship. Israel passed the Law of Return in 1950 and the Nationality Law in 1952. Both laws transformed the relationship between territory and membership in the political community in Israel. Ethnicity granted Jews automatic citizenship in the state. Based on the Law of Return, all Jews, no matter where, are potential Israeli citizens and can realize this potential whenever they decide. Palestinian inhabitants, however, had to meet particular conditions in order to become Israelis. The Nationality Law, in addressing those inhabitants who were not entitled to citizenship by way of return, established a narrowly defined territoriality-residence as a central condition for granting Israeli citizenship. In particular, Palestinians had to prove that they did not leave their houses "from the day of the establishment of the state to the day this law comes into force, or [that they] entered Israel legally during that period" in order to become citizens. Those who fled their houses, even to neighboring villages, were not entitled to become citizens. Furthermore, Palestinians should have registered themselves in the population register under the Registration of Residence Ordinance on March 1, 1949. As many Palestinians who had fled their homes did not register, fearing deportation, these people were not granted Israeli citizenship.

These measures facilitated constructing Palestinians Arabs as new immigrants in terms of their political rights and legal status. They also promoted constructing the present absentees as a legal category and dissolving them as a special social status group. The new conditions forced many IDPs to start campaigning for citizenship in order to overcome the threat of deportation. Winning Israeli citizenship became a more pressing problem than fighting for their property. On the other hand, the exclusion of many IDPs from Israeli citizenship made it impossible for them to reclaim their houses. Many could not appeal to Israeli courts, as they feared deportation.[40]

Remaining without their property and not being granted Israeli citizenship have been the conditions that IDPs had to face after the 1948 war. Many IDPs sought to be "naturalized," as if they were new immigrants. The

Israeli Nationality Law grants citizenship by naturalization, although that "is not a right but a privilege dependent on the discretion of the Minister of Interior."[41] Palestinians had to meet six conditions in order to become Israeli citizens. As a result, the privilege of naturalization became a successful tool to tame and control the Arab community in Israel. Naturalization became part of a broader policy of "presencing" based on allegiance and loyalty.

Having to face an overwhelming reality, many IDPs viewed their incorporation into the Israeli state as citizens as a matter of Israeli "courtesy" and "generosity."[42] In their view, Israeli citizenship assured their presence in their homeland and enabled them to struggle for return to their homes from within the Israeli system.[43] But by becoming citizens, the IDPs were caught within the confines of citizenship. Their naturalization as citizens turned their demand for return into an internal Israeli problem that was treated by the Israeli legislative and judicial systems based on new rules of the game enacted by these institutions. The Knesset and the court system were integral parts of the Jewish state and sought to facilitate the consolidation of the state system. As a result, most appeals to the Knesset or the courts by Arab citizens were rejected, denied, or delayed.[44] Since the entire Arab population was ruled by a military government, military officers were, in most cases, the final arbitrators in Arab affairs. To block the effectiveness of civil appeals to the Knesset or the courts, the army turned security needs into a banner to wave whenever the civil institutions recognized some of the Arabs' basic needs. The army also destroyed and concealed any traces of the Arab existence in hundreds of villages. In two cases (Ikrit and Bir'am), this was done deliberately to block any court decision in favor of the IDPs.[45] Military governor Emanuel Mor wrote specifically that any High Court decision that favored the return of the IDPs to these two villages "may cause serious harm to state security and harm the interests of the IDF."[46] In another case, involving Al-Ghabsiya village, the army acted in direct opposition to a High Court ruling that demanded the IDPs' return to their original homes.[47]

As part of the Israeli policy of denying the IDPs a special status, the government took the responsibility over them from the UNRWA in 1952.[48] The IDP problem then became an internal Israeli issue, not a refugee problem, and therefore precluded external powers' interference.

The Israeli government also imposed on the UN Relief for Palestinian Refugees (UNRPR) and the International Committee of the Red Cross (ICRC), which extended humanitarian aid to the refugees, to distribute their aid to all needy people inside Israel, including Jews.[49] Israel insisted that Jews who emigrated from Arab countries to Israel were refugees who should be assisted in settling. The government thereby managed to blur the differences between refugees whom the government policy created and Jewish immigrants who arrived in Israel voluntarily and who were encouraged to do so by the government. The government also sought to end the direct involvement of international organizations in the lives of refugees: its agreement with the ICRC made the latter collect aid abroad and transfer it to the Israeli government, which transported it inside Israel and distributed it to the needy.[50]

The "Israelization" of the IDP problem and its framing as parallel to Jewish immigrants became an official Israeli policy that conditioned any treatment of the refugee problem. Palestinian IDPs were disconnected from the general Palestinian refugee problem, as reflected in Israeli-Palestinian negotiations since the Madrid conference in 1991. Israel managed to convince all the parties involved, except the IDPs themselves, that the IDP problem was an internal Israeli affair that must be solved within the Israeli system. Israel enclosed the IDPs within its citizenship and submitted their rights to its own rule, abolishing any right to their property as native inhabitants of the land.

Transfer, Resettlement, and Planning

Another important Israeli policy that aimed at dissolving the IDP problem was resettling them in other places so as to better control them. Under the humanitarian justification of family reunification, the government relocated IDPs according to its own interests and plans for Jewish settlement and development. It sought to reduce the concentration of IDPs in Arab cities and villages, relocating them in many "shelter villages." This resettlement followed three criteria: territory allotted was not within areas heavily populated by Jewish settlers; it was not too close to existing Jewish settlements; and it was deemed valueless to Jewish settlement and development.[51] Moreover, the government prevented creating any precedent by allowing IDPs to return to their original villages.[52] This was documented in a secret letter written by the governor of Nazareth in January 1949,[53] in which he referred to demands of IDPs from Lubia, Sagarah, and Hitin who lived in Nazareth, Sachnin, and Deir-Hanna: "These villages were mostly centers of resistance against our forces and are located in areas that are purely clean from Arab presence and are settled by Jews. Aside from the psychological dimension of returning population to centers of resistance in the past, Arabs or/and refugees should not be settled here in order not to harm the normal development of the Jewish settlements."[54]

One exception was the village of Aylaboon, whose residents were enabled to return as a result of pressure by the Catholic Church. Some refugees from Haifa, especially those who found refuge in Nazareth, as well as refugees from Acre who found refuge in neighboring villages were allowed to return but not to their homes, which were already occupied by Jewish immigrants. The returnees to Haifa and Acre were mostly placed in abandoned houses owned by other refugees as was also done to other IDPs.

In some cases, government officials sought to persuade IDPs to exchange their original homes for homes given to them by the government, which mostly belonged to other refugees.[55] In other cases, the Israeli government was willing to compensate IDPs for their original homes, an offer that some accepted but many others opposed.

The government not only continued its policy of land confiscation but also used administrative and legal means to limit the natural development and growth of Arab residential areas. This policy increased the number of IDPs, either by not recognizing dozens of residential locations and villages in its master planning policies or by demolishing "illegal" houses. In 1951, the Law of State's Property transferred all lands that belonged to the Mandate government to the Israeli state. In 1960, the Lands Administration Law granted the Israel Land Administration (ILA) the right to administer state lands, including those confiscated from Arabs.[56] In 1965, the Building and Construction Law granted Jewish planning councils at the regional and national levels the right to issue "district outline plans" that identified existing and projected built-up areas. The plans recognized only 123 Arab villages, ignoring many others that had existed long before the plans were set.[57] All the latter villages were defined as "unrecognized" and therefore illegal. They were then deprived of basic water, electricity, and telephone services as well as all governmental assistance. In many cases, houses were destroyed, creating more IDPs who had to find refuge in other villages. This problem was most acute in the south in Bedouin areas.

The Causes for the Reemergence of the IDP Issue

After having analyzed Israeli policies toward the IDPs, it might sound anachronistic to ask why the IDP problem reemerged. Nevertheless, it is an important question if we are to evaluate the influence it may have on future Israeli-Palestinian relations in general and Jewish-Arab relations in Israel in particular. The issue, of course, was never forgotten and was always in the background of Arab politics in Israel. The mounting emphasis on it has long- and short-term causes.

One long-term cause has been the fact that Israeli policies of control, containment, and de-Arabization through land confiscation and political delegitimation have never stopped.[58] They took different forms in different periods but never changed their real characteristics and goals. The patterns of relations that were determined by Prime Minister David Ben-Gurion in the early 1950s between the Jewish state and its Arab citizens have not undergone fundamental changes. Israeli political, military, and legal elites still view the Judaization of the entire geographical space of the state as a major goal that state institutions must pursue. The same elites block real and effective Arab representation in state institutions.

This position is supported by a strongly anti-Arab public opinion that views limiting the political rights of the Arab population as a legitimate goal. A public opinion poll in March 2002 revealed that 31 percent of Jewish Israelis favored transferring "Israeli Arabs" out of the country (as compared with 24 percent in 1991); 60 percent favored encouraging "Israeli Arabs" to leave the country; 61 percent thought that "Israeli Arabs" posed a security threat; and 24 percent thought that "Israeli Arabs" were not loyal to the state.[59]

In another poll in May 2003, 53 percent of Jewish Israelis opposed full equality for Arab citizens, 85 percent believed that "to be Jewish" is "important or very important" in order "to be a 'real Israeli,'" and 57 percent thought that "the Arabs should be encouraged to emigrate."[60] These results, which match the figures from the 1980s, mirror the antagonistic Israeli-Jewish public opinion toward Arabs that legitimates discriminatory policies.

Those policies consolidated the sense of danger among Arabs. The experiences of harassment, discrimination, and marginalization led to Arab counterstrategies to struggle for equality.[61] All studies indicate major changes in their political awareness and the consolidation of their oppositional consciousness toward Israeli policies.[62] Among the central pressing issues has been the confiscation of land and the decreasing spaces for housing and development. Both topics are most urgent within the IDP community. As a result, the more Israeli policies of land confiscation and Judaization of space increase, the more the Arab community in general and the IDPs in particular are provoked to adopt an active strategy to assert their rights to the land.

The rising IDP struggle for new Israeli policies has also been triggered by the land liberalization and privatization policies that have been proposed and sometimes adopted by Israeli state agencies such as the ILA. The idea of privatizing public land, especially lands that were given by state institutions to kibbutzim and moshavim, has gained momentum.[63] Since these agricultural communities were established on destroyed Arab villages, their lands belong to Palestinian refugees and IDPs. Their privatization would establish a new land regime in Israel, transforming the lands of the "nation" into "real estate." This shift, besides marking a serious change in Israeli political culture, would change the relationship between people and land. The Zionist ethos of "redeeming the land" would evaporate into the pockets of big real-estate companies. Moreover, the change would have a major impact on the IDP problem. As long as their land is owned by the state and its agencies, it is much easier to claim them back. Privatizing the ownership of the land would render the claim more complicated, since the land would be owned by private people who bought it "legally" from the state.[64] As a result, Arabs resent Israeli privatization policies and have organized seminars and rallies to campaign against it.[65] IDPs were the first to organize against these efforts, which explains their emergence as a central political force among the Arab community.

Another long-term cause for the reemergence of the IDP issue is the generational change taking place in Arab society in Israel, especially the rise of a new leadership of politicians, intellectuals, and professionals. The dominant leadership generation has developed organizational, intellectual, legal, and political tools that enable them to reframe Arab rights in Israel in a fashion that locates displacement as a central issue in any solution of the Israeli-Palestinian conflict. Second- and third-generation IDP leaders are active in relocating their problem at center stage in the Israeli and Palestinian public spheres. Since displacement and the lack of land for development affect many Arabs and since the young generation of IDPs that lost its lands completely suffers the most from the land shortages, they bring the issue to the fore. Arab citizens, especially of IDP origin, who seek to build or buy a house face tremendous difficulties establishing a family. This increases the psychological inclination of this cohort to mobilize in reaction to external triggers.[66] The IDPs of this generation are among those who turned al-Nakba day into a general Palestinian national memorial day. Al-Nakba day is commemorated by visits to destroyed villages, an act that conflates local displacement with the national loss of Palestine, turning the former into a central topic on the national agenda. The IDP's turned these visits not only into collective memorializing events but also into protests against what is being currently done with these lands.

The intensity of the problems that the displaced community faces is growing as the number of IDPs expands. Since most IDPs lost most, if not all, of their lands, they are in great need to purchase land for housing. Israeli land confiscation and regional planning have reduced the surplus land in Arab residential areas. Many villages and towns have no new land for housing. As a result, the drive to return and regain their land is related to existential problems in their villages of refuge. Return acquires a material need and is not only a matter of nostalgia or yearning.[67] Not answering such basic needs of a quarter of a million people is a recipe for explosion in the future.

The surfacing of the IDP problem in Israel is also connected to the rising international interest in IDPs in general and the changes in the political environment in the Middle East in the 1990s with the Madrid peace conference and Oslo accords. The overlooking of the status of the Palestinian IDPs by both Israel and the PLO led this community to criticize the negotiations. Although most Palestinians in Israel supported the peace process, IDPs feared that their problem would be overlooked in negotiations for the final status agreement. Activists in the IDP community started looking for avenues of activity to promote their issue and raise public awareness as to its centrality to any peaceful solution of the Israeli-Palestinian conflict. IDP leaders seek to put their problem on the political agenda of the negotiations, in cooperation with refugee organizations in the West Bank and Gaza Strip, such as Badil and Shaml. These common ventures should not be understood as a willingness of IDP leaders to give up their representative character to an external leadership. They are, rather, part of the refugee community's effort to mobilize against any compromise of their right of return. The mobilization of the general refugee communities may therefore be another reason behind the reemergence of the IDP problem on the public Israeli and Palestinian agenda.

Modes of Organization and Meanings of Return

The initial organizational infrastructure of the IDP community goes back to the 1950s, when local committees were organized based on communal affiliation. The displacement patterns of the IDPs were influenced by several factors,[68] notably the reuniting of the same village in one place. This pattern re-created the communal life of the village after it was disrupted by the war. Although this was not always possible, it preserved some aspects of the social fabric that existed before 1948. IDPs who originated from the same village preserved their common memories and experiences and organized their struggle for return based on their place of origin. Local committees were established, which appealed to the government and the army authorities, trying to persuade them to allow the residents to return home.[69] However, the local initiatives were not coordinated among the entire displaced community. Political and economic circumstances blocked any attempts to organize on a national basis. The nature of the Arab leadership that remained in Israel, which was mostly traditional and tribal and lacked the organizational tools necessary for collective mobilization, did not help in putting the IDP problem on the public agenda. This leadership concentrated on dealing with the harsh daily existential conditions. This pattern of behavior, which lasted until the first Land Day, on March 30, 1976, left all IDP issues to local initiatives, mostly based on village affiliation. Even when their problems were raised by the leadership of the Communist Party, the main political force in the Arab community at the time, it was not raised from the perspective of restorative justice but rather as part of an effort to win distributive equality within the existing hegemonic Israeli political order.

In contrast, a meeting in Nazareth in April 1992, comprising activists from local committees, decided to establish the Preparatory Committee for the Rights of Internally Displaced Palestinians (PCRIDP) in Israel. In its manifesto, published before the meeting, the Preparatory Committee warned the Palestinian leadership not to give up on the basic rights of the IDPs to return to their homes as part of the solution of the general Palestinian refugee problem. The committee claimed that the IDP issue "symbolizes the core of ethnic discrimination and of violation of Palestinian national rights."[70] The committee emphasized that there must be a relationship between solving their problem and establishing peace between Palestinians and Israelis: "The solution of this issue will strongly impact the establishment of coexistence based on proper parameters and standards." These declarations made the strategic lines of the committee clear. On the one hand, the IDPs are an integral part of the Palestinian people and of the refugee community. On the other hand, the committee would not leave the representation of the IDP problem to the Palestinian leadership. This line of thought reflected the dilemmas that IDPs faced.

In the internal deliberations on establishing the national committee of the IDPs, some participants emphasized the term "refugees." Others wanted to emphasize the special status of the IDPs in Israel. In the end, they selected the terms "uprooted" or "displaced." The naming of the problem was based on their awareness of the growing literature on worldwide IDPs. They also sought to distinguish their problem from the broader Palestinian refugee problem. In a central publication of the committee, its leaders stated:

Despite the national, historical, and geographic ties between the Palestinian people and the internally displaced, we must highlight the unique position of the internally displaced who have remained in the homeland. This is a special situation that is shared by the entire Palestinian minority in Israel. Internally displaced Palestinians hold Israeli citizenship, a fact that distinguishes us from all other refugee communities. The Israeli authorities deal with us as Israeli citizens, and apply Israeli laws to us. Yet we are subject to ethnic discrimination policies, despite this citizen status, and our rights as citizens are not equal to those of other Israeli citizens.

This differentiation demonstrates the dual positioning of the IDPs' identity. IDPs have also shown their awareness that this duality has been fully exploited by the Israeli government. On the one hand, they are Palestinians and are treated as such when it comes to their rights. On the other hand, the government does not consider the IDP problem as an integral part of the Palestinian refugee problem, since they are Israeli citizens and their problem is an internal Israeli affair.

In a conference in Tamra in March 1995 in which representatives from more than thirty displaced villages participated, the Preparatory Committee was reorganized in order to include more representatives from different villages. This became the National Committee for the Defense of the Rights of Internally Displaced Palestinians in Israel (NCDRIDP), which lobbied successfully among the Arab leadership in Israel to be recognized as the sole representative of the Palestinian IDPs. This was a crucial step in asserting the right of return of the IDPs as a central issue on the agenda of the Palestinian minority in Israel.

The leaflet announcing the establishment of the National Committee reasserted the inherent connection between IDPs and refugees: "The refugees of 1948, including the internal refugees still living in Israel, are the principal victims of the Israeli policy through the Zionist-Arab conflict." The National Committee announced also that the IDPs "were disappointed by the negotiations when it became clear that their major issue had been neglected in the Oslo accords of 1993, and in all the subsequent agreements and accords."[71] The National Committee justified its establishment on the grounds that disregarding their problem has "led to the development of local initiatives to organize the uprooted communities into local avid national committees to struggle for their right to return to their home villages."[72] A manifesto published in 1999 added: "We decided to handle our case alone, especially after the Madrid conference, which excluded the refugees in the homeland, an exclusion which was repeated by the Oslo accords."[73]

The National Committee played a central role in turning al-Nakba day into an official Palestinian memorial day in which the IDPs visit their villages and rally for their return. Furthermore, the committee organized with other Arab NGOs, such as the Follow-Up Committee for Arab Education in Israel, educational programs to raise the awareness of the Arab youth of the IDP problem. These efforts turned the IDP problem into a central issue in the Arab public agenda that cannot be overlooked in any peaceful settlement of the Palestinian refugee problem.

In March 2000, the National Committee organized another conference in Nazareth, which supported the right of return without concessions as the central goal of the IDPs. The committee utilized UN General Assembly Resolution 194 (December 11, 1948) to establish the right of IDPs for return to their original homes. The Israeli day of independence has been turned into a memorial day on which a return rally takes place. This rally is convened in a different displaced village every year, in which IDPs would commemorate their original villages and demonstrate their commitment to their historical, political, and moral rights to return to the same homes that they owned before 1948. The National Committee has initiated the establishment of a displacement museum, in which traditional and folkloristic devices and tools are turned into pieces of art and exposed to the wide public, to memorialize the legacy of the IDPs community.[74]

Strategies of Return

The IDPs' National Committee utilizes several strategies to promote its goals. As a social movement, it seeks to reframe displacement and infuse it into the Israeli-Palestinian agenda. The committee appropriates material and human resources and mobilizes them to achieve its goals. Four interrelated strategies promote the goal of return.

Reframing Internal Displacement

Establishing the National Committee for the Defense of the Rights of the Internally Displaced Palestinians in Israel and its registration in 2000 as a legal NGO is part of the IDPs' campaign to reassert their problem and raise it higher on the public agenda in Israel and in Palestinian society. Since the beginning of the 1990s, there has been clear systemization of the IDPs' political campaign, and public gatherings are covered in the local newspapers and reported to foreign press agencies.

A central achievement is their success in uniting all Arab parties in Israel behind their right to return to their homes. Beginning with the 1996 elections, all Arab parties listed the right of return of the IDPs as a central goal in their platforms.[75] The IDPs' National Committee also united many Arab heads of local councils behind their goal. Twenty-seven heads signed a petition to cancel the Israeli Law of Absentee Property.

The National Committee also invested efforts to bring the issue to Israeli public awareness by initiating gatherings, rallies, and demonstrations in the destroyed villages. It drew support from several Jewish organizations and figures who identify with the IDPs' right to a just solution. An example of such cooperation was *Al-Awda* (return) public march and rally in the destroyed village of al-Berweh on April 17, 2002, in which hundreds of Jewish activists participated. The IDPs' gatherings in destroyed villages sometimes led to clashes with the police or with the Jewish residents of the Arab villages who tried to prevent the IDPs from entering them. These clashes received more public attention when they were reported in the press.

Furthermore, there are ongoing efforts to lobby for the return of the residents of the three villages—Ikrit, Bir'am, and Al-Ghabsiya—that were evacuated by the Israeli army after the 1948 war. These IDPs still live in neighboring villages and cities, awaiting a just solution to their problem. The decisions of the Israeli High Court in the 1950s ordering the government to allow them back into their homes are utilized to lobby among Jewish parties such as Meretz and Labor. These efforts drafted some people to support the efforts of the IDPs to solve their problem.[76]

Deconstructing Israeli Denial Policies

Palestinian IDPs utilized the legal system in order to refute the security discourse used by the Israeli army to justify displacement and to enforce their return to their villages. This strategy has been most apparent in the case of Ikrit, Bir'am, and Al-Ghabsiya. For instance, on July 31, 1951, the Israeli High Court ruled that there is no reason that the residents of Ikrit could not go back to their homes.[77] However, the court added that the villagers could return "as long as no emergency decree" against it has been issued. This formulation opened the way for the military to avoid implementing the court order. In the same year, the residents of Bir'am appealed to the court, which ruled in January 1952 that they were entitled to return to their village. The right of the residents of the two villages to return was denied by the military governor. However, legal efforts did not stop. The residents of Al-Ghabsiya, whom the Israeli army evacuated in 1948, then allowed to return for two years until August 2, 1951, and then evacuated again, appealed to the High Court after their village was declared a closed military zone by Prime Minister Ben-Gurion. On November 30, 1951, the Israeli court approved their right to return to the village. However, when they tried to return, holding the court's ruling in their hands, Israeli forces blocked their way and refused to implement the ruling.

These three rulings have formed the legal ground on which the IDPs based their struggle. Although no other villagers went to the High Court with an appeal regarding return, hundreds of appeals were raised to the court by IDPs regarding their confiscated lands or destroyed houses. These efforts sometimes solved personal problems but did not meet the expectations of the IDPs to resolve their problem collectively. The Israeli government's lack of will to reach a solution with the residents of the three villages that won a clear ruling from the High Court exposed the weaknesses of litigation and the disrespect that the executive authority showed to court rulings when these did not match its national priorities.

The weakness of the court system faced with the hegemony of the national agencies responsible for Jewish settlement and the commitment of the former to the government's Judaizing policy have been proven several times since the 1950s. In 1972, the government of Golda Meir denied the right of the evicted residents from Ikrit and Bir'am to return to their villages. In 1977, Prime Minister Menachem Begin promised to return the evicted, but nothing happened. The issue remained pending until 1993, when the government appointed a committee, headed by Minister of Justice David Libai, to examine the issue. In 1995, the committee advised the government to allow the return of the evacuees to an area of 1,200 dunums in order to reestablish the Bir'am and Ikrit communities on the basis of long-term land leases. The committee emphasized that its recommendation to allow these IDPs to return was based on the understanding that their case was unique and not similar to any other case in Israel. The committee based its special treatment on the "governmental promises that were given to residents of Ikrit and Bir'am by the representatives of the government and the army since the date of their evacuation and governmental promises given by the government to the residents in a declaration in front of the High Court of Justice."[78]

This recommendation was welcomed by the residents despite the fact that it did not recognize their right to own the land and covered only a small portion of the area confiscated since 1948. However, Libai's recommendations were not approved by the government, which soon lost power.

Meanwhile, the evacuees of Ikrit petitioned the High Court, which gave the government time to examine the issue. The new government appointed in 1998 another committee, headed by Justice Minister Tzachi Hanegbi. The committee recommended that "no obstacles should be placed in the way of the return of the evacuees in the spirit of the Libai and Klugman recommendations, which provide a step forward and a strong basis for negotiations."[79] As a result of the election in 1999, another change occurred in the government, which again postponed dealing with the issue.

With the election of Ariel Sharon as prime minister in 2001, the issue received a new twist. On October 15, 2001, Sharon submitted an affidavit to the High Court rejecting any appeal by the evacuees to return to their homes. He declared that the lands were appropriated legally by the state and that the evicted residents and their descendants have no legal claim. He warned that "the precedent of returning the displaced persons to their villages would be used for propaganda and political purposes by the Palestinian Authority."[80] Sharon also warned that this issue should be viewed in the context of some 200,000 Israeli Palestinians who lost their homes during the 1948 war. This twist in the governmental position was supported by the political argument that the change in Israeli-Palestinian relations and the deterioration in the security situation were strong enough factors to release the government from its commitment to allow the evacuees of Ikrit and Bir'am to return to their lands. This position was affirmed by the High Court, which rejected the evacuees' appeal, submitted in1997.[81] Even though the court utilized a legalistic discourse to support its position, there is no doubt that it was conditioned by its tradition of not breaking with the official line of reasoning when it comes to Arab rights in Israel.[82] The long history of disappointments and the unwillingness of the Israeli government to deal seriously with the problem of the evacuees of Ikrit and Bir'am have provided a lesson for the rest of the IDPs. This tradition of ignoring the basic rights of these evacuees has also been a major factor in directing legal efforts toward internationalizing the IDP problem. One should note that the residents of Bir'am and Ikrit put all their efforts into the Israeli court system and did not favor internationalizing the IDP problem. They also sought to separate their case from the rest of the IDPs, believing that their case had a good chance of being solved by the Israeli High Court. The court's ruling in June 2003 closed the door on winning the case judicially and left it to the goodwill of the government. This experience was used by IDPs to support the position that Israeli policies toward Arabs have not changed fundamentally since 1948.

Revitalizing Activities of the Displaced

The efforts to counteract Israeli policies that aim at concealing the IDP problem involved educating the new Arab generations about this issue.

Introducing formal educational programs regarding IDPs into Arab schools is still impossible, since the Israeli Ministry of Education controls the Arab school system. Therefore, informal measures were adopted. Many Arab teachers are themselves IDPs. This has influenced their readiness to raise the issue in their own classes. In addition, the IDPs' National Committee organized visits of IDPs to schools to lecture on the problem and its history.

The most influential IDP activity is the organization of public rallies and visits to the destroyed villages. Since the mid-1990s, there has been a sharp rise in the number of visits of IDPs to their original villages as well as the institutionalization of al-Nakba marches as a day of protest on the eve of Israel's Independence Day. The IDPs' National Committee views this day as central to its efforts to mobilize the Arab community and raise the voices of those who lost their houses as a result of Israeli policies. In some cases, the residents have sought to rebuild or rehabilitate holy places—mosques, churches, and cemeteries—in their original villages as a marker of their historical and moral bond to concrete places. The public marches to the villages became an educational tool to commemorate displacement and infuse national awareness among younger generations that are expected to carry on with the struggle to return. The importance of this policy stems from the fact that most Arabs living in Israel today were born after the act of displacement took place and have no personal experience in their original villages. Constructing the memory of affiliations to the original places of habitation has become a central factor in the struggle for return.

Globalizing the Displacement Issue

Israeli policies toward the Arab community have led to the development of international strategies that expose Israel for not respecting the basic rights of its own citizens. Besides struggling for their rights through the Israeli legislative and judicial systems as citizens, the Arab community challenges Israel in international human-rights institutions. For example, several Arab NGOs lobbied against Israeli policies of discrimination in the UN Committee on Economic, Social and Cultural Rights (UNCESCR) and Habitat for Humanity, especially its Housing and Land Rights Committee.[83]

These NGOs, which included the National Committee for the Defense of the Rights of Internally Displaced Palestinians in Israel, persuaded UNCESCR to criticize Israel for its discriminatory policies against Arab citizens in general and against IDPs and the "unrecognized villages" in particular. In its concluding observations, UNCESCR stated:

The Committee expresses its concern over the plight of an estimated 200,000 uprooted "present absentees," Palestinian Arab citizens of Israel most of whom were forced to leave their villages during the 1948 war on the understanding that they would be allowed by the Government of Israel to return after the war.

Although a few have been given back their property, the vast majority continues to be displaced and dispossessed within the State because their lands were confiscated and not returned to them. . . . The Committee notes with deep concern that a significant proportion of Palestinian Arab citizens of Israel continue to live in unrecognized villages without access to water, electricity, sanitation and roads. Such an existence has caused extreme difficulties for the villagers in regard to their access to health care, education and employment opportunities. . . . The Committee expresses its grave concern about the situation of the Bedouin Palestinians settled in Israel. The number of Bedouins living below the poverty line, their living and housing conditions, their levels of malnutrition, unemployment and infant mortality are all significantly higher than the national averages. They have no access to water, electricity and sanitation and are subjected on a regular basis to land confiscations, house demolitions, fines for building "illegally," destruction of agricultural fields and trees, and systematic harassment and persecution by the Green Patrol. The Committee notes in particular that the Government's policy of settling Bedouins in seven "townships" has caused high levels of unemployment and loss of livelihood.[84]

These concerns were reasserted in its concluding observations, published in 2001. From the Arab NGOs' point of view, these comments were the harvest of several years of preparations and lobbying. It is the first time that an important international document pointed out directly the way in which Israeli policies discriminate against Palestinian citizens. This success was seen to be only a first step in a long process of advocacy and lobbying in the international arena.

These efforts mark the Palestinian IDPs' refusal to accept plans that aim at settling them in their current residential villages and paying them compensation. Even though some IDPs have accepted compensation, the vast majority refuses to reach separate deals with the government. Most IDPs demand repatriation and return to their original villages and houses. For example, the spokesman of the IDPs' national committee, Wakim Wakim, asserts that the IDPs insist on returning back to the same villages and houses from which they were deported[85] and claims that it is the basic and fundamental right of every displaced person to return to his or her home. Moreover, in reaction to the Geneva initiative formulated by Israeli and Palestinian peace activists in October 2003, the IDPs' national committee rejected once again any attempt to compromise the rights of refugees and IDPs. The committee expressed its fear that the agreement eliminates the right of return for all refugees, including IDPs, and insisted that "the right of return is a personal right of every refugee. It is not negotiable and cannot be delegated to anybody, be it persons or organizations, to negotiate in order to compromise the right of every refugee to go back to his home."[86]

Conclusion

The hope for return among Palestinians has been the nightmare that scares the Jewish population in Israel. Israel as a "Jewish state" has been unwilling to accept the legitimacy of the right of return. Furthermore, the Israeli public has not considered the right of return as a central issue that could block progress in the peace negotiations.[87] One of the explanations given for the lack of public debate on the Palestinian right of return is that, since Israelis view this issue as the most threatening, the public seeks to deny this threat. When asked whether they accepted the Clinton plan, which proposed Israel's absorbing tens of thousands of refugees for family unification and humanitarian reasons, 77 percent of Jewish respondents opposed this part of the plan and only 23.9 percent were ready to accept the return of a limited number of refugees to Israel.[88] These numbers reflect clearly the unwillingness of the Israeli public to accept or even take seriously the Palestinian demand for return of the refugees.

Like many other studies on the issue of return, this public opinion poll did not include any question on the issue of the Palestinian IDPs. Nevertheless, one could expect that the Israeli Jewish public would be divided among a minority of those who approve the return of some IDPs to their uninhabited villages or to neighboring areas; those who are willing to compensate them in lands and money; and those who reject the whole issue. Raising the right of return of the IDPs is interpreted in Israeli Jewish society as an attempt to reshuffle the consequences of the 1948 war. The evidence we have regarding Jewish public opinion about the Arab population in Israel in general shows clearly that national demands of the Arab community are less and less tolerated. The Palestinians in Israel are seen as a growing threat by an increasing number of Israeli Jews. The Jewish majority is more and more inclined to delegitimate Arab claims for equal rights and fair treatment and is increasingly willing to support drastic measures to cure the "internal danger."[89]

IDPs long sought to solve their problems within the Israeli state system. They accepted the Israel discourse of citizenship and tried to utilize their citizen rights to regain their lost property. However, this is changing. Their experience has shown that states that created a problem of IDPs in their territory based on ethno-national conflict tend not to respond seriously to such problems. The appropriation of IDP resources by the state is usually seen as a precondition to the viability of the state. Indeed, Don Peretz wrote that "abandoned property was one of the greatest contributions toward making Israel a viable state."[90] Arab lands form, from an Israeli point of view, a precondition to the Judaizing process.

Palestinian IDPs are fully aware of Israeli official policies and tactics. Some try to prove that Israel is discriminatory by pointing out that their return to their villages would not change the existing demographic balances inside Israel. Therefore, security and demographic arguments raised against their return are not serious.[91] Since Israeli objections to any just solution to their problem has to do with the ideological character of the state, they increasingly insist that the solution of the Palestinian refugee problem should include them and that it must be based on the general Palestinian right of return. The disappointment with Israeli policies toward IDPs and the inability to cure the problem in the Israeli court system explain the rise of an alternative discourse among IDPs and the institution-alizing of the IDP struggle for return. IDPs are increasingly becoming active players in preventing any political solution of the Israeli-Palestinian conflict that does not seriously address the refugee problem. Since IDPs increasingly believe that Israeli civil law does not enable a principled solu-tion to the problem of the displaced and since the displaced are not willing to give up on their struggle, their political mobilization and their lobbying efforts on international stages are growing stronger. Any overlooking of their problem in a future settlement of the Israeli-Palestinian conflict will instigate resentment and fuel the IDPs' struggle for a just solution of their problem. The means of the struggle remain hard to predict, although this study has alluded to possible options.

Notes

1. On the critique of the Oslo accord by Palestinian refugee communities, see Naseer Aruri, ed., *Palestinian Refugees: The Right of Return* (London: Pluto, 2001); Ingrid Jaradat-Gassner, *The Public Campaign for the Defense of the Palestinian Refugee Rights in Historical Palestine* (Bethlehem: Badil Resource Center, 2000).

2. Edward Said, *Peace and Its Discontents* (New York: Vintage, 1993); Said Abur-ish, *Arafat: From Defender to Dictator* (New York: Bloomsbury, 1998).

3. See the work of two central Palestinian NGOs that concentrate on refugee issues: Badil (www.badil.org) and Shaml (www.shaml.org).

4. See the Israeli Law of Absentee Property (1950), Knesset documents.

5. Salim Tamari, *Palestinian Refugee Negotiations: From Madrid to Oslo II* (Washing-ton, D.C.: Institute for Palestine Studies, 1996); Elia T. Zureik, *Palestinian Refugees and the Peace Process* (Washington, D.C.: Institute for Palestine Studies, 1996).

6. Majid Al-Haj, "Adjustment Patterns of the Arab Internal Refugees in Israel," *International Migration* 24:3 (September 1988): 651–74; Aharon Lisovski, "The Pres-ent Absentees in Israel," *The New Orient* 10 (1960): 187–90; Hassan Musa, "The Geographical Distribution of the Arab Refugees in Their Homeland: The Galilee Area 1948–1987," master's thesis, Haifa University, 1988; Mahmud Said, "Adjust-ment Patterns and Living Conditions of the Internal Arab Refugees in the Arab Host Villages in the North, 1948–1986," master's thesis, Hebrew University, 1991.

7. See details of the debate over internal displacement in UN circles in www .refugees.org/world/articles/displacement_rr00_6.htm. For more information on the worldwide IDP problems and the absence of codified protection, see Roberta Cohen and Francis M. Deng, *Masses in Flight: The Global Crisis of Internal Displacement* (Washington, D.C.: Brookings Institution, 1998); Roberta Cohen and Francis M. Deng, eds., *The Forsaken People: Case Studies of the Internally Displaced* (Washington, D.C.: Brookings Institution, 1998); David A. Korn, *Exodus Within Borders: An Intro-duction to the Crisis of Internal Displacement* (Washington, D.C.: Brookings Institution, 1999).

8. "Guiding Principles on Internal Displacement," http://www.reliefweb.int/ ocha_ol/pub/idp_gp/idp.html.

9. See Guy S. Goodwin-Gill, professor of international refugee law at Oxford

University, in *World Refugee Survey 2000*, www.refugee.org; Jean-Daniel Tauxe, director of operations for the International Committee of the Red Cross, in *International Herald Tribune*, March 1, 2002.

10. http://www.reliefweb.int/ocha_ol/pub/idp_gp/idp.html.

11. Convention relating to the status of refugees from 1951 and its protocol from 1967, which gave the UNHCR an international legal basis to protect refugees, www.unhcr.org.

12. Cohen and Deng, *Masses in Flight* 7.

13. Ibid.

14. Benny Morris, *The Birth of the Palestinian Refugee Problem, 1947–1949* (Cambridge: Cambridge University Press, 1987); Benny Morris, *1948 and After: Israel and the Palestinians* (Oxford: Clarendon, 1990); Ilan Pappé, *The Making of the Arab-Israeli Conflict, 1947–51* (London: I.B. Tauris, 1994); Nur Masalha, ed., *The Palestinians in Israel: Is Israel the State of All Its Citizens and "Absentees"?* (Haifa: Galilee Center for Social Research, 1993); Nur Masalha, *Expulsion of the Palestinians: The Concept of "Transfer" in Zionist Political Thought, 1882–1948* (Washington, D.C.: Institute for Palestine Studies, 1992); Tom Segev, *One Palestine Complete: Jews and Arabs under the British Mandate* (New York: Metropolitan, 2000).

15. Masalha, *Expulsion of the Palestinians*, 189–99.

16. Walid Khalidi, *All That Remains: The Palestinian Villages Occupied and Depopulated by Israel in 1948* (Washington, D.C.: Institute for Palestine Studies, 1992).

17. Nafez Nazzal provides many examples of cases in which the Israeli army differentiated between original inhabitants of a village and those who found refuge in it and asked the local population to make sure that refugees left their villages. See Nafez Nazzal, *The Palestinian Exodus from Galilee, 1948* (Beirut: Institute for Palestine Studies, 1978).

18. Al-Haj, "Adjustment Patterns," 654.

19. Joseph Schechtman, *The Arab Refugee Problem* (New York: Philosophical Library, 1952); Don Peretz, *Israel and the Palestinian Arabs* (Washington, D.C.: Middle East Institute, 1958).

20. Publication of the National Committee for the Rights of the Internally Displaced in Israel, 1995; Sami Smooha, *The Orientation and Politicization of the Arab Minority in Israel* (Haifa: University of Haifa, 1984), 79.

21. Hillel Cohen, *The Present Absentees: The Palestinian Refugees in Israel since 1948* (Jerusalem: Institute for Israeli Arab Studies, 2000), 21.

22. Badil, *Information and Discussion Brief* 9 (November 2002).

23. Benny Morris, *The Birth*; Nur Masalha, "Debate on the 1948 Exodus," *Journal of Palestine Studies* 21:1 (autumn 1991): 90–97; Nur Masalha, *Imperial Israel and the Palestinians: The Politics of Expansion* (London: Pluto, 2000); Yitzhak Oded, "Land Losses among Israel's Arab Villages," *New Outlook* 7:7 (September 1964): 19–25.

24. Ronit Barzily and Mustafa Kabha, *Refugees in Their Homeland: Internal Refugees in the State of Israel 1948–1996* (Givat Haviva: Institute for Peace Research, 1996); Sarah Osazki, *Ikrit and Bir'am: The Full Story* (Givat Haviva: Institute for Peace Research, 1993); Dahoud Bader, *El-Ghabsiya: Remains Ever in the Heart* (Association for the Defense of the Rights of the Displaced Persons in Israel, May 2002).

25. Emanuel Markovski, the first Israeli military governor of the triangle area, spoke about four thousand refugees whereas Goel Lavitski spoke about deporting 8,500 refugees after the triangle was transferred to Israel. IDF Archives, 841/72/721 and 843/72/721, respectively. Cited also in Cohen, *Present Absentees*, 40.

26. Sandi Kedar, "Israeli Law and the Redemption of Arab Land, 1948–1969," dissertation, Harvard Law School, 1996.

27. Aref Abu-Rabia, "The Bedouin Refugees in the Negev," *Refuge* 14:6 (Novem-

ber 1994); Harvey Lithwick, "An Urban Development Strategy for the Negev's Bedouin Community," *www.bgu.ac.il/bedouin/monograph-Harvey.doc.*

28. The website of the Association of Unrecognized Villages speaks of fifty-eight villages, nine of which are in the north and the rest in the Negev desert. See *www.assoc40.org.* The first laws on planning were passed by the Knesset in the 1960s. On the unrecognized villages, see interview with the head of the Committee of Forty, Muhammad Abu Al-Hayja, "Ayn Hawd and the 'Unrecognized Villages,'" *Journal of Palestine Studies* 31:1 (autumn 2001): 39–49.

29. Dan Horowitz and Moshe Lissak, *Trouble in Utopia: The Overburdened Polity of Israel* (Albany: State University of New York Press, 1989).

30. Sabri Jiryis, *The Arabs in Israel* (New York: Monthly Review Press, 1976), 7–9; Elia Zureik, *The Palestinians in Israel: A Study in Internal Colonialism* (London: Routledge and Kegan Paul, 1978); Nadim Rouhana, *Palestinian Citizens in an Ethnic Jewish State: Identities in Conflict* (New Haven, Conn.: Yale University Press, 1997).

31. Ian Lustick, *Arabs in the Jewish State: Israel's Control of a National Minority* (Austin: University of Texas Press, 1980).

32. On the social meaning of state law, see Menachem Mautner, "Law as Culture: Towards a New Research Paradigm" (Hebrew) in *Multiculturalism in a Jewish and Democratic State*, Menachem Mautner, Uri Sageh, and Ronen Shamir, eds. (Tel Aviv: Ramot, 1998), 545–87.

33. Joseph Raz, *Ethics in the Public Domain: Essays in the Morality of Law and Politics* (Oxford: Clarendon, 1994).

34. Baruch Kimmerling, *Zionism and Territory* (Berkeley, Calif.: Institute of International Studies, 1983).

35. Sabri Jiryis, "Arab Lands in Israel," *Journal of Palestine Studies* 2:4 (summer 1973): 86.

36. Arjun Appadurai, *Modernity at Large: Cultural Dimensions of Globalization* (Minneapolis: University of Minnesota Press, 1996).

37. Joseph Schechla, "The Invisible People Come to Light: Israel's 'Internally Displaced' and the 'Unrecognized Villages,'" *Journal of Palestine Studies* 31:1 (October 2001): 20–31.

38. Gilles Deleuze and Félix Guattari, *A Thousand Plateaus: Capitalism and Schizophrenia* (Minneapolis: University of Minnesota Press, 1987).

39. Jeremy Waldron, "Superseding Historical Injustice," *Ethics* 103 (1992): 4–28; Tamar Meisels, "Can Corrective Justice Ground Claims to Territory?" *The Journal of Political Philosophy* 11:1 (March 2003): 65–88.

40. On the impact of the citizenship law on the status of the Arab community in Israel, see David Kretzmer, *The Legal Status of the Arabs in Israel* (Boulder, Colo.: Westview, 1990).

41. Ibid., 39.

42. Charles Caiman, "Ahri ha-asson: Ha-aravim bi-midinat yisrael 1948–1950" (After the catastrophe: Arabs in Israel 1948–1950), *Annals of Research and Critique* 10 (Haifa: University of Haifa, 1984).

43. Personal interviews with IDPs in several villages.

44. Cohen, *Present Absentees*, 48–52.

45. Ibid., 116–32.

46. IDF archives 68/55/81, a letter from August 12, 1951, cited in ibid., 127.

47. Menahem Hofnung, *Israel: Bitahun hamidinah mul shilton hahok, 1948–1991* (Israel: State security versus the rule of law, 1948–1991) (Jerusalem: Magnes, 1991), 64–65.

48. Alexander Bligh, "From UNRWA to Israel: The 1952 Transfer of Responsibilities for the Refugees in Israel," *Refuge* 14:6 (November 1994): 7–10.

49. State of Israel archives Ministry of Welfare, 94/2146, "Summary on the Activities of the Coordination Agency with the International Aid Organizations," September 1949.

50. Cohen, *Present Absentees*, 54.

51. Alexander Bligh, "Israel and the Refugee Problem: From Exodus to Resettlement, 1948–52," *Middle Eastern Studies* 43:1 (1998): 123–47.

52. Badil, *Report to the Committee on Economic, Social and Cultural Rights*, April 23, 2001.

53. Elisha Shultz, quoted in Cohen, *Present Absentees*, 50.

54. State of Israel archives, Ministry of Minorities, file no. 297/59, cited in ibid.

55. Cohen, *Present Absentees* 28, 47–48; Al-Haj, "Adjustment Patterns."

56. The members of the Israel Land Administration's governing council are half governmental officials and half members of the Jewish National Fund. This arrangement, which ensures total Jewish control of the state's lands, was criticized by the High Court in a ruling in July 2001 that required the state to involve Arabs in the governing council (H.C. 6924/98, *The Association for Civil Rights in Israel v. The Government of Israel*). However, the state did not change its policies. For details, see Adalah, the Legal Center for Arab Minority Rights in Israel, *www.adalah.org/legaladvocacy.html*.

57. Rassem Khamaisi, *Planning and Housing Among the Arabs in Israel* (Tel Aviv: International Center for Peace in the Middle East, 1990); Rassem Khamaisi, "Manganonie hashlita bakarka' vi-yihud ha-mirehav bi-yisrael" (Mechanisms of land control and the Judaization of space in Israel), unpublished paper; M. Hill, "Urban and Regional Planning in Israel," in *Can Planning Replace Politics? The Israeli Experience*, Raphaella Bilski, ed. (The Hague: Martinus Nighoff, 1980), 259–82.

58. Lustick, *Arabs in the Jewish State*; Zureik, *The Palestinians in Israel*; Asad Ghanem, *The Palestinian-Arab Minority in Israel, 1948–2000* (Albany: State University of New York Press, 2001); Rouhana, *Palestinian Citizens*; Oren Yiftachel, *Guarding the Vineyard: Majd Al-Kurum as a Parable* (Beit Berl: Institute for Israeli Arab Studies, 1997).

59. Amnon Barzilai, "More Israeli Jews Favor Transferring of Palestinians, Israeli Arabs—Poll Finds," *Haaretz* English Edition, March 12, 2002, on the poll by the Jaffee Center for Strategic Studies.

60. The Israeli Democracy Institute's poll, *www.idi.org.il/english*. Despite these views, 49 percent denied that Israeli Arabs were discriminated against.

61. Nadim Rouhana, "The Political Transformation of the Palestinians in Israel: From Acquiescence to Challenge," *Journal of Palestine Studies* 18:3 (1989): 35–59.

62. Amal Jamal, "Ethnic Nationalism, Native Minorities and Politics: On the Dynamics of Constructing Inequality in Israel" (Hebrew) *Iyunim* (forthcoming).

63. Oren Yiftachel and Sandi Kedar, "Al otzma va-adamah: Mishtar in hayisraeli" (On land and power: Israeli land regime), *Theory and Criticism* 16 (spring 2000): 67–100; Sandi Kedar, "Zman rov, zman mi'ut: Karka', li'om ve-hukeiha-ba'alut bi-yisrael" (Majority time, minority time: Land, nationality and the laws of property in Israel), *Iyuni Mishpat* 21:3 (1998): 665–764; Arieh Shavit, "Whose Land Is This, Damn It?" *Haaretz* magazine, March 16 and 22, 1999.

64. Oren Yiftachel, "Binui uma vahalukat hamerhav ba'etnokratiya hiyisraelit: Karka'ot ufe'arim adatiyim" (Nation-Building and the allocation of space in the Israeli ethnocracy: Lands and ethnic differentiation), *Iyuni Mishpat* 21:3 (1998): 637–65.

65. Julia Kernochan, "Land Confiscation and Police Brutality in Um El Fahem," *Adalah Review* (fall 1999). On October 19, 2003, Adalah and the National Committee for Arab Mayors filed a petition to the Supreme Court against the Israel Land

Administration (ILA), the Minister of Finance, and the Minister of Industry and Trade challenging the legality of the ILA's decision regarding the massive distribution of lands in the north and the south of the country. According to the decision, discharged Israeli soldiers and persons who have completed one year of national service would be given a 90 percent discount on the price of leasing lands managed by the ILA. This decision would apply to 141 towns and villages in the Galilee and 157 in the Negev. None of these towns and villages, in both areas, are Arab. Adalah argued that the ILA's decision discriminates against Arab citizens, who are exempt from and do not serve in the army or perform national service. Arab citizens are completely excluded from the group that would enjoy this benefit, and thus, their rights to equality and to housing are violated.

66. Dan Rabinowitz and Khawla Abu Baker, *Hador hazakuf* (The stand-tall generation: The Palestinian citizens of Israel today) (Tel Aviv: Keter, 2002).

67. Wakim Wakim, "The 'Internally Displaced': Seeking Return within One's Own Land," *Journal of Palestine Studies* 31:1 (autumn 2001): 32–38.

68. Nihad Boqae'e, "Palestinian Internally Displaced Persons Inside Israel: Challenging the Solid Structures" (Bethlehem: Badil, 2003).

69. See Cohen, *Present Absentees*, on newly available archival materials in, e.g., State of Israel archives, Central Zionist archive, and IDF archive.

70. Leaflet of the National Committee for the Defense of the Rights of Internally Displaced Palestinians in Israel. Circulated document, no date, Shafa'amr.

71. Ibid.

72. Ibid.

73. Documents of the National Committee, Shafa'amr.

74. Interview with Wakim Wakim, head of the National Committee, November 13, 2003.

75. For example, Azmi Bishara, head of National Democratic Assembly, claimed that one of his party's goals was to realize the right of return of all Palestinian IDPs in Israel. *Haaretz*, May 29, 1998.

76. Osazki, *Ikrit and Bir'am*, 24–26.

77. HCJ 64/51, *Dauod et al. v. Minister of Defence et al.*, Supr. Cour. Rept. 5 (1117).

78. Cited in ibid., 4.

79. *Haaretz*, October 10, 2001.

80. Ibid., October 15, 2001.

81. HCJ 840/97, *Awni Sbeit et al. vs. Government of Israel et al.*

82. Ilan Saban, "The Impact of the Supreme Court on the Status of the Arabs in Israel" (Hebrew) *Mishpat Umimshal* 3:2 (July 1996): 541–70.

83. The NGOs include Adalah, Arab Human Rights Association, Itijah, and Mosawa.

84. *http://www.unhchr.ch/tbs/doc.nsf/(Symbol)/E.C.12.1.Add.27.En?OpenDocument*.

85. Interview, Wakim Wakim, October 7, 2002.

86. Leaflet released by the National Committee for the Defense of the Rights of Internally Displaced Palestinians in Israel, October 14, 2003.

87. Dan Zakay, Yechiel Klar, and Keren Sharvit, "Jewish Israelis on the 'Right of Return': Growing Awareness of the Issue's Importance," *Palestine-Israel Journal* 9:2 (2002): 58–66.

88. Peace Index, Tami Steinmetz Center for the Study of Peace, poll, December 2000.

89. Ori Nir, "We Can't Just Be Shooed Away," *Haaretz* English edition, April 25, 2002.

90. Don Peretz, *Israel and the Palestinian Arabs* (Washington, D.C.: Middle East Institute, 1958), cited in Zureik, *The Palestinians in Israel*, 116.

91. Interview with Wakim, October 7, 2002.

Chapter 8
No Refuge for Refugees:
The Insecure Exile of Palestinians in
Kuwait

Ann M. Lesch

Some 750,000 Palestinians became exiles in 1948, when they were expelled from their homes. They gained refuge—a safe haven—in a few countries, but remained unwanted outsiders in many more places. In some instances, they formed diasporas, communities in exile through which they could retain ties to people and places at home or to other communities struggling to be formed abroad. Throughout the post-1948 period, however, they remained legally refugees.[1]

Their status therefore has been ambiguous in exile. Their right to return is enshrined in international law, but their ability to return is blocked. Moreover, at least 200,000 Palestinians were displaced after the 1967 war, and Israel has prevented thousands more from returning to the occupied territories.

For Palestinians, Kuwait became a refuge where they could prosper economically and maintain a vibrant community life. As a diasporic community, they assisted compatriots living in refugee camps or under Israeli occupation and supported the Palestinian national movement. But their status remained that of outsiders: legally refugees, technically in the same category as other migrant workers, and virtually ineligible to become Kuwaiti citizens, they nonetheless developed a sense of permanent attachment to Kuwait.

Although tensions gradually emerged, Palestinians were unprepared for the mass expulsion in 1991 that ended Kuwait's role as a refuge and uprooted their community. That expulsion underlined the impossible dilemma facing Palestinians. Their status contrasts markedly with that of migrant laborers who can return home and whose governments represent their interests. Homeless and stateless, Palestinians remain aliens and often

unwelcome guests. Indeed, one is struck by the parallel with the views articulated by the early Zionist Leo Pinsker: to him, a Jew could not be a native
or a foreigner but was condemned to be a homeless alien living in dangerous insecurity.[2]

Some have likened the Palestinians' status in Kuwait to "middleman
minorities" such as Jews in Europe, Indians in East Africa, and Japanese in
the United States.[3] In some instances, members of the group initially consider themselves "sojourners," temporary residents who plan to save
enough to go home. Over time, they may be relatively successful, filling
specialized niches and starting to feel linked to the host country. Yet they
remain strangers, banned from owning land and/or prevented from
becoming citizens. In either case, they cannot translate economic success
into political influence. In fact, their success and communal distinctiveness
breed suspicion. Increasing competition for jobs with the expanding indigenous middle class further marginalizes them. Paradoxically, while the host
society blocks their full integration, it also accuses them of disloyalty.
Although many aspects of the "middleman minority" concept do not fit
the Palestinian case, those key aspects do appear relevant in approaching
the Palestinian status in Kuwait.

Palestinians' Status in the Arab World

Each Arab government established its own rules for Palestinians who fled
to its territory, either as a country of first refuge or as a country of subsequent migration.[4] Only Jordan extended citizenship to Palestinians. Lebanon denied refugees access to permanent employment or public
education. Syria granted Palestinians access to jobs and schools, whereas
Egypt confined Palestinians to the Gaza Strip. The few Palestinians who
resided inside Egypt found their access to education, employment, and
property increasingly curtailed.

Starting in 1957–58, Syria, Lebanon, and Egypt issued refugee travel documents (laissez-passers) that allowed Palestinians to go abroad to study or
work. This resulted in a torrent of job seekers flowing to the rapidly developing Gulf, which lacked skilled indigenous workforces. Gulf governments
classified Palestinians as temporary residents, like other "guest workers"
from abroad, which meant that the government could deport them and
they had no legal rights.

Nonetheless, in 1965 the League of Arab States affirmed that Palestinians' status differed from that of other migrant laborers. The Casablanca
Protocol called on Arab governments to guarantee Palestinians full residency rights, the same right to work as citizens, and freedom of movement
within and among Arab countries.[5] However, Kuwait, Lebanon, and Libya
tabled reservations, and no Arab government passed the laws necessary to

bring the protocol into force. Ultimately, the Arab League suspended the protocol in 1991, after the Gulf War.

Migration to Kuwait

Kuwait's discovery of oil coincided with the Palestinian flight in 1948. Kuwait welcomed Palestinians, because their skills were indispensable and because its leaders felt obliged to help Palestinians following their defeat and flight. Palestinian teachers,[6] civil servants, and laborers played central roles in creating and staffing its bureaucratic and oil-producing infrastructures. Initially, a few hundred young men won contracts from educational and public works institutions, fields that the emir prioritized for investment.[7] Many more Palestinians smuggled themselves across the border from Iraq to work in construction, the oil fields, and agriculture.[8]

As a result of Kuwait's open-door policy toward labor immigration, its population doubled between 1949 and 1957, with expatriates suddenly reaching 45 percent of the total population. Palestinians/Jordanians constituted 16 percent of the foreigners and 7.3 percent of the entire population.[9] This influx led the government to introduce visa and labor regulations, which were not seriously enforced.[10]

The Palestinian population grew rapidly, from 15,173 in 1957 to about 37,400 in 1961 and 77,712 in 1965, then constituting 31.4 percent of the expatriates and 16.6 percent of the total population.[11] These Palestinians filled essential positions as technicians, teachers, pharmacists, doctors, and engineers.[12]

After 1967, important "push" factors propelled Palestinians to the Gulf. Israel's occupation of the West Bank and Gaza and the civil wars in Jordan (1970–71) and Lebanon (1975–90) propelled movement to the Gulf. Moreover, the booming oil economy exerted a powerful attraction: countries like Kuwait spent their windfall profits on infrastructure, commercial development, and the service sector. "Pull" factors were nearly as strong as "push" factors during the 1970s.

By 1970, Palestinians numbered 147,696 in Kuwait: 38 percent of all foreigners and 20 percent of the entire population. In that year, Kuwaitis became a minority, constituting 47 percent of the population and only a quarter of the labor force. The Palestinian community increased to 204,178 in 1975[13] and doubled to 400,000 in 1990, a mere fifteen years later. The Palestinian economic center of gravity clearly shifted to the Gulf. The Palestinians in Kuwait, in particular, were the wealthiest and seemingly the most stable community, providing crucial financial support for Palestinians back home or in refugee camps.

Family Migration

The initial immigrants were overwhelmingly men who left their families in their home village, town, or refugee camp. Migrants relied heavily on family and village networks to find lodgings and jobs and create a community life. In 1957, women constituted a quarter of the Palestinians and often worked as teachers or medical personnel. As travel eased in the late 1950s, families joined the male breadwinner.[14]

Family migration escalated after the 1967 war.[15] Men brought their families, since they were afraid to leave them under Israeli military rule. Insecure conditions in Jordan, which culminated in the 1970–71 civil war, also induced them to relocate their families to Kuwait. In 1975, almost half the Palestinians in Kuwait were female, and 69 percent of the registered births by foreigners were Palestinian babies.[16]

Palestinians created a family-centered life in Kuwait. Their children were born and educated there and often married other Kuwait-based Palestinians. Their diversified social structure ranged from wealthy businessmen and well-off professionals to small-scale shop owners and mid-level civil servants. This contrasted sharply with other foreign workers, who generally came without their families and did not put down roots.

The Palestinians' sense of rootedness led to resentment at discriminatory treatment, particularly by the younger generation. The first generation might tolerate discrimination, but the second generation sought rights comparable to the native-born. In addition to being annoyed by Kuwaitis' sense of entitlement,[17] Palestinians resented the police who patrolled their segregated neighborhoods and chafed at the unequal educational and employment opportunities. They lived with the fear that their Kuwaiti sponsors would take advantage of them financially and even deport them, on any pretext.[18] Despite these risks and resentments, they were "the most cohesive, successful, and politically conscious single Palestinian community in exile."[19]

Kuwaiti Regulations

As full independence neared in 1961, the Kuwaiti government sought to differentiate between citizens and foreigners. The emir's decrees in 1948 and the citizenship law in 1959 established criteria by which foreigners could become Kuwaiti. Some two thousand Palestinians gained Kuwaiti citizenship as a reward for outstanding services to the kingdom. These included the emir's doctors, some senior civil servants, and a few wealthy businessmen.[20]

Deportation

The citizenship law empowered the government to deport an alien if a court recommended the expulsion of a convicted felon, if the alien had no means of sustenance, or if the Ministry of Interior objected to his or her presence "for security or moral reasons."[21] The entire family had to leave, paying for their transportation. Otherwise, they could be held indefinitely in the deportation center.[22] This created problems for Gazans, whose Egyptian laissez-passers did not allow them to enter either Egypt or Gaza (after 1967). Palestinians holding Lebanese or Syrian laissez-passers could not return there if their travel permits had expired. Nonetheless, deportation affected Palestinians less than expatriates from other countries, as it was politically difficult for the government to expel the stateless Palestinians.

The *Kafala* (Sponsorship) System

In 1960, a law on commercial companies required 51 percent Kuwaiti ownership of all businesses and full Kuwaiti ownership of banks and financial institutions. This created valuable "welfare" benefits for Kuwaiti citizens: by merely lending his or her name, the Kuwaiti might gain as much as 51 percent of the profits.[23] Even a permit to drive a taxi required a Kuwaiti sponsor (*kafil*). Foreigners could not own property, thereby compelling them to rent apartments from Kuwaitis, only in certain neighborhoods. One Palestinian complained: "You could not own anything in Kuwait other than certain types of personal property like a car or furniture. You could not own real estate of any kind. You could not own a business. Palestinians who did own businesses had to have a Kuwaiti partner who was given a majority share. For nothing, no investment, no work, nothing, the Kuwaiti took 51 percent of everything produced by that business."[24] Some Kuwaiti academics decried this system for undermining Kuwaitis' work ethic and leading Kuwaitis to perceive their high standard of living as a right, rather than a reward for their individual efforts.[25] This, in turn, deepened their dependency on the expatriate community.

Kuwaitization

As more Kuwaitis gained secondary or university educations and entered the job market, they replaced Palestinians and other foreigners in the most senior positions. This pressure for Kuwaitization occurred just as young Palestinians, brought up in Kuwait, sought either to break out of menial positions that their fathers had originally accepted and establish themselves in middle-class occupations or to replicate the living standards of their professional parents. Kuwaitis' sense of being besieged mounted, even though the 1959 labor law prioritized hiring Kuwaitis, the 1960 civil service law barred foreigners from senior posts, the 1964 labor law limited foreigners' contracts to five years, a 1969 law linking visas to work permits, and foreigners could not be voting members of unions.[26] Even though Kuwaitis had preferential access to government jobs, with secure tenure, high salaries,[27] and liberal retirement benefits, Kuwaitis' felt besieged.[28]

Kuwaitis were particularly concerned by the Palestinians' well entrenched presence. In 1975, for example, Palestinians constituted 28 percent of all engineers, 37 percent of doctors and pharmacists, 25 percent of nurses, 28 percent of accountants, and 30 percent of teachers.[29] They were the most influential single community in the upper and middle economic levels, outnumbering Kuwaitis in those occupations.

By the 1980s, more Kuwaitis joined the professions. They had preferential access to Kuwait University, exclusive access to the teachers' training institutes,[30] generous support for advanced study abroad, and guaranteed jobs upon graduation.[31] Until the severe drop in oil prices in 1986, the overall economic growth meant that employing more Kuwaitis had little effect on Palestinians.[32] The drop in oil prices, however, caused unemployment among both Kuwaitis and Palestinians and led to the first systematic plan to reduce the number of foreign workers and residents.

Restrictions on Education

Soon after Palestinian families began to enter Kuwait in substantial numbers, the government worried that Palestinian children were overrunning the public schools. It introduced quotas in 1965: foreigners could total no more than a quarter of the students in public schools and in Kuwait University, which opened the next year. In 1968, this quota was slashed to 10 percent. In 1979, the government instituted an even more drastic restriction: persons who arrived after 1961 and who were not employed by the ministries of health or education could not enroll their children in government schools.[33]

These restrictions forced Palestinians to send their children to private schools. From 1968 to 1976, the government alleviated the problem by allowing the PLO to use public school buildings in the late afternoon and early evening for primary and intermediary level instruction.[34] Secondary-level students[35] competed for the limited openings in public schools or attended private schools, which received a 50 percent tuition subsidy from the government for enrolling them. The General Union of Palestinian Women (GUPW) sponsored tuition subsidies that assisted three hundred children in 1983–84 and three thousand in 1986–87.[36]

Acceptance into Kuwait University became particularly difficult. In 1983, for example, only 350 of the four thousand Palestinian high school graduates entered the university. Another one thousand managed to go to the United States or elsewhere to study, largely at their parents' expense.[37] In 1986, Palestinians won two hundred of the merely 276 slots at Kuwait University set aside for non-Kuwaitis. Almost no Palestinians entered the medical or engineering faculties, and Palestinians were banned from other programs, notably the teachers' training institutes. These restrictions, intended to discourage Palestinians from bringing their families to Kuwait, caused enormous resentment. Resentment was compounded by a Palestinian's need to earn at least a 89 GPA to enter the university, whereas a Kuwaiti needed only a 65 GPA. Ghabra stressed the "obsession with education" on the part of Palestinians. Lacking land and statehood, their survival strategy focused on professional attainment: "Investment in the mind . . . became a way of survival."[38] Denial of access to education caused acute stress and forced them to devise complex strategies to achieve that vital goal.

The Demographic Threat

Immigration and natural increase swelled the numbers of Palestinians living in Kuwait. By 1990, there were at least 400,000 Palestinians as against 600,000 full Kuwaiti citizens.[39] Although Asians outnumbered Palestinians, Kuwaitis were concerned that Palestinians would soon outnumber the full citizens, a demographic transformation with enormous political implications. Palestinians were difficult to dislodge, unlike other migrant workers, because of their unique political status. Even the requirement that foreigners leave when they retired and the restriction on the residency of adult sons had little impact on the overall numbers of Palestinians, because they found ways to circumvent those laws.[40] It was only unemployment that induced Palestinians to leave. Thus, an estimated fifty thousand Jordanians/Palestinians left during the 1985–90 economic downturn.[41]

Government planners sought to reduce the absolute number of foreigners, not just restrict their growth. The 1985 census revealed that 70 percent of Kuwait's population was foreign, coming from forty-eight countries: the 1.82 million residents included 550,000 Kuwaitis, 200,000 *bidoon* (indigenous residents lacking citizenship), and 1.07 million foreigners.[42] Kuwaitis (including *bidoon*) constituted 14 percent of the workforce.[43] Despite Kuwaitization policies, the expatriate share had grown from 78 percent in 1980 to 86 percent in 1985–86.[44]

The parliamentary election campaign in 1985 focused on this crisis, as anxieties caused by the Iran-Iraq war, the Iranian revolution, the Lebanese civil war, and the expulsion of the PLO from Lebanon increased Kuwaitis' fear that regional tensions could affect their country. The official demographic plan for 1985 to 1990 outlined measures to achieve a 50:50 ratio by restricting immigration and enforcing the expulsion of nonworkers, retirees, and adult family members.

Although Kuwait controlled the behavior of migrant laborers, their sheer number, combined with their diverse cultures, challenged its identity. Anh Nga Longva argues that, by 1981,[45] "Kuwaitis' capacity for cultural absorption seemed to have reached a point of saturation. Drowning in the midst of aliens from East and West, the small native population was desperately looking for ways to shield itself and to preserve a sense of cultural identity."[45]

Palestinians were the one group that could outweigh Kuwaitis. Palestinians had large and growing families, a multigenerational presence, and a vibrant society. Their cohesion and influence—along with their deepening perception of Kuwait as their home, in which they were entitled to certain benefits—threatened Kuwaitis. A Palestinian commented on this concern: "While we lived a good life in Kuwait, it was a segregated life. . . . While other foreign workers were also limited in rights, the difference for them was that they had a country to return to. They were in Kuwait for a temporary period of time, to earn money and go home. We Palestinians saw Kuwait as our home. We had no other place to go to. We invested everything we had in Kuwait—our time, our talent, our best effort. . . . But the Kuwaitis . . . over time . . . resented our loyalty to Kuwait and the fact that we saw it as home."[46]

Political Tensions

This sense of threat was exacerbated by political strains between the Palestinians' political leadership and the Kuwaiti regime. The government initially tolerated Palestinian political activism, since it was channeled into the Palestinian cause and not directed at Kuwait's governing system. Salah Khalaf noted that, when Fatah was founded in Kuwait in the late 1950s, its organizers were not persecuted, as they did not threaten "the authority and stability of the regime."[47]

Permitted Political Activities

When Fatah gained control over the Palestine Liberation Organization (PLO) in the late 1960s, Palestinians living in Kuwait made vital financial contributions to the national movement. They set up branches of the Palestine Red Crescent Society, General Union of Palestinian Women, General Union of Palestinian Students (GUPS), the Martyrs Foundation, and other organizations that funded welfare and medical programs in the occupied territories.

Palestinians were active in family, village, and town organizations. A "plethora of clubs and associations—clan or village *diwans*, women's and student organizations, unions, publications and political groups—attest[ed] both to an intense community activity and to a profound attachment to their roots."[48] A Palestinian economist even asserted that the Palestinians working in the Gulf—especially in Kuwait—provided "life support to the rest of the Palestinian body politic."[49]

Government Backing of the PLO

The Kuwait government endorsed these activities by deducting 5 percent from the salaries of Palestinian employees as a "tax" paid to the Palestine

National Fund.[50] The government aided the PLO and UNRWA (United Nation Relief and Works Agency) and assisted hospitals and other services in the occupied territories.[51] Moreover, it consistently backed the PLO and Fatah in diplomatic forums. However, in 1989, the sudden budget deficit forced Kuwait to reduce its aid programs by 39 percent and cut the PLO's share by more than half; that caused widespread resentment among Palestinians.[52]

The local PLO/Fatah office worked closely with the government to curtail radical groups, since it did not want to jeopardize the community's status. In particular, Fatah sought to limit the influence of the Popular Front for the Liberation of Palestine (PFLP) and keep Abu Nidal cadres out of Kuwait.[53] Despite these efforts, the government refused to reopen the special PLO schools, out of concern that they fostered a strong national consciousness and legitimized the Palestinians' special status.

The tacit accord that Palestinians not bring intra-Palestinian and intra-Arab discord onto Kuwaiti soil lasted over thirty years. The accord broke down with the Iraqi invasion on August 2, 1990.

The Trauma of Occupation

The Iraqi occupation of Kuwait severed relations between Kuwaitis and Palestinians, relations that had been based on mutual economic needs rather than deep-seated social or political ties.[54] Many Kuwaitis suddenly viewed Palestinians as a "fifth column" in their midst and declared them persona non grata.

A large part of Kuwaiti anger derived from the stance of the PLO: Arafat's failure to condemn the occupation, his efforts to mediate between Iraq and Gulf governments, and his embrace of Saddam Hussein just before the 1991 war. Kuwaitis were furious that their long-standing aid to the Palestinian cause was "rewarded" this way. Even though the Palestinian officials living in Kuwait strongly condemned the invasion, their voices were not heard.

Kuwaitis also blamed the PLO for the actions of the Arab Liberation Force (the Iraqi-controlled Palestinian militia) and Abu al-Abbas's Popular Liberation Front, whose members came from Baghdad to man roadblocks, participate in *al-jaish al-sha'abi*, and assist Iraqis in torture chambers.[55] Most Kuwaitis did not realize that local Palestinian officials restrained young Palestinians from looting abandoned property, refused to join demonstrations backing Iraq, and prevented locally based Palestinians from joining the *jaish*. Some Palestinians actively assisted the Kuwaiti resistance and protected Kuwaiti friends.[56] When local Fatah leaders rejected the order to join the *jaish* in January 1991, issued by the PLO office in Baghdad, Iraqi security harassed senior PLO/Fatah leader Ali al-Hasan and assassinated the head of Fatah, Rafiq Qiblawi, on January 18, 1991.[57]

Many Kuwaitis criticized Palestinians for returning to work, using Iraqi dinars, taking Iraqi ID cards, and changing the license plates on their cars, even though Palestinians had no way to refuse those demands. Kuwaitis hid their cars inside their residential compounds, whereas Palestinians lived in exposed apartment blocks, with their cars parked on the street. Kuwaitis accessed an underground network of funds and food supplies coordinated by the resistance movement; this network did not extend to all the *bidoon* or Palestinian areas.[58] (There was, nonetheless, some coordination and cooperation in providing essential supplies.) Palestinian shopkeepers had to enter Iraq to buy supplies; Palestinians had to shop in those stores and queue outside bakeries for bread. Kuwaitis viewed those everyday acts as support for the occupation, and threatened revenge.[59]

Palestinians were caught between Iraq's threat to kill them if they did not work and Kuwaiti threats to kill them if they did work. Even the exiled Kuwaiti government's stance contradicted the resistance movement's demands: In early August, the emir had called on Palestinians to maintain water, electricity, and public health services that were vital to the population. Nonetheless, most Palestinians quit work by October, terrified by the conflicting pressures.[60]

Kuwaitis were furious when Palestinians sent their children to school, a gesture that appeared to accept the occupation. Although some Palestinians may have seen it as a way to enter schools that were previously inaccessible to them, the primary Palestinian calculus was quite different: education was vital to their survival and had to continue under any circumstances. Kuwaitis were also unaware that Iraq fired most Palestinian teachers during September; eventually, nearly all schools closed.[61]

Recrimination and Expulsion

After Iraqi forces were expelled from Kuwait in February 1991, many Kuwaitis viewed Palestinians as their enemy, responsible for the destruction of their country. From a Kuwaiti perspective, Palestinians were ungrateful and disloyal guests who could no longer be tolerated in their midst. A government spokesman averred in January 1991 that "the loyalties of Palestinians resident in Kuwait [are] suspect and need to be determined."[62] Resistance graffiti threatened expulsion: "Jordan, 1970; Lebanon, 1982; Kuwait, 1990."[63]

Actions taken against Palestinians (and foreigners who were citizens of states that had tilted toward Iraq) included kidnapping and killing individuals and collective punishment against the entire community.[64] Palestinians did not anticipate these attacks; they welcomed the liberation and expected to return to their jobs and normal lives.

Killings

Some four hundred young Palestinians were immediately kidnapped from their homes or off the streets; six hundred were seized in the first two weeks.[65] Kuwaiti soldiers, state security police, resistance members, civilian vigilante groups, and royal "death squads" killed at random and targeted individuals, particularly doctors and teachers who had worked during the occupation.[66]

Collective Punishment

The government instituted comprehensive collective punishments against the Palestinian community. It banned Palestinians from their previous government jobs (including in the health and educational sectors), forbade them from entering utility sites (for example, power and water plants) where many had previously worked, and denied them back pay for the period of the Iraqi occupation.[67] The government pressured private businessmen to fire Palestinians and not hire those who had lost public-sector jobs. It was not until August 1991 that Palestinians could access their bank accounts or obtain severance pay; in the meantime, they were in dire financial straits.

The government hassled Palestinians when they reregistered their cars and billed them for rent, electricity, and water since August 1990. In retaliation for sending their children to school at the beginning of the occupation, it banned all Palestinian children from government schools and blocked currently enrolled students from completing their studies at the university.[68]

The government closed all Palestinian institutions, preventing them from assisting their compatriots. A banner briefly displayed at the entrance to the burned Fatah office read: "Anyone who is a Palestinian is a traitor. This is the home of the enemy collaborators against Kuwait."[69] These measures destroyed the ability of Palestinians to sustain themselves, educate their children, and maintain community activities.

Expulsion

At the time of the invasion, 30,000 of the more than 400,000 Palestinians were abroad on summer holidays. During the fall of 1990, more than 200,000 fled by land to or through Jordan. By December 1990, 120,000 to 150,000 Palestinians remained, approximately equal in number to the remaining Kuwaitis.[70]

After liberation, Palestinians were initially trapped: unable to support themselves while unable to find a dignified way to leave. Security forces placed many Palestinians in the Talha deportation center. Typically, the police then confiscated the family members' passports and ordered them all to fly to Amman at their own expense.[71]

In August 1991, the Ministry of Interior began to issue exit visas, which were necessary to obtain back salaries and severance pay. Palestinians could not leave until they had paid all their debts, including gas, electricity, and phone bills. As a result, many were destitute by the time of departure. Some twenty thousand Palestinians left in August and September 1991, seeking to reach Jordan in time to enroll their children in school. Many more left in October, just before the November deadline for obtaining temporary residence permits.[72] Most drove overland to Jordan, their cars and pickup trucks laden with household goods.

The Remnant

By the end of 1991, only 70,000 Palestinians remained in Kuwait, a number that later shrank to 35,000. Entire districts were deserted; a decade later, the government demolished the empty apartment complexes in Hawalli. Although the remaining Palestinians numbered less than 10 percent of the pre-occupation community, they continued to be viewed as a security threat. They survived on one-year permits, with no guarantee of renewal. When state security assumed direct control over residency visas in 1996, the rate of denial increased markedly and many individuals were targeted for deportation.[73] Political and extra-judicial torture, killings, and disappearances continued into the mid-1990s, and ID-checking roadblocks remained pervasive.[74] An asylum seeker described passing through roadblocks as playing Russian roulette, since the police could act with complete impunity.[75]

Palestinians who carried Jordanian passports had the option of "returning" to Jordan, even though two-thirds had been born in Kuwait and most of the rest came from the West Bank.[76] These 300,000 "returnees" constituted 10 percent of the 3.2 million Jordanian population. A few Palestinians returned to the West Bank and Gaza Strip, but only if they still carried valid residency cards.[77] Fewer still gained political asylum in the United States, Canada, Europe, or Australia.

These exit options were not available to Gazans who carried Egyptian travel documents and lacked Israeli permits that allowed them to live in the Gaza Strip.[78] Egypt banned them from entering without separate visitor's visas, and Jordan only let them transit to another country. In 1990, thirty thousand Palestinians with Egyptian documents lived in Kuwait. About seven thousand managed to leave during the Iraqi occupation. Afterward, some were deported to Iraq, others smuggled themselves out, and many were placed indefinitely in the deportation center. By 2000, Kuwait had granted temporary residence permits to five thousand Gazans, but left the remaining two thousand in legal limbo.[79] They lived in destitute conditions, with no access to medical and social welfare benefits or schools, working in low-paying under-the-table jobs and dependent on funds sent by relatives from abroad.

No Refuge

Ever since 1948, Palestinians have faced daunting difficulties in finding places to live and work without the constant fear of renewed displacement and loss. As stateless exiles, they lack basic human rights that others take for granted. As a marginalized people, discriminated against by their hosts, their sense of a distinctive identity as exiles has been reinforced over time rather than diminished.

The untenable situation that faced Palestinians who resided in Kuwait illustrates this acute problem. They devised survival strategies that enabled them to meet their material and cultural needs in a relatively welcoming but still insecure environment. However, the very success of those strategies undermined their status vis-à-vis the host country. The large size of this cohesive and vibrant community was perceived as a threat by the host government and triggered measures to diminish its size and its economic strength. The Iraqi occupation caused Kuwaiti public opinion to label the Palestinians a fifth column. As traitors, they should be expelled. That mass expulsion "solved" the demographic problem and eliminated the perceived threat to Kuwaiti identity that they posed. The mounting tensions were explainable by the shifting demographics, but expulsion was only feasible in the context of an upheaval that transformed the political and social order.

In this sense, their dilemma resembled that of the "middlemen minorities" mentioned earlier. Japanese living in the United States were denied citizenship and pushed into particular economic niches, only to be accused of disloyalty during World War II and forcibly detained and relocated. Jews were expelled and ultimately exterminated in parts of Europe, having been denied equal rights and excluded from owning land and entering mainstream occupations. Indians in East Africa were successful in trade during British colonial rule, but were expelled in large numbers afterward, even when they acquired citizenship. While the specifics and nuances of these situations varied, they share the pattern of a relatively well-off minority coming into increasing competition with indigenous peoples and lacking political and legal rights by which to protect its status.[80]

Issues of return and statehood take on particular urgency for Palestinians in this context.[81] Kuwait's inability to provide a secure exilic home underlines the untenability of living in exile as well as the insecurity of an unassimilable minority group. Already in the 1970s, Salah Khalaf had commented on his insecurity as a Palestinian in Kuwait with an Egyptian travel document:[82] "A stateless people are a people without recourse, without defense. It is hardly surprising that we seek our identity, indeed our very existence, in symbols such as a passport or a flag."[82] With statehood, Khalaf argued, Palestinians who remain outside the Palestinian state can "live in the Arab state of their choice, without complexes and without anxiety! They would finally be treated on an equal footing with all those who have a passport to show. And if they feel threatened for one reason or another, they would always have the option of packing their bags and going back to Palestine, where they wouldn't be treated as pariahs."[83] It is ironic that Khalaf echoed the cry of early Zionists like Leo Pinsker that statehood in their original homeland was the only way to end the unnatural condition of the Jewish people as unwanted aliens. Life in the diaspora could not be stable without a center that could uphold their legal and political rights. The insecure exile of the Palestinians in Kuwait confirms the validity of that perspective and underlines the urgency of the Palestinian quest for independence on their own soil.

Statehood is therefore one essential condition for reducing the insecurity of exile. Two other measures could also ease the Palestinians' predicament: a stable provision for permanent residency in Arab host countries and recognition of the legal right of return.

Permanent residency, including the right to work, was inherent in the provisions of the Casablanca Protocol (1965) but was never implemented. Enabling Palestinians to obtain permanent residency would lessen their sense of insecurity and their fear of deportation. As permanent residents, they would be able to own property, obtain social security, educational, health, and retirement benefits, and pass on their residency to their children.[84] This would be an extended version of the "temporary protection" doctrine under international law, short of permanent resettlement but addressing refugees' real needs to work, travel freely, live where they choose, and reunite with family members.[85]

Finally, renewed recognition of the legal right to return would reduce the pain of exile. As a realistic matter, few Palestinians would be able to return home, but provision would need to be made for compensation for properties lost in 1948 or 1967 and for the moral cost of over fifty years of displacement. Moreover, restitution for certain properties, along the lines of settlements in Central and Eastern Europe in the 1990s, would enable refugees to gain a fair income from their property without displacing the post-1948 Jewish residents.

A blend of practical measures—statehood, permanent residency abroad, and controlled implementation of the right of return—would help to heal the decades-old wound, end the insecurity of exile, and restore the moral balance in the region.

Notes

1. Under international law, they retain their legal status as refugees even when they gain citizenship in a country of refuge. Sari Hanafi, "Rethinking the Palestin-

ians Abroad as a Diaspora: The Relationships Between the Diaspora and the Palestinian Territories," in *Anthropology of the Diaspora*, Andre Misho, ed. (Stanford, Calif.: Stanford University Press, 2003), 14–15 (draft pagination).

2. The Russian Leo Pinsker (1821–91), who founded the Lovers of Zion Movement, wrote: "The foreigner claims hospitality, which he can repay in the same coin in his own country. The Jew can make no such return; consequently, he can make no claim to hospitality. . . . Since the Jew is nowhere at home . . . he remains an alien everywhere. That he himself . . . was born in the country does not alter this fact in the least" (*Auto-Emancipation*, quoted in Arthur Hertzberg, ed., *The Zionist Idea* [Westport, Conn.: Greenwood, 1959], 186–87).

3. See Edna Bonacich, "A Theory of Middleman Minorities," *American Sociological Review* 38 (1973): 583–94; Edna Bonacich and John Modell, *The Economic Basis of Ethnic Solidarity: Small Business in the Japanese American Community* (Berkeley: University of California Press, 1980); Walter P. Zenner, *Minorities in the Middle: A Cross-Cultural Analysis* (Albany: State University of New York Press, 1991).

4. Laurie Brand, *Palestinians in the Arab World: Institution Building and the Search for State* (New York: Columbia University Press, 1988); Bassma Kodmani-Darwish, *La Diaspora palestinienne* (Paris: Presses Universitaires de France, 1997); Elia Zureik, *Palestinian Refugees and the Peace Process* (Institute for Palestine Studies, 1996), www.ciaonet.org/wps/zue01/.

5. The Protocol for the Treatment of Palestinians in Arab States, adopted by the Council of Foreign Ministers, cited in Human Rights Watch, *Policy on the Right of Return* (New York, 2001), 2, http://www.hrw.org/campaigns/israel/return/arab-rtr.htm; Abbas Shiblak, "Residency Status and Civil Rights of Palestinian Refugees," *Journal of Palestine Studies* 99 (spring 1996): 38.

6. Kuwait recruited the first four Palestinian teachers in 1937 to staff the first two public schools. Shamlan V. Alessa, *The Manpower Problem in Kuwait* (London: Kegan Paul International, 1981), 57.

7. The government sent recruiters to scout for qualified personnel and offer incentives to attract them. Salah Khalaf related how the director of instruction came to Gaza and hired him away from his teaching position in 1959. Abu Iyad with Eric Rouleau, *My Home, My Land* (New York: Times Books, 1978), 28. Alessa (*Manpower Problem*, 44) notes that in the 1950s the government provided high wages, rent-free homes, free water and utilities, and sometimes free cars to much-needed managers and academics.

8. Shafeeq N. Ghabra, *Palestinians in Kuwait: The Family and the Politics of Survival* (Boulder, Colo.: Westview, 1987), 66. He points out that, until June 1961, Britain controlled visas to Kuwait through its consulates in Jerusalem and Baghdad. Persons who lacked formal contracts could not get visas and therefore had to take the "underground railway" through Iraq, depicted in harrowing detail by Ghassan Kanafani in "Men in the Sun."

9. Low-skilled laborers from Iraq and Iran outnumbered Palestinians. Brand (*Palestinians in the Arab World*, 115–16) says that 95 percent of the "Jordanians" were really Palestinian. Abdul-Reda Assiri, *The Government and Politics of Kuwait* (Kuwait: n.p., 1996), 138; Hassan Ali al-Ebraheem, *Kuwait and the Gulf* (Washington, D.C.: Croom Helm, 1984), 71; Peter Mansfield, *Kuwait* (London: Hutchison, 1990), 43, 45; Sharon Stanton Russell, "Politics and Ideology in Migration Policy Formulation: The Case of Kuwait," *International Migration Review* 23:1 (1989): 27; Yann Le Troquer and Rozenn Hommery al-Oudat, "From Kuwait to Jordan: The Palestinians' Third Exodus," *Journal of Palestine Studies* 111 (spring 1999): 37–38; see also their "Du Koweït à Jordanie: Le Retour suspendu des Palestinians," *Revue d'études palestiniennes* 14 (winter 1998): 54–70.

10. A labor office opened in 1954 and the Ministry of Labor and Social Affairs in 1955, which issued work permits. At that point, 60 percent of the workers had entered Kuwait illegally. Alessa, *Manpower Problem*, 32.

11. Brand, *Palestinians in the Arab World*, 115; Alessa, *Manpower Problem*, 34; Le Troquer and al-Oudat, "From Kuwait," 38, give slightly lower figures.

12. Ghabra, *Palestinians in Kuwait*, 76.

13. That figure includes all Jordanian passport holders. Brand, *Palestinians in the Arab World*, 116, and Alessa, *Manpower Problem*, 34; Le Troquer and al-Oudat's figures ("From Kuwait," p. 38) are slightly lower. Al-Ebraheem (*Kuwait*, 73) notes that Arabs were 42 percent of the population in 1975 and 80 percent of the expatriates. Jordanians/Palestinians far outnumbered Egyptians, who were the next largest Arab community, at 6 percent of the total population and 11.6 percent of the foreigners. Walid E. Moubarak, "Kuwait's Quest for Security, 1961–1973" (dissertation, Indiana University, 1979), 132, 135 on the overall figures in Kuwait.

14. By 1965, a third of the Palestinians in Kuwait were female (Alessa, *Manpower Problem*, 34). This pattern was evident in the political asylum cases I reviewed as an expert witness. For example, A.Q.'s parents fled from Ramleh to Syria in 1948, where they became UNRWA-registered refugees. A.Q.'s father used his Syrian-issued travel document to go to Kuwait in 1958, bringing his family there in 1963. In 1957, J.I.'s father left Rafidia, a village near Nablus, to work as an engineer in Kuwait; his family joined him in 1961.

15. Asylum seeker A.D., born in Nablus in May 1967, was only a month old when his parents and five siblings fled to Jordan and then to Kuwait. M.Q.'s parents fled Gaza after the war, on Egyptian laissez-passers. On three-year (renewable) temporary residency permits, they entered Kuwait, where they opened a grocery store. M.Q. and his siblings were born in Kuwait.

16. Another indication of their settled presence was that only 10 percent sent part of their salaries to nonresident wives and children; Le Troquer and al-Oudat, "From Kuwait," 50 n 19. Brand, *Palestinians in the Arab World*, 116; Alessa, *Manpower Problem*, 34; Philippe Gorokhoff, "Les Palestiniens au Kowëit," *Migrations et changements sociaux dans l'Orient arabe* (Beirut: CERMOC, 1985), 41, cited by Le Troquer and al-Oudat, "From Kuwait," 49 n 5. By way of contrast, the male/female gender ratio in Saudi Arabia for foreigners was 8:1 in 1985, as against 1.5:1 in Kuwait; Baquer Salman al-Najjar, "Population Policies in the Countries of the Gulf Co-operation Council," *Immigrants and Minorities* 12:2 (July 1993): 208, 210.

17. Asylum seekers reported that, if a Kuwaiti child wanted to sit in the front row in school, the Palestinian child would have to move to the back; if a bus was crowded, a Palestinian would stand when Kuwaitis entered; Kuwaitis would be served first in queues. See Anh Nga Longva, *Walls Built on Sand: Migration, Exclusion, and Society in Kuwait* (Boulder, Colo.: Westview, 1997), on this "studied deference" (179) and "submissiveness" (181) to Kuwaitis, which further reinforced the Kuwaiti ethos of dominance. Moubarak, "Kuwait's Quest," 144–47.

18. All foreign workers felt this fear of sudden deportation. Asylum seeker A.T. described how Kuwaiti sponsors took advantage of the *kafala* (sponsorship) system to pay Palestinians less than Kuwaitis and give them more difficult assignments. One contractor who owed him money even tried to get the police to deport him.

19. George T. Abed, "The Palestinians and the Gulf Crisis," *Journal of Palestine Studies* 68 (winter 1991): 37. Respected Palestinian leader Ali al-Hasan commented bitterly after the Gulf War that life had looked nice on the surface, but was really apartheid like South Africa (interview in Kuwait, May 27, 1991).

20. They included Khalid al-Hasan, general secretary of the Municipal Council Board, and Abd al-Muhsin al-Qattan, general inspector in the Ministry of Electric-

ity, both of whom became active in Fatah. Ghabra, *Palestinians in Kuwait*, 43, 47; Mansfield, *Kuwait*, 47, 61; Longva, *Walls*, 48. Naturalized citizens still faced disabilities: They only gained the right to vote in 1996. the families of full citizens must have resided in Kuwait since 1898 (1948 decree), later changed to 1920 (1959 law). That law limited the number of naturalized citizens to fifty per year. Moubarak (*Kuwait's Quest*, 140–41) notes that only 13,570 persons and their dependents were granted citizenship from 1961 to 1973, of whom 168 were Palestinian. That was far fewer than the 1,655 Iraqis and 1,320 Iranians who gained Kuwaiti citizenship.

21. Anh Nga Longva, "Keeping Migrant Workers in Check: The Kafala System in the Gulf," *Middle East Report* (summer 1999): 20–22; and idem, *Walls*, 97.

22. U.S. Department of State, *Country Report on Human Rights Practices* (1990), 1550, reported that some persons held in the deportation center had been there at least five years.

23. Mary Ann Tétreault, "Kuwait: The Morning After," *Current History* 91:561 (January 1992): 8; Longva, *Walls*, 78. Asylum seeker H.Y.'s father ran a trucking business, owned by a Kuwaiti, and another asylum seeker worked in his uncle's grocery store, licensed by a Kuwaiti. In some cases, both parties contributed capital and divided the annual profits. In other cases, the expatriate provided all the capital, expertise, labor, and management; the Kuwaiti signed the documents to register the business, rent the premises, and hire laborers (Longva, *Walls*, 68; Alessa, *Manpower Problem*, 45).

24. Asylum affidavit by A.T. Palestinians lived primarily in Hawalli, Nugra, and Farwaniyya. In 1981, 73 percent of the Hawalli residents were foreign, whereas only 21 percent of the residents of Jahra (a lower-class *bidoon* area [*bidoom* are indigenous residents lacking citizenship]) were foreign; Al-Ebraheem, *Kuwait*, 72. New suburbs for Kuwaitis had superior infrastructure and schools; Alessa, *Manpower Problem*, 47. Shaw J. Dallal describes the Hawalli "ghetto" in *Scattered Like Seeds* (Syracuse, N.Y.: Syracuse University Press, 1998).

25. Alessa, *Manpower Problem*, 54; Assiri, *Government*, (1996), 139–40.

26. Alessa, *Manpower Problem*, 46; Crystal, 59, 60; Longva, *Walls*, 78.

27. Alessa (*Manpower Problem*, 44) notes that in the late 1970s, an illiterate Kuwaiti school guard earned three times as much as an Arab high school teacher with a BA/BSc degree. Longva (*Walls*, 55), however, indicates that the monthly salaries in 1983 of Kuwaitis, Lebanese, and Syrians were 412–48 Kuwaiti dinars (KD), followed by Palestinians, Europeans, and Americans, at 358–62 KD, then Egyptians at 251 KD, and Indians, Pakistanis, and Bangladeshis at 192–201 KD.

28. Le Troquer and al-Oudat, "From Kuwait," 42. The Palestinian share of the teaching staff had been 50 percent in 1965, when only 10 percent of the teachers were Kuwaiti. See also Al-Ebraheem, *Kuwait*, 76; Alessa, *Manpower Problem*, 19–23. Alessa (4) notes that Palestinian Jordanians (22.5 percent of the foreign labor force in Kuwait) held 41 percent of the clerical positions in the government and 35 percent of professional and executive positions in the government; they were 21 percent of workers in sales and manufacturing; only 9 percent of service workers; and 2 percent of workers in agriculture, fishing, and animal husbandry.

29. Brand gives the Palestinian share as 30 percent of teachers in 1975, whereas Jacqueline S. Ismail, in *Kuwait* (Syracuse, N.Y.: Syracuse University Press, 1982), 137, says 25 percent. Ismail notes that Kuwaitis constituted 32 percent of the teachers in 1971–72 but only 28 percent in 1988–89: the absolute number of Kuwaiti teachers had increased, but the number of schools had also grown and the demand for teachers had increased.

30. Alessa notes (*Manpower Problem*, 24, 69) Kuwaitis' low demand for teachers' training and the difficulty of persuading them to enroll in vocational schools, in

contrast to commercial schools. Teaching was unattractive to Kuwaiti males, as it involved hard work and long hours. The government offered 35 percent salary bonuses to persuade Kuwaitis to become teachers. Kuwaitis also rejected becoming nurses, carpenters, and plumbers, but clerical staffs were 44 percent Kuwaiti.

31. Longva (*Walls*, 65) states that Kuwait University made new Kuwaiti Ph.D. holders deans and professors, displacing senior expatriates.

32. Alessa (*Manpower Problem*, 19–23) points out that although the number of Kuwaitis in administration, management, and professions more than doubled from 1970 to 1985, their share of those categories did not increase.

33. Ghabra, *Palestinians in Kuwait*, 140; Brand, *Palestinians in the Arab World*, 120. In 1978–79 (Alessa, *Manpower Problem*, 58, 61), after special Palestinian schools were closed but just before these new restrictions, 32 percent of the students in public schools were foreign and 18.4 percent were Palestinian. The next largest group was Egyptian; they constituted 2 percent of all students.

34. Brand, *Palestinians in the Arab World*, 114; Moubarak, "Kuwait's Quest," 143; Alessa, *Manpower Problem*, 62. The PLO operated (under Kuwaiti government supervision) eight schools with 4,721 children in 1968, which grew to twenty-two schools with 16,000 children in 1975–76. Asylum seeker A.D., born in 1967, resented this system: Palestinian children started school a year later than Kuwaiti children, attended classes from 4 p.m. to 9 p.m., and were not provided with free meals or school buses.

35. Two secondary Palestinian schools with 1,396 students served male students in 1976 (Alessa, *Manpower Problem*, 62). Female Palestinians attended regular Kuwaiti secondary schools.

36. Brand, *Palestinians in the Arab World*, 121.

37. Ghabra, *Palestinians in Kuwait*, 105, 141; Brand, *Palestinians in the Arab World*, 121. In 1985, 4,264 Palestinians graduated from secondary school; 7–10 percent entered Kuwait University. Among asylum seekers, A.D. studied mechanical engineering in the United States; A.T., engineering in Egypt and then in the United States; J.I., civil engineering in India. The brother of I.S. had a GPA of 86, three marks short of the minimum to enter Kuwait University; instead, he studied in the United States. Family and town organizations, the Fund for Palestinian Higher Education, and GUPW raised money for scholarships to enable students to study abroad. For example, the Hebron Fund financed thirty students from 1976 to 1985.

38. Ghabra, *Palestinians in Kuwait*, 76; Longva, *Walls*, 158; Moubarak, "Kuwait's Quest," 143. Ghabra makes an interesting comparison with the Jewish diaspora's emphasis on human capital (77).

39. Longva (*Walls*, 30) gives the total in 1990 as 510,000 Palestinians and 552,000 Asians (of diverse nationalities), with the Jordanian/Palestinian profile typical of a long-term residency rather than transient labor. Seventy-eight percent lived in family units, and 21 percent were in the labor force. In contrast, only 15–16 percent of Egyptians, Sri Lankans, and Filipinos lived in family units, whereas 84 percent were in the labor force.

40. A 1978 law to restrict family immigration also had little effect. Ismail, *Kuwait*, 143.

41. Russell, "Politics and Ideology," 721, citing her "International Migration in Europe, Central Asia, The Middle East and North Africa" (World Bank, Population and Human Resources Division, 1992). Some 126,000 Asians entered Kuwait during that period, many taking jobs at the bottom of the service sector that Palestinians and other Arabs rejected. Andrzej Kapiszewski, *Nationals and Expatriates* (Reading, U.K.: Ithaca, 2001), on Asian migrants.

42. Al-Najjar, "Population Policies," 202, 207, 210. If *bidoon* were counted as Kuwaitis, foreigners would amount to 60 percent of the population.

43. Tétreault, "Kuwait: The Morning After," 9.

44. *News from Middle East Watch*, November 16, 1990, 9. Kuwaitis were still only 15 percent of physicians and 10 percent of nurses and lab technicians, most of whom came from Asia.

45. Longva, *Walls*, 124; Moubarak, "Kuwait's Quest," 136, 138.

46. Asylum affidavit of A.A.T., 1994.

47. Abu Iyad, *My Home*, 38–39, 45. Fatah's Yasir Arafat was an engineer in the Ministry of Public Works, Faruq al-Qaddumi headed a department in the Ministry of Public Health, and Khalil Ibrahim al-Wazir (Abu Jihad) and Salah Khalaf (Abu Iyad) were secondary school teachers.

48. Le Troquer and al-Oudat, "From Kuwait," 42. Family, village, and town organizations are detailed in Ghabra, *Palestinians in Kuwait*. Brand details the PLO-linked organizations.

49. George T. Abed, "The Palestinians and the Gulf Crisis," *Journal of Palestine Studies* 68 (winter 1991): 36.

50. This totaled $122.5 million, 1965–89. Abdul-Reda Assiri, *Kuwait's Foreign Policy* (Boulder, Colo.: Westview, 1990), 40.

51. Mansfield, *Kuwait*, 66; Assiri (*Kuwait's Foreign Policy*, 147) states that Kuwait contributed $701 million to the PLO, 1964–1989; $15 million to the occupied territories, 1978–83; $3 million to victims of the civil war in Jordan, 1970; $1 million to Palestinians in Lebanon, 1981; $600,000 to UNRWA in 1981 and 1984; $300,000 to the Arab Institute in Jerusalem, 1981; and $5 million for the intifada, 1988.

52. In 1988, the PLO received $49.8 million, which was reduced to $24.9 million in 1989; Assiri, *Government*, 147. This was one factor in the PLO's failure to rally to Kuwait's defense in 1990.

53. The government allowed the PFLP to open an office in Kuwait, after it mediated tensions between Fatah and PFLP in 1988 (Assiri, *Government*, 52). Abu Nidal operatives killed the head of the PLO office in Kuwait in 1978 and tried to kill the next head in 1980; the group also attacked Kuwaiti diplomats abroad in 1982 (ibid., 158, 160; Kapiszewski, *Nationals*, 138).

54. For information on the occupation period and the PLO's stance, see Ann M. Lesch, "Palestinians in Kuwait," *Journal of Palestine Studies* 80 (summer 1991): 42–54; Lesch, "Contrasting Reactions to the Persian Gulf Crisis," *The Middle East Journal* 45:1 (winter 1991); Ghabra, "The Iraqi Occupation of Kuwait; An Eyewitness Account," *Journal of Palestine Studies* 78 (winter 1991): 112–25; Ghabra, "Palestinians in Kuwait; Victims of Conflict," *Middle East International* 397 (April 5, 1991): 21; Physicians for Human Rights, *Iraq-Occupied Kuwait: The Health Care Situation* (Somerville, Mass., March 1991); The Economist Intelligence Unit, *Iraq Country Report* 1 (London, 1991); interviews with PLO officials Ali al-Hasan (May 27, 1991) and Suhail Khoury (May 28, 1991) and Kuwaiti human-rights activists Mubarak al-Adwani (May 21, 1991) and Sa'ud al-Enezy (May 26, 1991).

55. The Iraq established *al-jaish al-sha'abi* as a neighborhood guard force, in which Iraqis and some *bidoon* were forced to participate. The Palestine embassy and homes of senior Palestinian officials were protected by forty Palestine Liberation Army soldiers, brought from Baghdad at the embassy's request. Kuwaitis saw those guards as proof of the PLO's collaboration with Iraq (interview with embassy official Suhail Khoury, May 28, 1991).

56. For example, eighteen-year-old H.Y., who became a volunteer firefighter, smuggled guns out of a Kuwaiti friend's home by pretending to enter to investigate a fire. A.M., an air-traffic controller, smuggled Kuwaitis out of the airport on August 3, slipped Kuwaitis through roadblocks, and brought munitions to fighters. Others protected the property of Kuwaiti neighbors and businesses.

57. Interview with Ali al-Hasan, May 27, 1991.

58. Ali al-Hasan (May 27, 1991) said that he asked Kuwaitis to help Palestinians financially so that they would not need to work. The Palestinian Martyrs' Foundation aided eleven thousand families whose breadwinners were unemployed. Mubarak al-Adwani (May 21, 1991), who was active in the resistance, said that he did not dare enter the segregated *bidoon* and Palestinian neighborhoods to provide food and money, for fear of being captured by Iraqi security forces.

59. A.T. said that, while buying food at a store, a Kuwaiti woman threatened: "When the Sabah family returns, we'll get our revenge."

60. The Kuwaiti supervisor told A.N. to report to a government dental clinic on August 2, 1990, and later instructed him to work at Mubarak al-Kabir Hospital. When they last talked by phone, on October 10, she said that the situation was out of control (i.e., Iraqis were running the hospital) and A.N. should do what he thought best. Caught between the Iraqis, who killed doctors who refused to treat Iraqi soldiers, and the resistance, which threatened to kill him for working, A.N. fled the country. Iraqi officials similarly forced bank employee M.A.T. to work, which led to death threats by the resistance; he quit on September 9 and fled through Jordan to the United States.

61. Some three thousand Palestinian teachers and five thousand children showed up when schools opened on September 1, 1990. Kuwaitis were particularly infuriated when 1,500 Palestinians registered for Kuwait University; it actually did not open because of the faculty boycott. In November, Iraq ordered teachers to report for work anywhere in Iraq, a measure that led the remaining teachers to hide or flee.

62. The Economist Intelligence Unit, *Iraq Country Report* 1 (London, 1991), 7.

63. Asylum affidavit by A.T.

64. Human Rights Watch/Middle East (HRW), *A Victory Turned Sour* (New York, September 1991); National Committee for Defending Palestinian Human Rights in Kuwait, *Memorandum on the Situation of the Palestinians in Kuwait* (Kuwait, May 1991); Michael Dumper, "End of an Era," *Journal of Palestine Studies* 81 (autumn 1991): 120–23; Lawyers Committee for Human Rights, *Laying the Foundations: Human Rights in Kuwait* (New York, 1993); interviews, Palestinian embassy (May 28, 1991) and Siham Khalil (May 27, 1991).

65. *The Independent* (London), March 4, 1991; a U.S. diplomat quoted in the *Washington Post*, March 15, 1991; Office of Asylum Affairs, U.S. State Department, advisory opinion (November 1998) concerning H.Y. Basil ("Rambo"), son of the crown prince (the martial law governor), led one vigilante group. Examples include M.Q., age fifteen, kidnapped the day after liberation while he celebrated on the street with friends: a Kuwaiti civilian looked at his ID, called him a traitor, and hauled him to a police station, where he was beaten and sodomized for three days. Civilians stopped H.Y.'s brother at a checkpoint; they fractured his arm and forced a bottle into his rectum. Frequently, men who drove their cars to buy gas never returned home; their bodies were found later on the roadside. The Riqqa cemetery logbook listed forty-nine unidentified bodies "killed" or "executed" during March 1991.

66. For example, Dr. Nazmi Salim Khurshaid, a fifteen-year physician in the health ministry, was seized during a meeting in the hospital and beaten to death in the military prison; dentist Dr. Salim Mukhtar was shot dead in his car; and the female director of a secondary school was killed after being tortured for a week. HRW's *A Victory Turned Sour* provides details.

67. Tétreault, "Kuwait: The Morning After," 8. Kuwaitis received back pay promptly and were exempted from paying for utilities during the occupation.

68. Three hundred Palestinians had been enrolled at the university. Younger pupils could not afford $4,500-a-year private schools. Dumper, "End of an Era," 121.

69. *New York Times*, March 4, 1991. The institutions closed included the Palestine embassy, Fatah office, Palestine Red Crescent Society, Martyrs Foundation, GUPW, and GUPS.

70. Another sixty thousand foreigners were also stuck in Kuwait. Figures from Ghabra, "The Iraqi Occupation," 124.

71. Interview with a mother in May 1991. The father had lived in Kuwait since 1959; their nine children had grown up there. Without their passports they could not sell their shop, car, and furniture in order to finance the flight and their resettlement. The Lawyers Committee for Human Rights (*Laying the Foundations*, 31–33) estimated that ten thousand people from many nationalities were deported by the end of 1992. When the International Committee of the Red Cross visited the deportation prison in December 1992, its 566 detainees included forty-seven Palestinians with Jordanian passports and nine Palestinians with Egyptian travel documents.

72. The deadline was later extended until June 1992. Without the permit, illegal residents faced a $7-a-day fine, detention, and/or deportation. The fine might be waived if the person agreed to leave.

73. U.S. State Department, human-rights report, 1998. The Talha deportation center closed in 1997–98; deportees were subsequently housed in the state security facility.

74. Fifteen-year-old M.Q. was pulled off public buses four times in 1992–93 going to or from school for questioning in police stations, as the police computer labeled him a "collaborator." He was so traumatized that he failed his senior year. When he turned eighteen, his uncle's Kuwaiti *kafil* sponsored his temporary residency, but the Ministry of Interior refused to renew it in 1999 and detained him in the state security office, where he was blindfolded, beaten, and cursed as a traitor and Palestinian dog. His uncle bribed officials to release him, after which he fled to the United States.

75. Affidavit of A.Q., who held poorly paid private-sector jobs after 1991 and finally left with his family in 1999.

76. That figure includes many who left Kuwait in 1990, before or during the Iraqi occupation. Le Troquer and al-Oudat, "From Kuwait"; Lamia Radi, "Les Palestiniens due Koweit en Jordanie," *Monde Arabe: Maghreb-Machrek* 144 (April–June 1994): 55–66; Gil Feiler, "Palestinian Employment Prospects," *The Middle East Journal* 47:4 (autumn 1993).

77. A total of 23,981 went to the West Bank and 3,380 went to the Gaza Strip (Le Troquer and al-Oudat, "From Kuwait," 49 n 10). Palestine Human Rights Information Center, "A Bittersweet Coming Home: The Experience of Palestinians Returning from the Gulf," *From the Field* (October 1993), states that thirty thousand to forty thousand returned to the occupied territories from *all* the Gulf States, of whom three-quarters came from Kuwait: 86 percent of those who went to the West Bank and 62 percent of those who went to the Gaza Strip came from Kuwait. Daoud Kuttab assesses the anticipated negative impact of losing remittances, "In the Aftermath of the War," *Journal of Palestinian Studies* 20:4 80 (summer 1991): 115–23.

78. If they left Gaza before June 1967, they never held Israeli residency permits. If they left afterward, they would lose the permits if they did not return frequently to renew them. Their children and grandchildren, born outside Gaza, had no right to live in Gaza.

79. Kuwait threatened to deport them but, under international pressure, agreed that they could remain. Office of Asylum Affairs, U.S. State Department, advisory opinion November 1998, for H.Y.

80. Ultimately, Japanese gained citizenship rights in the United States, many Indians returned to East Africa, and Jews secured citizenship rights in Western Europe and a political identity through the creation of Israel.

81. "Return" was not really feasible for most European Jews and Indians and was difficult for Japanese; "statehood" became the preferred option for many Jews.

82. Abu Iyad, *My Home*, 40.

83. Ibid., 224.

84. Proposed in 1981 by Alessa, *Manpower Problem*, 110. He also proposed that skilled, professional Arabs gain permanent residency after five years and citizenship after ten years.

85. Susan M. Akram, "Temporary Protection and Its Applicability to the Palestinian Refugee Case," *Brief* 4 (Bethlehem: Badil, n.d.), 6.

Chapter 9
The Vision of Return: Reflections on the Mass Immigration to Israel from the Former Soviet Union

Ze'ev Khanin

The traditional Jewish concept of aliyah (literally, "ascent" in Hebrew), the process of Jewish return from exile (the Diaspora) to the land of their forefathers and never-forgotten motherland of Jewish civilization, became a cornerstone of Zionist ideology. In the spirit of this ideology, Israel officially defines as an *oleh* (a repatriate or returnee) and grants immediate full citizenship to any Jew who decided to move to Israel from any country of the world. However, from the very beginning, Israel, as a modern liberal democratic state, had to broaden substantially the legal meaning of the *oleh* category. According to the Israeli Law of Return, adopted in 1950 with amendments in 1954 and 1970, *oleh* status and the relevant rights and obligations are available not only to Jews but also to non-Jewish spouses of Jews and descendants of mixed families in the second and third generations. This broad definition of *oleh* (plural, *olim*) far exceeds the traditional halachic definition of a Jew, which was also incorporated into the Law of Return, as a person who was born to a Jewish mother or converted to Judaism. According to tradition, such conversion also means joining the Jewish people in ethnic terms. This way, the idea of aliyah as the Jewish return to the historical homeland is different from immigration, meaning the simple resettlement in a foreign country, because it expresses the essence of modern Jewish nationalism and is part of the political identity of a revitalized Jewish statehood in the Land of Israel/Palestine.

Russian Jews were important since the dawn of the Zionist movement and were often a critical part of this trend. Jewish immigrants from Russia and other Eastern European countries had a great impact on the social demography of the Jewish population of Israel and Israeli society as a whole. Since the eighteenth century, with the aliyah of Yehuda Hasid, Jews of Russian origin have played an important role in the history of Palestinian Jewry. Jewish Zionist immigration from Russia, which started with the repatriation of the Bilu group in 1882, experienced variations but never ended, even during World Wars I and II. According to Jewish Agency data, about 1.1 million repatriates came to the Land of Israel from Russia/USSR/CIS (Commonwealth of Independent States) in the twentieth century alone.[1] The breakdown of the Soviet Union and subsequent mass Jewish emigration from the USSR and its successor states turned Israel into the largest center of Russian-speaking Jewry in the world. As of 2002, about one million Israelis of USSR/CIS origin make up about 15 percent of the Israeli population.[2] Overall, about half of Israeli Jews are in some way related to Russia, the USSR, or their successor states.

This large group does not belong to one *edah*, a term used to define subethnic and ethnic Jewish communities that enjoy special status in the Israeli socioeconomic and political hierarchy. There are substantial differences not only between "Russian Sefardis," who are originally from Central Asia and the Caucasus, and "Russian Ashkenazis," who are from Russia north of the Caucasus and Ukraine, Moldova, Byelorussia, and the Baltics. Moreover, there are important differences between the waves of immigration, concerning not only culture, preservation of religious tradition, and ethnic identity but also the vision of the Land and the State of Israel and their place in Jewish public consciousness.

The Historical Legacy and Contemporary Implications

From this point of view, we may define some major categories among Jewish repatriates from Russian Eastern Europe. The first category is represented by those who came before the establishment of the state and during the first decades of statehood and whose vision of return to the homeland of their forefathers was motivated by the various streams of practical Zionism of the early twentieth century. These people played a crucial role in constructing the political systems, economic infrastructure, and cultural codes of the Jewish national home in Palestine and the State of Israel as well as of the local version of the melting pot of Jewish Diaspora on the basis of Zionist Hebrew culture.

Soon after the Bolshevik revolution in Russia, however, Jews who remained there became separated from Zionist activities for fifty years. They were also separated from Israel and the rest of the Jewish world. This was because, starting in the 1920s, Soviet authorities suppressed Zionist organizations and organized Jewish life. Thus, those Soviet Jews who, after a long separation, began to come en masse to Israel in the late 1960s and 1970s and then again in the 1990s were not only different from Israelis whose roots were in Asia, Africa, or Western Europe; in terms of language, identity, and culture, they were also very different from the descendants of those who came from Russia in the first decades of the twentieth century to (re-)establish the Jewish home. Thus, if Russian origin was identified previously with mainstream Israeli politics and society, Russian-speaking immigrants of the 1970s, and especially of the 1990s, had their own cultural and political values and interests that were different from those of the earlier immigrants. Consequently, they captured an autonomous niche in the Israeli political structure and made a substantial impact on local politics, society, and collective identity. The arrival of this educated and highly qualified group not only promoted the rapid development of high-tech and military industries, education, culture, and health-care systems but also opened new internal and external markets. The immigration of hundreds of thousands of people with different cultural backgrounds became a challenge to Israeli society, contributing to the current tense ideological discussions about the future of Israel as the Jewish state.

These Jews were a product of the Soviet system and a target of discrimination by those authorities. This included the long-term suppression of the main means of Jewish national identification (religion, culture, education) and the suppression of any seeds of organized Jewish life. However, this subethnic entity of Eastern European Jewish life, although deeply assimilated, Russified, and considerably alienated from Jewish culture, still enjoyed a specific form of Jewish identity. This identity was formed by what remained of local Jewish cultural traditions and by pressure from the local social and political environment as well as self-determination as Jews in ethnic terms, deeply rooted in social memory and experience. This Soviet Jewish identity was formed by an imbalance between the negative and positive sources of their national consciousness. Whereas the negative element (opposition between "us" and "them") was nurtured intensely by the state and by administrative and popular anti-Semitism, positive sources of identity—culture, traditions, religion, language—were disappearing swiftly.

These conditions made such factors as historical memory and political identification much more important: on the one hand, the memory of the Holocaust and the interpretation of its consequences; on the other hand, attitudes toward the State of Israel. Over time, these two issues—one the source of crisis and the other a means of resolving the crisis—merged into a national consciousness that actively absorbed the vestiges of national tradition and filled the void of Soviet Jewish identity. Soviet propaganda equated Zionism with fascism, but for Soviet Jews, fascist terror and Arab terror and the struggle against Nazism and Israel's struggle for survival merged into a unified worldview. Thus, in April and September 1972, refuseniks organized crowded meetings in Babi Yar devoted to both the twenty-ninth anniversary of the Warsaw Ghetto uprising and to the memory of Israeli athletes who were killed by Arab terrorists during the Olympic games in Munich.[3] This view toward terrorism by Arabs, some of whose leaders cooperated with German fascists during World War II, as a prolongation of the Holocaust was an important factor in Soviet Jewish identity and remained after the Soviet Union disappeared. An Israeli Russian intellectual declared: "Many . . . [Soviet] Jews agree on one point: there is no way to forgive the Germans' crimes. Equally, it is impossible to buy an armistice from professional killers who want to annihilate us under the green banner of Islam. . . . The enemy will not let us ransom ourselves, neither with gold, nor with territories, nor with 'humanitarian concessions.' "[4]

Zionist feeling was widespread among Soviet Jews after World War II. This had little in common with the "far-flung Zionist underground" that the KGB invented for the Soviet leadership. Few Soviet Jews participated, in the full sense of the term, in Zionist political activity. The Zionism of even the most nationally oriented Soviet Jews was not so much acquired as it was an inner, emotional tie to Israel. This form of popular Zionism, in many ways a product of public and state anti-Semitism, was integral to the value system that nurtured Jewish national and ethnic consciousness. Characteristic of popular Zionism was an expatriate mentality, a view that Jews living in the USSR would always be seen by the local Slavic population as strangers and that their real homeland was Israel. There were numerous examples of these aspirations. On February 26, 1949, for example, a large group of Jews met in the yard of the Kharkov synagogue, recently closed by the government. A woman declaimed: "They drove us out and closed the synagogue; they despise us; there is no help and no one will extend any. Only Chaim Weizmann, the president of Palestine, who is defending us in our native land, is our protector. We are here temporarily; we are guests here. . . . I am not afraid. I am a Jewess and I defend Jews. I declare outright that I do not want to live here."[5]

The Six-Day War, in 1967, was a dramatic catalyst for the Israel-centeredness of Soviet Jewish consciousness. Israel's victory evoked an outburst of Jewish national pride. Operative documents of the KGB informed Communist Party organs about the outburst of "Zionist" sentiment in numerous cities. Observers noted the desire of some Jewish youths to immediately "join the Israeli army fighting against the Arabs." Moreover, speaking at a closed meeting of top Communist Party officials, party politburo member Vladimir Shelest used as an example remarks made by "some Jewish Communists": "Our people [the Israelis] have reached the Suez Canal."[6] In general, the analysis of statements by "citizens of Jewish nationality with regard to events in the Middle East" led Soviet leaders to unpalatable conclusions: "The majority opinion is rapturous in nature, with praise of the Israeli government's 'resolute actions.' "[7] The feeling of this generation of Soviet Jews was indicated by Haim Spivakovskii of Kiev in his letter to the United Nations:

I am a Jew—not a member of the Russian intelligentsia or a Soviet citizen of Jewish origin—but a Jew first and foremost. A Jew by birth and, to a considerable degree, by upbringing and on the basis of my worldview as well. . . . On the basis of my awareness of belonging to Jewry, I declare my human and national right to leave and make my home in Israel. . . . The idea that we should come back and should re-create our state was my first idea [which] came to me just after I have learned about our Holocaust eighteen centuries ago, and about *galut* [exile]. . . . Among the issues concerning the Middle East . . . is the fate of the Arabs living in camps for displaced persons. They include one or two generations who have already been born outside of Palestine. Nevertheless, many think of them as having been deprived of their motherland, in spite of the fact that fourteen Arab states surround them and that their historical motherland literally begins after Amman. I, however, have one, sole historical Motherland [namely, Israel]. . . . After all, I, too, am a descendant of displaced persons, only in the seventieth generation.[8]

The majority of the representatives of the wave of Jewish immigration to Israel in the 1970s largely shared this deeply positive, romanticized view of Israel, which existed at the mass level and was a key source nourishing Soviet Jewish national consciousness. The majority of this group of immigrants and their ideological and intellectual elite, some of whom participated in the underground Zionist movement, were partisans of the idea of *kibbutz galuyot* (melting pot of the Jewish Diaspora) in Israel. However, their identity included contradictory elements. On the one hand, the majority demonstrated strong Zionist aspirations and came to Israel to be an undivided part of the local Jewish society. On the other hand, many combined the crises of the traditional "Zionism of distress" with a classical approach to the Jewish Diaspora as the place from which Jews needed to be physically rescued. Thus, they had some "new Zionist" ideas to suggest to Israeli society: combining ethnic Russian Jewish values (high educational, culture, and technical progress-oriented standards and post–Six Day War Russian Jewish nationalism) with the Zionist political identity of Israel.[9]

However, this elite group met with little interest from either the Israeli establishment or the Russian Jewish immigrant masses. In practical terms, this meant that Russian Jewish immigrants of the "second wave" were ready to accept the existing rules of the game, dictated by the melting-pot philosophy.[10]

Jewish immigrants of the third wave, who started to come in great numbers in the 1990s, were quite different from those of the 1970s. Their philosophy was more relaxed toward ideological issues, including Zionism. As one immigrant put it: "My Zionism comes from the fact that I live in this country, pay taxes, and my son serves in the Israeli army."[11] It would be incorrect, however, to say that these immigrants were and are largely motivated by economic reasons and lack Zionist sentiment. The reasons for the huge Russian Jewish exodus were much more complicated than that, and national motives enjoyed a respectable place among them. One nonmaterial factor was the effect of "lost and obtained Motherland": the transnational USSR was vanishing in the late 1980s and early 1990s into ethnic national states of Ukrainians, Russians, Georgians, Estonians, Uzbeks, and so on. Although they all asserted the U.S.-model of nation-building, many chose ethnic nationalism. This made many Jews think seriously about their ethnic and national identity, making a choice in favor of repatriation to Israel. Vadim Feldman, a founder of the informal Jewish movement in Ukraine in the late 1980s, noted an indicative case. He, as a journalist, interviewed a fourteen-year-old Ukrainian boy who lived next door to a newly opened Jewish school in Kiev. The journalist asked the boy whether he knew that Jews were leaving the USSR and Ukraine, where they had lived for at least a thousand years, and what he thought about this. The reply was shocking. "It was probably good for [the Jews] to be on a visit [here in Ukraine], but it is always better at home," said the boy. In our discussion, Feldman noted: "I have spent all my life in Ukraine. My grand-parents, all my predecessors lived and were buried here, and I think that this country is my homeland. However, this fourteen-year-old boy thinks that he is my host. . . . Although we [Jews] may consider ourselves citizens of this country, the titular population will never accept it, and nothing can be done about it. That is the reason for the Jewish exodus to Israel: it started and it cannot be stopped."[12]

These external circumstances activated latent national feelings in a certain part of the largely assimilated Russian Jewish immigrants of the early 1990s. These feelings acquired an ideological expression at the level of the cultural and political elites of the groups of Jewish activists, who had first appeared during perestroika. These people witnessed the explosion of political ethnicity in the Soviet Union, which split local societies not only along cultural lines but also along social, political, and class lines. Many Russian Jews of this generation participated in the process of reviving the Eastern European Jewish movement, which involved the establishment of schools, associations, and communities, and involvement in party politics in the USSR and the post-Soviet states. Thus, they did not see any ideological problem in applying to Israel their experience with organizational and political activity and did not consider that preserving Russian (or Soviet) Jewish identity in Israel and the Diaspora in any way contradicted Zionism.

It was also important that the beginning of mass aliyah in the 1990s occurred simultaneously with the legitimization in Israeli society of the idea of multiculturalism and social heterogeneity. Thus, the melting-pot perspective that had pressured the previous wave of Russian immigrants was not an obstacle to the recognition of a Russian-Jewish-Israeli identity. However, the "new Zionist" ideology of this group included Israeli patriotism and Jewish nationalism as important values. Furthermore, many Russian Jewish immigrants of this wave were dissatisfied with the shortage, as they saw it, of Jewish content and a growing postmodernist atmosphere in Israel.[13] This critical view was especially popular among those who joined the Jewish national movement between 1981 and 1987, when emigration was blocked, and shortly after it was allowed, and who composed a substantial part of the ideological and political leadership of the 1990s immigrants. Velvl Tchernin, a noted Yiddish poet, activist of the Moscow Zionist underground in the 1980s, and currently lecturer at Bar-Ilan University, summarized the feelings of disappointment with what they found in Israel: "Maybe the problem is that I am too Jewish and too little Israeli. I expect Israel not to be a surrogate of America—in this case I would better go to America, in order to get an original—but a realization of a sort of national dream, shared by my forefathers in shtetls of the Poltava and Kiev areas. Maybe that was what formed my priorities as well as the priorities of many other Israelis, who are still too Jewish."[14]

The situation changed again in the latter part of the 1990s, when a new group of immigrants from the CIS started to flow into Israel. Non-Jews and their highly assimilated Jewish family members are a substantial and still-growing part of these immigrants. Many representatives of this category of immigrants, headed by a marginal group of the 1990s Russian Jewish elite, participate in the trend toward a post-Zionist identity.

The Land of Israel in the Identity of the Russian Jews

To summarize, the varieties of Jewish identity among immigrants from the USSR/CIS, including those eligible to immigrate to Israel but who do not qualify in Israel as Jews, can be traced to the different meanings that Judaism and Israel had for the people before emigrating. The vision of return to the historical homeland was an aspect of their ethnic, national, cultural, and religious identity. This identity displayed various and often contradictory features. We must define at least five groups of contemporary Soviet and post-Soviet Jewry.[15]

1. Soviet Jewish identity was a result of the forced transformation of the (neo)traditional identity of Ashkenazi Eastern European Jewry (including its nationalist Yiddishist and Zionist angles) under the Soviet regime. This identification included the high value placed on ethnic Jewish affiliation, normally registered in internal identity cards; a very limited (or almost no) impact of the Jewish religion, despite a strongly negative view toward conversion to Christianity or Islam; and the high ethnic and symbolic value of the Yiddish language (although only the elder generation could communicate in this language) and remnants of Yiddish culture. This model of identification was neither Israel-centrist nor anti-Zionist and, at some point, included Israel as a positive image. This model weakened during the Soviet era as ethnic and cultural assimilation proceeded. However, those Jews who lived in areas appended to the USSR during World War II and who survived the Holocaust were better able to preserve their traditional Jewish identity, culture, and some elements of their communal infrastruc-

ture, including Zionist structures, than their counterparts who had lived in the USSR since the Bolshevik revolution.

2. A Hebrew or Israel-centrist model of identity first appeared in the form of a "Russian new Zionism" after the Six-Day War and, in the 1960s–1980s, was mainly represented by various underground Zionist movements (political, culturalist, and religious) and Hebrew language circles. After the massive repatriation of most of these activists to Israel in the 1970s and late 1980s, this model was mainly reproduced by activities in Israeli cultural and educational institutions. The Hebrew model was appropriated by young and middle-aged Russian Jews and is not identical to Israeli Jewish identity, where Hebrew is merely a national symbol.

3. The traditional identity of Oriental (Russian Sefardis) Jewish communities—Bukhara, Mountain, Georgian Jews, and others—demonstrates their low level of acculturation into Russian culture and their high level of preservation of their traditions, strong intra-communal solidarity, "natural" religiosity, and mastering of their native languages. The Land (much more than the State) of Israel had an important symbolic meaning for their identity. These communities, although representing only 6 percent of Soviet Jewry, composed about 40 percent of Russian immigrants in the 1960s–1980s. In Israel, this group often demonstrates models of social, cultural, and political behavior different from those of immigrants from the Slavic republics.

4. The "Diaspora-centered" Jewish identity, which includes an indifferent and sometimes even hostile approach to practical Zionism. The religious version of this identity is represented with a relatively new phenomenon of non- and anti-Zionist Jewish orthodoxy, modeling *haredi* communities in Israel, the United States, and Europe. The ideology of these relatively small groups (mainly composed of foreign citizens who live in the CIS and local Jews who returned to Judaism) includes the symbolic importance of the "Land of Israel" but normally rejects the contemporary Israeli Zionist state. In its secular version, this identity is shared by various neo-Yiddishist or spiritualist Judaism groups. This model, which is mainly spreading among intellectuals of Jewish and ethnically mixed origin, concentrates on the Yiddish language and culture as the material base for Jewish ethnic national identity without any specific reference to the Land or State of Israel.

5. Assimilationism is represented mainly among those Jews and persons of mixed origin who are totally integrated into and acculturated to Russian culture and Russian society, although they do have an understanding of their specific origin and sometimes even demonstrate Jewish sentiments. This anti-Zionist model usually comes from understanding that "Jews are Russian intelligentsia."

All these groups, which are represented now within the "Russian" immigrant community and its elite, construct the public and ideological agenda of this entity: the meaning of "repatriation," Zionism and national identity issues, the role of their Russian roots, and the national, cultural, and ethnic status of the Land and State of Israel as well as the approach to the Palestinian Arabs inside and outside the Green Line.

For many Russian Jews who had a deeply positive, even romanticized view of Israel that nourished Soviet Jewish national consciousness, the meeting with real Israeli society was an uneasy experience. The connection between *Yerushalayim shel mala* (Israel-related mythology and symbols) and *Yerushalayim shel mata* (the Israeli reality) was especially difficult for the Russian Jewish Zionist elite, both secular and religious. Immigrants of the second wave (1960s–1980s) and especially their intellectual and cultural elites experienced strong identity crises. These crises resulted from many factors: realizing the difference between imperial Soviet culture and the provincial character of Israeli culture; disappointment with the lack of Jewish content in Israeli political and social culture; and the lack of readiness of the local elite to dialogue with them and that elite's unwillingness to take seriously the immigrants' "new Zionism" and their solutions to crises of the traditional Israeli "Zionism of distress." Alexander Voronel, a prominent representative of this group and editor of *Twenty-Two*, a leading forum of the "new Russian Zionists" in Israel, commented: "The participants in the new 'Jewish revolution' in Russia exaggerated their intellectualism, rather than nationalism. . . . Former dissidents found 'justice' lacking in Israel. Technocrats found technical progress lacking in the country. People with strong Jewish roots found the 'Jewish spirit' (*Yiddishkait*) lacking there. Finally, religious neophytes found Judaism painfully lacking in the Jewish state."[16]

That might be a reason (together with many others) that more than a fifth of the most nationalistic Russian Jewish repatriates of the 1970s–1980s (those who immigrated from Ukraine, Byelorussia, and the Baltic states) left Israel ten to fifteen years after their immigration.

The situation changed in 1989, when the gates for Soviet Jewish emigration opened. Many of those hundreds of thousands of Russian Jews were, even more than previous immigrants, assimilated, Russified, and considerably alienated from Jewish culture, although they did have a specific form of Jewish consciousness. They had usually never had relations with any organized Jewish cultural or Zionist activities in their country of origin. As a result, a misleading stereotype of non-Zionist aliyah was created, which, in the spirit of the post-Zionist aspirations of a substantial part of the Israeli political, cultural, and intellectual elite, was characterized as immigration (*hagirah*) rather than returning home (aliyah). This stereotype usually insisted that this immigration lacked any national content and was motivated almost exclusively by pragmatic considerations. The picture, however, is more complicated than that.

Thus, emigration was an important facet of Jewish national life in the postwar USSR in general. Both the historical memory and the social experience of local Jewry led Jews to view emigration as the optimal form of national behavior. Among the factors that influenced this trend was the fact that many were survivors or descendants of survivors of the Holocaust. As a consequence, the Jewish psyche activated social reflexes of ethnic self-preservation during critical periods that led to migratory behavior. In 1990–91, this was strengthened by the "lost and obtained" homeland effect, since the transnational USSR dissolved into fifteen ethnic national post-Soviet states.[17] These trends can also be illustrated by sociological studies conducted in 1990–92 among potential emigrants within the USSR and new Russian immigrants in Israel. Economic reasons for emigration were stressed by 20–40 percent of respondents. Seventy percent mentioned lack of positive life prospects, disappointment in Soviet ideals and values, and the wish to reach the historical motherland. More than half emphasized anti-Semitism, political instability, and fear of totalitarianism, and 30–40 percent pointed to their desire to live a Jewish life in their national state.[18] Studies conducted in the late 1990s also showed the diversity of pull and push factors for Russian Jewish immigration to Israel, although the relative weight of economic and personal motives in 1996–2000 constantly grew at the expense of national, cultural, religious, and political considerations.[19]

In general, these reasons for leaving the USSR and post-Soviet states as well as various understandings of the sense of coming to the Land of Israel (in terms of immigration or repatriation) and the vision of national identity of the Israeli state fit with three trends in the immigrant community: assimilation, integration, and isolation.[20] The first trend, more popular among immigrants with a strong Jewish identity, is toward almost complete integration and acculturation in the native Jewish Israeli environment. Such an identity was prominent among immigrants of the early 1990s, the majority of whom, according to polls, felt Jewish or Israeli rather than Russian. The opposite, isolationist trend reflects attitudes of non-Jewish immigrants and members of ethnically mixed families, including assimilated Jewish relatives. These people are often negative toward Jewishness and Israel and lack a readiness to integrate into Israeli society.[21] This trend is most visible among recent newcomers, approximately 50 percent of whom are non-Jews. Thus, according to the same polls, of those who arrived in 1997–99, 62 percent considered themselves Russian and only 38 percent felt Jewish or Israeli.[22] Finally, a middle-of-the-road group exists, consisting of both Jewish and ethnically mixed groups that seek "integration without acculturation,"[23] preserving a base for sectarian Russian cultural and political institutions as a legitimized peripheral phenomenon of local political pluralism.

All these trends are reflected on the organizational level through three major new immigrant parties: Yisrael Beiteinu of Avigdor Lieberman, Yisrael b'Aliyah of Natan Sharansky, and Habhira Hademocratit of Roman Bronfman. These are now parts of mainstream political movements—Ihud Haleumi, Likud, and Meretz, respectively. The split among Jewish, non-Jewish, and moderate groups may be seen through the disagreement within the Russian-speaking immigrant community regarding the question of the Jewish character of the state. According to a poll in November 1999, 48.8 percent of all respondents were worried that Israel might lose its Jewish essence and Jewish ethnic majority; 21.6 percent and 11.4 percent, respectively, either would welcome this or did not care, and 18.2 percent did not have a definite opinion.[24]

The future prospects for these trends are ambiguous. Some experts, while not underestimating the problem, still consider non-Jewish immigrants from the CIS to be "socially still a part of the Jewish community of the country."[25] On the other hand, many see this sort of ethnic national diversity within the new immigrants as a long-term phenomenon. This opinion may be strengthened by the results of a poll of potential emigrants to Israel—students of the Hebrew language schools (*ulpanim*) in the CIS. According to this study, conducted in December 2001, only 45 percent of the potential immigrants were halachic Jews, while 35 and 20 percent, respectively, represented the second (children) and third (grandchildren) generations of mixed marriages. Unsurprisingly, although 80 percent of halachic Jews declared a strong Jewish identity, only half of the second generation and a quarter of the third generation felt a strong sense of Jewishness.[26]

In turn, various groups in Israeli society developed different models to approach Russian Jewish immigrants, based on their social status and their own vision of the State of Israel. It is a "common understanding" in Israel that the Russian aliyah received the best possible treatment, mainly because of the favorable policies and public opinion in response to this immigration. The encouragement of aliyah is the country's mission, and it grants immediate citizenship to any immigrating Jew and his or her immediate non-Jewish relatives. The long-awaited mass immigration of Soviet Jews was especially welcomed by the Israeli establishment, and they were defined as "an ideal set of newcomers as any host country could want" and "the best thing that happened to this country during recent decades."[27] On the societal level, however, the approach to this immigration was more varied and ranged from unquestionable enthusiasm to open negativism. Various ethnic and social and demographic groups had different opinions about these new immigrants, opinions that changed in the course of the 1990s. Thus, several public opinion polls in the early 1990s showed that the older, educated, high-income, and Ashkenazi population expressed the most positive attitudes toward them.[28] This differed from the negative attitudes of many members of Sephardi communities, which reflected a sort of ethnic-social competition between the two groups. At that time, they competed for the same low-strata jobs and for state welfare resources. On the level of leadership, this negative attitude was expressed by veterans of the Black Panther movement and, more recently, by some activists in the Rainbow-Democratic-Mizrahi movement.

However, as the social and economic advancement of the Russian aliyah progressed, a substantial part of this aliyah found itself competing with the Ashkenazi middle class, which demonstrated an increasingly negative attitude toward the new immigrants. One result was an unprecedented campaign against aliyah from the CIS, which began in the mass media and some government organs in 1993–94 and peaked in late 1995. It was an important reason for the creation of an independent Russian party in 1995 and for its success in the 1996 elections.[29]

By the end of the 1990s, ethnic social cleavages reflected in Israeli Jewish attitudes toward Russian immigrants became more diverse and, to a large extent, intersected with internal ethnic social divisions among the immigrants themselves. These divisions were clear in 1999–2000, when there was public discussion of changing the Law of Return. This started in October 1999 with the declaration by the Minister of Diaspora Affairs Rabbi Michael Melchior that the existing version of the Law of Return had become a channel for massive non-Jewish immigration to Israel. The issue heated up after provocative declarations by ultraorthodox Yahadut ha-Tora (Torah Judaism) MK (member of Knesset) Rabbi Shmuel Halpert, who called non-Jewish immigrants "the fifth column" in Israeli society,[30] and hostile anti-Russian proclamations by Shas politicians David Benizri and Moshe Abutbul. Though Prime Minister Ehud Barak, Absorption Minister Yuli (Yael) Tamir, and other senior officials strongly condemned these statements and rejected the idea of changing the Law of Return, public discussion became more tenacious.

Russian immigrants demonstrated a clear split in their positions on this issue, depending on their different understandings of the essence and meaning of the Jewish return to Israel. Thus, a left-wing group represented by Russian immigrant Habhira Hademocratit party chair Roman Bronfman declared its disagreement with any changes in the Law of Return. However, Avigdor Lieberman, on behalf of right-wing Yisrael Beiteinu, supported changes in the law, which, according to this party, had become a channel to bring to Israel people "whose relation to the Jewish people is very questionable." Finally, Natan Sharansky, leader of the moderate Yisrael b'Aliyah, demonstrated a centrist position by admitting that "the immigration of non-Jews is indeed a problem" and "the Law of Return does need some urgent changes, which, however, should not touch its essence."[31]

This split reflected a long history of cleavages among Zionist, non-Zionist, and anti-Zionist groups within the USSR and its successor states, which continued when they reached Israel. One subject of heated discussion that clearly reflected their different visions of their immigration to Israel was the idea of the separation of state and religion. Thus, the post-Zionist and non-Zionist groups demanded a change in the status quo of state and religion to favor secularism and the "separation of religion from politics."[32] In contrast, Lieberman's camp argued that "the Jewish character of Israel should be preserved, and thus it is impossible to separate religion from the state."[33] For their part, the centrist Yisrael b'Aliyah leaders tried to maintain a communal consensus and abstained, when possible, on the critical issues of secular-religious relations. The party's platform challenged religious coercion and demanded the introduction of civil marriage, while simultaneously proclaiming the "party's respect for Jewish tradition and the status of the religious community in Israel."[34]

In sum, while the general Israeli public's approach to Russian immigrants reflects "divided attitudes in a divided society,"[35] new immigrants' visions of Israeli society have proved to be quite diverse as well.

Whose Land? Jews, Arabs, and Slavs

Jewish *olim* from the USSR and CIS also had to revise their vision of the historical homeland and their understanding of the national character of the state in relationship to another local reality of the western Land of Israel—a large and rapidly growing Arabic-speaking population, meaning Arab citizens of Israel as well as the Arab population of Judaea, Samaria, and Gaza.

Among the Arab citizens of Israel, one can identify two viewpoints concerning (post-) Soviet Jewish immigrants. On the societal level, the Israeli Arab public demonstrates a spectrum of opinions toward those immigrants, ranging from indifference to moderate negativism or hatred, especially among marginal groups such as Arab youth in criminalized areas of Lod and Ramla. However, some Druze and Arab Christians and, to a lesser extent, Muslims with a strong Israeli identity were initially ready to see a positive aspect to Russian Jewish repatriation. A curious feature of this trend was the establishment of a "Russian" Yisrael b'Aliyah Party branch in a Druze village in the Upper Galilee. Another Israeli "Russian" Yisrael Beiteinu Party (the leading part of the extreme right Yihud Leumi bloc) also received support among Israeli Arabic-speaking voters, mainly a few Christians and Druze.[36] Besides many other more instrumental reasons, this support, as some Israeli ethnic minority leaders confessed,[37] is often based on the perspective that only a strong Jewish democratic state, rather than a Muslim one or even the "all-citizens state," could preserve their specific interests and the status as a minority.[38] The views of Russian immigrants toward the Palestinian population on both sides of the Green Line are mostly a result of three factors: the logic of the Arab-Israeli conflict; their past negative experiences in Russia; and the lack of positive personal relations with the Arabic-speaking population. In terms of the Arab-Israeli conflict, most Russian immigrants place themselves on the right side of the local political spectrum. Thus, according to some polls, even before the intifada began in September 2000, 75 percent of Russians in Israel strongly opposed withdrawal from the Golan Heights in any agreement with Syria (rising to 83 percent in September 2002),[39] and about 80 percent (as opposed to 65 percent of native Israelis) rejected any territorial compromise in Jerusalem.[40]

These feelings became stronger during the intifada: by December 2002, 45 percent of Russian-speaking Israelis opposed the establishment of a Palestinian state even if Arab terror would stop completely and Arafat would disappear from the public arena. Over 80 percent of Russian Jews were convinced that the peace process with the Palestinians would not succeed.[41] Not surprisingly, these views were reflected in their attitudes toward Israeli Arabs. Opinion polls in 1993 and 2000 showed that three-quarters of Russian-speaking immigrants mistrusted Arabs and Muslims in general,[42] and 54 percent of them were not sure that their Muslim Arab counterparts were loyal citizens of Israel and should be granted the same rights as "loyal" ethnic groups.[43]

These orientations to the Arab-Israeli conflict were formed in the country of origin. According to Zvi Gitelman, they resulted from three factors: opposition to the Soviet government's pro-Arab and anti-Israel foreign policy, which had its domestic counterpart in brutal anti-Semitism and discrimination against Jews; negative experiences from contacts with the Arab and Muslim diaspora in the USSR, especially Muslim Arab students on university campuses; and anti-Russian inclinations in the Muslim republics and their opposition to "imperial culture," with which Ashkenazi Jews were identified.[44] However, it would be incorrect to assume that anti-Arab aspirations are an inherent feature of Soviet Jewish consciousness. Sociological studies of public opinion among new immigrants show a more sophisticated picture. For instance, in a study of Russian-speaking immigrant students in *ulpanim* conducted in 1997, the respondents were asked to define their views toward Israeli Arabs and Arabs and Muslims in general.[45] The views of these people, who had normally spent less than a year in Israel, ranged from extremely negative ("Arabs mean terror and hatred," "Arabs are aggressive and militant anti-Semites") to extremely positive ("Arabs are our neighbors and possible partners and friends," "Arabs are good people and brothers of Jews," and even "Israeli Arabs are peaceful, industrious, hospitable, devoted friends, open and trustful"). Only one-third of the immigrants showed an openly negative approach to Arabs; the expressions of the other two-thirds were neutral or positive.

Thus, one could assume that the mutual understanding between Israeli Russian Jews and Israeli Arabs was not totally impossible. However, despite the fact that the attitude of the Israeli Arab elite toward Russian immigrants was also diverse, the Arab majority since the early 1990s has regarded them as a threat to their political and economic prospects and to the status of the Arab minority.[46] That included awareness that massive immigration from the USSR would undermine the only tool of political pressure available to Arabs in a liberal democratic state, namely, the "demographic weapon."[47] In the second half of the 1990s, however, a significant section of the Israeli Arab elite converted from an overall critic of the ethnocentric, in their terms, Law of Return, to opponents of its change. The reason for this shift was their hope that secular and mostly non-Zionist Russian aliyah, with its substantial and growing share of non-Jews, might be an ally for Israeli Arabs in their struggle to transform Israel from a Jewish state into a state for all its citizens.[48] These expectations quickly proved to be wrong, especially after the start of the intifada. A potential for a peace camp among the Russian aliyah did exist, mainly represented by non-Jews and their assimilated Jewish family members, as well as a minor, but still significant, group among the Russian-speaking political and intellectual elite. However, the peace camp diminished dramatically in proportion to the increase in Palestinian terror.

It should be noted that, for certain objective reasons, the proportion of Russian immigrants who have been the target of terrorist attacks is higher than among native Israelis. According to Sharansky, new Russian immigrants (who are mainly concentrated in big cities, and many of whom cannot afford a private car, especially during their first years in the country, thus becoming disproportionately bus riders) compose about 40 percent of all bus-bomb victims.[49] In fact, the peace camp among new immigrants almost totally disappeared after the bombing of the Delfinarium nightclub in Tel Aviv in May 2001, in which terrorists killed twenty young people. That nightclub was frequented particularly by young Russians. The community's feelings were summarized by a Russian language newspaper: "It was hard to imagine an action more likely to discredit the just cause of the Palestinians in the eyes of the world community and especially Russian opinion."[50]

However, there were some exceptions, represented by marginal Russian anti-Semitic groups. The first indications of the establishment of these groups came in the late 1990s. During the 2003 elections, the topic of "discrimination against non-Jews in a cohesive Jewish state" was openly exploited not only by Meretz-Habhira Hademocratit but also by two immigrant parties that did not pass the 1.5 percent electoral threshold. These were Ezrakh u-Medina of Alexandr Zinker and the Progressive Liberal Democratic Party (Leeder), known as the Israeli branch of the ultranationalist Liberal Democratic party in Russia, headed by Vladimir Zhirinovsky.[51] These parties were the political wings of several non-Jewish Russian immigrant associations, whose appearance on the Israeli public stage was promoted by strengthening post-Zionist trends in Israeli public opinion and the secular-religious "war of cultures" of the late 1990s.[52] Yisrael b'Aliyah's campaign in 1999 under the slogan *MVD pod nash control* (Ministry of Interior under our control), which was mainly addressed to the feelings of non-Jewish immigrants and members of ethnically mixed families, who constituted 35–40 percent of the new immigrant community, also contributed to this trend.[53]

As a result, much more aggressive associations appeared in the early twenty-first century, including the Russian community, which demanded "cultural autonomy for ethnic Russians in Israel,"[54] and the Slavic Union. The latter marked its appearance with a campaign of criticism of, as its leaders put it, the "forced assimilation of Israeli Russians through the procedure of religious conversion" to Judaism, demanded that the Russian language be granted an official status, and demanded state subsidies for special schools with Russian language, literature, and history curricula. Slavic Union head Aleksei Korobov separated the interests and visions of ethnic Russians in Israel from the interests and visions of the Land and State of Israel expressed by Russian-speaking Jewish *olim*, stating that these two Russian groups were on different sides of the political barricades.[55] The Slavic Union leaders not only articulated their nonacceptance of Israel as the Jewish state but also, contrary to other immigrant groups, openly supported Palestinian Arabs in their war with Israel, called on ethnic Russians not to serve in the Israeli army, and urged them to vote for Hadash, the Arab Communist party. Not receiving any real support within Israel, the party sent a delegation to Ramallah, where they met with Arafat's governor. There, Korobov expressed the Slavic Union's support for "the struggle of Palestinian Arabs with Zionist aggressors" and proclaimed that his organization aimed to create "one state for two nations."[56] Similar sentiments were expressed by representatives of other radical anti-Israeli immigrant groups in the late 1990s. Finally, the indications of the same social and political dynamics are reflected through indications of anti-Semitism (not just anti-Zionism), mainly on the part of newly arrived young Russians, over 60 percent of whom are not Jewish, which has also become a milieu for aggressive and pro-Fascist youth movements.

The future prospects of these trends are ambiguous. Some experts, not underestimating the problem, consider non-Jewish immigrants from the CIS to be "socially still a part of the Jewish community of the country"; others see this ethnic national diversity within the new immigrants as a long-term phenomenon.[57] All this further complicates social and political controversies in Israeli society and is going to be a long-term factor, which Israel as the Jewish democratic state will have to face in this century.

Conclusion

Besides substantial differences among the ethnic and culture groups of Israeli society, there has been even more diversity among different waves of immigration from Russia and the USSR in terms of culture, preservation of religious tradition, ethnic identity, and the vision of the Land and State of Israel. First were those who came before the establishment of the State of Israel and during the first decades after its establishment, who carried a relatively classical Zionist vision of the Land of Israel. Second were those Soviet Jews who, after a long separation, came en masse in the late 1960s and 1970s and whose "new Russian Zionist" vision of return was motivated by Soviet governmental and societal anti-Semitism, the memory of the Holocaust, and the impact of the Israeli victory in the Six-Day War. Third were Russian Jewish immigrants and their non-Jewish family members, who started to arrive in large numbers in the 1990s and who demonstrated more diverse visions of the Land of Israel, ranging from religious Zionism and ethnic New (Russian) Zionism to post-Zionism and even anti-Zionism among some marginal groups.

As a result, the new immigrant community in Israel features almost the entire spectrum of opinions that exist in Israeli society. Although this mostly reflects trends rather than clear-cut differences, each new immigrant movement vocalizes various political trends within the community: politically left and anticlerical, right-wing and secular-religious status-quo oriented, and centrist. Furthermore, while the majority of Russian-speaking immigrants and their elites share an ideology that combines classical Zionist and neo-Zionist approaches, the political priorities of a marginal section of this group push it in a post-Zionist direction. Finally, each party personalizes ethnic communal, ethnic national, and class interests. The new immigrant community is split over the same issues as Israeli society in general, thus reflecting their political integration into that society.

Notes

1. Alex Prilutsky, "Vek Russkoi alii" (The age of Russian aliyah), *Vesti,* January 2, 2000.

2. Shlomo Groman and Mark Kotlyarshi, "Aliya prodolzhayetsia—nesmotria ni na chto" (Aliyah is going on—in spite of everything), *Vesti,* May 12, 2002.

3. For details, see Vladimir Khanin, *Documents on Ukrainian Jewish Identity and Emigration, 1944–1990* (London: Frank Cass, 2002), esp. docs. 61 and 71.

4. Aleksandr Riman, "'I ostalsia Yakov odin,' ili svideitel' obvinenia" ("And Ya'acov left alone," or the witness of the charge), *Vesti-2,* August 29, 2002, 9.

5. "Report on the Work of the UkSSR Commissioner of the Council of the Affairs of Religious Cults for January–March 1949, Kiev, 18 May 1949," Central State Archive of Public Organizations of Ukraine, Fond 1, Opis' 23, file 5667, 152–53.

6. Quoted in Michael Mitsel, "Vystupaiut ochen' ot'iavlenno dersko sionistskie elementary (Shtrikhi k politicheskomu potretu P.E. Shelest)," in *Jewish History and Jewish Culture in the Ukraine,* Gelii Aronov et al., eds. (Kiev: Kiev Institute for Jewish Studies, 1996), 3:137–42.

7. Top-secret report, submitted to the Communist Party of Ukraine Central Committee, "On the Desire of Some Individuals of Jewish Nationality to Leave for

Permanent Residence in Israel and Reactions to Events in the Middle East," June 16, 1967, TsDAGOU, F. 1, Op. 24, d. 6289, 11.4–7.

8. TsDAGOU, F. 1, Op. 29, d. 494, 11.76–79. For the full text, see Vladimir Khanin, *Documents*, doc. 48.

9. Noted Soviet Jewish dissident Natan Sharansky later summarized this viewpoint: "Zionism does not mean that Jews have to forget their Diaspora tradition and culture. Neither do they have to come to Israel because they suffer in the place of their origin, but rather are attracted by better conditions in this country." Quoted in Vladimir Khanin, "The New Russian Jewish Diaspora and 'Russian' Party Politics in Israel," *Nationalism & Ethnic Politics* 8:4 (December 2002): 46.

10. Rafail Nudelman, "Hanisayon lekhadesh hatsionut: Bein aliyat shnot hashiv'im la-aliyat shnot hatshi'im" (Attempts to renew Zionism: Between the aliya of the 1970s and the 1990s), *Yehudei Brit Ha-Mo'etzot Ba-Ma'avar* 4:19 (2000): 67–84.

11. Quoted in Alexander Bovin, "Piat' let sredi evreev i midovtsev" (Five years among Jews and foreign office officials) (Moscow: Progress, 2000), 174.

12. Interview in Kiev, January 1999.

13. According to a poll commissioned by Yisrael B'aliya on the eve of the 1996 elections, such opinions were shared by about 45 percent of respondents: Vadim Rotenberg, "Samoindentificatsia rossiiskogo evreistva: Popytka analiza" (Self-identification of Russian Jewry: An attempt at analysis), http://www.machanaim .org.il.

14. Velvl Tchernin, "Kak prekrasno eto derevo: Ramyshlenya o sovremennoi izrail'skoii literatute" (What a beautiful tree is that! Thoughts about modern Israeli literature), *Ierusalimskie khoiniki* (Jerusalem Chronicles), http://www.rjews.net/ gazeta/chernin.html.

15. Vladimir Khanin, "Social Consciousness and the Problem of Jewish Identity of Ukrainian Jewry," *Contemporary Jewry* 19 (1998): 120–50; Rozalina Ryvkina, *Russian Jews: Who Are They?* (Russian) (Moscow: Opos, 2000).

16. Alexander Voronel, "Sub'ektivnye zametki" (Subjective notes), *Vesti-Okna*, October 9, 2003, 14. See also Alek Epstein and Nina Kheimets, "Immigrant Intelligentsia and Its Second Generation: Cultural Segregation as a Road to Social Integration?" *Journal of International Migration and Integration* 1:4 (2000): 461–76.

17. For details, see Vladimir (Ze'ev) Khanin, "The Contemporary Ukrainian Jewish Community: Social, Demographic, and Political Changes," in *Demographic Shifts in the Jewish World: Forecasts and Implications*, Irit Keynan, ed.; collection of position papers presented by the Jewish Agency to the Third Herzliya Conference, "The New Strategic Landscape: Trends, Challenges, and Responses" (Herzliya: Institute for Policy and Strategy, Lauder School of Government, December 2002), 29–37; Valery Chervyakov, Zvi Gitelman, and Vladimir Shapiro, "The National Consciousness of Russian Jews," in ibid., 39–52.

18. David Aptekman, "Jewish Emigration from the USSR, 1990–1992: Trends and Motivations," *Jews in Eastern Europe* 1:20 (summer 1993): 15–34; and Vladimir Khanin, "The Ukrainian Exodus," *W.R.E. Oxford Journal of Opinion and International Affairs* (December 1991): 5–8.

19. See David Aptekman, Boris Biletsky, Leonid Goldman, and Alexandr Shraiber, *Ten Years of Big Aliya: Sociological Essays* (Jerusalem: Aliya Association, 1999).

20. Narspi Zilberg and Eliezer Leshem, "Imagined and Real Community: Russian-Language Press and Renewal of Communal Life in Israel of Immigrants from the CIS," *Hevra Verevakha* 1 (1997): 9–27; Moshe Lyssak and Eliezer Leshem, "The Russian Intelligentsia in Israel: Between Ghettoization and Integration," *Israel Affairs* 2:2 (1995): 20–36.

21. Aleksei Kozulin and Alex Venger, "Immigration without Adaptation: The Psychological World of Russian Immigrants in Israel," *Mind, Culture and Activity* 1:4 (1994): 230–38.

22. Yochanan Peres and Sabina Lissitsa, "Unity and Cleavages in Israeli Society: Initial Report—Immigrants from the Former Soviet Union and Veterans in Israel," *Israeli Sociology* 3:1 (March 2001): 7–30.

23. This phenomenon was discussed by Tamar Horowitz, "Integration Without Acculturation," *Soviet Jewish Affairs* 12:3 (1982): 19–23; and Vadim Rotenberg, "On Self-Determination of Jews from the Former Soviet Union Now Living in Israel" (Hebrew), *Yehudei Brit Ha-Moetzot Ba-Ma'avar* 4:19 (2000): 213–20.

24. Results of the Institute for Social and Political Research (Tel Aviv) poll are published at http://www.ispr/all.html.

25. See "Jewish Education and National Identity of Russian-Speaking Jews of Israel and the Diaspora," in collection of papers from the inauguration conference of the Association for Jewish Education in Russian, Seminar Oranim, Qiryat Tivon, Israel, May 5–6, 1999.

26. Eliezer Leshem, "Seker proyekt 'ha-zeut ha-yehudit' shlav alef ba-hama" (Study of the Project "Jewish identity," Stage A, in the CIS) (Jerusalem: Jewish Agency for Israel, August 2002).

27. Eliezer Feldman, *"Russkii Izrail": Mezhdu dvukh pol'usov* ("The Russian Israel": Between two poles) (Moscow: Market DS, 2003), 169–74.

28. Eliezer Leshem, "The Israeli Public Attitudes Toward the New Immigrants of the 1990s," in *Immigration to Israel: Sociological Perspective*, Elazar Leshem and Judith T. Shuval, eds. (New Brunswick, N.J.: Transaction Publishers, 1998), 307–27; and Joseph Shvarzword and Michael Tur Kaspa, "Preserved Threat and Social Dominance as Determination of Prejudice Toward Russian and Ethiopian Immigrants in Israel" (Hebrew), *Magamot* 4 (December 1997): 504–27.

29. Vladimir Khanin, "Israeli 'Russian' Parties and the New Immigrant Vote," *Israel Affairs* 7:2–3 (winter/spring 2001): 101–34.

30. *Vesti*, November 11, 1999; *Jerusalem Post*, January 12, 2000.

31. Sofia Ron, "Dva raskola, tri partii I Zakon o vozvrashchenii," *Vesti-2*, December 2, 1999.

32. See also Roman Bronfman, "A Non-Parliament Proclamation," *Vesti*, June 1, 2000.

33. Shlomo Briman, "Lieberman and Sharansky: The Open Dialogue," *Vesti*, May 31, 2000.

34. *Yisrael b'Aliyah: Two Years on the Political Map* (Jerusalem: Yisrael b'Aliyah, 1998), 12–16.

35. Majid Al-Haj, "Soviet Immigrants as Viewed by Jews and Arabs: Divided Attitudes in a Divided Country," in Leshem and Shuval, *Immigration to Israel*, 211–28.

36. Interview with MK Dr. Yurii Shtern (Yihud Leumi), Jerusalem, June 2003.

37. Author's interview with Mendi Sfuaj, chairman of the "Non-Jews for the State of Israel" movement, Lod, November 2003. He illustrated this opinion with the fact that 64 percent of those Golan Heights Druze who participated in Israeli 2003 parliamentary elections voted for the Yisrael Beiteinu–Ihud Haleumi party of Avigdor Lieberman, which strongly opposes any territorial concessions to Syria. Another Israeli ethnic minority leader, chairman of the Druze Zionist Council, Yusuf Nasser Adin, addressing the delegates of the 34th Zionist Congress (Jerusalem, June 17–20, 2002), called on Diaspora Jews to be concerned about "our [Israeli] difficult demographic situation" and thus "to come to Israel for the Third Temple of the Jewish Nation."

38. Crimean Tatars, who returned en masse in the 1990s to the Crimean penin-

sula after decades of deportation, demonstrate a similar case. According to their leaders, only Ukrainian suzerainty over the Autonomous Republic of Crimea and strengthening the Ukrainian national identity of the state can guarantee their ethnic cultural rights as well as their economic and political status in the Crimean Russian environment. See Irina Pribytkova, "Examination of the Citizenship Issue on the Return and Reintegration of the Formerly Deported Peoples of Crimea," in *Sociology in Ukraine*, Natalia Panina et al., eds. (Kiev: Institute of Sociology of the National Academy of Sciences of Ukraine, 2002), 244–305; and Vladimir Yevtuh, "The Dynamics of Interethnic Relations in Crimea," in ibid., 401–12.

39. "Israel's Russian Community Divided over Putin Victory," *Newsroom*, April 3, 2000; ISPR poll, http://prcenter-news.ru/news2004/4_apr_israel_putin.htm, accessed November 15, 2004.

40. *Vesti*, May 8, 2000.

41. *Maariv*, December 6, 2002.

42. Gallup polls quoted in Tamar Horowitz, "Ideology, Identity, Disappointment: Major Factor of Electoral Behavior of the FSU Immigrants," in *Israeli Elections 1999* (Hebrew), Asher Arian and Mose Sami, eds. (Jerusalem: Israeli Democracy Institute, 1999), 164; and "Israel's Russian Community Divided over Putin Victory," *Newsroom*, April 3, 2000.

43. See Yochanan Peres, *Integration of New Repatriates from the CIS in Israel: The First Steps* (Hebrew) (Tel Aviv University, Department of Sociology, 1992).

44. Zvi Gitelman, *Immigration and Identity* (New York: David and Susan Wilstein Jewish Policy Study, 1995).

45. Moshe Kenningstei, "Values and Stereotypes of 'Russian' Immigrants: An Ethnic Methodological Research," in *Migration Processes and Their Influence on Israeli Society*, Andrei Fedorchenko and Alek Epstein, eds. (Moscow: Hebrew University of Jerusalem, Moscow Institute for Israeli and Middle Eastern Studies, and Open University of Israel, 2000), 289–90.

46. Al-Haj, "Soviet Immigrants as Viewed by Jews and Arabs," 211–28.

47. According to the Israeli Central Bureau of Statistics (ICBS), in 1990, the first year of the "big Aliya" from the USSR, Jews composed 81.9 percent of the Israeli population, while Arab and non-Arab Muslims, Christians, and Druze composed 18.2 percent. Although total fertility in the 1990s for Muslim Israelis was almost double that of Jewish Israelis (4.6/4.7 births per woman versus 2.6/2.7) and the Arabs witnessed substantial population growth in absolute figures, the Arabic-speaking population's share in 2003 barely improved, becoming 20 percent versus 80 percent Jews. That was largely because of the aliyah of about 930,000 Russian Jews and their non-Jewish family members in 1989–2003, who composed about 14 percent of the population (see ICBS, http://www.cbs.gov.il/israel_in_figures). Arab immigration to "Israel proper" (within the Green Line) from the West Bank, Gaza, Jordan, and some other Arab countries was estimated for those years at 150,000–180,000 persons (Arnon Sofer, *Israeli Demographics 2000–2020: Dangers and Opportunities* (Haifa: The National Security Studies Center, 2002).

48. See Majid Al-Haj, "The Status of the Palestinians within Israel under the Shadow of the Intifada," keynote speech, Center for Strategic Studies (Jordan), August 27, 2002.

49. As quoted by Victoria Martynova, "The Theory of Directed Explosion," *Vesti*, January 30, 2003.

50. *Trud*, June 2, 2001.

51. For details, see Vladimir Khanin, "'Russian' Community and Immigrant Party Politics at the 2003 Elections," in *Israel at the Polls, 2003*, Shmuel Sandler and Ben Mollow, eds. (London: Frank Cass, 2004).

52. For more details, see Vladimir Khanin, *The "Russians" and Power in the State of Israel: Establishment of the USSR/CIS Immigrant Community and Its Impact on the Political Structure of the Country* (Russian) (Moscow: Institute for Israel and Middle Eastern Studies, 2003), esp. chap. 6.

53. Khanin, "Israeli 'Russian' Parties," 124–25.

54. Asia Entova, "Ours or Not Ours?" (Russian) *Russkii Zhurnal*, May 7, 2003, www.russ.ru.

55. Quoted in Entova, "Ours or Not Ours?"

56. Natasha Mozgovaia, "From Russia with Disappointment," (Hebrew) *Yediot Ahronot*, February 14, 2002, 22–23.

57. "Jewish Education and National Identity of Russian-Speaking Jews of Israel and the Diaspora," papers from the inaugural conference of the Association for Jewish Education in Russian, Seminar Oranim, Qiryat Tivon, Israel, May 5–6, 1999.

Part IV
Property Issues for Arab and Jewish Migrants and Refugees

Chapter 10
Palestinian and Mizrahi Jewish Property Claims in Discourse and Diplomacy

Michael R. Fischbach

A central focus of the Palestinian and Jewish grievances that emerged from the Arab-Israeli war in 1948 was the claims for compensation and restitution by Palestinians for property abandoned in what became Israel in 1948, on the one hand, and the claims lodged by Jewish emigrants from Arab countries for property left in or confiscated by those countries during and after 1948. These two sets of property losses and claims became a major issue for the refugees and emigrants themselves as well as for the wider Arab-Israeli conflict. Their importance was felt on two levels beyond the obvious deleterious socioeconomic impact that these property losses represented for those property owners who were affected. First, these two sets of losses quickly came to occupy important positions in the narratives of catastrophe and the return of exiles created by Arabs, especially the Palestinians, and Jews, including the Mizrahi Jews who lost property, and the government of Israel. Second, a number of parties used the property-claims questions as important ingredients in their overall diplomatic approach to the Arab-Israeli conflict. Both of these served to keep the two property-claims issues from being resolved, which in turn served to perpetuate the conflict.

This chapter examines the question of Palestinian and Mizrahi Jewish property claims after 1948 with an eye toward understanding their broader significance for the aggrieved parties and for the Arab-Israeli conflict as a whole. Beyond detailing the origins of these two sets of property claims and the amounts claimed, the chapter aims at understanding how these two issues have featured in the Palestinian and Mizrahi Jewish discourses of catastrophe and return and how they have affected the diplomatic course of the Arab-Israeli conflict.

Origins of the Property Claims

The 1948 war led to drastic demographic changes in the new State of Israel and the surrounding Arab world. These changes engendered the two different property-claims issues. Although the numbers themselves have become a source of controversy, at least 726,000 Palestinian Arabs fled or were driven out of their homes by Jewish forces during the fighting that raged in Palestine from the late autumn of 1947 to the end of 1948, leaving Israel a state overwhelmingly populated by Jews. In the process, these new exiles left behind homes, businesses, farmland, and movable property and found themselves refugees in a number of Arab countries. Largely as result of rising anti-Zionist feelings and violence directed at them in parts of the Arab world, several hundred thousands of Jews (mostly Mizrahim of Middle Eastern or Sephardic ancestry but including some Ashkenazim as well) emigrated from Arab countries during and after 1948, including 250,000–300,000 or more who fled without free access to their movable and immovable property. Many of these Jews immigrated to Israel. These figures do not include several hundred thousand others who later emigrated from Arab countries like Morocco under much less duress.

Although some parties, most notably the State of Israel, politically linked resolution of the Palestinians' property claims with those of Mizrahi Jews, the two sets of claims are not directly comparable.[1] A brief examination of each set of claims illustrates this. The Palestinian refugees lost their property as the result of war in their homeland. Armed conflict broke out between Zionist forces and those of Palestinian and other Arab forces in the wake of the United Nations' adoption of the 1947 plan to partition Palestine into separate Jewish and Arab states. Some Palestinians left in advance of the fighting, especially the refugees from towns and cities, generally considered middle class; others fled from actual fighting or the capture of their communities by Jewish forces; others were expelled by these forces. Their sudden flight allowed them little or no time to carry movable assets or dispose of landed property prior to leaving. Their country, British-ruled Palestine, ceased to exist in a juridical sense as of May 15, 1948, which left the bulk of the refugees stateless. After the war, nearly all were barred by Israel from returning to their homes and property. Israel quickly agreed to pay compensation to the refugees for some of their abandoned property, but most refugees demanded repatriation and property restitution rather than exile and compensation.

A key factor of Palestinian refugee property claims is the fact that the United Nations historically has assumed a significant level of responsibility for alleviating the plight of the refugees, given its intimate involvement in the causes that led to their exile. In addition to defining the exiles as "refugees," the world body has called for indemnifying them for their losses. Even before the war, UN General Assembly Resolution 181 (II) of November 29, 1947 (the partition resolution), anticipated the fate of Palestinian property in the proposed new Jewish state, and vice versa. It stated that the new Jewish authorities could expropriate Palestinian property only for "public purposes" and that they must compensate the owners for the land. The same would be true for Jewish property in the Arab state. According to Section I.C.2.8.: "No expropriation of land owned by an Arab in the Jewish state shall be allowed except for public purposes. In all cases of expropriation full compensation as fixed by the Supreme Court [of the Jewish State] shall be paid previous to dispossession." UN mediator Count Folke Bernadotte was also concerned about the refugees' lost property and noted in his September 1948 report to the UN: "There have been numerous reports from reliable sources of large-scale looting, pillaging and plundering, and of instances of destruction of villages without military necessity. The liability of the Provisional Government of Israel to restore private property to its Arab owners and to indemnify those owners for property wantonly destroyed is clear irrespective of any indemnities which the Provisional Government may claim from the Arab States." In December 1948, the UN General Assembly passed its landmark Resolution 194 (III), which created the United Nations Conciliation Commission for Palestine (UNCCP). That resolution also laid the basis for the decades-old UN call for compensating the refugees for abandoned property: "the refugees wishing to return to their homes and live at peace with their neighbors should be permitted to do so at the earliest practicable date, and that compensation should be paid for the property of those choosing not to return and for the loss of or damage to property which, under principles of international law or in equity, should be made good by the Governments or authorities responsible." Over the decades, the UNCCP exerted considerable efforts on behalf of refugee compensation and eventually produced the most thorough documentation of the scope and value of individual refugee losses ever assembled by any party, even though no compensation regime has ever been accepted by the parties to the conflict.

The origins of Mizrahi Jewish property losses and claims as well as the international responses to them differ from those of the Palestinians in certain key aspects. Jews rarely left Arab countries because those countries were the scenes of military conflict or because they were expelled by Arab forces. This applies to Jews from Syria, Lebanon, Iraq, Yemen, and Libya who emigrated in 1948 and the two decades thereafter. Their flight was not the result of armed conflict in those countries but was a by-product of the armed conflict between Jews and Arabs in Palestine and hostile anti-Zionist and anti-Jewish attitudes and actions found in the surrounding Arab world. Most chose to leave but did so under conditions of severe duress and violent intimidation. A notable exception to these generalizations about voluntary departure from noncombat situations was the expulsion from Egypt of Jews holding British and French citizenship as well as "stateless" Jews during the wartime conditions of October and November 1956. Another exception concerned Palestinian Jews whom Jordanian forces expelled from those parts of Palestine held by the Arab Legion, although, properly speaking, they are not part of the wider phenomenon of Mizrahi property losses. Some Mizrahim were forced to forfeit their Arab nationality or were declared "stateless" upon emigration, but most regained some type of citizenship rights, especially the more than 250,000 who settled in Israel and were granted Israeli citizenship. Other Mizrahim departed for Italy, France, and other countries, including Arab countries (in the case of some Syrian Jews who left for Lebanon). In the process, many had their property seized under a variety of different laws and thus had to leave behind both personal and communal movable and immovable property.

A more important difference between the case of the Palestinians and the Mizrahim lies in the UN and other international attitudes toward the two cases. The UN has never adopted resolutions or programs to deal with their property claims. Similarly, it has not linked these claims with the resolution of the Palestinians' own claims. The attitude of the United States has been more nuanced and has fluctuated. Initially, some American officials felt that a peaceful solution to the Arab-Israeli conflict should involve mutual compensation: "It certainly would be desirable to have property settlements accomplished for both the Arab and Jewish properties involved. However, it is hard to see how this can be done except within a framework of a general settlement of the Arab-Israeli conflict."[2] They did not exert any efforts on behalf of Mizrahi property claims, however, or any efforts at linking the two questions. More recently, President Bill Clinton may have signaled a change in U.S. policy when in 2000 he openly called for an international fund that could compensate both Palestinian refugees and Mizrahi Jews for their respective property losses.[3]

This discussion of the similarities and differences between the two property-claims cases does not in any way elevate one over the other in any moral sense. It also does not ignore the fact that the two issues are linked in a historical sense to the outcome of the 1948 war, nor does it detract in any way from the painful losses sustained both by Palestinian Arabs and Mizrahi Jews who left their homes and lost their property under difficult circumstances. It simply serves as a useful background to the rest of this chapter, which examines the ways that these two different cases have factored into the respective parties' worldviews and into the diplomatic history of conflict resolution.

Amounts Claimed

A variety of figures have emerged over the years, and it is beyond the scope of this study to discuss this aspect of the property-claims issues in detail. Suffice to say that some of the best estimates have been based on serious research (as opposed to political and media speculation) and indicate sizable losses to both communities, but particularly the Palestinians. A sample of such studies is presented below:

The figures are noteworthy in several ways. First, the amounts cited for Palestinian claims vary widely. Israeli figures generally are lower because they are based on a narrow definition of what constituted abandoned property. The figures generated by the UNCCP are higher because it used a broader definition. This was particularly true for the individual assessment of property losses that the UNCCP completed in 1964. Arab and Palestinian reckonings of the refugees' losses are usually higher than that because they considered a broad definition of abandoned property that included the value of communal property, movable property, houses of worship, and other types of property. Second, figures for Mizrahi property vary widely.

TABLE 10.1. Sample of Estimates of Palestinian Refugee Property Losses

Author of Estimate	Value of Land	Total Losses
Israeli Government, Weitz-Danin-Lifshits Committee, 1948	£I102,832,000 (gross) (1948 currency)	—
Israeli Government, Ministry of Justice, Land Assessment Division, 1962	more than £P140,000,000 (1947 currency)	—
Arab League, 1956	£UK1,726,000,000 (includes buildings) (uncertain date of currency)	£UK1,933,000,000
UNCCP, 1951	£P100,383,784 (1947 currency)	£P120,383,784
UNCCP, 1964	£P204,660,190 (1947 currency)	—
Yusif Sayigh, 1966	£P403,400,000 (1947 currency)	£P752,700,000
Sami Hadawi and Atif Kubursi, 1988	£P528,900,000 (1947 currency)	£P748,050,000

Sources: Israel State Archives (ISA) 2445/3, "Report on a Settlement of the Arab Refugee [Issue]" (November 25, 1948), appendix 9; Central Zionist Archives (CZA), A246/57, "Comments on Value Assessments of Absentee Landed Property" (November 12, 1962); J. Khoury, *Arab Property and Blocked Accounts in Occupied Palestine* (Cairo: League of Arab States, General Secretary, Palestine section, 1956), 20; United Nations Secretariat Archives (UNSA) DAG 13–3, UNCCP/Refugee Office/Land Specialist/Box 35/1951/Reports: J.M. Berncastle/MCP/3/51/9, "Valuation of Abandoned Arab Land in Israel" (August 14, 1951); UNSA DAG 13–3, UNCCP/Principal Secretary/Records Relating to the Technical Office/Box 16/1952–57/Land Identification Project/Jarvis Report/A/AC.25/W.83 ADD 1, "Initial Report of the Commission's Land Expert on the Identification and Valuation of Arab Refugee Property Holdings in Israel" (September 10, 1962); Yusif 'Abdullah Sayigh, *al-Iqtisad al-Isra'ili* (The Israeli Economy) (Cairo: League of Arab States, Institute for Higher Arab Studies, 1966),107–10; Sami Hadawi, *Palestinian Rights and Losses in 1948: A Comprehensive Study*, part 5: An Economic Assessment of Total Palestinian Losses by Dr. Atef [*sic*] Kubursi (London: Saqi, 1988), 113, 187.

TABLE 10.2. Sample of Estimates of Mizrahi Jewish Property Losses

Author of Estimate	Value of Land	Total Losses
Israeli Government, Ministry of Finance, Foreign Claims Registration Office, 1952	—	$US86,870,456 (includes non-Mizrahi Jewish property in Arab countries) (1952 currency)
Israeli Government, Ministry of Finance, Foreign Claims Registration Office, 1956	—	$US103,373,000 (includes non-Mizrahi Jewish property in Arab countries) (1956 currency)
Itamar Levin, 2001	—	$US6,000,000,000– 10,000,000,000 (2001 currency)

Sources: ISA (130) 1848/hts/9, "Overall Summary of the Work of the Foreign Claims Registration Office as of 31 December 1950"; ISA (130) 2401/22, "Claims for Jewish Property Frozen in Arab States" (October 6, 1952); ISA (130) 2401/22, memorandum of 5 November 1952; *Jerusalem Post* (October 9, 1952), in Joseph Schechtman, *On Wings of Eagles: The Plight, Exodus, and Homecoming of Oriental Jews* (New York and London: Thomas Yoseloff, 1961), 123; Itamar Levin, *Locked Doors: The Seizure of Jewish Property in Arab Countries* (Westport, Conn.: Praeger, 2001), xv–xvi.

The major divide here lies in the estimates generated by the Israeli government in the 1950s and those produced more recently by nongovernmental Jewish organizations and individual researchers. The former are based on questionnaires issued to Mizrahi immigrants. Israeli authorities admitted that the response to its campaign to register losses was low. By contrast, the figures generated by Jewish NGOs and individuals are not restricted to the losses suffered by Mizrahi immigrants to Israel but reflect total Mizrahi losses. While larger, however, these figures are based on less precise sources of data. Finally, the amount of Mizrahi Jewish losses is smaller than that of the Palestinians, at least according to a secret internal sample study of Jewish claims done by the Israeli Ministry of Foreign Affairs. That study stated that the Palestinian claims were larger by a figure of 22:1.[4] The implications of this difference are enormous.

Property Claims and the Discourse of Catastrophe and Return

More germane to this study than the amounts claimed is an examination of how these claims have played a role in the formation of the discourses of catastrophe and return for both the Palestinians and Mizrahi Jews. Devastating property losses inform the respective discourses quite significantly; however, such claims have played a comparatively more important role in the Palestinian notion of return than the comparable Mizrahi notion. One reason is the ongoing statelessness of the Palestinian refugees, in contrast to most Mizrahi emigrants from Arab countries, who were consciously absorbed into the Israeli polity. While not erasing property losses from their individual and even community visions of self, this did alter the ways that the Mizrahim constructed political understandings of catastrophe and return. In addition, both sets of claims issues became entangled with the wider political ebb and flow of the Arab-Israeli conflict. This contributed to the incorporation of the property losses into the respective nationalist discourses.

The central event in the Palestinian national saga is al-Nakba (the "catastrophe" or "disaster") of 1948. More than half of Palestine's Arab population was uprooted and dispersed into exile. Not only did they lose their homeland in a political sense and become stateless refugees; they also lost their actual homes and other forms of movable and immovable property. For Palestinian peasants, in particular, the catastrophe of abandoning their farmland was more than simply a psychological or even financial loss. It constituted the loss of a way of life and was a socioeconomic shock of the highest order. Bereft of land in exile, they no longer possessed the landed means of production with which to reconstitute their existence. The international community and the host Arab governments provided assistance but not land. The refugees' enduring poverty in exile is thus directly traceable to their property losses. The fact that they by and large remained stateless and were not integrated into the surrounding national polities compounded their attachment to their lost land, both in a personal and a national sense. *Al-ard* (land), in the Palestinian discourse, thus refers both to land as homeland and land as immovable private and communal property. The centrality of the refugees' property losses to their vision of catastrophe and loss is reflected in one of the most enduring and powerful images of the Palestinian exile: the image of the refugee holding on to the key to his house, or the deed testifying to her ownership of land in the lost homeland.

This connection to lost property remains central, even though studies historically have shown that not all refugees lost land during their flight. UN estimates from the 1950s and 1960s ranged between 40 and 66 percent. The UNRWA (UN Relief and Works Agency) distributed questionnaires on this subject to 84,000 heads of refugee families in Jordan (including the West Bank), apparently in late 1950. This represented some 340,000 persons. The UNCCP then tallied the results for 8,400 questionnaires that were randomly selected and extrapolated cumulative results from this statistical sample. The results were instructive. Some 66 percent of refugee families in Jordan (55,400) claimed that they had abandoned land, while 59 percent (49,500 families) claimed that they had lost homes.[5] UNCCP land expert Frank E. Jarvis later estimated in the mid-1960s that 348,300 of 904,000—39.6 percent—refugees registered with the UNRWA had owned land in Palestine. He also thought that the percentage of the total refugee population that owned land but were not registered UNRWA refugees stood at 1.5 per cent.[6]

Settlement of their property claims similarly has been integrally bound up in the Palestinians' vision of their *haqq al-'awda* (right of return). Based on their own firm convictions as well as the UN's calls for repatriation and compensation, Palestinian refugees have made their property claims a central ingredient of their understanding of return. Return means the physical return of refugees and restitution of their lost property. The refugees thus view return as going back to *al-ard* in both senses of the word. Return to the land means repatriation to the political homeland as well as the individual homestead. The fact that Israel and the United States have consistently opposed large-scale repatriation and have focused instead on the payment of compensation for lost property and refugee resettlement in the Arab world only deepens the refugees' connection between return and land. They have steadfastly maintained that any compensation that Israel eventually does pay cannot negate the right of return.

Mizrahi property claims have played a different role in their discourse on catastrophe and return. This role has been a complicated one, as expertly analyzed by Yehouda Shenhav. A central feature shaping the Mizrahi discourse is that many of them settled in Israel. Upon arrival, they were granted citizenship rights and settled on land in a new country that was desperate for immigrants. Their dominant discourse in their new country not only stressed communal virtues (even communal ownership of land) but was anxious to overlook the horrors of individual immigrants' past and stress instead the new Zionist future. In the Zionist saga, *ha-arets* (the land) refers to the national patrimony, as distinct from land as immovable property (*karka'* or *adama*). While it did not extend to compensation for lost property (as some Mizrahim demanded), this absorption into a self-consciously Zionist society served partially to transform their story in official Zionist discourse from one of personal and communal loss to a success story: the dramatic homecoming of Mizrahi communities, revived and sustained with global Jewish assistance. For some Mizrahim, however, their property claims have occupied a more important place in their own communal vision of catastrophe. Their flight from Arab lands impoverished some who had formerly been quite wealthy and thus exacerbated the cultural and political discrimination they faced upon arriving in a country dominated by Ashkenazim. Indeed, the Israeli government's attitude toward their claims, combined with Jewish nongovernmental organizations' concern with Ashkenazi claims for reparations and restitution from Germany, drove several Mizrahi organizations to stress their own losses. Thus, the property issue factored into and exacerbated some Mizrahi Jews' feelings of discrimination in Israel.

Mizrahi concepts of return are even more different from comparable

Palestinian concepts. "Return" in the dominant Zionist discourse refers not to return to their lost homes and property in their countries of origin but the return of Jews to Zion. Zionist, non-Zionist, and anti-Zionist Mizrahim are united in the fact that none discuss return to the Arab world. Since many Mizrahim ended up in Israel, they became subject to, if not always participants in, the dominant Zionist views about return. For much of the global Zionist community, the successful "return" of these communities (the *edot ha-mizrah,* "communities of the East") to Eretz Israel overshadowed the property losses they suffered. Those Mizrahim who have resisted this hegemonic discourse have often done so by focusing on the institutional discrimination they have faced in modern Israel as people with one foot in two worlds: a Western-style Zionist polity and the Islamic world whence they originated. "Return" has a distinctly contradictory ring to some Mizrahim.

For both Palestinians and Mizrahim, unresolved property claims influenced their respective national discourses, although in different ways. Where the claims affected both groups in similar ways was in the fact that both they and a number of other regional and international parties used— some would say, exploited—their claims for their own purposes relating to the Arab-Israeli conflict.

Diplomatic Use and Exploitation of Property Claims

The property claims of both Palestinians and Mizrahim have also been used and exploited for political and diplomatic purposes by a variety of parties in the decades since 1948. Such uses are intertwined with their respective discourses on catastrophe and return and exist in symbiotic relationship with them. Some Palestinians initially used their refusal to accept compensation for lost property as a symbol of their refusal to accept their refugee status as permanent. This attitude was later adopted by the Palestine Liberation Organization (PLO) in the 1960s. The PLO refused to discuss anything more than the return of the refugees via armed struggle. It considered any talk of compensation as tantamount to recognition of Israel's takeover of Palestinian land by force. Refusal to accept compensation was a badge of steadfastness. Indeed, the PLO even refused to attend meetings called by the Arab League to examine the refugee property question in 1966 and 1967, stating at the time that "[it] does not believe in an evaluation of property nor does it recognize anything called Israel."[7]

By the turn of the twenty-first century, however, the PLO's official negotiating position vis-à-vis the refugees had changed. Israeli-PLO talks on final status issues during the 1990s led the PLO to develop a specific negotiating position and collect statistics for enumeration of refugee losses. By the late 1990s, the PLO position on the refugees included the possibility that some might not return, but still demanded restitution of property, not compensation: "Moreover, real property owned by the refugees at the time of their expulsion should be restored to its lawful Palestinian owners or their successors. International law regards private ownership as sacrosanct. Accordingly, the various discriminatory laws and administrative schemes, notably the Absentee Property Law, enacted by the Israeli authorities since 1948 to seize the property of the refugees and transfer it to the state of Israel, its agencies, or to the hands of Jewish individuals must be repealed and the seized property should be restored whether the refugee chooses to return or not."[8] The PLO worked with the UNCCP and the UN Secretariat archives in New York from 1997 to 2000 to transfer the UNCCP's records on Palestinian refugee property into a computerized database for potential use in determining individual refugees' losses. PLO negotiators carried out studies of the scope and value of refugee property, both globally and in cities such as Jerusalem and Haifa.

PLO policy underwent further refinement by the time Palestinian negotiators presented a detailed proposal on abandoned refugee property at the last round of public Israeli-Palestinian talks held in Taba in January 2001. This proposal outlined two overall policies toward refugee property: restitution of lost land for refugees who would be repatriated to Israel and compensation for those persons' lost movable property; and compensation for both movable and immovable property for nonreturning refugees. On the first point, the Palestinian position paper was brief and noted only:

27. Real property owned by a returning [repatriated to Israel] refugee at the time of his or her displacement shall be restored to the refugee or his or her lawful successors.
28. In cases where, according to criteria determined by the [proposed] Repatriation Commission, it is impossible, impracticable or inequitable to restore the property to its refugee owner, the refugee shall [be] restituted in-kind with property within Israel, equal in size and/ or value to the land and other property that they lost.[9]

Returnees would receive compensation for lost movable property. PLO negotiators envisioned that most refugees would be resettled and not repatriated, and the proposal went into great detail about the modalities of compensation in a manner that suggested that such payments would be directed at resettled refugees. At heart, their idea was that all refugees are entitled to individual compensation (unless the particular land in question had been collectively owned prior to 1948, in which case compensation payments would go to the proposed Palestinian state); all refugees, including those without property claims, would receive compensation for pain and suffering; Israel should provide the funds for compensation; these funds should be paid into an international fund; compensation would be disbursed by a international compensation commission that would enumerate refugee losses and oversee the actual process of compensation. This fund would determine the current value of movable and immovable property and would use records of the UNCCP and the Israeli Custodian of Absentee Property to determine prima facie evidence of ownership. The Palestinian document also proposed that, once restitution and compensation had been accomplished in their entirety, the parties shall consider that the refugee problem has been fully resolved. Both sides would therefore end all claims related to that problem.

Not all Palestinians accepted the PLO's vision of compensation. Even after the PLO moved in this direction, others have continued to refuse the notion of compensation, pushing instead for restitution and return. In 2000, Shaykh Ikrima Sabri, the mufti of Jerusalem, stated that he had issued a fatwa (Islamic juridical ruling) barring Muslims from accepting compensation for their lost property. Sabri equated compensation with sale of the land, something he claimed was forbidden inasmuch as Palestine was a holy land.[10] Others have feared that the PLO will eventually accept a compensation package that is too low or one that is paid on a global rather than an individual basis. Groups like the Palestinian Society for the Protection of Human Rights and the Environment (LAWE) and the BADIL Resource Center for Palestinian Residency and Refugee Rights have tried a variety of ways to secure what they feel is an equitable solution to the refugees' property claims and have raised refugee property rights to a new level of public awareness to prevent any future Israeli-PLO compensation deal from short-changing the refugees.

In the past, Palestinians were not all opposed to the idea of compensation for nationalist reasons. Some lobbied against compensation for more personal grounds. Americans, Israelis, UN officials, and some Palestinians in the early 1950s were of the opinion that the wealthy refugees were mainly concerned with obtaining personal compensation for their lost property, not with the wider national dimensions of the refugee problem. They believed that these propertied refugees were blocking movement toward compensation or a negotiated settlement out of concern that compensation would be paid on a collective rather than an individual basis.[11]

Beyond the Palestinians themselves, the Arab world has also used or exploited the refugee property issue, especially in its discussions with and within the United Nations. The refugees' property became a major stick with which the Arab states sought to beat Israel in their ongoing diplomatic struggle with the Jewish state. One week after General Assembly Resolution 273 (III) of May 11, 1949, admitted Israel to the UN, the Arab delegations to the UN sent a letter to the UNCCP demanding that Israel abrogate its legislation sequestering abandoned refugee property. They continued to demand solutions to various aspects of the refugee problem, including their property claims, in advance of wider talks on Arab-Israeli peace. In 1953, the Arab states also raised the idea of the UN establishing a "property custodian" to supervise the refugees' property, instead of the Israeli government. Their struggle for such a proposal brought them into direct clashes with the Americans. Eventually, they changed tactics and demanded that the UN create a property fund that would manage the income that Israel generated from its use of the refugees' land. This effort finally succeeded in 1981, when the General Assembly passed Resolution 36/146 C. The resolution read in part:

Considering that the Palestinian Arab refugees are entitled to their property in conformity with the principles of justice and equity, *Recalling*, in particular, its resolution 394 (V) of 14 December 1950, in which it directed the United Nations Conciliation Commission for Palestine . . . to prescribe measures for the protection of the rights, property and interests of the Palestinian Arab refugees. . . . [The General Assembly] *Requests* the Secretary-General to take all appropriate steps, in consultation with the United Nations Conciliation Commission for Palestine, for the protection and administration of Arab property, assets and property rights in Israel, and to establish a fund for the receipt of income derived therefrom, on behalf of their rightful owners.

The Arabs also used the refugees' property claims as a way of demonstrating their solidarity with the Palestinian cause when dealing with the UNCCP. Arab states demanded copies of the UNCCP records on Palestinian refugee losses beginning in 1953 so that they could use them for their own purposes. The UNCCP finally decided in late 1972 to allow relevant parties to purchase copies of its microfilmed records. Egypt eventually received two sets of films in 1974 and 1975, as did Jordan in 1974 and the PLO in 1984. As discussed above, the PLO later worked with the UN Secretariat archives in creating a computerized database using the UNCCP materials. The Jordanian government also produced its own computerized database in 1999–2001 from its films and other documents in its possession, for possible future use.

The United States similarly has used the property-claims issue in its approaches to resolving the Arab-Israeli conflict. The Americans always agreed that Israel must pay compensation to the refugees. They believed that compensation would thereafter serve as the primary financial vehicle for effecting the resettlement of Palestinian refugees in the Arab world. From the beginning, American officials believed that the best solution to the refugee problem was resettlement in the Arab world. As part of this solution, compensation payments would constitute a major vehicle for financing such a scheme. As early as May 1949, the Department of State delivered a memorandum to President Harry S Truman entitled "Palestine Refugee Problem: Financing Repatriation and Resettlement of Palestine Refugees," which suggested precisely this. Several weeks later, the Central Intelligence Agency drafted a memorandum that similarly called for refugee resettlement. Although not mentioning compensation specifically, the memorandum did state that the costs of resettlement ultimately would be cheaper for the United States than continued regional instability.

Over the decades, the United States continued to support the notion of compensation, although the question largely dropped from the diplomatic radar screens because of the vicissitudes of the Arab-Israeli conflict after 1956 and especially after 1967. Yet, in light of Israeli-PLO negotiations in the 1990s, the American government has returned to active consideration of the compensation question. It continues to view compensation as a vehicle for financing whatever final status agreement Israel and the PLO reach. At the Camp David II talks in July 2000, Clinton publicly discussed the compensation question and spoke of creating an international fund for such purposes.[12]

Israel has long used both sets of property claims as part of its diplomatic warfare with the Arab world. As early as 1949, the Israeli government agreed to compensate the refugees, although with limitations. Yet in the early 1950s, it used its willingness to pay compensation—or not to pay—as leverage in trying to force the Arab world to negotiate a wider peace settlement. Foreign Minister Moshe Sharett told the UNCCP in July 1950 that "no useful purpose would be served by the subject of compensation . . . being torn out of the general context and treated in isolation from the rest." He also ordered Israel's ambassador to the UN and the United States, Abba Eban, to tell the UNCCP that it should convey to the Arabs an Israeli threat: the Arabs' refusal to come to the negotiating table was liable to prompt Israel to withdraw its compensation offer.[13]

Over the years, the Israelis also insisted that compensation must be paid globally, not to individual refugees. This would assist in resettling the bulk of the poorer refugees. However, they sometimes tried to entice individual refugees to strike compensation deals when it served their interests. Israeli negotiators dangled compensation in front of the Jordanians in 1950 as an incentive to sign a peace treaty with the Jewish state. Later, Israel began a secret program to pay compensation to individual refugees, in third countries like Cyprus, starting in 1963.[14]

The second way that Israel used the property question was by linking compensation of the Palestinians with compensation of the Mizrahim.[15] Although it had earlier linked Palestinian compensation with return of property owned by Jews in the Arab-controlled West Bank, Gaza, and other locales, it stated in March 1951 that any future payments to Palestinians would be reduced by an amount equal to what the Mizrahim abandoned in Arab countries. The reasoning was that Israel absorbed these penniless Mizrahim at great cost to itself, even though the Jewish Agency was responsible for financing immigration. The Israeli government began gathering data on Mizrahi losses specifically in Arab countries in 1949. Disappointed with the low response rate among Mizrahi immigrants in Israel, it carried out a second registration in 1952.[16] It later undertook registrations of Iraqi and Egyptian Mizrahi property in 1956 and 1957, respectively, and established an office in the Ministry of Justice to maintain records on Mizrahi property in 1969.[17]

The demand for reciprocal compensation became a bedrock claim of the Israeli government for decades. With the beginning of direct bilateral talks with the Palestinians in the early 1990s, however, Israel began shifting its thinking. By the time of the Taba talks in January 2001, Israeli negotiators finally conceded that Mizrahi property claims no longer would be part of its final arrangement with the Palestinians, although they still argued for compensating the Mizrahim from an international fund. The Israeli position paper at Taba noted: "Although the issue of compensation to former Jewish refugees from Arab countries is not part of the bilateral Israeli-Palestinian agreement, in recognition of their suffering and losses, the parties pledge to cooperate in pursuing an equitable and just resolution to the issue."[18]

Finally, Mizrahi nongovernmental organizations have long lobbied for compensation for their abandoned or confiscated property. Various groups and individuals began pushing for recognition of their claims, especially as it became clear that the Israeli government was using the issue as a way to reduce what it owed the Palestinians, rather than championing the cause in order to benefit individual Mizrahim (especially those who did not settle in Israel). As early as 1949, the International League for Saving Arabian Jewry raised the question of Mizrahi property with the Israeli government, appealing for the government to factor this into its relations with the UNCCP.[19] Despite the fact that it publicly championed the Mizrahi claims and even gathered statistics detailing their losses, the government decided to use this issue as political capital in dealing with the Arab world and its claims for Palestinian compensation. This in turn prompted various Jewish NGOs to undertake their own campaigns to quantify Mizrahi losses and lobby for relief. At times, Mizrahi activists were quite vocal in their anger at the Israeli government for its decision to save the issue for future negotiations rather than push for resolution of their claims. Jewish NGOs collected their own statistics. In 1957, for instance, several NGOs that were not even exclusively Mizrahi—the World Jewish Congress, the American Joint Distribution Committee, the Alliance Israélite Universelle, and the American Jewish Committee—founded the Joint Committee (Central Registry of Jewish Losses in Egypt) to record Jewish property losses in Egypt.

In the past thirty years, a number of Jewish NGOs have renewed their focus on the property issue. This was partly due to the success of various Jewish groups to obtain reparations and property restitution relating to Ashkenazi losses in Europe during the Holocaust. Another reason has been the desire to demonstrate that there are "other Jews" in the world who similarly endured traumatic experiences in the twentieth century. Finally, the rise of Israeli-PLO negotiations in the 1990s prompted other groups to form in order to champion their cause in advance of a final status deal. The Foreign Ministry–funded World Organization of Jews from Arab Countries (WOJAC), active from 1975 to 1999, raised awareness of Mizrahi property claims although it supported the government's policy of advocating these claims itself with an eye toward incorporating them into a future Israeli-Palestinian deal.[20] So, too, have other NGOs such as the World Jewish Congress (WJC), the American Sephardi Federation (ASF), and the International Committee of Jews from Arab Lands (formed by the WJC and ASF). Most recently, several Jewish NGOs and the Israeli government agreed to work together on this issue, and the group Justice for Jews from Arab Countries emerged in 2002. Still, some Mizrahim, including within WOJAC and the Mizrahi Democratic Rainbow Coalition, have objected to leaving this issue simply in the hands of the Israeli government or joint organizations to handle. They fear that individual Mizrahim might not receive compensation as part of an Israeli-PLO deal, particularly those Mizrahim who live outside Israel.

A Joint Resolution?

The tortured history of the property issues, and especially the recent activity by a number of parties preparing for possible negotiations, raises the question: Will the two sets of claims be addressed together in any final resolution of the Arab-Israeli conflict, despite their inherent differences? During the past fifty years, that conflict has become a truly international dispute on a variety of levels. Despite its origins as a struggle between Zionist Jews and Palestinian Arabs for control of Palestine/Israel, it widened to include and affect the destinies of Jews and Arabs throughout the Middle East and the wider world. While the two sets of property claims are different in many ways, what is similar is the fact that both Palestinian refugees and Mizrahi Jewish emigrants from Arab countries lost property for reasons related to the struggle between Zionism and the Arab world; both have factored these losses into their discourse of exile and return; both have seen others use and even exploit their trauma as part of the diplomatic twists and turns of the Arab-Israeli conflict; and both have found their claims for compensation or restitution linked with the other's claims, whether they like it or not.

The reality has long been that the two issues have followed a parallel course in the minds of many. This does not suggest that they should have been linked; it merely recognizes what has occurred historically. Supporters of Israel have long claimed that the dual population exodus constituted a social and economic exchange: the Arab world's Jews for Israel's Arabs, Jewish property for Arab property. Palestinian partisans have countered that they and their plight have nothing to do with Mizrahi claims against sovereign Arab states like Iraq and that the "Arab Jews" can seek redress directly from those states. The Zionist argument subsumes the human aspect of the problem into a wider national one and refuses to acknowledge that, in the end, individuals on both sides remain bereft of their property. The Palestinian argument refuses to acknowledge the wider historical interconnectedness between the two sets of losses within the context of Zionist-Arab hostility and the subsequent inability of Mizrahi Jews (especially citizens of Israel) simply to fly back to the Arab countries of their origin and demand compensation.

Despite its failures, the onset of the peace process in the 1990s prompted all sides to begin thinking in terms of a comprehensive approach to ending the Arab-Israeli conflict. The Madrid process not only set in motion bilateral Arab-Israeli negotiations but also a multilateral track that aimed at tackling overarching regional problems that defy mere bilateral solutions. In so doing, peacemakers were cognizant that a lasting peace would require rising to a new level of awareness. The Oslo peace process, for all its faults, managed to allow the sets of property claims to be discussed publicly, in connection with one another and with other aspects of the peace process. The 1990s thus ushered in a process whereby a joint resolution to the twin property questions is possible, indeed likely.

Conclusion

The property claims of Palestinians and Mizrahi Jews have played vital roles in their respective national discourses as well as in the ways that they, and others, have used and exploited property claims during the past fifty years. As noted, this and other levels of similarity do not suggest that the two property-claims issues are comparable in terms of origin, amounts claimed, or political uses, or that they should have been linked. What is beyond doubt, however, is that both groups emerged from the tragedy of 1948 with significant property losses alongside their collective communal and personal traumas.

Overall, there may be two particularly significant levels of comparison. First, their respective internal discourses, their own understandings of "victimhood," have viewed their recent past in terms of traumatic emigration, loss of livelihood, impoverishment, and global inaction. Second, the ways in which the two property issues became linked and became entangled in the wider diplomatic machinations of the Arab-Israeli conflict over the decades have led both claims issues to remain unresolved despite the suffering of individual claimants. In this, the Palestinians and Mizrahi Jews have a common past and perhaps a common future.

Notes

This chapter is based on my *Records of Dispossession: Palestinian Refugee Property and the Arab-Israeli Conflict* (New York: Columbia University Press, 2003). I would like to acknowledge the financial support of a Research and Writing Grant from the John D. and Catherine T. MacArthur Foundation, given through the Friends of the Institute for Palestine Studies; the Institute for Palestine Studies; and a Rashkind Endowment Grant and Walter Williams Craigie Teaching Endowment Grant, both from Randolph-Macon College.

1. Yehouda Shenhav was the first scholar to study this linkage specifically and systematically. I am grateful for the help he provided me on this topic. See his "The Jews of Iraq, Zionist Ideology, and the Property of the Palestinian Refugees of 1948: An Anomaly of National Accounting," *International Journal of Middle East Studies* 31:4 (November 1999): 605–30; "Kehilot ve mahozot shel zikaron mizrahi" (Communities and districts of Mizrahi memory) (unpublished manuscript, Van Leer Institute and Tel Aviv University, 2000); and "Ethnicity and National Memory: World Organization of Jews from Arab Countries (WOJAC)," *British Journal of Middle Eastern Studies* 29 (2002): 25–55.

2. United States National Archives and Records Administration (NARA), RG 59, 887.411/3–2751, "The Position of the Jews of Iraq" (April 5, 1951).

3. *Jerusalem Post*, international edition, April 1, 2001.

4. Itamar Levin, *Locked Doors: The Seizure of Jewish Property in Arab Countries* (Westport, Conn.: Praeger, 2001), 223.

5. United Nations Secretariat Archives (UNSA), DAG 13–3, UNCCP; Subgroup: Office of the Principal Secretary. Series: Records Relating to Compensation/Box 18/1949–51/Working Papers; Document: W/60, "Sampling Survey of Abandoned Property Claimed by Arab Refugees" (April 12, 1951).

6. NARA RG 59, POL 27–14 PAL/UN, USUN to Department of State (January 14, 1966).

7. *The New York Times*, July 17, 1966; NARA RG 59, POL 3 PAL/UN, Amman to secretary of state (March 29, 1966), Beirut to secretary of state (March 30, 1966), Beirut to secretary of state (April 6, 1966), Cairo to secretary of state (July 12, 1966); RG 59, REF 3 UNRWA, Beirut to Department of State (February 27, 1967).

8. See the website of the PLO Negotiations Affairs Department, www.nadplo.org/permanent/refugees.html.

9. *Journal of Palestine Studies* 31:2 (winter 2002): 150.

10. Agence France-Presse news service, July 25, 2000.

11. For example, see Israeli thinking on this in Israel State Archives, *Documents on the Foreign Policy of Israel*, Vol. 6, Yemina Rosenthal, ed. (Jerusalem: Israel State Archives), 151–56; Document: "Report on the Visit of L. Jones in Israel" (March 11–14, 1951); Avi Shlaim, *Collusion Across the Jordan: King Abdullah, the Zionist Movement, and the Partition of Palestine* (New York: Columbia University Press, 1988), 551.

12. NARA RG 59, Lot File 53D468/Records of the Bureau of Near Eastern, South Asian, and African Affairs/McGhee Files 1945–53/Box 18; Document: "Palestine Refugee Problem: Financing Repatriation and Resettlement of Palestine Refugees" (May 4, 1949); ibid.; Document: "Intelligence Memorandum No. 180" (May 31, 1949).

13. UNSA DAG 13–3, UNCCP; Subgroup: Office of the Principal Secretary. Series: Records Relating to Compensation/Box 18/1950/Compensation; Document: "Letter dated 9 July 1950 addressed to the Chair of the Conciliation Commission by the Foreign Minister of Israel" (July 13, 1950); *Documents on the Foreign Policy of Israel*, 5:502. Sharett to Eban (August 27, 1950).

14. *Newsweek*, April 8, 1963; NARA RG 59, REF PAL, New York to secretary of state (July 3, 1963), Tel Aviv to secretary of state (July 8, 1963), Nicosia to Department of State (July 11, 1963), Nicosia to Department of State (July 18, 1963); RG 59, REF ARAB, Tel Aviv to secretary of state (August 30, 1963); NARA RG 59, REF

ARAB, Tel Aviv to secretary of state (August 30, 1963); RG 59, REF PAL, Tel Aviv to Department of State (November 7, 1963).

15. See Shenhav, "The Jews of Iraq."

16. ISA (130) 2401/22, "Claims for Jewish Property Frozen in Arab States" (October 6, 1952), and memorandum of November 5, 1952); ISA (130) 2401/22, "Claims for Jewish Property Frozen in Arab States" (October 6, 1952); ISA (130) 2401/22/1, Director of UN Department of Ministry of Foreign Affairs to Washington (November 5, 1952); ISA (130) 2401/22, memorandum of November 5, 1952; *Jerusalem Post* (October 9, 1952), in Joseph Schechtman, *On Wings of Eagles: The Plight, Exodus, and Homecoming of Oriental Jews* (New York: Thomas Yoseloff, 1961), 123; ISA (130) 2563/7, Foreign Currency Department to Ministry of Foreign Affairs (February 20, 1956).

17. *Divrei ha-Knesset* (26), 1050 (February 10, 1959); Itamar Levin, *Confiscated Wealth: The Fate of Jewish Property in Arab Lands,* Policy Forum No. 22 (Jerusalem: Institute of the World Jewish Congress, 2000), 19; Levin, *Locked Doors,* 63–64; Avi Machlis, "Compensation for Jews Who Fled Arab Countries," *Jewish Telegraphic Agency,* in *Jewish News of Greater Phoenix* 52 (August 25, 2000): 50, www.jewishaz.com/jewishnews/000825/fled.shtml.

18. Israeli Proposal on Palestinian Refugees, cited in *Journal of Palestine Studies* 31:2 (winter 2002): 150.

19. NARA RG 59, 867N.48/3–2249, Jerusalem to Department of State (March 22, 1949).

20. See Shenhav, "Ethnicity and National Memory."

Chapter 11
Arab Jews, Population Exchange, and the Palestinian Right of Return

Yehouda Shenhav

In July 2000, U.S. president Bill Clinton announced that an agreement had been reached at the Camp David summit to recognize the Jews from the Arab countries as "refugees" and that an international fund would provide compensation for the property they left behind when they immigrated to Israel during the 1950s. The immediate political significance of this declaration was to help Israel's prime minister at the time, Ehud Barak, to mobilize Shas's voters (the majority of whom are of Arab descent) in support of the peace process. However, the underlying logic—defining the Jews from Arab countries as refugees—responded to a deeper political theory that was developed in Israel in the 1950s to counterbalance the collective rights of the Palestinian refugees. It is not surprising, therefore, that Palestinians around the world reacted with dismay and rage to this announcement. In its contemporary garb, this "population exchange" theory was proposed to abdicate Israel's responsibility for the expulsion of Palestinians in 1948 and 1967, alleviate demands to compensate the Palestinian refugees, and serve as a bargaining chip against their right of return. For all practical purposes, the population exchange initiative was used to legitimize Israel's wrongdoing with regard to the transfer of the Palestinian refugees in 1948.

In this chapter, I lay out the political history of the population exchange theory, focus on the alleged nexus between the Palestinian refugees and the Jews from Arab countries, and challenge the validity of the theory by examining its logic, historical ramifications, and moral standing in contemporary Israeli political culture. I do not analyze the causes and political ramifications of the Palestinians' flight, since other chapters in this volume address that crucial issue. I do, however, note that most Jewish Israelis treat the right of return as a black box, as a sealed-off package, unwilling to consider the many ways in which this can be discussed, interpreted, negotiated, and solved. This was manifested in Barak's negotiating strategy in Camp

David, where he and his underlings refused to conduct any serious discussions about return or repatriation of refugees.

However, Jewish refusal to engage in political dialogue regarding the right of return is not uniform and can be roughly separated into three categories. These categories are neither exhaustive nor mutually exclusive but capture most discursive strategies used in Israel today. First, there is the mainstream response that denies any Israeli responsibility for the refugee problem, notably canonical Zionist historiography that attributes the Palestinians' mass exodus to orders that were ostensibly issued by Arab leaders, asking the Palestinians to flee their homes and villages.[1] Second, there are those (mainly on the Zionist Left) who acknowledge Israel's partial moral and political responsibility for the refugee problem but reject the right of return, arguing that it would end Israel's existence as a Jewish state. Third, there are those who brush off Israel's responsibility and invoke the population exchange argument, suggesting that the Middle East has witnessed a de facto population transfer in which the Palestinian refugees "fled" from Palestine and Jews "fled" from Arab countries.

I focus on this third discursive strategy, first examining practices of the Israeli government and the World Organization of Jews from Arab Countries (WOJAC). Based on these analyses, I show the fallacies associated with the usage of this population exchange theory and draw theoretical conclusions about the modus operandi of the state and its apparatuses.

Population Exchange as a Policy of Constructed Ambiguity

Prior to the immigration of Arab Jews, the Israeli government agreed to take back a limited number of Palestinian refugees.[2] The government avoided the term "population exchange" to avoid any explicit discourse about the refugee problem. During the 1950s, however, the government realized that it could use the Arab Jews as a bargaining chip against the Palestinians, first to relinquish responsibility to compensate the 1948 refugees for their property and then to block the demands for return.[3]

Mention of transfer and the exchange of Palestinians and Arab Jews existed in the Zionist lexicon as early as the 1930s. Whereas Zionist discourse used the "transfer" idea with regard to the Palestinians, it used "population exchange" in relation to the Arab Jews. For example, in 1937, at the World Congress of Poalei Tsion, a senior Mapamnik, Aharon Ziesling, urged that efforts be made to effect a population exchange between Palestine and the Arab states. David Ben-Gurion did not reject the idea out of hand. Similar proposals were voiced by American Zionists and by local leaders of the Labor movement.

In 1938 and 1939, wealthy Dutch capitalists corresponded with Zionist officials concerning a possible transfer of Palestinians to Iraq and Iraqi Jews to Palestine. Jewish capital would develop parts of Iraq so that the deal could go through. The initiative came ostensibly from non-Jewish circles in Holland, but the correspondence shows clearly that Zionist officials were involved, among them Dov Hoz (head of the political department of the Histadrut federation of labor until 1941) and Abel Hertzberg (president of the Zionist organization in Amsterdam). The Jews in Iraq were not consulted. It is not clear what became of the plan, although one can infer from the correspondence that at a certain stage the highest officials—Ben-Gurion, Moshe Sharett, and Pinhas Rutenberg—reacted coldly and with a pronounced lack of interest.[4]

Although these events are of historical interest, they are, finally, episodes that contrast sharply with the interest that Zionism took in the Jews of Iraq, beginning in 1941–42. That is, the population exchange theory was deemed less relevant as long as there was no interest in the immigration of Arab Jews to Palestine/Israel. During World War II, as the mass murder of Jews in Europe was increasingly confirmed, the Zionist movement turned its gaze upon the Arab Jews as candidates for immigration. In 1942, Ben-Gurion described at a meeting of Jewish experts and leaders a demographic plan to bring a million Jews to Palestine, known as *Tochnit Ha'milion*. He singled out the Middle Eastern Jews: "Our Zionist policy must now pay special attention to the Jewish groups in the Arab countries."[5] In July 1943, Eliahu Dobkin, head of the Jewish Agency's immigration department, presented a map of the Arab Jews. Explaining their importance for the demographic question in Palestine, Dobkin emphasized that "many of the Jews in Europe will perish in the Holocaust and the Jews of Russia are locked in. Therefore, the quantitative value of these three-quarters of a million [Arab] Jews has risen to the level of a highly valuable political factor within the framework of world Jewry. . . . The primary task we face is to rescue this Jewry, [and] the time has come to mount an assault on this Jewry for a Zionist conquest."[6] These statements marked the beginning of a discourse on the Arab Jews as potential immigrants to Palestine.[7] In 1948, Joseph Schechtman, a member of the Jewish Agency's actions committee in the United States, published a proposal to solve the refugee problem on the basis of the Greco-Turkish model in the Treaty of Lausanne of 1923, including a trade-off exchange with the Arab Jews.[8] The model conceptualized the 1948 war as an event in the vagaries of world history; its adoption would abdicate Israel from any responsibility regarding the Palestinian refugees.

However, only in the early 1950s did a great number of Arab Jews arrive in Israel. The Iraqi immigration in 1950–51 was pivotal to the reemergence of the population exchange theory. In March 1950, Iraq enacted a denaturalization law—valid for one year—that enabled Jews to leave after renouncing their citizenship. Approximately 120,000 Jews were brought by air to Israel from Iraq between May 1950 and June 1951.[9] In this context, the population exchange theory became entangled with another state theory to be labeled as the "property exchange" theory.[10]

Police Minister Behor Shitrit was the first to raise the question of the "situation of Iraq's Jews" in the Israeli cabinet, in March 1949. He was worried about the condition of the Jews in Iraq after Zionism had been outlawed; at one stage, he proposed that the property of Israeli Arabs be held hostage for the Jewish property in Iraq, but this idea was rejected by the foreign ministry. At the end of that month, the Knesset debated the situation of the Jews in the Arab countries. Eliahu Eliachar, from the Sephardi list, asserted that in addressing the refugee issue, the government must take into account the transfer to Israel of Jews who would want to make that move: "This bargaining chip was given to our government by Divine Providence so that we can take preventive measures."[11]

In July 1949, the British government, fearing the decline of its influence in the Middle East, proposed a population exchange and tried to persuade Iraqi prime minister Nuri Sa'id to settle 100,000 Palestinian refugees in Iraq. The British Foreign Office wrote to its legations in the Middle East about an "arrangement whereby Iraqi Jews moved into Israel, received compensation for their property from the Israeli government, while the Arab refugees were installed with the property in Iraq."[12] The British Foreign Office believed that "the Israeli government would find it hard to resist an opportunity of bringing a substantial number of Jews to Israel."[13] In return, Sa'id demanded that half the Palestinian refugees be settled in Palestine and the rest in the Arab states. If the refugee arrangement were fair, he said, the Iraqi government would permit a voluntary move by Iraqi Jews to Palestine. Under the terms of the plan, an international committee was to assess the value of the property left behind by the Palestinian refugees who would be settled in Iraq, and they would receive restitution drawn from the property of the Iraqi Jews who would be sent to Palestine.[14] Although Zionist circles at the time accepted transfer or population exchange as solutions to the conflict, the proposal did not generate an Israeli response.

In September 1949, Shitrit again raised in the cabinet "the problem of the Jews in the Arab countries." He asked whether the foreign ministry had taken steps to assist them: "I would like to know if . . . it is possible to arrive at some agreement on a *transfer* [emphasis added] in terms of both property and people, and to take up the matter with the UN institutions and inform the world. . . . They are our brothers, and it is our duty to rescue them."[15] This question exasperated Foreign Minister Sharett, who retorted brusquely: "This is actually a query and not a subject being put forward for discussion. . . . If Mr. Shitrit takes an interest in matters of immigration—he need not bother the cabinet with this—there is a special institution for it, and there they would inform him of the difficulties being encountered in getting the people here. . . . They will explain to you why it is impossible to bring Jews from Iraq at this time."[16] Sharett's response exposes two facets of the relationship between the state and its institutions. First, he tells Shitrit that there are other institutions, rather than the government, that deal with immigration. By relegating the responsibility to the Jewish Agency, which can deal with the immigrants without determining their status, the government blurs the boundaries between state and society. At the same time, Sharett says that the state proper (that is, the foreign ministry) will deal with the matter if a peace treaty is achieved (in relation to negotiation between sovereign states).

In this discussion, Sharett spoke for the first time about the Jewish property in the Arab countries. He cited the absence of a peace treaty with Iraq as the reason for his rejecting cooperation with the government in Baghdad: "To address at this time the question of transferring the property of the Jews to Israel—that would be naive. We are talking about an agreement, about establishing peace, and we are not budging—will we suddenly succeed in removing the question of the Jews from that framework and getting the Arab states to accept an agreement regarding the Jews who reside in those countries? I am not blessed with that kind of diplomatic skill! Such thinking is quixotic."[17] For the sake of balance, Sharett pointed out that hundreds of families had arrived in Israel from Egypt and were being provided with housing by the government. It was apparently not by chance that Sharett linked these new arrivals with the Palestinian property in Israel: "I met one of these families that had already settled in one of the abandoned [Palestinian] villages—people who had come from Egypt just a day or two before." The discussion ended without the prime minister and foreign minister having to address Shitrit's question about a transfer. However, Sharett's linkage of Jewish property and Arab property was in time developed into a political practice of the government as well as of several Jewish organizations. It demonstrates that the practice of population exchange preceded explicit acknowledgment of it. The usage of Palestinian property for the partial housing of Arab Jews (although in very small numbers) shows that the state did not shy away from implementing this theory de facto.

In October 1949, the world and Israeli press reported the Iraqi-British plan for a population exchange (for example, *Davar*, October 16, 1949). The publicity embarrassed the other Arab leaders and caused a stir in the Palestinian refugee camps. The British ambassador to Iraq informed the Foreign Office that Palestinian refugees would not agree to settle in Iraq. The Iraqi delegate to the United Nations also lost no time in denying that Iraq would take in 100,000 refugees; he claimed that Zionist sources were behind the reports.[18] Even though internal documents show that the plan was known to various levels of the Israeli administration,[19] Israel immediately rejected it. At a cabinet meeting, the ministers pressed the foreign minister and prime minister for information.[20] Sharett replied: "What does

an exchange mean—we cannot solve the problem of the Arab refugees on
the basis of an exchange, we do not have enough Jews to match the number
of the Arab refugees." "In my eyes," Ben-Gurion added, "all the talk about
an exchange is strange. Clearly, if the Iraqi Jews are able to leave, we will
receive them and we will not ask questions about an exchange or not an
exchange; about property or about an absence of property."[21] Israeli
sources further claimed that "Iraq is casting an eye on the Jewish property"
and that Baghdad had floated the exchange idea as a trial balloon. Nevertheless, Shitrit reiterated his exchange proposal, writing to the finance
minister: "If an official proposal is made to our government about a population exchange, we should accept the offer."[22] Ignoring such signals, Ben-
Gurion and Sharett constructed a policy based on ambiguity. They understood the heavy price that Israel would have to pay if it entered into concrete agreements regarding the Palestinians. They would have to
acknowledge responsibility for the refugee problem, allow the return of
Palestinian refugees, and/or compensate them for their property. Sharett
told the British ambassador to Israel that the idea of exchanging 100,000
homeless (Palestinian) refugees for 100,000 (Jewish) refugees who would
leave their assets behind was read in Israel as extortion.[23]

In late October 1949, the cabinet held a special meeting on the situation
of Iraq's Jews in which Foreign Minister Sharett responded:

> On the question of a *population exchange*, it was reported in the press, purportedly
> citing the spokesman of the Survey Group, that the Prime Minister of Iraq has alleg-
> edly made such an offer. We asked the Survey Group about the truth of this report.
> We received an official reply that in the course of a conversation Nuri Sa'id had
> 'thrown out' an idea along the lines of a possible exchange of Iraq's Jews for the
> Arab refugees. . . . Agreeing to this would mean, in my opinion, our agreement to
> have the property of Iraq's Jews confiscated by the Iraqi Treasury in return for the
> Arab property we have confiscated here, and then we assume responsibility for com-
> pensating the Jews of Iraq on account of the Arabs' property, as against the Jews'
> property there. That would create a dangerous precedent with regard to Egypt and
> other countries. It could also be construed to mean that every Arab country under-
> takes to accept refugees only to the extent that it has Jews.[24] [emphasis is mine]

Sharett's concern was over a possible future claim of compensation by
Iraq's Jews, should the Israeli government agree to a transfer deal. The possibility of extricating the Iraqi Jews together with their property was lost in
his accounting logic: "This would be a dangerous precedent vis-à-vis other
countries. We will be confronted by tens of thousands of people who will
arrive, naked and destitute, demanding that we give them property. This
could entangle us in an inextricable impasse."[25]

In the meantime, Moshe Sasson, vice-consul at the Israeli legation in Ath-
ens in the early 1950s, was busy working out a proposal for a population
and property exchange involving Israeli Arabs and Libyan Jews. Sasson
noted its importance as a "lesson" for the Palestinian refugees who were

still seeking to reenter Israel.[26] At this point, the concepts of population exchange and transfer (of Israeli Palestinians out of Israel) became associated, if not synonymous. Yet Israel kept its policy ambiguous despite these scattered, sometimes uncoordinated, efforts. In April 1950, following the enactment of the denaturalization law, attempts were made on behalf of the State of Israel to extract the Jewish property in Iraq unilaterally. Ezra Danin, an adviser to the foreign ministry, reported that the prime minister had asked him to trade the property of Israeli Palestinians listed as "present" and "non-absentees," who "will want to leave" because "they have not been able to adapt to the Jewish state," for the property of Iraqi Jews. Danin wrote to the finance minister: "I have been asked by Messrs. Y. Palmon and Z. Lief, in the name of the Prime Minister and the Foreign Minister, to try to examine whether the possibility exists to exchange property of *non-absentee* [emphasis in the original] Israeli Arabs for property of Jews in Iraq. It was emphasized that the examination will be carried out with regard to Iraq and not the other Arab states, and that no attempt should be made to involve property of absentee Arabs in this matter."[27] Danin was a member of Ben-Gurion's transfer committee, which proposed to expel "present" Israeli Arabis.[28] Ze'ev Lief, an adviser on land and borders in the prime minister's office and an ardent activist in the efforts to transfer Israel's Palestinians, had already moved to implement the proposal.[29] In a note to the prime minister, foreign minister, and finance minister, Lief wrote: "As a first means, I would advise instructing our representative in Persia to contact Jewish circles in Iraq and have them desist from the wholesale liquidation of assets at depressed prices and hint to them that the prospect exists that they will be able to liquidate their property at better terms on an exchange basis."[30] Nothing was done with Lief's request, but Danin arranged with several Palestinian families to leave Israel. His emissaries went to Iran to organize a property exchange from there, but their efforts fell through because the proposals sounded suspicious to Iraqi Jews. Reports about discrimination against the Arab Jews and bureaucratic obstacles in Israel deterred them from investing in the country or transferring capital there.[31] Still, it is not clear whether the attempts at a unilateral extraction of property were serious. In September 1950, after the organized departure of Jews from Iraq had begun and with the Israeli government no longer feeling threatened by an explicit exchange agreement, Sharett acknowledged publicly that the Iraqi proposal had been a genuine diplomatic option.[32] This acknowledgment, however, did not change Israel's policy of ambiguity.

The transfer idea, as I argued earlier, was not alien to Zionist thinking; it was manifested in both praxis and ideology before and after the Iraqi Jews were brought to Israel. At the time, the Israeli government's ambiguous position regarding the transfer offers was motivated by demographic fear. The government believed that officially agreeing to population exchange would create a "dangerous" precedent.[33] In the government's estimate, there were three times as many Palestinian refugees as there were Jews in the Arab states, who totaled 200,000 Jews since the possibility of bringing the Maghreb Jews to Israel had not yet arisen.[34] The Israeli government feared that a population exchange that rested on a numerical basis would obligate Israel to repatriate the "surplus refugees." Indeed, the United Nations' Morton plan called for the settlement of thousands of such "surplus" refugees in internationalized Jerusalem.[35] This possibility, combined with information that Egypt refused to admit Palestinian refugees, deterred the Israeli government. The foreign ministry maintained that only if Iraq agreed to absorb 300,000 to 400,000 Palestinian refugees in return for the Iraqi Jews could Israel contemplate accepting the transfer agreement.[36] Thus, government officials were careful not to make explicit claims about population exchange and keep the state's position ambiguous.

Population Exchange and Property Exchange Juxtaposed

Even though Israel kept its position on population exchange vague, it formally adopted a property exchange theory. In March 1951, a year after Iraq's Jews had been given the opportunity to leave, about 105,000 Jews had registered to emigrate. However, only 35,000 had actually left. The rest, having renounced their citizenship, were waiting. On March 10, Prime Minister Sa'id submitted a bill to the parliament to impound and freeze the Jews' property. To prevent transactions from being carried out in the period between the bill's enactment into law and its implementation, the finance ministry shut down the country's banks for three days and the police sealed stores owned by Jews, confiscated their vehicles and other items, and searched the homes of merchants and jewelers. This law freezing Jewish assets relieved the Israeli government of the need to make a formal declaration of support for a population exchange; henceforth it could refer to any such exchange of property and people as a spontaneous occurrence. Sharett briefed the cabinet on the law and its implications: . . . "The question that arises is what we can do. Approaches to England and France are possible, of course, but . . . they could say: You took the property of the Arabs who left Palestine and entrusted it to a custodian, they are doing the same."[37] On March 19, Sharett apprised the Knesset of the government's reaction to Iraq's action. He officially and unequivocally fused the two accounts into a single equation:

The Government of Israel . . . views this episode of plunder in the spirit of the law as the continuation of the malicious regime of dispossession that has always prevailed in Iraq vis-à-vis defenseless and helpless minorities . . . By freezing the assets of tens of thousands of Jews who are immigrating to Israel—today stateless but citizens of Israel immediately upon their immigration—the Government of Iraq has opened an account between it and the Government of Israel. We already have an account with the Arab world, namely the account of the compensation that accrues to the Arabs who left the territory of Israel and abandoned their property. . . . The act now committed by the Kingdom of Iraq . . . forces us to link the two accounts. . . . We will take into account the value of the Jewish property that has been frozen in Iraq with respect to the compensation we have undertaken to pay the Arabs who abandoned property in Israel.[38]

Now the foreign ministry was ready to inform the UN Conciliation Commission for Palestine (UNCCP) that the government was committed to contribute toward a resolution of the refugee problem, but added: "It will be unable to honor that commitment if in addition to its other commitments to absorb new immigrants it will find itself having to undertake the rehabilitation of 100,000 Iraqi Jews."[39]

This was a crucial moment in the history of the population exchange theory. The State of Israel understood that the Arab Jews could serve as pawns in the demographic war if they could be linked to the Palestinian refugees in a formula of national accounting. Sharett's statement, which also seemed to hold out the promise of compensation for Iraqi Jews, was aimed at both the Iraqi Jews and the international community. It was necessary to send a message to the Iraqi Jews, as they had assailed the Zionist activists for doing nothing to salvage the community's property. The statement—whose implications Sharett would later disavow—had the intended effect of assuaging the concern of the Iraqi Jews, but also of generating high expectations among them. They were now convinced that they would receive restitution from the Israeli government for the property that they were leaving behind.[40] Yitzhak Raphael, head of the Jewish Agency's aliyah department, who was also a recipient of the cable, noted with satisfaction in his diary that Sharett's statement had mitigated the sense of discrimination among the Iraqi Jews.[41]

At the same time, the foreign ministry's Shamay Kahane cautioned Sharett that "we have to take into account that the registration of claims may generate illusions among the new immigrants, and they are liable to demand that the Government of Israel pay them compensation from the funds of the [Arabs'] abandoned property."[42] The foreign ministry sent an internal memorandum to the director general of the prime minister's office explaining that the registration of property claims had the sole purpose of creating a bargaining chip on the Palestinian issue. The memorandum added that it was crucial to uphold the principle of group compensation and not individual payments, which many refugees demanded. "We will not, then," the document noted, "be able to take the opposite approach with the Iraqi Jewish immigrants without opening the gates to a flood of private claims from tens of thousands of Arab refugees who once owned any property in the Land of Israel."[43] In short, the foreign ministry's proposal—which was put into practice—was to make the Iraqi immigrants hostage of the Israeli government. The Palestinians' abandoned property remained in the hands of the state's custodian general, while Iraq's freeze of Jewish property was invoked as an excuse to justify the confiscation of Palestinian assets.

As noted, Sharett's Knesset statement was also intended as a message to the great powers. Although he had previously opposed the exchange option, the frozen property in Iraq afforded him a golden opportunity to lock the skeleton of the Palestinians' rights into a closet. Even though Sharett knew that plundered Palestinian property was vastly more valuable than Jewish property in Iraq, he allowed the foreign ministry to "release" exaggerated appraisals of the respective worth of the two accounts. In a cable to the Israeli legation in Paris, Walter Eytan noted: "The mutual release of frozen deposits should include Iraq. . . . The value of the frozen deposits of Arabs in Israel is estimated at five and a half million pounds, whereas the value of the frozen deposits of the Jews in Iraq is at least twenty million and perhaps even thirty to forty million."[44]

On March 27, 1951, when Sharett met with U.S. undersecretary of state George McGhee,[45] he reasserted the government's promise and insinuated that German reparations to Israel could facilitate that. On May 1, 1951, the United States announced that, if the Israeli government took positive action to accelerate the transfer of Palestinians' frozen property, it could approach Baghdad with a similar request.[46] In its reply, Israel rejected the comparison but reiterated its readiness to pay restitution for the "abandoned property" as part of a peace agreement.[47] Britain, too, maintained that the Iraqis' impounding of Jewish property was not an original idea: Israel had set the precedent. No attempt to effect a settlement would be useful, the British believed, unless Israel either unfroze the refugees' property or paid compensation.[48]

The Israeli government's creation of the linked property account was a singular act—something of a historic milepost—that constructed a zero-sum equation between the Arab Jews and the Palestinian refugees. The political theory that underlay this equation rested on the robbery of the Palestinian property and on the nationalization of Jewish Iraqi property. The Israeli government "appropriated" the property of all Iraqi Jews in order to utilize it—rhetorically, symbolically, and judicially—as state property. Files in the state archive containing the foreign ministry's correspondence on this property bear the telltale heading "Protection of Israeli Property."[49]

Sharett's declaration that the question of Jewish property would be taken into account in the future was put to an empirical test four times: in 1951, the mid-1950s, the 1970s during negotiations with Egypt, and the 1990s Oslo era. In 1951, a government commission began to document Jewish property in Iraq. Archival documents show that the commission was not created out of concern for that property; its report was intended to buffer the Israeli government in the face of future claims for compensation resulting from the nationalization of Palestinian property by the custodian general. The officials who established the commission, seeking to conceal the manipulation, wrote: "It is proposed not to announce, at least for the time being, that registration of the personal claims is being carried out with the aim of deducting the value of the Jewish property frozen in Iraq from the payment of compensation for the abandoned Arab property."[50] In October 1955, public pressure forced the government to establish another commission to reregister Iraqi immigrants' claims. Its December 1956 report was ignored by the foreign ministry.[51] Officials suggested that an extra-governmental body register the claims, in order to avert the government's having to assume responsibility vis-à-vis the Iraqi Jews. On the eve of the commission's establishment, the prime minister ordered that Iraqi immigrants who presented claims not be asked about movables they had left behind, since "their registration is liable to conflict with our policy of restitution to the Arab refugees, which is confined solely to immovables."[52]

The property exchange theory forestalled any possibility of individual claims for compensation and made use of the assets of Arab Jews as if they were state property, at the disposal of the State of Israel. The submission of private-property claims of individuals—for example, to the Egyptian government within the auspices of the peace agreement—would weaken the state in future negotiations with the Palestinians.

WOJAC's Discourse on Population Exchange

Whereas in the early 1950s the government accepted the property exchange theory, it denied formal adoption of the population exchange theory. However, this idea reemerged in the 1970s with the rise of the Palestinian national movement.[53] Pivotal to the resurgence of the theory was a Jewish organization known as WOJAC: World Organization of Jews from Arab Countries.[54] The organization was a voluntary state organ, supported by the foreign ministry and the Jewish Agency. When established in 1975, the foreign ministry told WOJAC that its connection should be kept secret. Whereas the state's practices were harder to decipher, WOJAC was clear and adamant about its objectives, and its discursive practices were easy to discern. It argued explicitly that Palestinian refugees should not be allowed back into Israel, since an involuntary population exchange had already taken place in the Middle East. Led by Mordechai Ben-Porat, a former Zionist leader in Iraq, a member of Moshe Dayan's Rafi Party, and a cabinet member, the organization adopted a resolution casting responsibility on the Arab governments.[55] Speaking at the UN General Assembly in December 1977, Ben-Porat stated that "the problem of the Arab and Jewish refugees in the Middle East can find its practical solution only within the framework of de facto exchanges of population, which have already taken place." Members of its executive committee established a direct linkage

between the establishment of WOJAC and activities of the Palestine Liberation Organization (PLO). As Dr. Jacques Barnes stated: "We are the Jewish
answer to the PLO . . . to the right of return. . . . [T]hat is why we exist."[56]
This was the root of President Clinton's statement in Camp David in July
2000.

The idea of defining Arab Jews as refugees was a major objective of
WOJAC. Ostensibly, the description of the Arab Jews as refugees was not
unreasonable in light of the fact that the term "refugee" became a central
concept in historical and sociological discourse and in international law
after World War II and was dominant in the Jewish world following the
Holocaust.[57] Thus, UN Security Council Resolution 242 of November 1967
referred to "a just settlement of the refugee problem" in the Middle East,
although in the 1970s the Arab states sought explicit mention of "Arab refugees in the Middle East." Under Israeli pressure, a working paper drawn
up by U.S. Secretary of State Cyrus Vance in 1977, ahead of the proposed
Geneva conference, stated that a solution would be found for the "refugee
problem" without specifying which refugees. However, WOJAC ultimately
failed in its attempt to win acceptance of the term "Jewish refugees."

WOJAC mobilized some Israeli politicians to endorse this concept, notably Labor Party Shimon Peres, who wrote in 1983:

Even in 1948—in the midst of the War of Independence—we asked the Arabs living
in the country not to leave, and not to pay heed to the incitement by the Mufti of
Jerusalem . . . to flee for fear of the terrible Jews. . . . These suffering people [refu-
gees of 1948] could easily have been accommodated in their countries of residence—and not perpetuate their misery. Another aspect of the refugee problem in
the Middle East is the Jewish aspect. The State of Israel saw it as its sacred, supreme
duty to bring all the Jews of the Arab countries to Israel, and to allow them to share
in building the land, in founding a dynamic and creative society, and in forming a
new Jewish-Israeli man. To a great extent, we can see these two processes—the
transfer of the Arab residents from Israel to the Arab countries, and the ingathering
of Arab Jewry in Israel—as an informal population exchange.[58]

It should be noticed that Peres's letter displays the contradictions
endemic to the population exchange theory. Whereas he depicts the
uprooting of the Palestinian refugees as a voluntary act, he is careful not to
go so far as to argue that the Arab Jews were expelled from Arab countries.
However, WOJAC's refugee exchange theory presupposed implicitly and
explicitly that Arab Jews became refugees from their countries of origin.

This was most radically presented by Ya'akov Meron, a justice ministry
official and one of WOJAC's most articulate spokesmen. Meron took the
unequivocal position not only that the model of Jewish-Muslim relations
was distinctly antagonistic but that the Jews were expelled from the Arab
countries.[59] Meron took issue with the Zionist saga, which, he contended,
was not subjected to a critical assessment until the removal of the Labor
Party from power in 1977.[60] That saga, he argued, gave rise to romantic

labels such as Operation Magic Carpet and Operation Ezra and Nehemia, which underscored the positive aspect of Zionist immigration to Israel and overshadowed the fact that the Jews emigrated because of "an Arab policy of expulsion."[61] Refugee status produced by a coordinated Arab expulsion diminishes the importance of Zionist activity to remove the Jews from the Arab countries. Even the more moderate position, holding that the Jews in those countries were caught up in turbulent events and became refugees because of historical circumstances, contests the classic Zionist account by all but eliminating the role attributed to Zionist consciousness as a reason for Jews to move to Israel. For example, Moshe Sasson, a Damascus-born foreign ministry official, said he wanted to set the record straight: "The fact is, and it must be stated, and stated frankly and simply, that the struggle between the Jewish national movement and the Arab national movement was a central factor that left its mark and influenced the relations of the regime or the Arab movement in one country or another toward the Jews. . . . It was the conflict that was influential."[62]

Meron's thesis also shed a problematic light on reports by Zionist activists in Arab countries and on the tremendous difficulty they encountered in their efforts to bring the Jews to Israel. Shlomo Hillel, for example, described the difficulties he and his colleagues faced in trying to remove the Jews from Iraq via illegal immigration in 1950.[63] So does Yosef Meir, who writes about the distress of the Iraqi government at the movement of Jews to Iran and about its attempts to prevent the process.[64] Likewise, Hillel and Ben-Porat describe their attempts to persuade Sa'id and Suweidi to let them remove the country's Jews and take them to Israel. Some writers place (with exaggeration) the onset of Zionist activity in the Arab countries in the 1920s, long before Jewish-Muslim relations begin to be described as antagonistic. The genre of Zionist underground literature emphasized the elements of escape, of Jews being smuggled out, and of mystery—they did not hint at the possibility of expulsion.

Indeed, the expulsion-refugee thesis within WOJAC generated strong sentiments and reactions. In a discussion about what to name the new organization, Ben-Porat, then a deputy speaker of the Knesset, pondered: "The question here . . . [is] whether to introduce the word refugees, Jewish refugees, or not. . . . There is some sensitivity here in Israel, as to why we call ourselves refugees. There is a second approach that says—it is not only an approach, it is the truth—we all arrived here as refugees [and] afterward we rehabilitated ourselves and became citizens of Israel."[65] Ben-Porat admitted that the foreign ministry was not pleased with his references to Jewish refugees in the Middle East: "I will not say that I met with any great enthusiasm from the foreign ministry or from the government concerning the proposal. Their reply was: it is a two-edged sword."[66] Ben-Porat outlined the dilemma in his search for a compromise formula:

We must not say that the Jews immigrated to Israel only on account of the suppression. . . . But on the other hand we must also not say that it was only on account of the yearning for Israel. . . . [B]oth of those elements played a part in their immigration to Israel. We must ground it historically . . . that the Jews arrived in Israel as refugees . . . [and] went through the agonies of absorption. . . . We want to ground it in documentation, how the Jews who arrived in Israel, how they lived in transit camps, huts . . . in order to prove that it was not only the Arab refugees who lived in camps . . . , but that our Jews [also] suffered greatly.

Elsewhere Ben Porat pursues this line of confusion:

We want to be emissaries for the State of Israel, for Israel's policy. That is our goal and that is where we have to direct our activity . . . to tell ourselves and the whole world that a movement of populations occurred here, or that it led to an exchange of populations, and not voluntarily or because of propaganda. Let us say, not because of Zionist propaganda. . . . We have to find the right balance in this argument, between leaving due to distress and leaving due to yearning, and to find the right formula, because you have to take into account the ears of the Gentiles. . . . So that obliges us to emphasize precisely the aspect of distress. . . . [67]

The major dissenter from WOJAC's refugee argument was the Tunisia-born Knesset member Mathilda Gez: "There are another twelve million Jews dispersed in the diaspora. If we appear as refugees, how can we go before them and talk about immigration based on the Zionist idea? . . . Do I have to deny my Zionism today because of my rights to Tunisia? Absolutely not. . . . So I do not want us to blur the issue."[68] Gez, then, declined to discard the Zionist, pan-Jewish interest and viewed the Jewish Diaspora through a proto-Zionist lens, that is, as potentially Zionist until the anticipated immigration to Israel. Yehuda Nini, professor of Jewish history, further stated: "I urge caution. . . . The problem is very delicate, very complicated. . . . I do not think that the question of an organization of Jews from Arab countries should be linked . . . to the matter of Palestinian refugees. . . . We did not create the problem of the Palestinian refugees."[69] A lively discussion ensued, focusing on the dichotomy between their own definition as refugees and Zionist yearning, which provided a narrow conceptual space regarding the possibilities for getting to Israel. Ben-Porat contested the notion that Arab Jews were "proto-Zionists": "No one will persuade me . . . that if I had given them the choice of coming with a proper passport, [and coming] whenever [they] wanted with their property, that 120,000 would have come from Iraq or that all the Jews of Egypt would have come. . . . The persecutions played a part here. They definitely expanded the matter . . . [and] gave rise to the question of the yearning."[70]

But Shimon Avizemer argued: "We know that there was no Zionist movement in these countries. There was Zionism, there was Judaism, there was ideology, [but] there was no movement, no organization, no framework . . . as there was in Europe. . . . The persecutions were a catalyst, a catalyzing force for the love, the Zionism, the Judaism that burned in them all the time. . . . They came to the Land of Israel because no other country accepted them."[71]

Opposition to the definition of Arab Jews as refugees intensified. Shlomo Hillel, who was active in the Zionist underground in Iraq and was the architect of the mass escape known as Operation Meikelberg, said years later: "I do not regard the exodus of Jews from Arab countries as refugees. I do not accept that. The Jews in the Arab countries came because they wanted to come."[72] Similarly, Meretz's Ran Cohen declared emotionally in the Knesset on July 29, 1987:

> I proclaim: I am not a refugee. I did not come to this country as a refugee. I stole across borders. I underwent a great deal of torment. So did my family. So did my friends. And I have no need for anyone to define the Jews of the East as a refugee Jewry. For some reason, that definition is applied only to Eastern Jewry. . . . Can anyone say that we, the Jews from the Arab lands, came here only for negative reasons, and that the force of Zionism, the power of attraction of this land and the idea of redemption played no part among us? Why? Only because we have to be portrayed as wretched, so that this wretchedness will also be synonymous with what we lived through there and what we are living through today?[73]

Professor Shlomo Ben-Ami, foreign minister in Ehud Barak's government during the second Camp David meeting, speaking at a national conference of WOJAC, was unsparing in his description of the dilemma: "From the advent of Zionism, the Jews from Arab countries have been struggling for their place in the Zionist dream. As part of that struggle for a place in the Zionist dream, they contend that Zionism was not invented by the Jews of Central and Eastern Europe. . . . If that is the case. . . . there is a yearning of the Jews from the Arab lands since ancient times to leave those countries and come to the Land of Zion and Jerusalem to build a homeland."[74] Ben-Ami concluded, "Those who dreamt of going up to Israel since the days of the Babylonian Talmud have no case" to claim that they are refugees.

The refugeeism discourse also generated reactions from the Palestinian and Arab world. A report compiled by the Research Division of Military Intelligence that was sent to WOJAC in June 1975 forecast (partially accurately) that at the forthcoming Arab summit meeting, the PLO would submit a proposal to allow Jews from Arab states to return to their home countries. The report stated: "There are many expressions of commiseration and solidarity with the [Arab Jews]. The accepted Arab viewpoint sees the Jews from Arab countries who are living in Israel as a population that suffers discrimination because of its Eastern origins and lives in harsh economic conditions. This, according to the Arabs, demonstrates concretely that Israel is racist not only outwardly but inwardly as well."[75] In January 1979, Radio Baghdad, in a Hebrew language broadcast, called on all Jews of Iraqi origin "to return home," promising that they could live as citizens with equal rights in Iraq. The broadcast claimed that people of Iraqi origin suffered discrimination in Israel at the hands of the Ashkenazim and that this injustice would be rectified when they returned to Iraq.[76] With these comments, Radio Baghdad broke the Zionist taboo and smoothly reflected on the contradiction in defining the Arab Jews as refugees.

Thus, even though WOJAC set out to bolster the Zionist position and assist Israel's battle against Palestinian nationalism, it accomplished the opposite by rendering the Zionist position fragile and fluid; challenging Israel's official historiography regarding the arrival of the Arab Jews to Israel; and keeping the Palestinian refugee problem on the negotiating table. The Israeli foreign office was fearful of a chain reaction in which Jews would take legal action against Arab countries and that in return would encourage Palestinians to file suits against the Israeli government for lost property. Furthermore, WOJAC's explicit discussion of the refugees (by invoking the population exchange theory) negated the government policy of maintaining ambiguity.

Thus, despite the seemingly productive dowry that WOJAC offered the State of Israel, the foreign ministry reacted with great dismay. Officials warned against a public endorsement of the theory. However, WOJAC ignored the ministry's demands even when their statement prompted Farouk Kaddoumi, head of the PLO's political department, to send greetings to WOJAC urging Arab Jews to return to their countries of origin. The foreign ministry's worst fears were thus realized, and it immediately reprimanded the WOJAC executive. An official, Max Varone, even reprimanded WOJAC in public for acting as "a separate entity parallel to the PLO." The foreign ministry, he concluded, would not permit WOJAC "to become a state within a state."[77] This statement attests again to the practice of the state vis-à-vis its institutions. At first, the foreign ministry contracts out a certain "propaganda activity" to WOJAC precisely in order to blur the boundaries of the state, but when the state believes that it is losing control, it reasserts the power of the state. Indeed, WOJAC closed down in 1999 when the state discontinued its financial support.

Conclusion

The state of Israel, like any other state, is a conglomerate of entities, institutions, and decision makers who make political action multiple, contradictory, and often nebulous. In this particular case, the state was composed—in addition to the government—of two "outsourcing" organizations: the Jewish Agency and the World Organization of Jews from Arab Countries. The two quasi-governmental organizations enabled the government to blur its practices but at the same time made them explicit and unequivocal. This was more than the foreign ministry bargained for. In order to assert its sovereignty and mask its (often unintended) policies, the government had to reappropriate its control and redraw the boundaries between "itself" and those institutions. More concretely, the government, which kept its own policy vague, was threatened by WOJAC's explicit formulation and decided to end its support of the organization.

Despite the tension between WOJAC and the government, there was one a priori political strategy that was fairly consistent. This was the government's nondecision to maintain an ambiguous policy regarding the exchange of population, which I labeled "constructed ambiguity." The population exchange theory emerged out of political practice rather than the other way around. At the end of the 1948 war, the government faced international pressure to take back Palestinian refugees and compensate them for the property confiscated by the general custodian of Israel. From 1948 to 1950, Ben-Gurion and Sharett kept the official position rather vague. Constructed ambiguity kept all options open. It could be applied, and it could be denied, as opportunities rose. Only with the immigration of the Arab Jews to Israel were more vehement voices about transfer or exchange heard. Even with the establishment of WOJAC, government officials hesitated to talk about a population exchange, as opposed to a property exchange. They also worried about using the term "refugees" for Jewish immigrants from Arab countries. And they ultimately discontinued funding to WOJAC in order to reassert the state's control and reappropriate political action.

In the early 2000s, we have witnessed renewed efforts to define the Arab Jews as refugees. Bobby Brown, Diaspora affairs adviser to Prime Minister Barak, engineered this policy, along with such Jewish organizations as the World Jewish Congress and the World Federation of Sephardic Jews. Nonetheless, their organization, called Justice for Jews from Arab Countries, did not gain broad support. Israeli politicians understand that this argument is a double-edged sword and causes more risks to Israel than positive outcomes, although Jewish organizations have not yet internalized this lesson.

The Palestinian claim for the right of return is serious and, whatever its outcome, should not be brushed away. The definition of the Arab Jews as refugees and the discursive use of population exchange is a manipulative technique to avoid direct and courageous talks on the right of return. It is a strategy to abdicate moral and political responsibility. The reasons and motivations by which the Arab Jews immigrated to Israel are diverse. Some were coerced by the conditions in Arab countries and as a result of Zionism and Arab nationalism. Some came voluntarily and intentionally. Others were brought against their own will by the Zionist movement and Jewish organizations. Whatever the motivation, it should not be equated with the Palestinian inhabitants of Palestine prior to 1948. The linkage between those populations and their properties is a manipulative practice of the state and should be abandoned from the political discourse. As Jan Abu Shakrah argued, the (legitimate) Jewish claims for compensation for property loss do not arise from the same occurrence as Palestinian refugee claims. Jewish losses were not at the hands of Palestinian refugees nor did Arab Jews cause Palestinian dispossession, although they benefited from it.[78]

It is time that Israel adopts some version of a truth-and-reconciliation commission that will face its past and admit its own wrongdoings. I believe that this is an essential element of any agreement with the Palestinians. The depiction of Arab Jews as refugees, as Clinton did in Camp David, is an obstacle to the peace process.

Notes

I thank Gil Eyal, Adriana Kemp, Shoham Melamed, and Yossi Yonah for useful comments on an earlier draft of this chapter.

1. For extensive discussion, see Benny Morris, "The Causes and Character of the Arab Exodus from Palestine: The Israeli Defense Forces Intelligence Branch Analysis of June 1948," *Middle Eastern Studies* 22 (1986): 5–19; and idem, *The Birth of the Palestinian Refugee Problem, 1947–1949* (Cambridge: Cambridge University Press, 1987).

2. Shulamit Carmi and Henry Rosenfeld, "When Most Israeli Cabinet Members Have Decided Not to Block the Option of Return of Palestinian Refugees" (Hebrew), *Medina ve Hevra* 2 (2002).

3. Yehouda Shenhav, "The Jews of Iraq, Zionist Ideology, and the Property of the Palestinian Refugees of 1948: An Anomaly of National Accounting," *International Journal of Middle East Studies* 31:4 (November 1999): 605–30; and idem, "Kehilot ve mahozot shel zikaron mizrahi" (Communities and districts of Mizrahi memory) (unpublished paper, Van Leer Institute and Tel Aviv University, 2000).

4. I received the relevant documents from Bracha Eshel, who found them in the Lavon Institute in an old file that had been catalogued under the heading "Holland, Individuals." Yehouda Shenhav, *The Arab Jews: Nationalism, Religion, and Ethnicity* (Hebrew) (Tel Aviv: Am Oved, 2003).

5. Dvora Hacohen, *From Fantasy to Reality: Ben-Gurion's Plan for Mass Immigration, 1942–1945* (Hebrew) (Tel Aviv: Ministry of Defense, 1994), 212.

6. Ibid., 211.

7. Yehouda Shenhav, "The Phenomenology of Colonialism and the Politics of 'Difference': European Zionist Emissaries and Arab-Jews in Colonial Abadan," *Social Identities* 8:4 (2002): 1–23; idem, *Arab Jews*.

8. Joseph B. Schechtman, *Population Transfers in Asia* (New York: Hallsby Press, 1949); Daphne Tsimhoni, "The Diplomatic Background to the Operation of the Immigration of Iraq's Jews 1950–1951" (Hebrew), in *Studies in the History and Culture of Iraqi Jewry*, Yitzhak Avishur, ed. (Or Yehuda: Center for the Heritage of Babylonian Jewry, 1991), 89–113. Proponents of this theory, particularly members of WOJAC, cite the Lausanne treaty as their base line (e.g. Malka Hillel Shulewitz and Raphael Israeli, "Exchanges of Populations Worldwide: The First World War to the 1990s," in *The Forgotten Millions: The Modern Jewish Exodus from Arab Lands*, Malka Hillel Shulewitz, ed. (London: Cassell, 1999). According to the treaty, more than a million individuals and 350,000 individuals became "Greeks" and "Turks," respectively. However, as Renee Hirschon shows, the "Greek" refugees defined themselves as refugees even fifty years after their arrival to Greece (*Heirs of the Greek Catastrophe* [Oxford: Oxford University Press, 1989]); also Emanuel Marx, "Refu-

gee Compensation: Why the Parties Have Been Unable to Agree and Why It Is Important to Compensate Refugees for Losses," in *The Palestinian Refugees: Old Problem—New Solutions* (Norman: University of Oklahoma Press, 2001), 102–8.

9. There are different accounts for this mass exodus. For mainstream Zionist historiography, albeit meticulous and informative, see Esther Meir, *The Zionist Movement and the Jews of Iraq 1941–1950* (Hebrew) (Tel Aviv: Am Oved, 1993); idem, "Conflicting Worlds: The Encounter between Zionist Emissaries and the Jews of Iraq during the 1940s and early 1950s" (Hebrew), in *Israel in the Great Wave of Immigration, 1948–1953*, Dalia Ofer, ed. (Jerusalem: Yad Ben Zvi, 1996). Esther Meir-Glitzenstein, "The Riddle of the Mass Immigration from Iraq," *Pe'amin* 71 (1997): 25–53 (Hebrew), 1997. For critical accounts, see Abbas Shiblak, *The Lure of Zion: The Case of the Iraqi Jews* (London: Al Saqi Books, 1986); Shlomo Swirski, *Seeds of Inequality* (Tel Aviv: Breirot, 1995) (Hebrew); Shenhav, "Jews of Iraq."

10. Shenhav, "Jews of Iraq"; idem, "Ethnicity and National Memory: World Organization of Jews from Arab Countries (WOJAC)," *British Journal of Middle Eastern Studies* 29 (2002): 25–55.

11. Tsimhoni, "Diplomatic Background," 94.

12. Shiblak, *The Lure of Zion*, 83.

13. Ibid.

14. Tsimhoni, "Diplomatic Background."

15. Minutes of cabinet meeting, 35, September 6,1949.

16. Ibid.

17. Shenhav, "Jews of Iraq," 613.

18. Fadil al-Jamali, *New York Times*, October 31, 1949; Schechtman, *Population Transfers*.

19. For example, a document from R. Gordon, director of the Foreign Ministry's International Institutions Division, to the ministry's director-general states that the chairman of the Survey Group "reconfirmed to me that the Prime Minister of Iraq indeed said this" (Foreign Ministry 2384/4 from November 17, 1949).

20. Records of the First Government, October 18, 1949.

21. Records of the First Government, October 25, 1949.

22. Foreign Ministry (130)/2563/8, October 26, 1949.

23. Tsimhoni, "Diplomatic Background."

24. Shenhav, "Jews of Iraq," 615.

25. Ibid.

26. Uzi Benziman and Mansour Atallah, *Subtenants* (Hebrew) (Jerusalem: Keter, 1992).

27. Foreign Ministry 2387/4, June 20, 1950.

28. Benziman and Mansour, *Subtenants*.

29. In 1950, for example, Lief proposed moving the residents of the large village of Kara in Wadi Ara across the border and compensating them for their property. Such ideas were not an isolated phenomenon (Benziman and Mansour, *Subtenants*).

30. Foreign Ministry 2387/4, June 21, 1950.

31. Benziman and Mansour, *Subtenants*.

32. Cabinet Record 67, September 7, 1950.

33. See an article in this spirit in the Labor movement daily *Davar*, October 17, 1949: "Is There Any Substance to the Iraqi Proposal?"

34. See, for example, *Yediot Ahronot*, October 28, 1949. Only after the arrival in Israel of the Maghreb Jews did the number of Jews from Arab countries in Israel match the number of Palestinian refugees. Speaking to the 32nd UN General Assembly on October 17, 1977, Foreign Minister Moshe Dayan put the number of

Arab refugees at 590,000 and the number of Jewish "refugees" at 600,000, including the North African Jews.

35. Morton (British Foreign Office) was the deputy chairman of the UN Economic Survey Mission, headed by Gordon Clapp. The Israeli press perceived Morton's proposal for the refugees' resettlement as a "trial balloon of the Foreign Office" (*Haaretz*, October 19, 1949).

36. Memorandum of the director of the International Institutions Division (Foreign Ministry 2384/4, November 17, 1949).

37. Cabinet Records 35, March 15, 1951.

38. Knesset Record, Third Session of the First Knesset, viii, 1358–59.

39. (130) 2387/4, March 25, 1951.

40. Foreign Ministry, Document 93, 191.

41. (130) 2387/4, March 21, 1951.

42. (130) 2387/4, April 2, 1951.

43. (130) 1963, October 16, 1951.

44. Foreign Ministry, Document 388, 648 (September 16 1951). The foreign office knew that the value of the Palestinian property was much larger than Jewish property in Iraq (Shenhav, "Jews of Iraq"; idem, *Arab Jews*).

45. Foreign Ministry, Document 99, 199.

46. Foreign Ministry, Document 150, 149.

47. Foreign Ministry, Document 240, 410.

48. Moshe Gat, *A Jewish Community in Crisis: The Exodus from Iraq 1948–1951* (Hebrew) (Jerusalem: Zalman Shazar Center, 1989); Elie Kedourie, "The Break between Muslims and Jews in Iraq," in *Jews among Arabs: Contracts and Boundaries*, Mark R. Cohen and Abraham L. Udobitch, eds. (Princeton: Darwin Press, 19), 21–33.

49. Foreign Ministry, International Institutions Division, 1963/1.

50. Foreign Ministry (130) 2563/6I, May 30, 1951. See also document of the Custodian General's Office (130) 2563/5, July 9, 1952.

51. Gat, *Jewish Community in Crisis*, 221.

52. Shenhav, "Jews of Iraq," 622.

53. Shenhav, *Arab Jews*.

54. Shenhav, "Ethnicity and National Memory."

55. The organization's executive formulated three major political assertions, all of which were intended to offset the main three claims of the Palestinian national movement: (1) that of the historical nature of a Jewish national and religious presence in the Middle East (known as the primordiality thesis; Shenhav, "Ethnicity and National Memory"); (2) that the Middle East had witnessed a de facto mutual population exchange of Arab refugees and Jewish refugees (the population exchange thesis); and (3) that the property of these Arabs and Jews could be counterbalanced due to the population exchange (the property exchange thesis). These three theses gained additional attention after the peace treaty with Egypt and the resurgence of the debate regarding the Palestinian refugees in the 1990s.

56. Shenhav, "Ethnicity and National Memory," 33.

57. WOJAC consistently placed this concept in an international context; e.g., Malka Hillel Shulewitz and Raphael Israeli, "Exchanges of Populations Worldwide: The First World War to the 1990s," in *The Forgotten Millions: The Modern Jewish Exodus from Arab Lands*, Malka Hillel Shulewitz, ed. (London: Cassell, 1999), 126–41.

58. Shulewitz, *The Forgotten Millions*, appendix.

59. Ya'akov Meron, "The Expulsion of the Jews from Arab Countries: The Palestinians' Attitude toward It and Their Claims," in *The Forgotten Millions*, Shulewitz, ed., 83–125.

60. Meron criticized the Labor Zionists' hegemonic position, which blocked Revisionist arguments. The result, he maintains, was that Israel's political stand vis-à-vis the Arab world was weakened; only Menachem Begin's election in 1977 enabled the overthrow of that dominion of memory.

61. Meron, "Expulsion," 83. Meron's expulsion thesis is exceptional even among Zionist researchers on Iraqi Jewry (Esther Meir, *The Zionist Movement and the Jewis of Iraq 1941–1950* [Tel Aviv: Am Oved, 1993][Hebrew]); Gat, *A Jewish Community in Crisis*), researchers on Jews in Islamic lands in general (Norman Stillman, "Middle Eastern and North African Jewries Confront Modernity: Orientation, Disorientation, Reorientation," in *Sephardi and Middle Eastern Jewries: History and Culture in the Modern Era* [Bloomington: Indiana University Press, 1996]), and, of course, more radical scholars (Shiblak, *The Lure of Zion*).

62. November 28, 1978; Shenhav, "Ethnicity and National Memory," 39.

63. Shlomo Hillel, *Operation Babylon* (Tel Aviv: *Yediot Ahronot* and Ministry of Defense, 1985).

64. Yosef Meir, *Beyond Desert: the Pioneer Underground in Iraq* (Tel Aviv: Ministry of Defense, 1973).

65. Shenhav, "Ethnicity and National Memory," 39.

66. February 1, 1976; Shenhav, "Ethnicity and National Memory," 39.

67. Afterward, as a cabinet minister in the Begin government, Ben-Porat chaired the ministerial committee to resolve the problem of the refugees (by settling them in populated locales). That committee replaced the term "refugee camps" with the term "hotbeds of distress" (minutes of WOJAC's Content Committee, June 23, 1983).

68. Shenhav, "Ethnicity and National Memory," 39.

69. June 6, 1975; Shenhav, *Arab Jews*, 180.

70. Shenhav, *Arab Jews*, 180.

71. Ibid.

72. Conference at Tel Aviv University, June 6, 1998.

73. Shenhav, *Arab Jews*, 182.

74. Tel Aviv, December 16, 1993; Shenhav, *Arab Jews*, 183.

75. Intelligence Branch/Research 660/0550, June 1, 1975; Shenhav, *Arab Jews*, 184.

76. January 29, 1979; Shenhav, *Arab Jews*, 184.

77. Shenhav, *Arab Jews*, 202.

78. Jan Abu Shakrah, "Deconstructing the Link: Palestinian Refugees and Jewish Immigrants from Arab Countries," in *Palestinian Refugees: The Right of Return*, Naseer Aruri, ed. (London: Pluto, 2001), 214.

Chapter 12
Palestinian Refugee Property Claims: Compensation and Restitution

Salim Tamari

Assessment of refugee property losses should be tackled in the wider context of addressing refugee grievances, which include residency options, rehabilitation, restitution, and repatriation. In this chapter, I will isolate the issues of property compensation and restitution for analytic purposes and with the assumption that this approach will be part of the larger body of refugee claims. My working assumption is that it is essential to distinguish between the constellation of issues related to refugee rehabilitation, residency, and compensation for states undertaking refugee absorption, on the one hand (including Israel and the future Palestinian state), and issues of property compensation/restitution, on the other hand. This approach is obviously problematic, since Israel and some European countries have proposed that a package be comprehensive and that an international fund deal with refugee claims for material compensation. In addition, Israel proposed in the first and second Refugee Working Group (RWG) plenary meetings in the context of multilateral negotiations that refugee property claims be dealt with in relation to an exchange with Jewish refugee property claims in the Arab countries, notably Iraq and Egypt.[1] This position was flatly rejected by the Palestinian side, which adopted the position that these claims should be dealt with on a bilateral basis with the respective Arab states concerned.

Similarly, the proposal for creating an international fund for compensation—while suitable for certain aspects of refugee rehabilitation, including support for states undergoing revalidation—has been deemed unacceptable for several reasons:

It takes the issue of refugee property out of the domain of Israel's legal accountability and transfers it into the realm of international voluntary donations.

It absolves the State of Israel from accountability for property that it has appropriated for Jewish immigrants with the resultant ethnic displacement. That rewards this displacement.

It establishes a false parallel between the rights of Palestinian refugees and those of Jewish immigrants. To the extent that Arab Jews were expelled from their countries of origin, those claims of lost property should be dealt with bilaterally between the respective Arab states and these Jewish emigrants, including those who did not go to Israel but rather sought refuge in other European countries and the United States.

Scope of the Problem

Palestinian refugee property includes the bulk of private and public real estate, buildings, communal/public property, and *waqf* (Islamic religious endowment) property acquired by Israel in two broad areas: land within the territory designated for the Jewish state in the 1947 partition plan; and areas added to the State of Israel by military conquest and consolidated by the armistice agreement of 1949.

Land acquired in the 1967 war, which may be consolidated by any future accord to be signed by Israel and the Palestine Liberation Organization (PLO) is not within the scope of this chapter. A distinction should be made between claims of compensation/restitution for public/state property within the boundaries of the Jewish state according to the partition plan and those areas that were annexed in 1949 to the expanded Jewish state. For example, railway lines, public buildings, and forest land in the Jaffa area, which was designated as part of the Arab state, would be subject to compensation claims, whereas the same categories of properties in Haifa would not. Compensation/restitution claims for refugee property would apply to those who were displaced either during and after the war of 1948 or in its immediate aftermath and found themselves outside the boundaries of the state and those Palestinian refugees who became citizens of the state but whose land was taken over by the state involuntarily.[2]

Until recently, most studies of refugee compensation claims have focused on the issue of valorization of lost property. One of the first to address this issue seriously was Sami Hadawi in his *Palestinian Rights and Losses*.[3] The assessment was based on his work with the United Nations Conciliation Commission for Palestine (UNCCP) and contained a critique of the UN's categories, which were based essentially on tax declarations. In Hadawi's estimates, those properties amounted to $11.5 billion in 1990 prices.[4] Since then, Atef Qubursi and Yusif Sayigh separately attempted to update and refine these assessments. Among the international assessors, Frank Lewis came up with supplementary assessment for agricultural lands, which amounted to $2.3–2.8 billion in 1993 prices.[5] Nevertheless, global figures for property losses, as we shall see, must be subjected to assumptions that are rarely clarified in these estimates. For example, do they include *waqf* properties? Do they include public and communal properties in the area designated as the land of the Jewish state in the partition plan? If not, would they include such properties in the areas that were de facto annexed to the State of Israel by virtue of the armistice of 1949? These and many other questions should be clarified before we attempt to assess the value of lost Arab property in Palestine.

The procedure for filing compensation claims will also have to take into account several factors that are related to the passage of time, as well as bureaucratic steps, which are bound to result in inequities.

First, poorer refugees are less equipped than better-off claimants with documentation and authentication for their property. Landless refugees and former sharecroppers (about 20–25 percent of all rural refugees) do not have any land claims but do have claims of material grievances—now recognized by a number of important precedents. Since a compensatory fund is likely to be based on an Israeli or international fund with finite resources, refugees with more substantial land claims are more likely to benefit from such a fund than those with little or no such claims. In other words, richer claimants who are already living comfortably will get the lion's share of this compensation, rather than poorer refugees who suffered more in the war itself and subsequently in the refugee camps.

Second, unlike the situation in Germany after World War II or the former Yugoslavia in the 1990s, where refugee claims were supported by a coalition of international forces favorable to their predicament, no similar compulsion impels the State of Israel today to deliver on any obligations it will incur toward the Palestinians either during the negotiating process itself or in the implementation of an agreement. Indeed, the current Israeli position under the Sharon government is that Palestinian refugee property has already been "exchanged" for the losses of Jewish emigrants from Arab countries (sometimes Iran is added for good measure) after the war of 1948.

Third, bureaucratic setup for most procedures of compensation means that the state and agencies representing the refugees (including the battery of international lawyers acting on their behalf) will siphon off the bulk of those benefits owed to their clients/subjects.

The gradual opening of important data archives that delineate the nature of property and land claims as well as the social composition and distribution of Palestinian refugee population has made the issue of documenting refugee claims much more feasible than at any previous time. We can say without exaggeration that these databases—and the UNRWA (United Nations Relief and Works Agency) and UNCCP files in particular—contain the most extensive and reasonably reliable information about the social attributes as well as socioeconomic and property claims of the

Palestinian refugees, more reliable than similar data on any other refugee population in modern history.

Problems Inherent in the Documentation of Property Claims

But these databases are not without problems, which include missing components, lack of longitudinal depth, and lack of proper access. Most important for the purpose of this analysis, these databases tend to reinforce an element of unjust distribution of claims for historical losses. I will discuss this component of bias for each database separately.

Biases in the UNRWA Archives

Archives of the UNRWA contain demographic data, prepared for the purpose of the administration of welfare among refugee populations, for nearly 3.8 individual refugees in five refugee areas: Palestine (West Bank and Gaza), Jordan, Syria, and Lebanon. Most of these data are available in a computerized data system known as the Unified Registration System (URS) since 1979 and updated from field offices on a daily basis. A more extensive data source is contained in a subsystem of the URS covering elaborate attributes of the most destitute of the refugee population households (about 15 percent of total households in the URS) originally known as "special hardship cases."

A separate, but noncomputerized, source of data is the family files. These are currently (2003) prepared for digitization (and hence searchability). They contain data on the original process of registration of refugee families, reasons for flight from Palestine in 1948—as reported in 1950 by the head of household—and changes that affected the family fortunes in the process of relocation to the host countries. They also contain a key section, but not properly or systematically entered, on losses incurred by the refugee family as a result of the war of 1948 and documentation of these losses—again, not systematically provided.

Together these databases provide an extensive picture of the demographic profile of refugee families, their composition, their educational achievement, their health conditions, and their habitat and location. The data are relatively accurate (compared to census data gathered by the state) and very detailed.

What are the main pitfalls in the UNRWA databases?

1. It is basically a record of poor refugees. The professional strata, the middle classes, and a substantial section of skilled workers are absent, as are the bulk of the landed elements, namely, the people with the most substantial compensation claims.
2. It does not cover refugees who settled outside the "confrontation

states"—Syria, Lebanon, Jordan, and the Palestinian territories. That is, refugees in Egypt, the Gulf States, North Africa, and abroad do not appear in the record; nor do "internal refugees" from Israel.

3. It has no historical depth. That is, the UNRWA data are not longitudinal. Computerized data are continuously being replenished with updating and deletion and expunging of earlier information. People who die, who move outside the system, whose records are a few years old, and so forth are removed from the record. This may be essential for the purposes of administering welfare dispensation, but it is a disaster for proper examination of social change, mobility, and the evolution of the refugee problem.

4. An important component of these data, the family files, is not computerized and therefore not searchable. This includes data about original claims and conditions of flight. Recent commitments (in the summer of 2003) by certain European states—most notably, Denmark—to extend the computerization of the UNRWA archives will improve this situation considerably.

5. Self-reporting of property losses does not lend itself to authentication and therefore to the external legitimizing of these claims. By contrast, social conditions and claims for current material assistance are rigorously investigated since they fall under the mandate of the UNRWA as a service provider for the health, educational, and welfare needs of refugees.

Biases in the UNCCP Records

The UNCCP database in New York is currently digitized and contains the most elaborate record of Palestinian refugee property and land losses in the war of 1948, systematically gathered by an expert land team from 1951 to 1961. The records are for individual (personal) title deeds and for communal and religious endowments. They are tabulated by title-deed owner, size of land, and locational coordinates. They contain map linkages for easy determination of location.

One of the most important features of the UNCCP land records is that exact replicas of the database are owned by the five regional Arab states (as well as Palestine) in addition to Israel. Thus, claims based on this source are verifiable and subject to immediate authentication. Its verifiability is further buttressed by the fact that the land records are all derived from regional land-registry offices (the Tapu), currently located in Israeli territories.

But the UNCCP database has a number of pitfalls in terms of its applicability to material claims by refugees.[6] First, it does not cover the conditions of hundreds of thousands of refugees who were either landless or sharecroppers with long-term cropping contracts with landlords. It also does not cover the claims of former peasants who lost their property because it was not properly registered in the Tapu.

Second, it is a record frozen in one moment of history. It does not reflect changes in the status of properties, real estate, and land plots since 1948. These changes include confiscation, leases, and resale by the State of Israel and by some former owners, and changes in the physical status of the property, such as changes in agricultural land into urban property and the abolishing of *waqf* land and its transformation into state, communal, or private property.

Third, large areas of refugee property do not appear in the UNCCP records. Those include a substantial area of southern Palestine (the Negev area), which was deemed communal property as a result of common law practices of Bedouin tribes. Significant sections of urban real estate (for example, Jaffa) are also missing for obscure administrative reasons. Areas not surveyed and settled into the land registry by 1947 are included, but proper coordinates for their location make those sections of the UNCCP in need of modification. This is true of areas in West Jerusalem, which have been digitized most recently by the mapping section in Orient House.

Fourth, a technical problem with the UNCCP record is the lack of bilingual entries. Since Arabic names are transliterated, this may produce problems of recognition.

Integrating the Demographic and Property Databases

At the risk of oversimplification, we can say that while the URS (UNRWA) constitutes a demographic record of poor refugees in the countries of the Arab East, the UNCCP records provide a basis for claims by the propertied classes. There is obviously a substantial degree of overlap in the two social categories, but this overlap is deceptive. The UNRWA records, intended primarily as a frame for the provision of welfare services for camp and non-camp needy refugees, need substantial modification before they can become a suitable frame for compensatory claims. In contrast, the UNCCP was established for exactly this purpose. Having said that, there is a lot to be gained from the creation of a single digitized database from the two sources of refugee archives; such an integration would help in rectifying the absence of a "poor refugee" component in the UNCCP archives and would supplement the UNRWA-URS with a property record that has so far been poorly documented in the family files. It will also help buttress the UNRWA records with an important element of replicability and verifiability—a condition that has been perceived as lacking (at least by the Israelis and Americans) in the UNRWA files.

One assisting factor is that both the URS and the UNCCP records have individual coding features that can act as the linkages between the two data sets. In order to integrate the two archives, certain measures have to be taken:

A political decision on the part of the PLO that an integrated data set should be created as a basis for refugee compensation claims.

A joint committee made up of UNRWA and UNCCP technical staff to work out conceptual and technical modalities for the integrated framework.

The protocols for codes of identification of individual and collective (family, communal) refugee units must be approved by the Arab host countries and Israel, since those parties' cooperation will be needed to facilitate this technical process.

The Issue of Equity in Refugee Property Claims

The Palestinians have hesitated in developing a strategy for compensation/ restitution, since that might lead to questions about the resilience of the leadership in defending refugee political rights. Israel has used this absence as an instrument in claiming that the Palestinians have been using the refugee issues as a means of (potential) demographic destabilization of the Jewish state. Some Palestinians (for example, Rashid Khalidi) have put forth the position that Israeli acceptance of moral culpability for the dispossession of the refugee will be the basis of a historical settlement of this issue,[7] but most Palestinian negotiators on refugees have taken the position that a combination of options must obtain (restitution, repatriation, naturalization, and compensation) in order for closure on the refugees to be achieved. In all of these cases, the refugees themselves should be an essential party to the determination of their future based on concrete choices.

From time to time, diplomats and many supporters of Israel, as well as Israeli representatives, have suggested that Palestinian property claims should be considered in conjunction with Jewish global claims for property lost in Arab states in the 1950s. The rationale for this position lies in the assumption that the Israeli-Palestinian refugee settlement will be part of a wider process of negotiating the Arab-Israeli conflict. But if this is the case, it makes equal sense to bring the issue of German-Israeli reparations into this global picture: first, because these reparations can set important precedents for the ways and means of implementing refugee compensation; and second, because Palestinian refugees were themselves the indirect victims of the German displacement of Jews.

Separating Refugee Repatriation from Refugee Compensation

I argue that it is essential to distinguish and separate the issue of resolving the future repatriation of refugees from the question of the disposition of their property. Considerations dealing with the question of residency emanating from repatriation (return, naturalization, settlement) are likely to affect some refugees, while issues of compensation will affect all refugees. In the former case, the modalities of the practical implementation of the right of return were discussed at Taba in December 2000: return to Palestine, to Israel, to territories ceded to the future Palestinian state naturalization in the current host country, and resettlement in a third country. The issue of material compensation, on the other hand, needs to be addressed in terms of documentation of property claims and compensating losses in life chances—for example, employment, normality, and physical and psychological suffering.

One significant feature of the compensatory paradigm, if taken on the basis of documented losses of property, is that it tends to replicate a highly skewed social structure: a claims strategy in which refugees will simply reiterate their demands for compensation on the basis of material property losses is highly favorable to the owners of large estates and their descendants and very unfavorable to those who were either landless or had small properties, the latter constituting the vast majority of refugees. Furthermore, if we assume that the collective fund for restitution will be limited and considerably smaller than the actual value of dispossessed land and real estate, this inequity will be further accentuated.

The Issue of Demographic Attrition

Two essential historical factors contribute to the process of inequity in compensation claims:

First, refugees with smaller property (those households that individually used to possess less than 50 dunams) will have property claims that are extremely fragmented and divided into parts by demographic attrition, four generations later. One can visualize interfamilial squabbles over such rights, whose return will be further reduced by the passage of time and the intervention of a battery of lawyers who will get the lion's share of such indemnities.

Second, establishing material claims for landless refugees and those with small amounts of property will be much more difficult to ascertain and authenticate than for those with substantial property. The rich have always been better at preserving their records than the poor in condition of war. Moreover, the UNCCP records—the most systematic of these records— have nothing to say about landless refugees and those sharecroppers whose land was unjustly appropriated by big landlords.

A Strategic Approach toward Material Compensation

Israeli acknowledgment of its role in the historical dispossession of Palestinian refugees in the war of 1948 should not be seen as an act of contrition in lieu of concrete settlement but as the first step in a process of negotiations over material settlement that will bring closure to the issue of the refugees. So far, with precious few exceptions (for example, Shlomo Ben-Ami in the Ottawa multilateral meeting in 1991 and Yossi Beilin's proposal for a joint narrative in Taba 2001), Israeli official pronouncements have been that Israel and its armed forces are not culpable for the displacement of the refugees in the 1948 war and that the appropriation of Palestinian absentee property is held in lieu of the "exchanged" Jewish property confiscated in Iraq, Egypt, Tunis, Lebanon, and so on.

I propose here a three-pronged approach to material compensation, which will follow a process of acknowledgment of historical injustice. The essential feature of this process is that it will give the refugees concrete options to chose from, including repatriation in Palestine, repatriation to areas of Israel that will be annexed to Palestine (on a swap basis), repatriation to Israel, naturalization in the host countries, and third-state migration. The compensation/restitution modalities apply independently to all of these options.

During the first stage, the PLO and Israel, in coordination with the Arab host governments, will agree on the procedures necessary to authenticate the documents needed to approve property claims. It is necessary at this stage to separate the procedures of repatriation/resettlement from those pertaining to material compensation. It is not the objective of this paper to address the question of repatriation/naturalization, which has been dealt with at length elsewhere.

For collective versus individual claims, it is essential that Palestinian refugees be able to have two venues for claims of material compensation. A collective claim will go for the state (for example, state to state), earmarked for the rehabilitation of repatriated refugees and the building of a national infrastructure (housing, roads, and economic and social base) for the absorption of refugees. Individual claims, on the other hand, will be cleared through an autonomous organization (possibly the UNRWA), which will assess, authenticate, and process individual claims for property losses. Refugees who are residents of countries outside the regional host countries will be able to file claims worldwide.

Restitution is an essential component of a just solution to the refugee problem. One major argument used against restitution of property is that such an act would dispossess current (that is, Israeli) occupants. But precedents in other areas, including Germany and Bosnia, indicate that a model of restitution would enable the owners to repossess their former properties while allowing for long-term leases for the current occupiers.

Precedents need to be examined in order to see which recent historical examples are appropriate. One of the most relevant cases in this regard is the Dayton peace agreement, concerning the repatriation of refugees from Bosnia and Herzegovina (1995), which involved millions of Bosnian, Serbian, and Croatian refugees. Although the schemes for repatriation and compensation were only partly successful, the Dayton agreement contained the three elements of success necessary for the Palestinian-Israeli case: international intervention by the European Union and the United States; border delineation; and a mechanism for repatriation of refugees and restitution/compensation for their lost properties, supervised by the UN High Commissioner for Refugees (UNHCR) and the UN International Task Force. One can learn from the benefits as well as the mistakes contained in this agreement. In a recent comparative study on repatriation and resettlement, Mick Dumper noted: "As a result [of the agreement] by 2000 only 10 percent of the Serbs from Croatia, 5 percent of Muslims and Croats from western Bosnia and Herzegovina and only 1 percent of those expelled by Serbs from eastern Bosnia and Herzegovina (Republica Srpska) returned to their homes."[8] This case is particularly relevant to the Palestinians because it involved the issues of borders, displacement, and restitution in a new state that ceased to be the national state of the original refugees. Most other international cases involving repatriation (for example, Guatemala, Afghanistan, Somalia) involve refugees' repatriation to the country that still represents them or third-party relocation.

As far as the cut-off point for property claims, it will enhance refugee claims to propose a strategy (successfully adapted in Yugoslavia, among other recent cases) in which landless refugees and those with minimal property claims (say, owners of areas under 40 dunams in rural areas and single properties in urban areas) group their claims into a single package deal in which they will receive a standard package of monetary compensation (or a number of standard packages) per family. Although on the surface, this proposal may not meet the standards of justice, its consequences meet conditions of fairness. For once, claimants will shorten prolonged waiting periods for the bureaucratic procedures of authentication of claims, which could take years and quite likely decades, judging from precedents. They will also ensure that the bulk of this compensation goes directly to the claimants and not to attorneys and bureaucrats representing them.

But there is a more important reason for adopting this procedure, already referred to above. Namely, the cumulative increase in the size of the households of those claimants, four generations after the event, will most likely ensure internal family disputes over individual rights that can be spared through the suggested procedure. It is quite likely that this procedure will allow a substantial proportion of Palestinian refugee property claimants (perhaps as many as 80 percent of the total refugees) to expedite their claims within months of the implementation of an accord on such claims, leaving room for effective concentration of legal and administrative resources for the remaining 20 percent.

Why is it possible to achieve an equitable resolution for refugee claims despite inequitable power relations between the protagonists? Now we come to the thorniest of the questions of equity raised above: Why would the State of Israel feel compelled to respond to these issues of justice and equity? So far, it has had three standard answers: that Israel is not account-able for the fate of refugees during the war; that Palestinian property con-fiscated from exiled refugees has been "exchanged" by the sequestered property of Jewish emigrants from Arab countries; and that the status of refugees is a humanitarian issue of global concern, largely the product of Arab countries themselves intent on perpetuating the conditions of misery for their own political objectives, and in this context Israel will contribute, voluntarily, to solving this situation through an international fund of com-pensation.

The first of these answers has already been superseded by the intellectual work of the New Israeli Historians, whose contribution has already become acceptable to important members of the Israeli establishment, such as Shlomo Gazit, Yossi Beilin, Shlomo Ben-Ami, and indeed, to public opin-ion worldwide. It is ironic that the same claims, when made by the victims themselves for decades, were seen as propaganda. It took the work of a few courageous Israeli scholars, especially renegade historian Benny Morris, to make this point acceptable.

The second response, concerning the exchange of property, has acquired recent weight since it has been officially adopted by both the Net-anyahu and Sharon governments. Nevertheless, it has been sufficiently challenged during the multilateral peace negotiations to warrant its shelv-ing. The main argument here is that Palestinian restitution claims cannot be reduced to the status of "generic Arab claims" and pertain to Israeli actions during the war and its aftermath and that Jewish property claims belong to the arena of bilateral negotiations between Israel (or individual Jewish emigrants and refugees) and the concerned Arab states.

My main contention is that, despite the lack of equity in power relations, Israel will most likely respond to claims of accountability with regard to ref-ugee property for two important reasons.

First, Israel wants to achieve closure on the question of refugees more than any other issue. This is partly due to the need to bring about an "end of claims, end of conflict" resolution in negotiations, which was at the heart of the collapse of the Camp David/Taba negotiations in 2000 and which is impossible without addressing refugee property claims. It is also to forestall individual refugee claims for property rights by making a collec-tive deal on this issue with the PLO/PNA (Palestinian National Authority) acting on behalf of the global refugee population.

Second, Israel seeks the ultimate legitimacy and its acceptance as a state within the Arab world. It is impossible to do this without resolving the refu-gee claims, especially as far as Jordan, Syria, and Lebanon are concerned.

Israel will most likely resist any deal that will involve the repatriation of refugees inside Israeli territory and will insist that refugees be either repatriated to the future Palestinian state or naturalized in the host country. Even if a symbolic deal is struck over repatriation of refugees to Israel, the Israelis will try to undermine it in the process of implementation.

But even here, there is room for flexibility. If the process of naturalization of refugees in the Arab states is to succeed, Israel must be party to this absorption. Having said this, it will make more practical sense for the Palestinians to insist that refugee repatriation in the context of implementing Resolution 194 be accomplished primarily in territories in Israel to be annexed or swapped to the Palestinian state.

Notes

1. S. Tamari, *Palestinian Refugee Negotiations: From Madrid to Oslo* (Washington, D.C.: Institute for Palestine Studies, 1996), 6.

2. Amal Jamal analyzes their situation and claims in "The Palestinian IDPs in Israel and the Predicament of Return," in this volume.

3. Sami Hadawi, *Palestinian Rights and Losses* (London: Al Saqi, 1985).

4. See Ruth Klinov, "Reparations and Rehabilitation of Palestinian Refugees," paper presented at the Max Planck Institute's conference on Palestinian refugees, Heidelberg, July 11, 2003.

5. Klinov, "Reparations," 18–19.

6. For a discussion of these flaws, see Elia Zureik and Salim Tamari, eds., *Reinterpreting the Historical Record: The Uses of Palestinian Refugee Archives for Social Science and Policy Analysis* (Jerusalem: Institute of Jerusalem Studies, 2001).

7. Rashid Khalidi, "Toward a Solution," in *Palestinian Refugees: Their Problem and Future* (Washington, D.C.: Center for Policy Analysis on Palestine, October 1994), 24–25.

8. Mick Dumper, "Comparative Perspectives on Repatriation and Resettlement of Palestinian Refugees: The Cases of Guatemala, Bosnia and Afghanistan," unpublished paper, 7.

Part V
The Refugee Issue
in Context

Chapter 13
Truth and Reconciliation: The Right of Return in the Context of Past Injustice

Nadim N. Rouhana

One remarkable feature of the conflict between Israel and the Palestinians is that, while each side has constructed its own identity solidly around a homeland between the Jordan River and the Mediterranean Sea, each side has also failed to imagine, let alone articulate, the other's place within this same identity space. While this failure is symmetrical in that it occurred on both sides, its antecedents, dynamics, and consequences are determined by the asymmetrical nature of relations between the forceful imposition of the colonizer and the modes of resistance of the uprooted and the exiled, and by the asymmetrical power relations between the two. But despite the failure to imagine the homeland with a place for the other in it, both the Zionist movement and the Palestinian national movement constructed, again asymmetrically, some features of the other's identity that were consistent with and subservient to usurpation and control on the Zionist side and to the various modes of resistance on the Palestinian side.

While the failure to imagine a place for the other is not uncharacteristic of intense social conflicts, the glaring failure to do that during a "peace process" that lasted almost a decade in the 1990s requires renewed examination of old assumptions. The fact that the peace process proceeded with the strong support of the international community, enjoyed the backing of the majority in each society, and reached its peak after years of intense, unprecedented unofficial diplomacy generously financed by American foundations and European governments must raise urgent questions: What is it about this conflict that makes it defy settlement? Is reconciliation based on a historic compromise even a realistic or possible goal? And what are the avenues for making a breakthrough? The questions become even sharper in light of the fact that the collapse of the peace process is bringing the conflict to a level of violence that now entails war crimes and that has the potential for even more serious war crimes, including ethnic cleansing.

My main arguments in this chapter: first, this conflict's resistance to resolution is inherent in its nature. The conflict is over the homeland itself, as both a territorial space and a space of symbolic meaning, and it is between an undefeated (and perhaps undefeatable) homeland nation and an ongoing colonization project in which the colony itself, the motherland of the indigenous nation, was transformed into the colonizer's only homeland. I will argue that this conflict carries the seeds of escalation that can lead to (further) war crimes and crimes against humanity. My second argument is that reconciliation between Zionism and the Palestinian national movement is unattainable, and reconciliation between Israelis and Palestinians cannot at this stage in history be a realistic goal because of irreconcilable differences regarding the right of return, which in turn reflect an irreconcilable past and divergent visions of the future. Third, I argue that a peaceful settlement, but not reconciliation, is imaginable but that it requires historic and controversial compromises within each community, in the one about the right of return and in the other about the requirement to recognize the Jewish character of Israel, and that the agreement between the parties will be based on these internal compromises.

In advancing these arguments, I maintain that a distinction should be drawn between a settlement based on power relations and reconciliation that is based on the recognition of mutual legitimacy.[1] Reconciliation in this kind of conflict, in which two groups claim the same homeland, guards against the reversal of the conflict to stages in which the very legitimacy of the Other is questioned. But reconciliation has its own requirements, to which I return later in this chapter.

Taking Over Another Nation's Homeland

Inherent in the dynamics of the conflict between the Zionist movement and the Palestinian national movement are the seeds of protracted conflict, use of force, escalation cycles, retreat of the weak, and continuous resistance. Inherent in the dynamics, too, are the seeds of extremism, the colonizers' war crimes, and the homeland nation's violent resistance and even terrorism.

Force has been a central component of the relationship with the Palestinians from the moment the Zionist idea was conceived. It was and it is still naive to think that it was possible to establish a Jewish state in the homeland of the Palestinians except by force. This is true regardless of whether the Arab inhabitants of Palestine at the time that the Zionist project started had developed a national identity or whether this identity developed later. In either case, the establishment of the Jewish state was achieved by force; the land was "liberated" from its indigenous Arab inhabitants. The use of force is embedded in the idea of Zionism itself, and the extent of the force is determined by the extent of resistance.[2] When dealing with the Arabs,

Israel internalized a culture of force and domination over the years. The occupation of the West Bank and Gaza in 1967, the ongoing project of Jewish settlement in these areas, and maintenance of the occupation against the will of the occupied were achieved by using brute force, oppression, and gross violations of human rights that penetrated into Israeli culture itself. Similarly, the Zionist Jewish identity of the state and its unconcealed discriminatory legal and constitutional expressions could not have been imposed on the indigenous population but by domination and force.

This protracted use of force became part and parcel of many Israelis' relationships with Palestinians. It has possibly become part of their very identity in light of the extent to which their collective existence has been defined by power over this most significant other in their national experience. Israelis' worldview of the Palestinians, and inevitably of themselves, is determined by forceful domination and the resulting justificatory distortions.

It is therefore no surprise that Israel sought and still seeks to impose its formula for the solution by force, a formula that is devised to solve Israel's problem of occupation—the problem of the occupiers—not that of the occupied Palestinians. Central to this formula is "getting rid of the Palestinians—the Arabs" through physical separation, maintaining a Jewish demographic domination and complete political control over the non-Jewish population, annexing parts of the occupied Palestinian lands, and stifling any emerging Palestinian entity. Again, such objectives can be achieved, if at all, only by force and imposition.

Resistance by the Homeland Nation to the Zionist Narrative of Return

Throughout their relationship with the Zionist movement and later with Israel, the Palestinian experience was shaped by various forms of resistance. Resistance, like return, and earlier liberation, formed a constitutive concept in their narrative but also a constitutive experience in their national history, perhaps equaled only in its importance by the predicament of exile. Resistance took different forms: violence, endurance, preserving the national narrative, and rejecting or "spoiling" unjust settlements determined by an extreme power imbalance. Perhaps one of the most effective and least evident forms of resistance was the preserving of the national narrative, at the core of which was the denial of the legitimacy of the Jewish state in the Palestinian homeland. This narrative is shared by all segments of Palestinian society, including a majority of the Palestinians in Israel.

The sense of threat that Palestinian resistance caused to Israel is minimal at the national security level (although suicide bombings introduce a sense of real insecurity at the public level). But the psychological threat that emanated from the challenge to the Zionist narrative was meaningful. The

Zionist narrative of return to the fatherland was founded on the denial of the relationship between the Palestinians and Palestine. Such a relationship, if validated, would reveal the historical injustice that was inflicted on the Palestinians by Israel's establishment and its direct responsibility for the destruction of Palestinian society, their dispersion, usurpation, and exile.

Zionism placed Israel (and before 1948, the Jewish political community in Palestine, known as the *yishuv*) in an inevitable position of feeling threatened. This threat emanated not only from Palestinian resistance but also from the Palestinians' very existence. It arose because the idea of a Jewish state is irreconcilable with the presence of large numbers of non-Jews. By definition, Arabs are in a state of resistance and their mere presence is threatening; Jews are in a state of being threatened. The psychological sense of threat emanating from the Arabs' existence became fused with other sources of fear: the historic trauma of the ghettoized European Jews; massacres, persecution, and humiliation, culminating in the Holocaust; real security threats, and the fears associated with frequent wars and protracted conflict. But the fear that is seldom examined in Israel is the fear that stems from having established a state in another people's homeland while the other people still claim the homeland for themselves.

Is Reconciliation between Israel and the Palestinian National Movement Attainable?

It is important to distinguish between political settlement and reconciliation. Political settlement seeks a formal termination of conflict based on mutual interests and is represented by reaching an agreement between the conflicting parties that reflects the power relations on the ground. A settlement does not necessarily reflect equitably the needs of the parties and often does not meet the weaker party's long-term interests. In conflict settlement, the agreement is reached by elites and, to a large extent, does not concern itself with relations between societies or with genuine mutual recognition between the parties. Accordingly, peace between the conflicting parties could be either cold or warm as long as their interests are met and they enjoy a tolerable coexistence.

Reconciliation is a qualitatively different process and seeks to achieve a kind of relationship between the parties that is founded on mutual legitimacy. The open, public, and socially based granting of legitimacy—as the culmination of the process—becomes the defining feature of the relationship and the cornerstone of mutual recognition and genuine security. As such, reconciliation, although it does not prevent strains in the relationship and future disputes between the parties, does guard against reversal of the relationship to a stage in which the very legitimacy of each side is questioned again. In this sense, reconciliation brings about a genuine end to the existential conflict between the parties, because the nature of the relationship between the societies is transformed in a process that is intertwined with psychological, social, and political changes. Despite its shortcomings, the reconciliation process in South Africa remains an example that is worthy of examination and studied emulation.

For genuine reconciliation to take root, four key issues must be addressed: truth, historical responsibility, justice, and restructuring the social and political relationship between the parties. The following section focuses on the requirements of truth and historical responsibility, which are rooted in the different narratives of Israelis and Palestinians.[3]

Historical Truth

Even within an ethical and theoretical framework of historicism that declines to judge historical knowledge as measured against fixed truths or fixed values that exist independently of a historical and cultural context, there are sufficient grounds for establishing the difference between truth and fiction, and even between right and might.[4] Within a "moderate historicist" framework, it will be possible to talk about historical truths (and consequently about historical responsibility and historical injustice) and examine the narratives of Palestinians and Israelis. Indeed, one of the far-reaching consequences of extreme historicity is to grant the two narratives, the Palestinian and the Zionist, equal moral grounding. Based on this assumed equality, it becomes possible to develop a formula about the right of return on the basis of recognizing the two narratives.[5] Such a formula can be predicated on the assumption that each party has its own narrative, its own version of history, and its own sense of victimization (supposedly derived from the other's treatment of its group members). These narratives, according to such formulas, are equally legitimate and each side can respect the other's narrative.[6]

Granting equal legitimacy to both narratives and symmetricizing an asymmetric conflict carries the danger of leading to erroneous conclusions, in addition to being ethically questionable. The fact that each side has its own narrative and a strong sense of victimization is not sufficient to justify maintaining that both narratives are equally valid or equally legitimate. These narratives themselves, and the sense of victimization, should be subjected to examination in the context of unequal power relations and the dynamics of dispossession and resistance. For example, white South Africans had their own narrative, and they, too, felt victimized while perpetrating one of the most heinous political systems in modern history.[7] Similarly, Protestant settlers in Northern Ireland and Serbs in Bosnia, who perpetrated gross human-rights violations, felt threatened and victimized and constructed narratives to justify their behavior. It is true that a narrative is experienced as valid, but the narratives of the perpetrator and the victim cannot be granted equal moral weight. A narrative, in principle, can be based on distortions, denials, and myths. These are all legitimate subjects of study and examination, particularly in the context of occupation, domination, and exploitation and in the context of resistance, defiance, and endurance.

As argued above, the spectacular breakdown of the Israeli-Palestinian peace process was rooted in the failure of each society to recognize basic truths and historical responsibilities. The peace process that started in the early 1990s, at least in the public perception, sought to end the conflict and achieve a historic compromise, although, paradoxically, as mentioned at the opening of this chapter, without developing a vision of the place of the Other in the desirable peace. Before the Camp David summit in July 2000, as well as in the negotiations that followed, ending the historical conflict between Israel and the Palestinians became a central theme in the formal Israeli political discourse on the required outcomes of the negotiations. But this requirement was never presented within a framework of reconciliation. Thus Israel sought an agreement that "closes the files" on all outstanding issues in the conflict. In other words, Israel sought to achieve the outcome of a negotiation process while pursuing a power relations–based settlement process. But a reconciliation process and outcome requires that each party face its own history vis-à-vis the other. Because the power relations are asymmetrical, each party has its own load of history—different in quantity and quality—to reckon with. The weightier load is that of the Israelis.

The Israelis will first have to recognize a simple historical truth: when the Zionist project started in the late nineteenth century, there was a Palestine and a people who lived in it as its indigenous population. It was their rightful homeland. Zionism sought to establish an exclusive Jewish state in Palestine while another group of people, a nation—or at least, a nation in formation—was already living there. Thus the Zionist goal could only have been achieved by force. Establishing a Jewish state in Palestine inevitably entailed uprooting the indigenous population. The debate on whether the Palestinians had developed a separate national identity before the Zionist settlers arrived is irrelevant to whether the land was taken from them by force.[8] How else could immigrants coming from various other parts of the world establish an exclusive state for themselves in another people's homeland? Furthermore, how would an exclusive Jewish state be established in Palestine without displacing the Palestinians, psychologically as well as politically, by making them refugees? The psychological displacement of the Palestinians was accomplished by treating them as if they were occupiers of their own land, as aliens, foreigners, or illegal inhabitants of the future Jewish state, or in connection with the Zionist movement's claim of a higher right to the land as given to the Jewish people by God.

This consciousness was not only compatible with the fulfillment of the

Zionist project but also was a prerequisite for the implementation of that project. Israel's denial of its responsibility for the plight of Palestinian refugees, which can be traced to this motivated consciousness, has to be faced to allow for reconciliation. The historical arguments that the expulsion of the Palestinians was the outcome of local circumstantial logic developed within the context of fierce fighting[9] is not compatible with the logic of establishing an exclusive Jewish state in a country inhabited by others. This engineered perception of the Palestinians is an important subject of investigation, because when Israel negotiates with the Palestinians it does not see them as the indigenous population of Palestine with natural rights over their own homeland and with whom a historic compromise has to be achieved. Many Israelis see them as hostile, threatening aliens who should be kept out and separated from the Jewish state.[10] They feel that any concessions Israel makes emanate from its own generosity and therefore should be accepted with gratitude—a logic that emanates from their position of domination and usurpation. This is the exact logic that has to be fundamentally challenged if reconciliation is to be seriously considered.

These views of Palestinians, their nationhood, relationship to the homeland, and the responsibility for their dispersion, which were constructed in the context of conflict, are engineered in a project not less spectacular than the project of establishing the Jewish state. The literature that employs only the context of conflict to explain this consciousness fails to do so because it de-historicizes and de-contextualizes the analysis and thus often erroneously symmetricizes the views of each party toward the other. The goals of the project of the Jewish state and the means it used are those that constituted a particular kind of consciousness dominated by denial and motivated ignorance about Palestinian history and experience. From the founding fathers to their modern heirs, thinking about the Palestinians was dominated by a sophisticated system of denial that ranged from denying the very existence of the Palestinians to denying their genuine relationship with Palestine. The national movement of the Jewish people—Zionism— sought to expropriate that relationship. This was not a goal for itself, for the Zionist movement had no reason to make the Palestinians or any other Arabs enemies except for the simple reason that they existed on the land of Palestine, the land that the movement claimed from Europe to be that of the Jewish people. Thus, the goal of expropriating this relationship, although only a secondary goal on the way to taking over the land, was still a central goal of Zionism.

This consciousness, involving Zionist expropriation of the relationship of the Palestinians with their homeland at its center, permeates Israeli knowledge-producing institutions (the educational system and academia), social institutions (the courts and the media), political discourse, language, national and historical time, space, geographical naming, and, to a large extent, the arts and literature, although a non-justificatory narrative leaks into these cultural institutions more than into others.

Israel's Views about the Right of Return

The mainstream Israeli narrative tells us that the Arab countries opened war on Israel in 1948, and many refugees fled voluntarily. Thus, Israel refuses to accept moral responsibility for the refugees' problem, which is why the Camp David negotiations did not go far on this issue. This narrative, however, does not address the question: Even if the refugees left on their own, why have they not been allowed to return? It ignores the fact that about five thousand Palestinians were killed as they attempted to cross the border from their refuge places in neighboring countries to go back to their homes, in the early years after 1948.[11] What are the moral foundations for preventing them from returning to their own homeland despite the United Nations resolutions in favor of their return? Even though the expulsion of the Palestinians in 1948 is one of the largest ethnic cleansing projects after World War II, the controversy over how many Palestinians were expelled in 1948 and how many left under duress of war is irrelevant to their basic right to return to their homeland and to Israel's responsibility for their plight. The debate is important only because of its relevance to the nature of responsibility that Israel should face, not to the Palestinians' basic right to return.

Facing these issues has strong moral, legal, and political implications for Israel and the core of Israeli identity. In order to avoid the moral implications, Israel developed a massive and sophisticated system of denial mechanisms and multilevel justifications to come to terms with its own history. Israel, inevitably, denies both the means by which the establishment of a Jewish state in another people's homeland was achieved and its consequences for the Palestinian people.

It is not surprising, therefore, that Israeli society has developed a national consensus on the issue of the right of return. However, underneath the national consensus there seems to have evolved, over the years, a range of views that has been underestimated by researchers and analysts. To reveal the range of views in each society, one has to examine a broader discourse on the right of return than the "practical return" of the Palestinian refugees to their original places inside Israel. In looking at the recent discourse, one can distinguish among practical, moral, and psychological dimensions of negotiation, with each of these dimensions further differentiated. It is becoming increasingly clear that reconciliation on this issue cannot be achieved without addressing all three dimensions, although, as I will argue, a settlement should be considered that leaves dealing with all dimensions to a later stage. These dimensions cannot be analyzed separately, and the discussion below should not be seen as reifying what I view as interrelated yet conceptually distinct levels of analysis.

The discussion is rather simplistic on the practical level, because it focuses on the number of refugees who should be allowed to return within the context of a peace agreement. Yet even on this level, questions of distributing the return of returnees over a number of years and developing criteria to determine which category of refugees will have priority to return to Israel, as opposed to the West Bank or Gaza, remain unexplored.[12] Furthermore, practical issues related to the nature of compensation and the source of compensation can also help fracture what on the surface appears to be a one-dimensional issue.

On the moral level, the question of historical responsibility and national narratives gain center stage. From a Palestinian point of view, recognizing Israeli responsibility for the refugees' fate is a sine qua non for an agreement that they can accept. Some Palestinians argue that this level is even more important than the practical level. In other words, while the practical implementation of the right of return can be negotiated, the right itself has to be recognized.[13]

But there are many ways by which Israelis are willing to formulate the issue of Israel's historical responsibility. Some formal and informal negotiations have discussed this issue. For example, a subgroup at the Taba negotiations composed of Yossi Beilin and Nabil Shaath reportedly developed some initial formulations.[14] Similarly, an unofficial Israeli-Palestinian working group on Israeli-Palestinian relations worked at length on this issue and published a working paper on the topic.[15]

Theoretically, it would be possible to distinguish among different levels of responsibility: partial responsibility shared with others, practical responsibility but not responsibility in principle, indirect responsibility, and so on. Similarly, different levels of justice and injustice can be identified: that injustice was done to Palestinians, that injustice was done by Israel but not intentionally, that injustice was done intentionally but in the context of war and hostilities, or that injustice was done intentionally but was inevitable.

The same arguments apply to historical truth as another major dimension in this context. However, this issue has not been subjected to systematic empirical research. Yet it is possible that the range of public views on this issue is broader than assumed.

The third dimension is the psychological, in which the experience of the Palestinians is validated. In this dimension, too, one can differentiate among various levels, such as recognizing the suffering of the refugees, recognizing that as a consequence of Israel's establishment Palestinians suffered, recognizing that there is another narrative, and recognizing that there are two valid narratives. It is worth mentioning that Ehud Barak experimented with this third dimension during his term as prime minister. For example, he told the Israeli Knesset in his first speech that Israel's "victory created hard realities for the Palestinian side. Many Palestinian families also lost their dear ones and many Palestinians are now refugees."[16] This is obviously far from recognizing the Palestinian experience or taking responsibility for it, but it does connect Israel's creation with the Palestinian plight.

When one considers all three dimensions of addressing the right of return, the assumption that Israeli society holds a uniform view on this issue becomes less compelling. But there is no systematic research that draws a picture of the distribution of views on all three dimensions. Yet despite the variation of views, the dominant discourse on all three dimensions is far from creating the appropriate ground for possible reconciliation based on truth and facing historical responsibility as described above.

Willingness to Engage in Reconciliation

Considering the factors that influence parties in conflict to get involved in a reconciliation process can help us estimate the willingness of Israelis and Palestinians to initiate such a process or even to be interested in it. As with respect to many other dimensions in this conflict, this willingness is not symmetrical. Yet reconciliation requires that the two parties be involved in a process that takes truth, historical responsibility, and past injustices as the points of departure. The outcome of negotiations and political changes becomes guided by this framework. But there is no guarantee that parties in conflict will be interested in a process guided by such a framework.

Willingness to embark on a mutual process of reconciliation depends on a number of factors that determine the extent of each party's interest in seeking reconciliation. Perhaps the most important factor is the power relations between the parties and the extent of power asymmetry. For each party, depending on its position in the power-relations matrix, reconciliation entails differing risks in terms of threats to national identity and national narrative, political restructuring, and permanent political loss. The risks for the high-power group are greater because, by definition, rectification of the injustice involves upsetting the status quo and ending the perpetrators' dominance. Thus, the costs of such a process are also asymmetrical in reverse: the cost for the high-power group is greater than the cost for the low-power group. Therefore, the more powerful party seeks to avoid such a process, and the weaker party, even when interested in the process, has no means to impose reconciliation.

Another major factor in considering reconciliation is whether the injustice can be undone and what the precise implications of undoing the injustice are for the dominant party. Thus, killing a person cannot be undone, but stealing a person's house or destroying it can largely be undone by returning the stolen house or rebuilding the destroyed one. On the collective level, eliminating an ethnic group cannot be undone, but expulsion and ethnic cleansing can. It might be harder to accept responsibility in cases where injustice can be partly undone, such as expulsion of an ethnic group that demands to return, than in cases where the injustice cannot be undone, such as in cases where the ethnic group has been eliminated or almost eliminated. Reconciliation might be harder in the first case because of the implications that facing the responsibility has for the perpetrators. These implications can be both political (in the broad sense, including legal) and psychological. In cases of ethnic cleansing such as in the former Yugoslavia, the political implications can involve such steps as power sharing, political transformation, and return of refugees; these consequences are usually framed in terms of existential threat to identity and to national security. However, in cases where the ethnic group has been eliminated or reduced to insignificant numbers, such as the Native Americans, facing responsibility does not involve a similar price.

The psychological implications for an injustice that can be undone are also serious. If the perpetrators do not intend to correct an injustice that can be corrected, recognizing the injustice has clear psychological implications for national identity, national narratives, historical myths, and self-image. When an injustice, such as genocide, cannot be undone, the perpetrators, if not forced, do not recognize the crime nor do they take moral responsibility for it. To this day, more than eighty-five years after it was committed, the Armenian genocide is still denied by Turkey—by both its government and its people.

Another factor is the clarity of the injustice and the moral issues involved in the conflict. The importance of the moral component, even if underestimated in international relations, cannot be overemphasized for the party on the receiving side of injustice. For a reconciliation process to be urged on the perpetrator, the moral case should be clear not only to the victim but to the international community as well. The more powerful party usually develops a system of defense mechanisms against moral arguments, and its members become almost immune to the moral case of their victims. Without the support of the international community for the moral cause of the low-power party, that party loses one of its few means of rectifying the power imbalance. Low power usually comes with less access to international media and fewer resources to invest in public relations, so the powerful party is in a better position to put out its version of the conflict story as "absolute fact." The low-power group often resorts to terrorism, the tool of the powerless, to protest the injustice to the international community, but paradoxically, these means contaminate the clarity of their moral case. Compare, for example, the simplicity and salience to the international community of the African National Congress's moral case against the South African apartheid system, with the ambiguity of the Tamils' case in Sri Lanka or the case of the Palestinians in their struggle. The international moral attitude against injustice can provide substantial pressure on the high-power group to engage in reconciliation.

The emergence of a new generation within the dominant group that did not commit the original wrongdoing but benefits from it can also increase the willingness of the high-power group to pay the cost of reconciliation. For one thing, the descendants of the perpetrators do not carry the same psychological burden as their forefathers; not that the psychological burden disappears, but it is lighter than that of those who actually committed the injustice. The longer the time that has elapsed, other things being equal, the easier it becomes for new generations to face their historical responsibility. However, if the injustice is ongoing, new generations become heavily invested in it, as happens with ongoing colonization.

In sum, the likelihood that a more powerful party will engage in a reconciliation process and willingly shoulder its political and psychological cost increases as the psychological and political implications of undoing an injustice become less onerous, the clarity of the moral case of the victims becomes stronger, international support for their cause grows, and the duration of time since the injustice was committed lengthens. From this analysis, it is apparent that it will be hard to convince Israelis of the value of reconciliation. To the contrary, this analysis suggests that Israel, even under a left-wing government, will have the popular backing to block any attempts to start such a process or even encourage the discourse of reconciliation. A short analysis of historical patterns of reconciliation can augment this conclusion.

Patterns of Historical Reconciliation

One can find four major patterns in the historical reconciliation experience in which perpetrators are motivated or compelled to face responsibility for historic injustice. None of these patterns, briefly mentioned in the next paragraphs, applies to a case in which there is a gross power asymmetry in favor of the perpetrator.

First, reconciliation becomes possible when external or internal forces defeat the perpetrating system and a democratic order is installed, for example, the defeat of Germany in World War II or the collapse of the Rumanian regime in the post-Communist era. Notice that defeat without replacing the existing regime is not sufficient, as in the case of defeated Yugoslavia under Milošević or defeated Iraq under Saddam Hussein. Similarly, the collapse of the regime and its replacement by an undemocratic regime is not sufficient. The system should be defeated on grounds that include its own injustice.

Second, reconciliation becomes possible when the existing (oppressive) system faces an imminent defeat that can only be circumvented by accepting profound political and social transformation, as in South Africa. In this case, the perpetrating system concluded that without transformation, the system might collapse and the interests of the powerful group could be irreparably damaged. The transformation itself came out of negotiations that preserved some of the interests of the powerful group.

Third, reconciliation becomes possible when the weaker party is either eliminated or reduced to a status that cannot significantly threaten the existing social and political order, such as the Native American population in the United States, Canada, and Australia. In this case, reconciliation is much less costly for the high-power group, because changing the narrative does not necessitate significant political restructuring. The elites in the high-power group who lead the revision of narratives are not required to give up any of the gains they acquired at the expense of those who were eliminated or reduced in numbers. The new generations—those that did not perpetrate the injustice—adopt a new narrative in return for psychological self-cleansing at very low cost.

Fourth, the conditions for historic reconciliation gradually develop in a democratic regime that committed injustice against racial or ethnic groups within its own sovereign jurisdiction. These conditions are usually created by the victims' struggle for equal inclusion within the system itself. The historic injustice of slavery in the midst of the largest Western democracy has not been completely reconciled, at least not by the slaves' descendants. Although the conditions for reconciliation have been gradually created in a long process that has transformed the face of American society and the place of the African American community within it, the debate over apology to the African American community and the proper compensation for material and psychological losses they endured has just started, almost 150 years after the formal end of slavery.

In summary, the Israeli-Palestinian case has some similarities to both the second and fourth patterns discussed in this section. However, major differences place the Israeli-Palestinian case outside any of the above patterns. Israeli society is too far from facing the truth about the establishment of Israel to discuss Israel's historical responsibility for the Palestinian catastrophe, introduce an element of justice into the framework of negotiations, and, above all, pay the bill of reconciliation in the coin of the political restructuring that it requires.

Achieving a Settlement—Compromises within Each Community

With the existing balance of power between Israelis and Palestinians, Palestinians cannot expect a just solution to be found for the Palestinian refugee problem in the foreseeable future. That is a simple conclusion that should be taken into consideration in Palestinian political thinking. A just solution can and must be advanced in the intellectual sphere and must penetrate into the political discourse of the communities. Reconciliation, based on justice, facing historical truth and responsibilities should remain the future goal of a relationship between Israelis and Palestinians, and ways and means of achieving it should be constantly examined. But in the absence of this possibility of a just solution, the question is whether a settlement can be reached between Israel and the Palestinians—without historic reconciliation. The Palestinians have not decided within their own community about the precise goal of the Palestinian national movement at this stage: to achieve justice—defined politically as a two-state solution with Israeli recognition of the Palestinian right of return and the implementation of this right (and increasingly as a one binational state over the whole territory of historical Palestine)—or to achieve a Palestinian state without the right of return in practice, but with the principle upheld according to a formula negotiated with Israel. In either case, the Palestinians will have to define the meaning of each choice.

The first choice will mean that Palestinians will have to de-Zionize Israel, either by defeating it or by persuading Israelis to give up Zionism, the idea of an exclusive Jewish state. Israeli recognition of the right of return means that Israel will have to relinquish its Zionist past and restructure its future as a binational state. This is what Israelis mean by the argument that "the right of return means the end of Israel," because for most Israelis "Israel" and the "Jewish state" are one and the same. This is the logic behind Israel's obsession with the internal demographic threat. The rise of the demographic discourse in Israel in the last few years, which coincided with increased awareness about the right of return[17] and the emergence of fanatic right-wing politics, is directly related to objections to the return of Palestinian refugees.[18]

But this option cannot be attained by negotiation. Israel will not voluntarily abandon its Zionist ideology and Jewish character, and Palestinians cannot achieve the unequivocal recognition of the right of return, let alone its implementation. If the Palestinian national movement insists that Israel recognize and implement the right of return—facing its history and recognizing its past—Palestinians will have to define their goals clearly to both Palestinians and Israelis. They will have to be able to envision and articulate a place in the country for the Jewish people in Israel that they can support. Palestinians will have to be open about the impossibility of attaining this goal in the near future by negotiation, and they will need to develop a strategy to achieve this goal that their constituency can understand. This requires ideological underpinnings that are not consistent with mainstream thought within the Palestinian national movement and its leadership at the present time.

In all likelihood, pursuit of this option will bring about, at least in the immediate future, an acceleration of trends toward extremism in Israeli society and politics and the intensification of the use of force and, in turn, of Palestinian resistance. It will open the door for more serious war crimes and an apartheid system, from which the struggle for one binational state will become the most natural option and political goal for the next generations of Palestinians and for many Israelis. But in the absence of a Palestinian secular national ideology that can advance such a vision, develop it into a political program, and devise the political means for pursuing its success, the intensity of force and resistance is more likely to strengthen extremist religious movements on the Palestinian side—the counterpart of extremist politics in Israel.

The second option is to define the goals of the Palestinian national movement as achieving a state in the West Bank and Gaza without reaching a historic reconciliation with Israel. Instead, the historic compromise will be within the Palestinian community, because the creation of such a state, without implementing the right of return and without changing Israel's Jewish character (and with the probability that Israel will insist on being recognized as the Jewish state), can only come at the expense of the Palestinian refugees and the Palestinians in Israel. Palestinian refugees will have to accept the offers of compensation and moving to the Palestinian state. Palestinians in Israel will have to pay the heavy price of unequal citizenship, but will seek to change Israel's Jewish identity.

This option leads to a settlement with Israel but not to reconciliation. This option does not represent a historic compromise with Israel, because Israel's legitimacy is not accepted and the right of return is not forfeited. The future will have to remain open for changes in the agreement by peaceful means and by mutual agreement. The Palestinians will not accept Israel's Jewish character but will live peacefully with Israel.

The moral and political choice between these two options is an internal Palestinian issue. The internal Palestinian debate about the right of return touches on these choices. Sari Nusseibeh has the right to argue that the right of return should be implemented within a Palestinian state, as do the Palestinians who signed the Geneva Accords with a group of left-wing Israeli politicians in December of 2003.[19] These Palestinians will need to have the moral courage to go to Palestinian refugees and explain the trade-off to them. The only logic they can use to explain this trade-off is the context of power relations. In the present context of power relations, they will argue, Palestinians can get an independent state in the West Bank and Gaza only if we give up the implementation of the right of return. Why? Because Israel, supported by force and international diplomacy, won't accept the Palestinian right of return. These Palestinians can pose a difficult moral choice: "Solve your problem in the context of a Palestinian state with the implementation of the right of return to the Palestinian state and compensation or continue the struggle against unmatched force, a struggle in which you are just, but weak." That is a legitimate question about which Palestinians will have to make a moral choice, not a tactical choice. But what is not legitimate is to have such a decision made without the participation of Palestinian refugees and Palestinians in Israel, the two Palestinian communities that pay the price for such a settlement.

These are not the only options Palestinians have. One possibility is to reach a fake "historic compromise" in which Israel pays lip service to its responsibility and develops a formula for recognizing the right of return that does not challenge the Israeli narrative and allows for the return of tens of thousands within the context of "family reunification." This will be the choice of a "diplomatic formulation of words" that will lead neither to settlement nor to reconciliation. The settlement based on such an option will be divisive and will ultimately break down over the interpretation of language. The other possibility is for Palestinians to turn inward and seek to empower their institutions and society without seeking reconciliation or establishing a state that is the outcome of an unacceptable political settlement.

But a political settlement based on compromise within Palestinian society will also require a compromise within Israeli society. As the powerful side, Israeli compromises are less painful. The compromise in Israel will be over the requirement for the recognition of Israel as a Jewish state. Israel, having the upper hand in the conflict, can afford to avoid difficult choices. But it is also becoming clear that the intifada is entrapping Israeli society as it is entrapping Palestinian society. The long struggle for Israel means a struggle to defeat the Palestinian national movement. But a homeland nation can be defeated only by extermination. Even ethnic cleansing and the imposition of an apartheid-like system would bring only a temporary defeat, because it only changes the nature of the conflict, not the conflict itself.

The hard choice for Israel in a political settlement of the kind described above is not to forfeit its Jewish character, because Israel will not. But a political settlement will require that Israel does not insist on Palestinian recognition of its Jewish identity and that it leaves open the future character of the state for the citizens of the country to determine. In Israel, this debate has yet to begin.

Notes

1. See Nadim Rouhana, "Identity and Power in the Reconciliation of National Conflict," in *The Social Psychology of Group Identity and Social Conflict: Theory, Application, and Practice*, Eagly, Baron, and Hamilton, eds. (Washington, D.C.: American Psychological Association, 2004). See also how this distinction is applied to the Israeli-Palestinian conflict in Rouhana, "Group Identity and Power Asymmetry in Reconciliation Processes: The Israeli-Palestinian Case," *Peace and Conflict: Journal of Peace Psychology* 10:1 (2004): 33–52.

2. One famous Israeli cultural maxim that reflects much of the relationship between Israel and the Palestinians is that Arabs—read Palestinians—understand

only the language of force. This reflects a relationship between the dominant and the dominated and the fact that the gains of land, property, and legitimacy were achieved by force.

Indeed the dynamics of force and resistance dictated by the Judaization project have been continuously at work and are inherent to the conflict. Their intensity has occasionally abated—for example, during the 1990s "peace process"—but when the Palestinians resisted Israeli and American pressure to accept Israel's proposals and when the second Intifada started, Israel's use of military force against the Palestinian population shifted into a classic escalatory cycle. That violent struggle has transformed the face of Israel's society and state (as well as that of Palestinian society and governance). That Intifada thus revealed a trend that had started several years earlier and whose ideological foundations fall within the range of Zionist thought, but that had not been fully expressed after Israel's establishment.

The new stage of force and resistance encouraged fanaticism in Israeli political thought and practice as was demonstrated in the reversal of the Oslo process, sharply negative changes in public-supported policies toward the Palestinian citizens in Israel, and the reawakening of dormant anti-democratic political ideas. The end result was that Israeli society reached a phase of unprecedented extremism with the potential for war crimes, ethnic cleansing, and openly racist policies and behavior toward Palestinians in both the occupied territories and Israel. See Nadim N. Rouhana and Nimer Sultany, "Redrawing the Boundaries of Citizenship: Israel's New Hegemony," *Journal of Palestinian Studies*, 33:1 (fall 2003): 5–22.

3. For a discussion of justice, see D. A. Crocker, "Transitional Justice and International Civil Society: Toward a Normative Framework," in *Constellations* 5 (1998): 492–517; idem, "Reckoning with Past Wrongs: A Normative Framework," in *Ethics & International Affairs* 13 (1999): 43–64; D. Little, "A Different Kind of Justice: Dealing with Human Rights Violations in Transitional Societies," in *Ethics & International Affairs* 13 (1999): 65–80. For discussion of justice in the context of the Israeli-Palestinian conflict, see R. Khalidi, "Attainable Justice: Elements of Solution to the Palestinian Refugee Issue," in *International Journal* 53 (1998): 233–52; and Rouhana, "Group Identity and Power Asymmetry." See also Y. Peled and N.N. Rouhana, "Transitional Justice and the Right of Return of the Palestinian Refugees," in *Theoretical Inquiries in Law* (2004).

4. T.L. Haskell, *Objectivity Is Not Neutrality: Explanatory Schemes in History* (Baltimore: Johns Hopkins University Press, 1998). See also J.E. Towes, "Salvaging Truth and Ethical Obligations From the Historicist Tide: Thomas Haskell's Moderate Historicism," in *History and Theory* 38 (1999): 348–64.

5. See, for example, Yossi Beilin's views about the significance of the Taba's negotiations regarding the right of return: "The wisdom of Taba was that we could refer to the two narratives in the evolving Palestinian refugee problem, without accepting either of them. The mere fact that we could refer to them and respect both narratives was enough to satisfy both sides that their stories is not being ignored." "Akiva Eldar Interviews Yossi Beilin and Nabil Shaath," *Palestine-Israel Journal* 9 (2002): 12–23.

6. Ibid.; see quotation from Yossi Beilin.

7. See Akenson's comparative study of Israel, South Africa, and Ulster: D.H. Akenson, *God's Peoples: Covenant and Land in South Africa, Israel, and Ulster* (Ithaca, N.Y.: Cornell University Press, 1992).

8. Actually, this debate is based on a covert assumption that if the Palestinians had not by that time developed a separate national identity, it would have been legitimate for the Zionist project to plan and implement establishing a Jewish state on their land.

9. This argument, advanced mainly by Benny Morris, *The Birth of the Palestinian Refugee Problem, 1947–1949* (Cambridge: Cambridge University Press, 1987), allows for a formula of sharing responsibility with the Palestinians over their catastrophe. The logic of circumstances can be blamed, and Israel's share in this responsibility is limited to these circumstances that develop within the context of war.

10. See Bar-Tal and Teichman's comprehensive review of research on Arab representation by Israel's public, media, literature, textbooks, and arts. D. Bar-Tal and Y. Teichman, *Stereotypes and Prejudice in Conflict: Arab Representation in Israeli Jewish Society* (Cambridge: Cambridge University Press, forthcoming).

11. Benny Morris, *Righteous Victims* (New York: Vintage, 1999).

12. See the study conducted at Tel Aviv University in March 2002 that surveyed 312 Israelis on related issues. D. Zakai, Y. Klar, and K. Sharvit, "Jewish Israelis on 'the Right of Return': Growing Awareness of the Issue's Importance," in *Palestine-Israel Journal* 9 (2002): 58–66.

13. See Peled and Rouhana, "Transitional Justice."

14. See, for example "Akiva Eldar Interviews Yossi Beilin and Nabil Shaath"; and Ian S. Lustick, "Negotiating Truth: The Holocaust, *Lehavdil,* and al-Nakba," in this volume.

15. J. Alpher and K. Shikaki, "Concept Paper: The Palestinian Refugee Problem and the Right of Return," in *Middle East Policy* 6 (1999): 167–89. Other unofficial groups worked on this subject, but authors presented separate Palestinian and Israeli views—for example, the project of the American Academy of Sciences produced papers by Shlomo Gazit and Rashid Khalidi. S. Gazit, *The Palestinian Refugee Problem,* Final Status Issue no. 2 (Jaffee Center for Strategic Studies, Tel Aviv University, 1995); R. Khalidi, "Observations on the Palestinian Right of Return," in *The Palestinian Right of Return: Two Views,* Emerging Issues, Occasional Paper Series of the Academy of Arts and Sciences, J. Boutwell, ed., 1–16 (Cambridge, Mass: American Academy of Sciences, 1990).

16. *Divrei HaKnesset,* September 8, 1999.

17. See Klar Zakai, and Sharvit, "Jewish Israelis," 58–66.

18. In September 2002, Minister of Labor and Social Welfare Shlomo Benizri (Shas) reconvened the Demography Council in order to find solutions to the "demographic problem," namely, the increase of Arab population and the decrease in the percentage of the Jewish population in Israel, in order to preserve the Jewish character of the state. The reconvening of the council after five years of inactivity sends a clear message that the growth of the Palestinian citizen population is a threat to the state and to its people. See Gideon Levy, "Wombs in the Service of the State," *Haaretz* English edition, September 9, 2002.

19. The Geneva Accord can be found at http://www.heskem.org.il. The accord argued for the return of Palestinian refugees into a Palestinian state in the West Bank and Gaza.

Chapter 14
The Visible and Invisible in the Israeli-Palestinian Conflict

Ilan Pappé

This chapter provides a retrospective look at the history of peacemaking in Palestine and Israel, for the sake of a better understanding of what lies ahead. Its main argument is that for various reasons, throughout the years an Israeli perception of what is a solution guided the peacemaking, while the Palestinian reading of the situation was totally neglected and rejected.

The result so far has been a peace process that focused on what is presented here as the visible and recent aspects of the conflict: the desire to reach a compromise over the fate of the West Bank and Gaza Strip, occupied by Israel in 1967, while sidelining what for the Palestinians is the heart of the matter, the 1948 war and the refugee problem. The Palestinian view deals with the more distant past and the less visible layers of the conflict, focusing on responsibility, guilt, and justice.

The way forward, given the dismal failure of all the peace efforts hitherto, is to push toward a reconciliation process that will focus on abstract issues such as fairness, justice, and guilt. This process will not be limited to compromises over borders, the nature of regimes, or other materialistic aspects of a political settlement. In fact, I argue that the possible achievements in the physical issues of land and borders are useless without significant progress on moral and legal grounds.

My departure point is that "fairness" and "justice" are no less important components of the future solution than armies and territories. This is not an attempt to present only an ethical reflection; it is much more the outcome of a functional approach to the conceptualization of a future solution. This approach gains increasing support on the ground, as the two-state solution in Palestine loses its feasibility and, to a certain extent, its credibility. In the various alternatives suggested, the main concern seems to focus on moral issues, no less than on materialistic questions of percentages of territory, sovereignty, and security. My guess is that moral issues will even override these practical aspects of a solution.

Historical Background

Power and knowledge go hand in hand, and hence in the West, one hears too often and too loud the conceptualization of "fairness" postulated by the occupier, the winner, and the victorious—in our case, the Israeli side. One hears little about the point of view of the other side, the subaltern Palestinian. This is why in the past British, United Nations (UN), American, and Israeli conceptualizations of fairness dominated the search for peace and were based mainly on the territorial dimension of the conflict while neglecting the questions of guilt, restitution, and justice. These perceptions of fairness are closely connected to questions of a homeland in the realm of possession, entitlement, and future control. In the second part of this chapter, I will argue that only the inclusion in a dominant position of the Palestinian concepts of fairness can construct notions of homeland conducive to the pacification of the conflict.

The Israel-Palestine conflict has been an object of reconciliation, mediation, and peace efforts ever since it erupted in the late nineteenth century. The first significant efforts were made by the British Empire during the Mandatory period. At that early period, one can distinguish between two stages. During the first state, until the 1930s, the various British initiators of dialogue wanted to construct under British auspices a political structure—a joint homeland—that would represent equally the small Jewish community and the Palestinian majority on the land of Palestine. The second stage, beginning in the mid-1930s, was mainly inspired by the principle of partition: dividing the territory between the two communities and the construction of two separate political structures. In the first stage, one can talk about a missed opportunity around 1928, when the Palestinian leadership agreed to discuss a joint federative structure, after years of rejecting any compromise; but the Zionist leadership, which had supported until that moment such a model, opposed it when it learned that the Palestinians consented to it—a typical mode of behavior that would repeat itself in 1947. Compromises, which challenged the very essence of Zionism, were accepted by the Jewish community only when it was absolutely clear that they would be rejected by the Palestinian side.[1]

The joint and equally divided political structure of 1928 included restrictions on Jewish immigration and was a basis for a binational state. It was totally forgotten when the UN—inspired by Zionist and British schemes—offered a partition plan in 1947. This partition left an equal number of Jews and Palestinians within the future Jewish state. Therefore we can say that in a way, the 1947 partition resolution offered a kaleidoscopic vision of a homeland divided into one binational state next to a uni-national one.[2] However, it is important to connect the Zionist acceptance to the prior knowledge of an assured Palestinian rejection.

As in 1928, so also in 1947 the Zionist leaders were offered a binational model. In 1928, they rejected it and were let off by the British. In 1947, they succeeded in creating the impression that they, unlike the Arab side, preferred such a binational state next to a purely Arab state, as stipulated by the partition resolution. As the Arab and Palestinian rejection persisted, their bluff was never called.

The Israeli scholar Simcha Flapan was adamant in his conviction that Zionist support for partition in 1947 stemmed from a clear knowledge about the general Arab rejectionist posture and the particular Palestinian refusal:[3] a very sensible act of historical deduction, but one that is difficult to substantiate with documents. It is quite clear nonetheless that a binational Palestinian-Jewish state—as offered by UN General Assembly Resolution 181—would have defeated the most basic Zionist aspirations and that the Jewish leadership of the day would have resorted to any possible means—destruction and transfer included—to make the state as purely Jewish as possible.

It is noteworthy that a few days before the UN partition resolution was adopted, the Zionist leadership discussed the issue, and a consensus emerged that, if Palestinians would remain within the future Jewish state, they would have to be granted full citizenship. Three months later, the military command of the Jewish community devised a plan for what we now call ethnic cleansing of the areas of the future Jewish state.[4]

Thus, a "fair" solution until 1948 was a binational state, either in all of Palestine or in part of it, while the other part was to belong to the indigenous population. This "fair" solution was unacceptable at the time to the Palestinians, who regarded the Zionists as Algerians regarded the Pieds Noir, with whom they had no desire to divide the land. But it was also totally unacceptable to the Zionist movement, whose leaders decided to de-Arabize any part of Palestine that would be allocated to them or that they would occupy. Yet in the international collective memory, the "fair" solution was accepted by Israel and rejected by the Arabs—a memory shaping attitudes especially in the West toward Palestinians as villains and Israelis as heroes.

Indeed, the future concepts of homeland in the context of Israel and Palestine would be closely associated with the international community's input into peace negotiations. This input in turn is influenced significantly by perceptions of right and wrong and assessments of past behavior.

What blinded the UN at the time was the organization's curious decision to opt for a solution that was adopted by the majority of its member states and not to seek consent between the two warring parties on the ground. The future homeland of both locals and newcomers was to be defined and brokered by outside forces, although never in history has this been a recipe for success.

Partition was institutionalized in November 1947 by the United Nations Special Committee on Palestine. The members of this committee did not know Palestine at all and, in a relatively short period, adopted the plan already offered by the Peel Royal Commission in 1937, which had been endorsed by the Zionist leadership. In essence, partition meant dividing the land into two states, while keeping between them an economic union and supervising them from abroad. This has remained the basis for the peace efforts. But already the initiators of the partition resolution recognized that not every issue in Palestine was divisible or negotiable on a rational basis. The resolution offered, contrary to its spirit, the internationalization of Jerusalem. The positions of both sides toward the city were born not in decision-making processes but in layers of conscience and consciousness. Even if those positions were not fully understood by the mediators, they realized that a solution could not be based on the divisibility of the visible but rather should emerge out of respect for the non-divisibility of the invisible, or less clearly visible, layers of the conflict.[5]

It was the first mediator after the Mandate, Count Folke Bernadotte, who tried to penetrate these deeper layers. He was appointed UN mediator on June 20, 1948, shortly after the 1948 war erupted. He offered two proposals to end the conflict by partitioning the land into two states. The difference between them was that in the second proposal, he suggested the annexation of Arab Palestine to Transjordan. In both proposals, he stipulated the unconditional repatriation of Palestinian refugees as a precondition for peace. He was ambivalent about Jerusalem, wanting it to be the Arab capital in the first proposal but preferring it to be international in the second. In any case, he seemed to place the refugees and Jerusalem at the center of the conflict and perceive these two dilemmas as indivisible problems, for which a comprehensive and just solution would be required.[6]

Even after Bernadotte's assassination by Jewish extremists in 1948, the Palestine Conciliation Commission, which was appointed to replace him, pursued the same policy. The three members of this commission wanted to build the future solution on three tiers: the partition of the land into two states (not according to the map of the partition resolution but in correspondence to the demographic distribution of Jews and Palestinians); the internationalization of Jerusalem; and the unconditional return of the refugees to their homes. The new mediators offered the three principles as a basis for negotiations. The Arab confrontational countries and the Palestinian leadership accepted this offer, during the UN peace conference in Lausanne in May 1949 and already in UN General Assembly Resolution 194, of December 1948. The offer was nonetheless buried by the intransigent prime minister David Ben-Gurion and his government in the summer of 1949. At first, the U.S. administration rebuked Israel for its policy and exerted economic pressure on it, but later the Jewish lobby succeeded in reorienting U.S. policy onto pro-Israeli tracks, where it has remained until today.[7]

There was a lull in peace efforts in the 1950s and 1960s, although schemes such as the Anglo-American Alpha program and the Johnston Plan were discussed.[8] These and more esoteric initiatives, almost all of them American, sought to adopt a businesslike approach to the conflict. This meant a great belief in partition according to the security interests of Israel and its Arab neighbors, while totally sidelining the Palestinians as partners for peace. The Palestinians were canceled as a political partner in the businesslike approach. They existed only as refugees whose fate was treated within the economic aspect of the American cold war against the Soviet Union. Their problem was to be solved within a new Marshall Plan for the Middle East. This plan promised U.S. aid to the area in order to improve the standard of living as the best means of containing Soviet encroachment. Under that plan, the refugees had to be resettled in Arab lands where they would serve as cheap labor for those states' development (and thereby also distance them from Israel's borders and consciousness).

Fortunately for the Palestinians, they had the Palestine Liberation Organization (PLO), a movement that, through guerrilla warfare and welfare systems, enabled the refugees to show enough resistance that Arab regimes left the refugees in their transitional camps, despite their perception as a destabilizing factor. The association of the PLO with the Soviet Union was another factor pushing the Palestinians, wherever they were, away from any prospective Pax Americana.

The June 1967 war and its consequences clarified in the most striking manner the gap between businesslike American and Israeli attitudes, on the one hand, and the Palestinian conceptualization of a fair solution, on the other. This chasm subsequently disabled any significant progress in the peace efforts. As I hope to show, the quantitative and divisible approach to the conflict can produce at best military and economic rearrangements and configurations that reflect the balance of power; at worst, it perpetuates past evils and injustices. Hence the occupier, Israel, remains in its previous role, and the Palestinians, the occupied, continue to live under the same oppression. Not even a very dramatic discourse of peace, dramatized by high-profile ceremonies on the White House lawn, can hide this reality.

Israel had occupied a large share of Palestine already in 1948—77 percent of it. It completed Palestine's takeover in response to the Arab attack in 1967. This total control of the land enabled American negotiators such as William Rogers and Henry Kissinger and Swedish UN mediators such as Gunnar Jarring to produce and market an equation they presented as the ultimate and fair solution. Territories for peace: an equation that was wholeheartedly endorsed by the pragmatic Israeli Labor movement. It is a strange formula: on one side of the equation is a quantitative and measurable variable; on the other, an abstract term, not easily conceptualized or even illustrated. It was less bizarre as a working basis for bilateral peace between Israel and its Arab neighbors; it operated quite well for a while in the cases of Egypt and Jordan. Yet we should remember that it produced

only a "cold peace" with these two countries, as it did not offer a comprehensive solution to the Palestine question. Indeed, what had this equation
to offer to the ultimate victims of the 1948 war, whose demand for justice
is the main fuel kindling the conflict's fire?

Justice is not only demanded by Palestinians; it is asked for by the Arab
world at large. Justice in the local regional context is a less abstract term
than it sounds. Justice for Palestinians is part of the reshaping of the postcolonial Middle East agenda. Even if Arab regimes tend to forget it, their
civil societies remind them of this particular context of the Palestine question. Peace with Israel, even in the case of Egyptians and Jordanians, means
reconciliation with the last colonial movement—even if it was also a
national movement—remaining on Middle Eastern soil. For those who
were not direct victims of this colonialism, it may be easier to reconcile,
because of economic interest or in recognition of the balance of power
with the Jewish state; but for its victims, not only from 1948 but also from
the continuous campaign of destruction of the Palestinian people, economic interests and balance of power can persuade only the few, the
uncommitted, but not the devoted many. They not only seek rectification
of past evils; they seek immunity from present and future devastation. It
has also taken a considerable effort for Israeli Jews to forsake their narrative
and even more so to accept their role as victimizers. But this is the key to
the solution, and I will later deal with mechanisms for such a process.

Thus, in the eyes of the Palestinians, a fair peace must be based on the
healing of past wounds and, far more important, security against future
destruction. Can territories assure that? Put differently, can a future solution be based on territorial dimensions alone?

The Oslo Discourse of Fairness

The architects of the Oslo accord thought it could be based on territorial
dimensions alone. They resold the merchandise of "peace for territories."
Hallowed concepts such as Israeli recognition of the PLO and autonomy
for the Palestinians were meant to strengthen the businesslike approach to
a solution. The solution was perpetuation, through indirect military control, of the Israeli occupation. This solution was overlaid with a dramatic
discourse of peace.[9]

I am not underestimating the progress made in Oslo, but one should
never forget the circumstances of the accord's birth, as these explain why
it was such a colossal failure. Dramatic changes in the global and regional
balance of power and an Israeli readiness to replace the Hashemites of Jordan with the PLO as a partner for peace opened the way to a complicated
variant of the "territories for peace" formula. Territories, and everything
else that is visible and quantifiable, would be divided between the two sides.
Thus, only the non-Jewish parts of post-1948 Palestine would be redivided

between Israel and a future Palestinian autonomous entity. Within this 23 percent of Palestine, the illegal Jewish settlements would be divided into 80 percent under Israeli control and 20 percent under Palestinian authority. And so on: most of the water resources to Israel, most of Jerusalem in Israeli hands. Peace, the quid pro quo, meant a stateless Palestinian state robbed of any say in its defense, foreign, and economic policies. As for the Palestinian right of return, according to the Israeli interpretation of Oslo, which is the one that counts, it should be forgotten and erased. This conceptualization of fairness was presented to the world at large in the summer of 2000 at Camp David.

For Palestinians, the Camp David summit was meant to produce the final stages in the Israeli withdrawal from the West Bank and the Gaza Strip according to UN Security Council Resolutions 242 and 338 and prepare the ground for new negotiations over a fair settlement on the basis of UN General Assembly Resolution 194—the return of the refugees, the internationalization of Jerusalem, and a full sovereign Palestinian state. Even the United States voted in favor of this resolution and continued to do so.

The Israeli Left, which regained power in 1999, regarded the Camp David summit as a stage for dictating to the Palestinians their concept of fairness: maximizing the divisibility of the visible—evacuating 90 percent of the occupied areas, 20 percent of the settlements, 50 percent of East Jerusalem—while demanding the end of Palestinian references to the invisible layers of the conflict: no right of return, no full sovereign Palestinian state, and no solution for the Palestinian minority inside Israel. After Camp David, fairness meant that as long as the Palestinians would not accept the Israeli dictate, occupation, exile, and discrimination would continue until the Palestinians would budge. With or without Ariel Sharon's violation of the sacredness of al-Haram al-Sharif, the second uprising broke out in the territories and in Israel in October 2000, and it will be with us for a very long time.

"Territories for peace" is no longer on the peace table, ever since the outbreak of the second intifada. The uprising spilled over into Israel itself, leading the Palestinian minority there to call for the de-Zionization of the Jewish state, allowing West Bankers to demand the Palestinization of Muslim and Christian Jerusalem, inducing the inhabitants of Gaza to raise arms against the continued occupation, and uniting refugees around the world in their call for the implementation of their right of return. What this last intifada makes abundantly clear is that, while the end of occupation is a precondition for peace, it is not peace itself. The Israeli peace camp is insulted by this. They feel that their leaders maximized the equation by offering most of the territories that Israel occupied in 1967. They demand now, as never before, Palestinian recognition of the Zionist narrative of the 1948 war: Israel has no responsibility for the making of the refugee problem, the Palestinian minority in Israel—now 20 percent of the population—is not part of the solution to the conflict, and Palestinians should recognize as forever Jewish the settlement belt encircling Jerusalem and planted in the heart of such Palestinian cities as Nablus and Khalil (Hebron).

Thus, the conceptualization of a future solution is tied to values such as fairness not less than to the eviction of territories. The post-territorial dimension of the solution is closely associated with the direct recognition by Israelis of their role as colonizers, expellers, oppressors, and occupiers.

This is a most difficult task for the Jewish society in Israel since it imagines itself to be the victim. This is done consciously and unconsciously by the national systems in Israel that cultivate through their discourses and conduct the fear of attributing to the Palestinians positive or even empathetic images. This particular dilemma was revealed in Israel in the early 1950s. The state system by then conveyed a negative stereotyping of everything that was Arab. It was the hated Other, symbolizing everything we, the Jews, are not. This juxtaposition ran into trouble when Israel encouraged about a million Arab Jews to immigrate. There was a conscious effort to de-Arabize these Arab immigrants: they were coached to scorn their mother tongue, reject Arab culture, and make an effort to be Europeanized.[10]

The other, complementary side of this coin was a systematic effort to deny acts of barbarism against the Palestinians and to attribute the ability to perpetuate such human abuses only to the other side. This particular dilemma can be seen in the way that Israeli historiography dealt with Jewish atrocities in the 1948 war and Jewish terrorism in the Mandatory period. Atrocities and terrorism are two modes of behavior that Israeli Orientalists attribute solely to the Palestinian resistance movement. Therefore they cannot be part of an analysis or description of chapters in Israel's past. One way out of this dilemma is to credit a particular political group, preferably an extremist one, with the same attributes as the enemy, while stressing the mainstream's moral national behavior. This is why Israel always admitted to the massacre in Deir Yassin, committed by the right-wing Irgun, but tried to hide the many other massacres carried out by the Haganah and later by the Israeli Defense Forces (IDF).[11]

Thus, a fair solution requires a new Israeli approach to the issue of victimhood. As I have written elsewhere, the Israeli TV series *Tekuma*, celebrating Israel's jubilee in 1998, was the first popular attempt to ponder the possibility that Jews were not only the ultimate victims of the twentieth century, but also victimizers. This was done by allocating space on TV to show, alongside the Zionist narrative, chapters from the Palestinian version of history. Although this was a very cautious attempt that did not deviate too much from the Zionist narrative, it was enough to bring the wrath of the entire political system on the series' editors and producers.[12]

Until such a recognition of the victimizing role they played becomes a vital and necessary station in the socialization of the Jews in Israel, no less than the horror destinations to which high school children in Israel are forced—and one hopes that at least some of them went by their own accord—to visit in Holocaust Europe, there is very little chance for progress on issues such as a fair solution in the construction of a future homeland for both Palestinians and Jews.

For Israeli Jews, recognizing the Palestinians as victims of their own evil is deeply traumatic, for it not only questions the very foundational myths of the State of Israel and its motto of "a state without a people for a people without a state" but also raises a whole panoply of ethical questions with significant implications for the future of the state. This fear on the Israeli side is the stronger of the two aversions and most destructive in the Jewish society's ability to turn a new leaf in its relationship with the Palestinians. The fear of allowing the other side to become a victim of the conflict would not be so fierce had this victimhood been related to natural and normal consequences of a long-lasting bloody conflict. From such a perspective, both sides are victims of the circumstances or any other amorphous, non-committal concept that absolves human beings and particularly politicians from taking responsibility. But what is demanded by the Palestinians—in fact, has become a condition sine qua non to many of them—is that Israel recognize them as victims of its own evil. The fear is deeply rooted in the way that Israelis choose to tell the story of 1948 and, more important, in how Israelis react to the way the Palestinian narrative tells the story of that year, the year of the Nakba.

In Israel, educators, historians, novelists, and cultural producers in general have all been involved in a campaign of denial and concealment. The horrors of 1948 were hidden from the public eye and from generations to come by those who committed them. Only at the end of 2000 did Gideon Levy, a voice in the wilderness, cry out in an article in *Haaretz*: How could you have lied to us for so many years? Very few ask this question now, and even fewer are willing to answer it.[13]

Historians and educators are the main villains in this case. In one way or another, they helped to construct and preserve a national narrative that eliminates the collective Palestinian memory. This elimination is no less violent than expulsion and destruction; it is the main constitutive element in the construction of collective Jewish identity in the state of Israel. It is manifested in the tales told by child minders on Independence Day and Passover, in the curriculum and textbooks in elementary and high schools, in the ceremonies of freshmen and the graduation of officers in the army. It is broadcast in the printed and electronic media as well as in the speeches and discourse of the politicians, in the way artists, novelists, and poets subject their works to the national narrative, and in the research produced by academics in the universities about the Israeli reality in the past and the present.

This act of symbolic violence and thought control intensified after October 2000. It is particularly evident now in the educational system and the media, but mostly in Israeli academia—a state of affairs that requires nonpartisan scholars in Israel and elsewhere to rethink what they can and should do in their relationship with an academia that supports oppression, occupation, and discrimination.

This self-control keeps even peacemakers in Israel from opening the Pandora's box of 1948 and the whole question of victimhood. This can be seen in the posture adopted by the Peace Now movement in Israel. For its members, peace and reconciliation are translated into the need for mutual recognition between the two national narratives, in a way that would eliminate the clash between them. The way to do it is to make divisible everything that is visible: land, resources, blame, and history into a pre-1967 mind-set when "we the Jews were right and just" and a post-1967 mind-set when "you the Palestinians were right and just."[14]

Viewed from this perspective, victimhood in the Israeli-Palestinian conflict can also be divided into those two historical periods. The same righteous approach of the Israeli peace camp applies to the early, more distant chapter in the history of the conflict as one before 1967, in which the Jews were the victims, and the chapter after 1967, in which the Palestinians were victims. The periodization is very important, since the earlier period is considered to be more crucial; thus, being Just then, in the formative period of the conflict, justifies the existence of Zionism and the whole Jewish project in Palestine. At the same time, it casts doubt on the wisdom and morality of Palestinian actions in that period. It obliterates from any discussion the ethnic cleansing carried out by the Jews in 1948: the destruction of four hundred Palestinian villages and neighborhoods, the expulsion of 700,000 Palestinians, and the massacre of several thousand Palestinians.[15] From this perspective, Israel deviated from the moral and just road after being forced to occupy the West Bank and the Gaza Strip. But this misbehavior does not cast any doubt on its very essence and justification.

But peace and mutual recognition entail bridging over the invisible—hence indivisible—layers of history, guilt, and injustice. Blame cannot be divided, not if peace and reconciliation mean respect for the Other's narrative. The Palestinian narrative is that of suffering, reconstructed on the basis of oral history: a continued exilic existence and rediscovered historical narratives read backward through the prism of contemporary hardships. In that narrative, Zionism or Israel is the absolute evil, the arch-villain as well as the ultimate victimizer. How can this image be divided in the businesslike approach to peace preached by American and Israeli peacemakers?

It cannot, of course. When peace is discussed in this context, one should appeal to ways in which communities of suffering worldwide reconcile with their victimizers. The narrative of suffering is an interpretative construct describing a collective evil in the past, employed for the political needs of a given community in the present in order to improve its conditions in the future. This is the tool employed by Jewish victims of the Holocaust, Native Americans, African Americans, Muslims in Bosnia, the African majority in South Africa, and Palestinians.

In order to avoid a reductionist view of the narrative of suffering, I will add that in the case of the Palestinians especially, as well as other communities that continue to live the aftereffects of the original action that led to this narrative, such a concept has also a redemptive value for the communities themselves. However, the way that this narrative is manipulated by cultural production and political actors for political ends is another issue.

This narrative is reproduced with the help of educational and media systems and a commemorative infrastructure of museums and ceremonies and is preserved by employing an adequate discourse of collective national memory. It can serve a community in conflict; it is more difficult as a means for reconciliation. In the case of the Palestinians, this takes the form especially of crowding the calendar with significant days that have to be commemorated: days such as the Balfour Declaration, the Declaration of Independence, the end of the Mandate, the partition resolution, and the day Fatah was founded. It is admittedly less a case of collective museums, as the Palestinians continue to lack such a basic infrastructure in the absence of a terra firma on which to establish commemorative rituals. For example, the mass graveyard of the Sabra and Chatila massacres has been used as a massive garbage dump for the past nineteen years. Every year it is cleared up in September, but it usually takes activists from outside the camp to generate some memorial event before it disintegrates into a dump again.[16] In one community, at least, PLO activists residing in Tunis between 1983 and 1993 had a corner in the living rooms of their private homes with a kind of a museum representing a narrative and a discourse of national identity.

While Palestinians live the memory of the Nakba, Israelis deny it out of fear. This Israeli fear plays a crucial role in the violence exercised daily in the Israeli struggle against the Palestinian narrative, the memory and the assumption of victimhood. Victimizing the other and negating its right to be a victim are intertwined processes of the same violence. Those who expelled Palestinians in 1948 deny that the ethnic cleansing that took place. So the self-declaration of being a victim is accompanied by the fear of losing the position of the Jew as the ultimate victim in modern history to the Other, the ultimate victim of Israel and Zionism.[17]

How can we deal with this fear, a subject that has to be encountered if the hypothesis of this chapter is accepted, that without such a confrontation there is very little hope for a different kind of coexistence or for the construction of a post-conflict reality? Let me suggest two possible but very different ways to approach this complex question of reconciliation.

Post-Conflictual Possibilities

The first and most difficult approach is legal. The very idea of considering the 1948 case in the realm of law and justice is anathema to most Jews in Israel, and hence outside pressure would be needed in order to adopt this approach.

Bringing onto the stage of international tribunals Israel's conduct in 1948 and ever since may deliver a message even to the peace camp in Israel that reconciliation entails recognition of war crimes and collective atrocities. This cannot be done from within, as any reference in the Israeli press to expulsion, massacre, or destruction in 1948 is usually denied and attributed to self-hate and service to the enemy in time of war.[18] This reaction encompasses academia, the media, and the educational system as well as political circles. The reaction shows what a powerful disincentive the current power structure poses. It reveals how deep the fear is that members of Israeli society would be implicated in actions, the likes of which have been condemned by the entire world, including prominent members of Israeli Jewish society.

Tribunals like this, even if they are staged public events, can teach us in advance about the mechanism of future settlement. For instance, how does one quantify the suffering? One of the best means of approaching this quantification of suffering was offered by the Israelis and Germans in their reparation agreement. That agreement included pensions calculated according to inflation across the years, estimations of real-estate values, and other aspects of individual loss. A different set of agreements was concluded about translating the collective loss into money, in the form of grants to the State of Israel. Salman Abu-Sitta has begun such thinking, giving us an idea on the real value of assets lost in the Nakba.[19]

A softer approach is to offer non-retributive paradigms of justice. Howard Zehr criticizes the pro-punishment judicial system.[20] One of the questions he raises is relevant to our discussion of the means by which Jews in Israel could overcome their fear of facing the past. Zehr asks, should justice focus on establishing guilt or should it focus on identifying needs and obligations? In other words, can it serve as a reregulator of life where life was once disrupted? According to Zehr, justice cannot be made to inflict suffering on victimizers, let alone their descendants, but can stop suffering from continuing.

Such a non-retributive panel was offered by the Truth and Reconciliation Commission headed by Bishop Desmond Tutu in South Africa. The power underlying this commission lies in its disinclination to inflict heavy penalties and in its insistence on discussing future relationships between different communities in South Africa. It ensures that victims are not transformed easily into victimizers themselves.

Another legal approach is offered by the American psychologist Joan

Fumia, who focuses on the transformation of attitudes in conflictual situations. She bases her work on the relationships that develop between offenders and victims in the American legal system, based on a recently introduced procedure that offers victim-offender mediation. This method involves a face-to-face meeting between offender and victim. The most important part of the procedure is the readiness of the offender to accept responsibility for the crime. Thus, the deed itself is not the focus of the process, but rather its consequences. The search is for restorative justice, which is defined as what the offender can do to ease the loss and suffering of the victim. It is not a substitute for criminal proceedings, just as in the case of Palestine it cannot be an alternative to actual compensation or repatriation but a supplement to any real solution. Fumia claims that this model was implemented successfully in South Africa.

Israeli responsibility for the Nakba, if it were to be discussed, which at the present stage is unlikely, as part of the attempt to reach a permanent settlement for the conflict, would obviously not reach an international court, as did the cases of Rwanda and ex-Yugoslavia. Or at least, this is what one can conclude, given how the Nakba is perceived by governments in the United States and Europe. These political actors have so far accepted the Israeli peace-camp perspective on the conflict, as elaborated above. However, the civil societies in America and in Europe as well as governments in Africa and Asia have different views on this, and the situation may change (the move to prosecute Ariel Sharon in a Belgian court is one such example). As long as this balance of power remains as it is now, one doubts the possibility of establishing a truth commission as in South Africa. But the demands of the 1948 Palestinian victims will remain in a dominant position on the peace agenda, whether or not this procedure is followed.

This outcry will continue to face the offenders. The fear of the offender would have to be taken into account in order for the settlement of the conflict to move from the division of the visible to the restoration of the invisible.

The second approach is educational and requires a dialectical recognition of both communities as communities of suffering. For this, the very natural process of negating the Other should be overcome first. The destruction of the collective memory of the Other, through the construction of one's own, is a central element in the formation of national identities. Violence, direct as well as symbolic, plays a crucial part in the way that collective memories are produced, reproduced, disseminated, and consumed within concrete historical power relations, interests, and conceptual possibilities and limitations. In the case of Palestine and Israel, control of the collective memory is part of the internal and external violence and of the counterviolence that each of the rival collectives applies to secure its existence. That is, the way the two sides construct their collective identity is a dialectical process whose impelling force is the total negation of the

Other. Within this dialectic, each side sees itself as a sole victim while totally negating the victimization of the Other. The violence used in order to conquer the centers of power relations and dynamics aims at positioning more effectively one's own narrative, interests, values, symbols, goals, and criteria while securing that those of the Other are marginalized, excluded, or destroyed. Incommensurability has the upper hand, and dialogue has no chance of finding a starting point. Collective self-constitution, negation of the legitimacy of the Other's otherness, victimizing the Other, and refusing to acknowledge the Other's suffering become inseparably bound up with each other. The self-proclaimed victimhood, the refusal to acknowledge the evil inflicted on the Other, and the insistence on being sole victim are fused into the kind of practice that reflects the position of the Other. In the case of Israeli/Palestinian coexistence, the struggle over the control of the memory of victimization is a matter of life and death, and suffering and death, as actuality and as memory, are philosophical, political, and existential issues.

It will not be easy to overcome such a powerful dialectical process in the case of Israel and Palestine, not least because of the point I have made concerning the disparity in blame, injustice, and victimizing between the two sides. The way to go about it is by treating the history of the conflict as a chain of victimization. The violence that bred the national awakening of the Jews and their search for a homeland in Palestine did not justify past or present evils inflicted by the movement or later the State of Israel on the Palestinians. While Zionism may not be a historical case of pure colonialism, it can still be defined as a colonial movement, and therefore the Palestinian violence and counterviolence cannot be judged in the same way as Zionist violence against Palestine should be assessed. In this sense, no injustice was inflicted by the Palestinians on the Israelis, as no injustice was inflicted by the Algerians on the French colonialists, although there certainly was violence. This, however, should not disable us from judging ethically the violence inflicted by Palestinians. The suicide bombs planted in the center of a civilian population can be condemned, while a more lenient attitude can be taken toward guerrilla attacks on soldiers within the occupied territories. But there was a European injustice inflicted upon the Jews that can be recognized as a first link in the chain of victimization.

In the reformulation of collective memory currently under way in South Africa, Africans are not diminishing the catastrophes that propelled white settlers to come to South Africa. While reintroducing the crimes of apartheid into the collective memory, the dialogue there creates space for the traumas that led whites to leave Europe in search of another homeland. Similarly, one cannot equate injustice and Palestinian resistance to Jewish expulsion and ethnic cleansing.

The demands from the Palestinians lie elsewhere in this approach. They comprise the need to avoid dwarfing or eliminating the role of the Holocaust in Jewish national identity and collective memory, on the one hand, and the end to instrumentalizing the Nakba in a way that obstructs the chances for peaceful dialogue, on the other. The demand not to instrumentalize the memories of both catastrophes is, of course, directed to both sides. Such a demand cannot be accepted unless the political structure of the future solution is a-national or binational. Only in such a political formation can one hope for non-ethnocentric, polyphonic reconstructions of the past that can produce in their turn more reflective and humanistic attitudes toward the suffering of both sides. This can happen in a state for all its citizens—a state born out of distaste for the nationalism and ethnicity that guided political formations in the past. It is difficult to accept how many victims may be necessary before such a break with past identities becomes possible. The comparative historical lessons are not very encouraging in this respect. Therefore, the by-products of the one-state solutions can be seen as an ideal model that would probably be implemented in a more restricted way on the ground. This is the difference between one-state and binational models. The latter imposes many restrictions on our hope for a multicultural and polyphonic future but is less rigid than the two-state solution as a political framework that allows deviations from being enslaved to national narratives and interpretations of reality.

The starting point is overcoming nationalism and ethnocentrism. Without this, no Palestinian-Israeli dialogue on historiographical, moral, and philosophical levels is possible. Critical theory and postmodern elaboration of the historical constitution of the subject, knowledge, identity, and memory, together with empirical studies, should impel this deconstruction and reformulation of the hegemonic Palestinian and Israeli narratives. The enemy here is not so much the hegemonic interpretation as it is the position of exclusivity demanded by one side or the other and by the denial of the Other's narrative. The demand for exclusivity in the case of the Holocaust is understandably a very touchy issue. The recognition of the universality of the Holocaust's memory and its expropriation from the hand of Zionism does not and should not diminish its uniqueness in the history of mankind. This uniqueness, however, is manifested inter alia also in the Nakba and the Palestinian suffering. Such an attitude contains new political possibilities currently overshadowed by both sides' one-dimensionality.

But those who go down this road will encounter many obstacles. Adopting a critical humanist or universal approach, which does not simply dismiss humanism, they will find themselves set apart from the accepted intellectual, cultural, and emotional levels within the history of their societies and may be pushed into eternal exile. On such marginal spots, can these people still be considered "Palestinians" or "Israelis"? This is but one question to be answered within this future dialogue.

Indeed, how will Israeli Jews challenging the Zionization of the Holocaust memory fare, and how could Palestinians openly challenge the national instrumentalization of the Nakba in direct clash with mainstream Palestinian conceptions of the Nakba memory?

In the 1990s, hopeful signs for the beginning of such a dialogue appeared on both sides. The New Historians in Israel challenged the foundational myth of the Jewish state while, on the Palestinian side, self-criticism emerged about the tendency to minimize the Holocaust memory and its universal implications. Edward Said, Azmi Bishara, and a few others deconstructed the way that Arab and Palestinian literature dwarfed, ignored, and at times denied the Holocaust memory as a constitutive element in the Jewish collective memory.[21] Edward Said wrote:

> What Israel does to the Palestinians it does against a background, not only of the long-standing Western tutelage over Palestine and Arabs . . . but also against a background of an equally long-standing and equally unfaltering anti-Semitism that in this century produced the Holocaust of the European Jews. . . . We cannot fail to connect the horrific history of anti-Semitic massacres to the establishment of Israel; nor can we fail to understand the depth, the extent and the overpowering legacy of its suffering and despair that informed the postwar Zionist movement. But it is no less appropriate for Europeans and Americans today, who support Israel because of the wrong committed against the Jews to realize that support for Israel has included, and still includes, support for the exile and dispossession of the Palestinian people.[22]

The universalization of the Holocaust memory, the deconstruction of this memory's manipulation by Zionism and the State of Israel, and the end to Holocaust denial and underrating on the Palestinian side can lead to the mutual sympathy that Said talked about. However, it may need more than this to persuade Israelis to recognize their role as victimizers. The self-image of victim had been deeply rooted in the collective conduct of the political elite in Israel from the very early years of the state. It is seen as the source for moral international and world Jewish support for the state, even when this image of the righteous Israel on the one hand and the David and Goliath myth on the other became ridiculous after the 1967 war, the 1982 invasion of Lebanon, and the intifada. Yet the fear is there of losing the position of the victim, next to the fear of facing the unpleasant past and its consequences, not far away from the fear, nourished by the political system and substantiated by Arab hostility, of being physically eliminated as a community.

Conclusion

The nuclear arsenal, the gigantic military complex, and the security service octopuses have all proved themselves useless in the face of the two intifadas and the guerrilla war in South Lebanon. They are useless as means of facing an ever frustrated and radical million Palestinian citizens of Israel, or a local initiative by refugees unable to contain their dismay in the face of an opportunist Palestinian authority or a crumbling PLO. None of the weapons that the real or imaginary fear produced can face the victims and their wrath. More and more victims are added daily to the Palestinian community of suffering, in the occupied territories and in Israel itself. The end of victimization and the recognition of the role of Israel as victimizer are the only useful means of reconciliation.

Thus, a post-conflictual homeland cannot be constructed on the basis of a division of the shared imagined homeland in accordance with a most unfair balance: 78 percent a Jewish state and 22 percent a Palestinian protectorate. It is even less thinkable as a solution when the offer on the international agenda involves dividing even the 22 percent by a further partition. A fair solution cannot allocate to Israel exclusive say in security, foreign policy, and economic matters. The future solution cannot include a Jewish state in which Palestinians are second-rate citizens, and it cannot perpetuate the occupation, even if it is described with new terminology.

Above all, a future constructed homeland cannot survive as a physical and political entity when an estimated four million Palestinian refugees and their right of return are erased from its agenda. A future homeland, from which the symbolic and actual violence are reduced or even extracted, is one in which the past evil of transfer is rectified by the repatriation of those who were expelled. This principle should be discussed as a practical solution taking into account demography, economy, cultural inclinations, and, above all, fears.

Notes

1. The 1928 episode was covered by Eliakim Rubenstein, "The Treatment of the Arab Question in Palestine in the Immediate Period after the 1929 Events and the Establishment of the Political Bureau: Political Aspect" (Hebrew), in *Jewish-Arab Relations in Mandatory Palestine: A New Approach to the Historical Research*, Ilan Pappé, ed. (Givat Haviva: Institute of Peace Research, 1995), 65–102.

2. On the circumstances that led to the resolution and its content, see Ilan Pappé, *The Making of the Arab-Israeli Conflict, 1947–1951* (London: I.B. Tauris, 1992), 16–46.

3. Simcha Flapan, *The Birth of Israel: Myth and Realities* (London: Croom Helm, 1979), 13–54.

4. Ilan Pappé, "Were They Expelled?: The History, Historiography and Relevance of the Refugee Problem," in *The Palestinian Exodus, 1948–1988*, Ghada Karmi and Eugene Cotran, eds. (London: Ithaca, 1999), 37–62.

5. I have dealt extensively with this issue in Ilan Pappé, "Angst, Oferschaft, Selbst- und Frembilder," in *Angst in eigenen Landen*, Rafik Schami, ed. (Zurich: Nagel and Kimche, 2001), 65–77.

6. Ilan Amitzur, *Bernadotte in Palestine 1948: A Study in Contemporary Humanitarian Knight-Errantry* (London: Macmillan, 1989).

7. See Pappé, *Making of the Arab-Israeli Conflict*, 203–43.

8. Avi Shlaim, *The Iron Wall: Israel and the Arab World* (New York: Norton, 2000), 109–10.

9. For a critique of Oslo, see Ilan Pappé, "Breaking the Mirror: Oslo and After," in *Looking Back at the June 1967 War,* Haim Gordon, ed. (Westport, Conn.: Praeger, 1999), 95–112.

10. See Ella Shohat, "Sprache in Speil: Erinnerugsframente einner Arabisched Juden," in Schami, *Angst,* 84–95.

11. See Ilan Pappé, "Fear, Victimhood, Self and Other," in *The MIT Electronic Journal of Middle East Studies* 1 (May 2001).

12. Ilan Pappé, "Israeli Television Fiftieth Anniversary Series: *Tekuma*: A Post-Zionist Review?" *Journal of Palestine Studies* 27:4 (Summer 1998): 99–105.

13. *Haaretz,* November 1, 2000.

14. I have elaborated on the Peace Now syndrome in "Post-Zionist Critique, Part I: The Academic Debate," *Journal of Palestine Studies* 26:2 (winter 1997): 29–41.

15. The scope of the tragedy is well described in a collection of articles: Ghada Karmi and Eugene Cotran, eds., *The Palestinian Exodus, 1948–1988* (London: Ithaca, 1999).

16. Robert Fisk, *The Independent,* September 16, 2000.

17. Ilan Gur-Ze'ev and Ilan Pappé, "Beyond the Destruction of the Other's Collective Memory: Blueprints for an Israeli-Palestinian Dialogue," *Theory Culture and Society* 20:1 (February 2003): 93–108.

18. Ilan Pappé, "I Profughi Palestinesi tra Storia e Storiografia," in *In Fuga: Guerre, Carestie e Migrazioni forzate nel Mondo Contemporaneo,* Marco Bultino, ed. (Naples: L'Ancora, 2001), 81–106.

19. Salman Abu-Sitta, "The Feasibility of the Right of Return," in Karmi and Cotran, *Palestinian Exodus,* 171–96.

20. Howard Zehr, *Changing Lenses: A New Focus for Crime and Justice* (Scottdale, Pa.: Herald, 1990).

21. All quoted in Gur-Ze'ev and Pappé, *Beyond the destruction,* 105–8.

22. Edward Said, *The Politics of Dispossession* (London: Chatto and Windus, 1994), 167.

Chapter 15
Reflections on the Right of Return: Divisible or Indivisible?

Gershon Shafir

Shelly Fried concludes his survey of all the Arab-Israeli peace conferences this way: "[T]he common denominator in all conferences from Lausanne to Taba was that the refugee problem was the main obstacle to reaching an agreement."[1] By way of explanation, Ilan Pappé argues vigorously in his chapter in this volume that the reason for the intractable character of the refugee issue is that it falls in the realm of the "invisible" issues (along with Jerusalem), since it requires the assumption of historical responsibility, and as such is associated with fairness, guilt, restitution, and, ultimately, justice.[2] The resolution to the plight of Palestinian refugees, consequently, is "indivisible," since it can only be comprehensive. The reason for the failure to tackle the tragedy of the Palestinian refugees is that the American and Israeli (including Peace Now) approaches have been businesslike: by seeking to trade territories for peace, they concentrated on the "visible" aspects of the conflict. Since the visible layer consists of the material substance of the conflict, it is treated as "divisible" and rationally negotiable while the demands in the realm of the invisible, namely, the right of return, are ignored if not outright dismissed.[3] Pappé suggests, and let me introduce a more frequently used terminology, that the resolution of the tragedy of the Palestinian refugees, now in the sixth decade of their displacement, is a moral concern that cannot be tackled with political tools; in this instance, morality and politics part ways. Pappé insists that any attempt to reduce the conflict to its divisible aspects, by ignoring core aspects of the homeland and the refugees' ties to it, is but a reflection of the Israeli-Palestinian power imbalance and is likely to perpetuate injustice.[4]

Pappé's view that national as well as colonial conflicts encompass multiple aspects and are waged on distinct levels is hardly controversial, but the ultimate preference he seems to give to the idealist or primordialist account of the nation, an approach usually associated with the views of

Ernst Renan and Anthony Smith, is puzzling. Moral dilemmas have practical aspects (and invariably political implications) and, therefore, are neither abstract nor indivisible. Both the visible and invisible aspects of the Israeli-Palestinian, as other, conflicts, are divisible, and in the past decade or so, considerable creativity has gone into constructing solutions that entailed acceptable divisions in other seemingly intractable national, ethnic, and late decolonization conflicts.

Most likely, the attempt to present an image of indivisibility, namely, to present an issue as primordial and incapable of negotiated or rational resolution, is a construction advanced and established with particular political objectives in mind. A successful construction creates a hegemonic view, one that purports to rule out alternative possibilities and, as we shall see, does so, in this case, by exclusive reliance on legality or, rather, legalism.

To what extent compromise does or does not serve morality, fairness, justice, and practical and political goals, and indeed, which issues should be constructed as divisible and which as indivisible, should not be presumed at the outset but be part of the discussion itself. I intend to explain, in contrast to Pappé, why the territories occupied in 1967 are best treated as indivisible whereas the refugees' rights should be treated as a divisible issue. In general, I will demonstrate that addressing side by side the issue of land and absent and present people will allow us to explore the refugee question more thoroughly.

Instead of accepting the intractable character of the refugee issues, I would like, as a first step, to examine the reasons for the circumstances and perceptions that made them appear so. In this quest, I am inspired in part by the poet Mourid Barghouti, who questioned the seemingly immutable and indivisible aspect of the refugee question, its symbolic dimension. In 1995, upon visiting his childhood village, Deir Ghassanah, near Ramallah, from which he had been absent for thirty years, Barghouti wrote in his memoir:

> I have always believed that it is in the interest of an occupation, any occupation, that the homeland should be transformed in the memory of the people into a bouquet of "symbols." Merely symbols. They will not allow us to develop our village so that it shares features with the city, or to move with our city into a contemporary space. Let us be frank: when we lived in the village did we not long for the city? Did we not long to leave small, simple, Deir Ghassanah for Ramallah, Jerusalem, and Nablus? Did we not wish that those cities would become like Cairo, Damascus, Baghdad, and Beirut? The longing is always for the new age.[5]

Barghouti not only draws attention to the political character of the backward-looking or nostalgic perspective but also illustrates the price exacted by adherence to this symbolic view. Barghouti the poet would give up the symbols that obstruct the entry into the new age that Palestinians would have chosen on their own, in the absence of occupation. Of course, the

Israeli occupation is very real; it is the defining experience for the majority of Palestinians, but even so, when it is allowed to single-handedly define Palestinian options, it narrows and rigidifies them.

In fact, not only the Palestinian but also the Israeli perspective on the refugee question is rigid and narrow. Since these views serve as each other's mirror image, each constraining and delimiting the other's options, they lead to "a dialogue of the deaf."[6] Indeed, in few other areas besides this could one speak of Israel and Palestinian perspectives in the singular. It seems to me that the root of this intractability in regard to the refugee question is found in the two peoples' and national movements' diametrically opposed formative experiences. Consequently, their moral epistemologies or, in one particular rendering, collective memories, are antithetical. The world looks different and is experienced differently by Israeli Jews and Palestinians.

As a second step, I intend to demonstrate that comparing the historical record of the Palestinian experiences of diaspora and settlement and ties with the land with the Jewish experience demonstrates that such bonds undergo significant changes and thus require that we examine more flexibly the relationship between the visible and invisible aspects of the conflict. Such openness will lead us to reformulate its divisible and indivisible aspects not as given but rather as choices, an approach I will adopt throughout this chapter.

Rapture and In/justice

In the Palestinian perspective, the era before the confrontation with Zionism is one of harmony; an original stage. Zionist colonialism destroyed the organic connection of Palestinians with their towns, villages, and fields— with their land. Return, consequently, would mean not rehabilitation and relocation but restitution and repatriation. This perspective finds its expression in the iconic formula of "return to one's home," in the layout of some of the refugee camps—made to correspond to villages of origin, and in the continued commemoration of ties with specific villages. Even the massive tome *All That Remains*, a publication of the Institute for Palestine Studies edited by Walid Khalidi, in which researchers from Bir Zeit University systematically catalogued the 418 Palestinian villages destroyed during and in the aftermath of the 1948 war, seems to have made little dent in this formula. In the Palestinian worldview, the concept of justice is primary, injustice is departure from it, and redress is expected to tip the scales back.

The Jewish experience in Eastern Europe, which propelled the Zionist movement, is the opposite: it holds that the world is fundamentally unjust. Their middleman minority status meant that Jews were routinely excluded and cyclically oppressed by moral orders based on double standards. This experience had been crystallized in a lachrymose view of history, in which Jews are the quintessential Other and, therefore, the perennial victim. The disenchantment with the Enlightenment and citizenship in many of the modern nation-states further reinforced this view. The quest from this Jewish perspective was to ease loss and reduce hardship, to make justice appear and prevail.

Among moral epistemologists, Kant holds the first perspective by asserting the supremacy of the moral law, which, he argues, is anchored in transcendental principle. John Rawls adheres to the same moral position but without its metaphysical deduction. In the process of formulating a notion of justice as emerging from an original position and, therefore, as prior to any robust notion of social good, he holds that "justice is the first virtue of social institutions."[7] Its primacy is indicated in treating justice as the "value of values" by which other standards are assessed.[8] As Michael Sandel points out, justice as fairness in Rawls's approach overcomes, or does not depend on, subjective conceptions of the good, but on its objective circumstances. Hume's account of such circumstances, which Rawls explicitly embraces, states that justice has to be addressed within circumstances of scarcity. Consequently, justice competes with other virtues and is no longer absolute.[9] Rawls himself seems to retreat to this view by holding that "justice is not to be confused with the all-inclusive vision of a good society," but is "essentially the elimination of arbitrary distinctions and the establishment . . . of a proper balance between competing claims."[10]

A contemporary articulation of the latter perspective is offered by Elizabeth Wolgast. She reminds us of the simple truth that once a rape or murder has been committed, it cannot be expunged, and harmony remains unattainable. Efforts to correct wrongs consequently lead to paradoxes (for example, punishing a murderer by death) and sometimes to further injustice. In this view, moral outrage is born out of a sense of injustice as the prior human condition and, therefore, propels us to search for remedies. To find them, we need to take many factors into consideration and thus rarely find a single answer. "Justice appears then as an indefinite corrective to injustice rather than something definable in its own right."[11] This makes the search for justice more, not less, moral and certainly more humane and necessarily divisible.

These Palestinian and Jewish experiences led to the prevalence of two different and foundational collective memories of in/justice: a restorative and a retributive one, respectively. These moral perspectives are based on contrasting lived experiences and seem irreconcilable, as long as the experiences themselves do not change. Conversely, once circumstances do change, the corresponding moral epistemology would not stay the same. The destruction of the Judaean state and Jewish dispersal gave rise to a messianic tradition whose purpose in antiquity, at first in the secular domain and gradually in the spiritual realm, was the restoration of the Kingdom of Judaea and the House of Israel. In its most dramatic and mediated version, this vision underlay the kabbalistic tradition itself. The vision of the original state in antiquity was replaced with a view that emphasizes the unjustness of the world and calls for a retributive justice. In short, to a significant degree, the difference between these moral perspectives is a function of the time frame and time scale. The nonessentialist character of these views, their rootedness in changing historical circumstances, is ironically illustrated by the similarity of the Palestinian perspective to the Judeo-Christian notion of original sin and of the resemblance of the Israeli and Jewish views to Greek tragedy, exemplified by Antigone's reaction, in which moral outrage is born out of a sense of injustice.

It might seem naive to present these perspectives without objections and alternatives but, as so many of the chapters in this volume attest, they have been shaped into hegemonic umbrellas, expressed in exclusivist legal language, under which the majorities of the respective groups repose (as I shall show in detail later). But while irreconcilable, they are not exclusive, and therefore instead of being viewed as maps of the world, they can and may be used as tools that may be applied in different domains, or to issues, allowing us to address certain grievances as indivisible (restorative) and others as divisible (retributive). Divisibility sometimes means not that we cut something into smaller but identical units, but rather that we divide the issue into separate spheres.

Following this approach, I wish to argue later that the allegedly invisible aspects of the conflict, the ones related to homeland—such as the Palestinian refugee tragedy—are far from being indivisible. There seem to be many divisible issues, ranging from the way we conceptualize the refugee problem to the particular conditions in which Palestinian refugees find themselves. Indeed, were these issues indivisible, this would remain a zero-sum game, and even the small and halting signs of progress we witnessed would not have been possible. Even Pappé recoils from the full logic of indivisibility at the end of his chapter and suggests that we put our trust in retributive justice.[12] In contrast, I argue later that a resolution of the Israeli-Palestinian conflict has to treat the territorial component of the conflict as indivisible.

Land: Less or More?

The experience of their relationship with land, the typical settler-colonial facet of this conflict, shaped central Palestinian and Jewish ideas and national presuppositions. Contradictory relationships to land led to contrary formative experiences: as colonizers, Jewish pioneers and settlers sought to augment the portion of Palestine they could possess; Palestinians, as colonized, saw more and more of their land pass into Zionist possession. The Labor Settlement Movement's (LSM) perspective was one of progressive gain, articulated in the slogan "one more dunam and one more goat"; the Palestinian was one of regression. Both sides evolved domino theories of their reciprocal relationship, but these theories were antithetical. Zionists developed a "cumulative" or "additive" perspective to land, Palestinian a "subtractive" one. For Jews, control over a land parcel provided a foothold, the basis for obtaining more; for Palestinians, land loss was a prelude to further loss, as the adversary became more entrenched and powerful. One side's gain was the other's loss: here the view of the conflict as a zero-sum-game was created, and the possibility of shared benefit undermined.

A typical recent, though somewhat caricatured, Palestinian perspective comes from Sami Al-Banna.[13] He compares the evolution of the various partition plans from the subtractive perspective. The United Nations partition plan said to the Palestinians: you are going to have 47 percent of the 100 percent that was originally yours. The 1993 Oslo agreement said to the Palestinians: you are going to have 22 percent of the 100 percent that was originally yours. Ehud Barak's "generous offer" to the Palestinians in 2000 said: we are going to give you 80 percent of 22 percent of 100 percent of the land that was originally yours. Finally, Sharon's peace plan to the Palestinians in 2000 said: we are going to give you 42 percent of 80 percent of 22 percent of 100 percent of the land that was originally yours, and this 42 percent will remain under continuous curfew.

A particularly painful aspect of this land-for-peace formulation from the Palestinian perspective is that by using the current possession of the land as the starting point instead of the respective groups' original relationship to land, the categories of who gives and who receives are reversed, and it is Israel that appears generous. When Israel "gives" Palestinians something they possessed in the first place, taking appears as giving, while in fact the giving is done by the Palestinians.

Though the cumulative Zionist approach seems avaricious, it was neither the most extreme strategy nor always the dominant one. The Revisionists and the LSM adopted different courses of action vis-à-vis the issue of land.[14] Jabotinsky's Revisionists evolved their views in response to the spiraling anti-Semitism of the interwar years that made the conditions of the Jewish masses desperate in Central and Eastern Europe. Laboring under this urgent need to rescue Eastern European Jewry, the Revisionists sought a historical shortcut, what Harkabi called a "historical big bang," to set things right all at once.[15] For example, they conceived of a hopelessly impractical plan to evacuate a million Jews to Palestine within twenty-five years. Such shortcuts called for the employment of diplomatic and military methods. Jabotinsky argued even earlier that not settlement and cultivation, but only military power could be the guarantor of national security and that therefore Zionist aims could only be accomplished from behind the iron wall of an independent Jewish military force.

The LSM leaders emphasized Jewish historical rights in Palestine but conceded that Jewish immigrants had "to earn" these rights in the present by gaining control of and developing the land. This strategy was the opposite of the militaristic one; in Baruch Kimmerling's words, it started with purchase and ownership, followed by presence through settlement, which laid the basis for sovereignty and ultimately leveraged into boundaries.[16] As the extent of Jewish settlement grew, so did the land allotted to the Jewish state from the 1937 Peel Plan to the partition of 1947, to the planned post-1993 partition plans, each time reinforcing the subtractive Palestinian perspective. The principal moral justification of the LSM was tailored to Jewish demographic potentials: after Jews were to become the majority—a process that the LSM, like most Zionists, viewed as inevitable and, during which, they were determined to suspend the operation of democracy—their wish would be the democratic choice, and the contradictions (democratic, socialist, and moral) created in the early phase of Jewish colonization would fade.

Since the use of military power would cancel the waiting period to attain a majority, the Revisionists had no use for the LSM's approach of "demographic suspension." Nor did they feel the need to tailor Jewish territorial aspirations in Palestine to the size of its Jewish population. The Revisionist moral maxim stated that Palestine did not need "to be earned" by Jews; it was theirs to take. In contrast to the alternatives of a binational state and the partition of the land, the Revisionists remained the steadfast adherents of greater Eretz Israel, to spread on both banks of the Jordan River.[17]

The core of the LSM's course of action was the appreciation of the relevance of demographic facts and processes, in the context of the general relations of forces, for the realization of its political aims. The LSM, in short, learned to deal with the disappointments caused by Jewish demographic potential in Palestine—limited initially by the preference of most Eastern European Jews to migrate to other destinations, and later by the tragic losses of the Holocaust—by imposing realistic self-limitations. In Harkabi's terminology, it agreed to give up the grand design of Jewish settlement in greater Eretz Israel and concentrated on the everyday policy of seeking a Jewish majority in a more limited expanse. In 1937, and again in 1947, a segment of the mainstream of the LSM was willing to accept the partition of Palestine between a Jewish and a Transjordanian or Palestinian state. The LSM's position was not adopted in recognition of Palestinian national aspirations. On the contrary, partition was acceded to precisely because such a strategy was capable of removing the Palestinian "demographic threat."

From the Palestinian perspective, the partition resolution was not only unjustified but also unfair: it gave the Jewish side 15 million dunams of land, although they only owned 1,678,000. In their perspective, "the parti-

tion plan was effectively a declaration of war against the Arabs of Palestine."[18]

The folly of the limitless "additive" process was revealed when Israel
transferred the colonization strategy perfected in Palestine to land that was
on the Egyptian side of the border by international law, thus risking and
harvesting Israel's most bitter and humiliating war in 1973. In the years
leading up to the war, Israeli preference for settlement over potential diplomatic solutions became ever clearer. The 1973 war raised serious questions as to the ability of colonization to achieve its declared aim of
achieving security, most dramatically illustrated by the fate of settlements
on the Golan Heights in the first hours of the 1973 war. But other groups,
later coalesced as Gush Emunim, were already waiting in the wings to justify
settlement in new terms, in order to continue and expand the venture
begun in the Labor era. The 1979 Camp David accord required full Israeli
withdrawal. Notwithstanding the fact that Israel ignored the British drawn
boundary between Egypt and Palestine until 1977, its withdrawal was
rationalized by reference to the need to respect the international boundary. This logic, however, allowed continued and ever increasing colonization in the West Bank, which was not demarcated in the same fashion. Each
stage of expansion, from military to suburban to messianic, from 1967
through 1977 to the post-1993 years, has only generated additional resistance. The Hebrew proverb *kol hamosif gorea*—probably best translated idi-
omatically as "the more we get, the worse off we are"—points up the
danger of such overreaching.

The resolution of the Israeli-Palestinian conflict through full Israeli withdrawal to the 1967 borders in the West Bank and Gaza has been on the
table for at least a decade. Israeli withdrawal to the 1967 borders, with the
possibility of strictly equivalent territorial exchanges, is only one of the preconditions for peace and recognition with the Arab world under the 2001
Saudi plan, which was endorsed by the Arab League in March 2002. But it
carries pregnant consequences for the adversarial epistemological experiences described above. Territorial withdrawal in which Israel shoulders the
full burden of territorial concessions would put an end to Israel's cumulative or additive territorial epistemology as well as to the Palestinian subtractive one. If the clock, at least this once, was turned back, the connection
between settlement and borders would be severed, signaling the conclusion of the colonial experience itself and undermining this epistemology
once and for all. By showing that Israel can no longer gain territorially,
revanchist movements would be discouraged in Israel. Such an outcome
would also bring the Palestinian experience in line with international practice, which, after 1945, did not sanction territorial expansion.[19] Finally,
complete territorial withdrawal would mean that the visible aspect—land
and the 1948 borders—would be made indivisible.

Rights of Refugees: Conceptual and Legal Issues

In other nationalist conflicts of majorities and minorities, and with greater intensity in conflicts between settlers and native peoples, the goal of sovereignty was bound up with the maintenance or formation of a numeric majority in the given territory. A typical expression of its pivotal place is Ben-Gurion's conclusion: "[T]he true conflict between us and the Arabs [is that] we both want to be the majority."[20] This "demographic interest" added another dimension to the asymmetrical struggle and perspective on the struggle's outcome: one in which the Zionist perspective was, as with regard to land, cumulative or additive, and the Palestinian subtractive. Every additional Jewish settler-immigrant to Palestine brought closer the day in which Jews would constitute the majority and could parlay it into sovereignty, and endangered the Palestinian hope to remain masters in their homes and attain political independence.

Diametrically opposed demographic perspectives held and still hold sway in the respective populations. The transformation of around 80 percent of the Palestinian population into refugees during the 1948 war did not end but only transformed this aspect of the conflict. The demographic dimension still plays a central role in shaping attitudes and options, and the conflict is played out as much in violent struggles as it is in ports of entry and exit and in maternity wards.

These opposing views have been hardened by being transformed into legal arguments, into rights. The arguments used by Zionists for the Jewish right of return prior to the Balfour Declaration were drawn from the Jewish moral epistemology, which required the ending of Jewish suffering, and the corresponding Christian mythology. Zionists were uncomfortable with their inability to explain under which general rule they were operating by claiming for Jews the right to return to Palestine while not according to, say, Muslims the right to return to Spain. Their understanding of the weakness of this special pleading was apparent from Herzl's desire to secure a charter from the Ottoman government and from the fact that as soon as the Balfour Declaration gave Jews an international legal commitment, the Zionist leadership, when speaking to non-Jews, almost entirely abandoned the ideological or historical arguments in favor of legal commitments that had been made and had to be abided by.[21] Not surprisingly, the right to return was codified directly in the foundational legal framework of Israel, where the right to return was enshrined in the Law of Return.

The same holds true for the Palestinian view. In the absence of other rights, the right of return has been the only right that the stateless and citizenship-less Palestinian refugees were able to demand be honored. Although for close to two decades, they deemed UN General Assembly Resolution 194 unsatisfactory because it did not explicitly spell out a Palestinian right to return, Palestinians eventually came to attribute such an interpretation to it.

A major reason for the apparently indivisible character of the refugee issue is not that it alone is bound up with fairness, responsibility, and justice, but rather that, like the topic of land, the two sides' versions are mirror images of each other. This is sometimes hard to tell since both are presented overly legalistically, but the legal framework that each side uses is rooted in a different legal framework. While seemingly mirroring each other, the two legal arguments operate within different frameworks: one international, the other national. Palestinians treat the question of refugees as an issue of human rights, Israelis as one of citizenship. We need to distinguish between them.[22]

Citizenship is a broad legal and social framework for membership in a political community. It has broadened over time. For example, T.H. Marshall distinguishes between three sets, or what in legal idiom we might term three generations, of citizenship rights: civil, political, and social. During the Enlightenment, the tradition of human rights emerged out of natural law philosophy. Human rights are universal, unalienable, and equal because they are anchored in a person by virtue of his or her humanity and not by virtue of his or her status in the body politic.[23] In spite of the long and expanding list of human rights, starting with the Universal Declaration and the International Covenant on Economic, Social and Cultural Rights, a recent survey of the internalization of the international human-rights norms narrows its focus to the "central core of right: the right to life (. . . define[d] as the right to be free from extrajudicial execution and disappearance) and the freedom from arbitrary arrest and detention" because these alone "have been most accepted as universal rights and not simply associated with a particular political ideology or system."[24] A recent manual on human rights, published under the auspices of UNESCO (UN Educational, Scientific, and Cultural Organization), surveys the cutting-edge areas of the human-rights debate and legislation. Some of the topics examined are the right to peace, democracy as a condition for other rights, the right to development, environmental protection, the right to health, workers' rights and women workers' rights, and rights of indigenous peoples.[25] In short, the purview of human rights is amorphous, but not even the broadest version provides for a right of return that overrides all other considerations. In fact, Amnesty International and many scholars studying refugees prefer to use the less sweeping and strict concept of "right to return."[26]

More significant, in spite of their universal character, their enforcement almost invariably is entrusted to national, not international, bodies. Refugees are people who cannot avail themselves of the protection of the country of which they are citizens, which they left out of fear and, hence, have become temporary beneficiaries of a special regime of international human rights. The significant problem is that questions relating to nationality and the entry into a state's territory touch on the sensitive area of sovereignty, and, while questions of refugees and of human rights in general are internationally conceived, enforcement is left to states even though refugees themselves "are subversive of the established primacy of the nation-state."[27] The central question in this context is the problem of denationalization either for the purpose or as the consequence of expulsion. Denationalization falls between the two frameworks. According to Amnesty International, "[W]hile international human rights standards with regard to nationality are less concrete than in some other areas of human rights," one of the human rights presumed in the past few decades, notwithstanding the "few signatories to the relevant international treaties," is the "right not to be arbitrarily deprived of one's nationality."[28] Denationalization, not surprisingly, is a particularly sensitive issue from the perspective of the nation-state. Having the fox guard the chicken coop has been counterproductive and no more so than in the Palestinian case.

By insisting on an unconditional right of return, Palestinians are presenting a particularly strong and sweeping human-rights case against the State of Israel; but with regard to admission of people to citizenship status, state immunity to the international application of liberal norms is especially strong. During the Camp David meeting in 2000, President Bill Clinton was cognizant of Israel's and other countries' right to absorb refugees according to their own policies and laws.[29] Even where the question facing states is one of asylum for individual refugees, states' foremost responsibility is to their citizens.[30]

One consequent difficulty is that, from the Palestinian perspective, the right of return is presented as an individual human right, a choice to be made by individuals whose rights have been violated.[31] But this is precisely a point of contention and possible transformation. For Israel it is a collective issue, one that infringes on citizenship and criteria for citizenship, which are defined by ethno-nationalism and religion. In fact, the Palestinian perspective is more complex than Friedman suggests: first, the right of return for all Palestinian refugees, namely, the issue of Palestinian national aspiration, has to be accepted by Israel before individual Palestinians can decide whether to exercise it.

There are many examples of mixing the different realms and applications of human rights and citizenship rights. Julie Peteet found that even Palestinians who have or would take advantage of opportunities to attain Lebanese citizenship demand the right to participate in the decision concerning their fate and the fate of refugees in general.[32] Similarly, Laleh Khalili demonstrates that refugees' commemorative practices are acted out with a clear political purpose in mind, to assert their demand for citizenship "as political participation in the polity to help determine their eventual fate as equal members of another polity," in a yet unborn state.[33] These observations demonstrate the sweeping, and highly unusual, use of the citizenship discourse. The desire to use the leverage of citizenship in a Palestinian state in order to decide whether to become Israeli citizens through the implementation of the right of return is a legal anomaly. Similarly, having acquired the citizenship of another country, whether the United States, France, the United Kingdom, or Jordan, signals that the person is no longer a refugee. To prevent such denationalization was indeed the primary reason for setting up and maintaining the refugee camps over the years.

The Palestinian and Israeli sides' perspectives have also been reversed with regard to the issues of return in the past century. The Zionist movement invoked, in various phrasings, the reigning post–World War I international principle of national self-determination to justify its atypical demand that collective immigration be recognized as return, but it now insists on the sovereignty of the Israeli state in deciding whom to make its citizens. The Palestinian leadership during Mandatory times was opposed to such a sweeping application of self-determination in the name of territorially based nationalism, but now relies on the growing post–World War II international regime of human rights to demand a sweeping definition of return. Whereas Zionism replaced its international with national prerogatives, the Palestinian perspective was transformed from a national to an international one. Each, however, stretches the boundaries of the international principles that seem to endow it with its respective right of return in the first place.

There was one school of thought that attempted to find a way around this dualism, this reliance on different legal traditions to justify intransigence. The binationalists formed Brit Shalom, a coterie of intellectuals led by Yehuda Magnes, Martin Buber, Hugo Bergman, Gershom Scholem, and Arthur Ruppin, in 1925. They conceded the importance of Palestine's large Arab population, numbering in the hundreds of thousands, and they admitted that attempts to overturn that demographically unfavorable reality would require imperialist support and the use of antidemocratic measures. Brit Shalom preferred to endorse the equality of Jewish and Palestinian national rights in Palestine to be exercised within a binational state. By arguing that cooperation with the Arab inhabitants of Palestine was more important than the creation of a Jewish majority, Brit Shalom members broke ranks with mainstream Zionism.

Brit Shalom endorsed equality between Palestinians and Jews but gave this idea a singular twist. By claiming that being a majority—whether Arab or Jewish—was no precondition for possessing national rights, Brit Shalom sought to overturn the modern doctrine of political sovereignty. Not surprisingly, Brit Shalom became an intellectual force to reckon with but remained an unpopular and negligible minority among Israelis, and it did not become attractive to Palestinians. Jews were opposed to Brit Shalom's views because of its declared willingness to forgo the demographic goals of the Jewish settler-immigrants and, therefore, their demand for sovereignty.

Palestinians were equally antagonistic, since Brit Shalom demanded the endorsement of equality of political rights between the two groups, in effect favoring the Jews, who made up only a small fraction of Palestine's population in the 1920s. They remained opposed for similar reasons to demographic parity, the revised goal of the League for Jewish-Arab Rapprochement, formed, in 1942, mostly by ex–Brit Shalom members and by Hashomer Hatzair. The political failure of this approach before 1948 was most succinctly expressed in Ruppin's words: "[W]hat we can receive [from the Arabs] we do not need, and what we need we cannot get."[34]

It would seem that this binationalist approach and solution, which received such limited support in the 1920s and 1940s, would do away with the distinction between human and citizenship rights by getting around the issue of denationalization and introducing into the post-national framework international norms of equal treatment, thereby opening the door to the return of Palestinian refugees. In fact, as the Jewish bi-nationalists learned, the principle of majority could not be suspended, because the majority would oppose it. Palestinians, who were the majority, remained opposed to granting rights regardless of the numeric ratio of the two populations. A new binational dispensation would replicate that dynamic: the Jewish majority would be equally opposed to changing the demographic ratio through a Palestinian right of return. Palestinian return is much more likely to a Palestinian state than to a binational one. The confrontation of the two rights of return is not likely to yield resolution. Therefore, it is elsewhere, in the context of the frameworks of transitional justice developed in the past decade, that we need to look for insight and inspiration.

Transitional Justice

The growing emphasis on human rights resulted from global changes ushered in by the fall of the USSR. This epoch-making event signaled the end of the "revolutionary era," namely, the expectation of radical and often violently effected changes. Ironically, the expectation of radical change had served as a barrier for more slow-paced reforms. As revolution gave way to reform, pent-up social and political pressures erupted in many places, and the attempts to resolve them frequently called for a new regime of human rights.

In many stalemated situations, new parties and approaches that were willing to be satisfied with partially new orders gained the upper hand. Compromises, which did not include undoing the past or the punishment of perpetrators, were effected as the price for transformation from authoritarian to democratic orders. Probably the best-known examples were the truth commissions. Since 1974, at least twenty-seven such officially sanctioned commissions have been established for a temporary duration in order to investigate past patterns of abuses (but not specific events).[35] Not only due to political stalemates but, in Priscilla Hayner's view, also "partly due to the limited reach of the courts, and partly out of a recognition that even successful prosecutions do not resolve the conflict and pain associated with past abuses, that transitional authorities have increasingly turned to official truth-seeking as a central component in their strategies to respond to past atrocities."[36] At the same time, Hayner's benchmark study of truth commissions holds that they are not based on a trade-off between truth and justice but on the minimum that can be attained. However, in some cases, after time passes, the immunity granted perpetrators is eroded or disregarded and new legal proceedings take place to further the cause of justice.[37] Though we probably have to take this conclusion with a grain of salt, since truth commissions in general divide truth from justice, and also keep in mind that a typical truth commission does not fit closely the circumstances of the birth of the Palestinian refugee question, the idea of a compromise or divisibility is indicative of possibilities for addressing this invisible aspect of the conflict.

A significant fruit of truth commissions' hearings is the creation of a single authoritative narrative that potentially can replace the conflicting and self-serving narratives, which played an important role in sustaining the conflict. Coexistence, as Ernst Renan argued in his seminal essay on the modern nation, requires not just common memories, much celebrated and studied in contemporary social sciences and humanities, but equally an ability to forget violence committed by one section of the population against another.[38] The same would seem to apply to neighboring populations. Forgetting, however, requires a new vantage point—for example, shared rights and a clean slate. For the Israeli Palestinian population, this would mean first-class citizenship and for refugees in camps, the return of a sizable number to Israel proper. Without a change of consciousness and the creation of a new framework for coexistence (for example, nonracialism in South Africa and nonsectarianism in Northern Ireland), the invisible aspects of the conflict will continue to overwhelm the visible ones.

Are Israelis ready for a truth commission on the 1948 war? In the past fifteen years or so, whole herds of "holy Zionist cows" have been slaughtered, but the one still grazing is the myth of the birth of the Palestinian refugee population. There seems to have been some progress in this area as well, as Benny Morris's well-known book[39] and some parts of the *Tekuma* TV program attest. An alternative form of such a commission—a historical commission, established by civil society actors, lawyers, historians, social scientists, and educators—could carry out part of the role played by truth commissions: the writing of a historical narrative that would be sufficiently elaborate and detailed so that both sides could view it as their own.[40] Barkan's analysis sees the fusion of polarized antagonistic histories as a key to the successful attempt to remedy past injustices. As with other commissions, the historical commission would not focus on a single event but on the pattern of conflict and abuse. In this case, its purview, for example, could encompass the Arab revolt of 1936, the 1948 war, the period of Israeli occupation after 1967, and the Palestinian intifadas.[41] It would not and could not seek to write an "end of history" type of narrative, but would look beyond the nationalistic versions of history and employ the considerable body of work created by Revisionist historians to detach history from the conflict as far as possible. It would not negotiate between versions but seek to integrate them. Its findings would be used by a group of experts to rewrite Israeli and Palestinian textbooks to reflect the findings.

A historical commission would not preempt the possibility of a truth commission to be established by future Israeli and Palestinian governments after the signing of a peace agreement. In this fashion, some of the most effective aspects of a truth commission could be employed. The appearance of Palestinian witnesses would be a truly cathartic experience for them and an educational one for the Israeli Jewish population and the rest of the world. The hearings would be broadcast on Israeli and Palestinian TV. The findings of the commission would, in the end, be expected to lead to an Israeli apology for its part in the creation of the refugees' plight, following a divisible approach to past injustice: the issuance of public apologies by the victimizers or their heirs.

Jews, in particular, have received such apologies from leaders of states— for example, Jacques Chirac and the Catholic Church. "[R]eligions around the world are [also] acknowledging and atoning for past sins. . . . Roman Catholics have apologized for their silence during the Holocaust, United Methodists for their massacre of American Indians during the Civil War, Southern Baptists for their support of slavery, and Lutherans for Martin Luther's anti-Jewish remarks."[42] Clinton apologized to Japanese Americans for their internment during World War II, and Ehud Barak apologized to the Mizrahi population in Israel for their mistreatment at the hands of the Labor movement.

As John Torpey points out in his study of reparations sought for acts of injustice perpetrated during World War II, for state terror prior to democratic transitions, and for legacies of colonialism: "The perfidy of the Nazi assault on European Jewry has emerged as a kind of gold standard against which to judge other cases of injustice and to which advocates seek to assimilate those instances of human cruelty and oppression for which they seek reparations."[43] Torpey concludes from his survey that "contrary to those who regard the Holocaust as a sponge of historical memory that sucks the juices out of commemorative and reparations projects, the very opposite is the case: the Holocaust has become the central metaphor for all politics concerned with 'making whole what has been smashed.'"[44] As a consequence, the emblematic status of the Holocaust "has helped others who have been subjected to state-sponsored mass atrocities to gain attention for those calamities."[45] The more thoroughly Palestinians acknowledge the genocidal horrors of the Holocaust and put an end to comparisons of Israeli practices in the occupied territories with Nazi atrocities, the more broadly may their demands be recognized as part of the current adjudication of claims in the context of transitional justice. Their demands would also not be isolated or placed in a narrower moral framework connected with anticolonial struggles but with the more widespread contemporary struggles against tyranny and for democracy. It would, finally, enhance the possibility of what Torpey calls, following Habermas, a "communicative history," namely, a "discourse ethics" of norms shared by participants.[46]

A particularly noteworthy example of this approach is Walid Khalidi's introduction to *All That Remains: The Palestinian Villages Occupied and Destroyed by Israel in 1948*. In his short but poignant introduction to this stark "dictionary of destroyed villages," Khalidi notes that "other peoples have suffered worse fates in history: to be dispossessed of one's patrimony, dispersed and pauperized, even on such a scale, is still more merciful than wholesale physical annihilation."[47] In addition to pointing out the colonial aspect of Zionism, Khalidi places the Palestinian question in a broader sweep of modern history. After describing the Palestinian villages as having been "wiped off the face of the earth," while their inhabitants "continue to be maligned for having suffered such dispossession," Khalidi lashes out at the cynicism of Western elites and public opinion, which hailed the victory of Zionism "as the very principles of democracy the violation of which made the Zionist revolution possible in the first place."[48] Khalidi does not intend this album as "a call for the reversal of the tide of history [or] for the delegitimization of Zionism" but "for a moment of introspection." He suggests that "if only on prudential grounds, the exultant builder could well take into his appraisal both the monument of his achievement and the debris left in its wake."[49]

Implementation

Let us to turn now to an examination of the practical level. In this context, the issue of Jewish immigration during the *yishuv* was connected with the country's "absorptive capacity." The Mandatory authorities, in accord with the conditions of their mandate, established a labor schedule, drawn up every six months, to regulate the number of immigration certifications issued to different classes of Jewish immigrants. The main classes were persons of independent means, professionals, small tradesmen, and artisans with capital and, finally, workers with definite prospects of employment. While the Zionist bodies accepted that immigration should be based on the economic absorptive capacity of Palestine, the size of the largest category of immigrants—workers without means—the Achilles' heel of Zionist colonization, remained a source of contention between the World Zionist Organization and the British authorities.

But after independence, Israel itself adopted a selective immigration policy. This consisted of a number of parts. As Tom Segev showed in his *1949: The First Israelis*,[50] the new state was overwhelmed by a massive immigration wave, which more than doubled its population within about two years.[50] At first, attempts were made to keep the doors wide open to all Jewish immigrants, including the old and the ailing. The justification was that the doors of the countries of origin might be slammed shut as the postwar era ended and whoever was not able to leave would remain trapped. While this argument carried considerable weight, eventually Israel slowed down immigration. In addition, the composition of the immigrant population underwent change. "The State of Israel . . . in the wake of the Holocaust and the barring of emigration from communist Eastern Europe, resorted to the hardly tapped demographic . . . potential of Middle Eastern and North African Jews," not so much to rescue them but to create a Jewish majority.[51]

In the late 1980s and the 1990s, when Jewish immigration from the USSR and later its successor states became possible, Israel welcomed those immigrants with open arms, in part to tilt the balance of the Jewish population in the favor of the Ashkenazim, who were about to become a minority among Israeli Jews. At the same time, and for many decades, Israel refused to admit Ethiopian Jews, whose Jewishness was questioned; it did admit them, ironically, only under the pressure of American Jewish organizations.[52] Finally, not only the Ashkenazi:Mizrahi ratio has changed in the immigrant population but, in the aftermath of replacing most Palestinians with overseas workers, the Jewish:non-Jewish ratio. In August 2000, the daily *Yediot Ahronot* concluded that "relative to the population, the number of labor migrants [in Israel] is the highest in the Western world."[53] Though the estimates greatly vary, overseas workers, documented and undocumented, constitute anywhere from 7 to 14 percent of the Israeli labor force.[54] Immigration to Israel was based on and regulated to a large extent by the Law of Return, but more mundane immigration dynamics—economic and sometimes political—have frequently interfered in its implementation. Palestinian return is likely to be similarly multifaceted.

If we could imagine a return of Palestinian refugees, what would it be like? The epistemological difference raises the following barrier: Palestinians insist on an Israeli recognition of the right of return. Simultaneously, and probably rightly, they assure Israelis that only a portion of the refugees will, in fact, choose to resettle in Israel. Israel, for its part, refuses to give what it views as a blank check and raises the specter of mass return. How can this gap be bridged?

One possible approach would call for Israel (maybe by its experienced but currently idle Ministry of Immigration and Absorption) to open offices in all Palestinian refugee camps and interview individual refugees as to their intentions. Those refugees who plan to settle in Israel would thereby have direct contact with Israeli officials and would gain a clear understanding of the citizenship terms under which they would settle there.

More broadly, the refugee population is not made of one cloth and, consequently, the resolution of their plight would be divisible into multiple options. Danny Rabinowitz has suggested an innovative approach, based on a number of distinctions: "between Palestinian refugees who lack citizenship and those who have received citizenship from any country since 1948, . . . according to their living conditions and their chances of rehabilitation in their current homes, . . . between those who were exiled in 1948 and family members who were born in exile, between the right to citizenship and the right of residence, and to link all of these distinctions to the matter of monetary compensation."[55] Two alternatives would be presented: one following the human-rights route and the other the citizenship route. For those who want to be resettled elsewhere, immediate compensation would be available; those choosing repatriation would be classified, as refugees commonly are, according to place of birth and hardship and would be allowed in according to a schedule. Simultaneously, with a view to the longer run, a truth commission would be established and would lead to an Israeli apology for its part in the expulsion of Palestinian residents and the creation of the refugee population.

Finally, the refugee issue is a global one, and there have been suggestions for global solutions by linking the human-rights and citizenship frameworks. Pierre Hassner ingeniously suggests that the primary candidates for gaining citizenship based on universal human rights are refugees. "It is precisely because they are citizens of nowhere that they are potential citizens of the world."[56] Refugees are frequently doubly marginal, initially within their home countries and subsequently in the interstate order. States, in fact, are frequently more likely to protect themselves against refugees than to protect the refugees themselves. The refugee and asylum problem—like the dangers of pollution, nuclear proliferation and genocide—can be addressed only by raising it above the monopoly of states to a global level.[57] In Hassner's view, the European Union could take the first step in that direction by according European citizenship not only to member-state citizens but also "to those Europeans who do not, or no longer, have a territorial state within the framework of which they may have access to the rights and duties of citizens." Thus the EU would offer the same haven to persecuted Europeans as Israel does for the Jewish diasporas.[58] Palestinian refugees would be prime candidates for a similar approach.

Conclusion

Palestinian and Israeli positions toward issues of land and people, toward the ratio of land and people, and today especially toward the issue of the right of return seem hard and rigid. These grew out of competing experiences that have given rise to competing moral epistemologies, cumulative for Israelis and subtractive for Palestinians—in short, leading to zero-sum legalistic approaches. As we have seen, two kinds of comparisons, a time series of evolving views of both peoples and between Jews and Palestinians, suggest that changing circumstances may lead and frequently have led to changes and even full reversals in positions with respect to these very same issues. We have not come across any indivisible issues, neither among the visible nor the invisible ones. It is much more accurate to conclude that it has been the lack of resolution over time and the limited options that led to the radicalization of the competing perspectives through their "legalization," namely, dressing them up in the language of ultimate rights. In fact, the frameworks of transitional justice, which in the past decade replaced the all-or-nothing language of revolutions, have made divisibility or compromise their hallmark. It would seem that the Israeli-Palestinian conflict, stalemated and therefore escalating, would be a prime example of the kind of conflict that would benefit from resolution through the instrumentalities of transitional justice: historical commission, truth commission, apology, on the route from remembering to resolving to forgetting. The very diverse context in which Palestinian refugees are found makes such a resolution practical. In one area, however, I suggest a different approach.

In the context of refugees and return, a new framework is required, a divisible one that builds on the experience of the 1990s and requires the two sides to meet each other part way. In contrast, with regard to land I suggest an indivisible approach: that Israel concede all occupied land, or its equivalent, conquered in the 1967 war not only to create a territorially contiguous and viable Palestinian state but also to undo Israel's colonial state-building strategy, which it does not seem to be able to abandon either in time of conflict or of purported peacemaking. In short, Israel would undo its expansionist or cumulative epistemology (and revanchist tendencies) and thus also end the Palestinian fear of further encroachment. This would make possible the formation not of competing but of complementary moral epistemologies, typical of peaceful neighbors.

Notes

I wish to thank Ian Lustick for his extensive, cogent, and astute comments and suggestions. I rethought and rewrote this chapter from a comparative framework following his recommendations.

1. Shelly Fried, "The Refugee Issue at the Peace Conferences, 1949–2000," *Palestine-Israel Journal* 9:2 (2002): 31.

2. Ilan Pappé, "The Visible and Invisible in the Israeli Palestinian Conflict," in this volume, 2, 6.

3. Ibid., 11.

4. Ibid., 7, 8.

5. Mourid Barghouti, *I Saw Ramallah* (New York: Anchor, 2003), 69.

6. Adina Friedman, "Unraveling the Right of Return," *Refuge* 21:2 (February 2003): 63.

7. John Rawls, *A Theory of Justice* (Cambridge, Mass.: Harvard University Press, 1971), 3, 26.

8. Michael J. Sandel, *Liberalism and the Limits of Justice* (Cambridge: Cambridge University Press, 1982), 16.

9. Ibid., 168.

10. Rawls, "Justice as Fairness," *Philosophical Review* 67 (April 1958): 165.

11. Elizabeth H. Wolgast, "Why Justice Isn't an Ideal," in *The Grammar of Justice*, Elizabeth H. Wolgast, ed. (Ithaca, N.Y.: Cornell University Press, 1987), 125–32, 146.

12. Pappé, "The Visible and Invisible," 20.

13. From e-mail of Sami Al-Banna.

14. Gershon Shafir, "Ideological Politics or the Politics of Demography: The Aftermath of the Six Day War," in *Critical Essays in Israeli Society, Politics, and Culture*, Ian S. Lustick and Barry Rubin, eds. (Albany: State University of New York Press, 1991), 41–61.

15. Yehoshafat Harkabi, *Israel's Fateful Decisions* (London: I.B.Tauris,1988), 69.

16. Baruch Kimmerling, *Zionism and Territory* (Berkeley, Calif.: Institute of International Studies, 1983).

17. Shafir, "Ideological Politics."

18. In Walid Salem, "Legitimization or Implementation?" *Palestine-Israel Journal* 9:4 (2002): 8.

19. Mark W. Zacher, "The Territorial Integrity Norm: International Boundaries and the Use of Force," *International Organization* 55:2 (spring 2001): 215–50.

20. Quoted in Yosef Gorny, *Zionism and the Arabs* (Oxford: Clarendon, 1987), 210.

21. I owe this observation to Ian Lustick.

22. See Gershon Shafir, *The Citizenship Debates: A Reader* (Minneapolis: University of Minnesota Press, 1998).

23. Lynn Hunt, "The Paradoxical Origins of Human Rights," in *Human Rights and Revolutions*, Jeffrey N. Wasserstrom, Lynn Hunt, and Marilyn B. Young, eds. (Lanham, Md.: Rowman and Littlefield, 2000), 3–5.

24. Thomas Risse, Stephan C. Ropp, and Kathryn Sikkink, eds., *The Power of Human Rights: International Norms and Domestic Change* (Cambridge: Cambridge University Press, 1999), 2.

25. Janusz Symonides, ed., *Human Rights: New Dimensions and Challenges* (Aldershot: Ashgate, 1988).

26. Amnesty International, *Nationality, Expulsion, Statelessness and the Right of Return* (New York, September 2000); Frances Nicholson and Patrick Twomey, eds., *Refugee Rights and Realities: Evolving International Concepts and Regimes* (Cambridge: Cambridge University Press, 1999), 4, 217.

27. Nicholson and Twomey, *Refugee Rights and Realities*, 8.

28. UN Sub-Commission on the Promotion and Protection of Human Rights, 1999; see Amnesty International, *Nationality*, 3.

29. Nazmi Ju'beh, "The Palestinian Refugee Problem and the Final Status Negotiations, *Palestine-Israel Journal* 9:2 (2002): 9.

30. Daniel Warner, "The Refugee State and State Protection," in *Refugee Rights and Realities: Evolving International Concepts and Regimes,* Frances Nicholson and Patrick Twomey, eds. (Cambridge: Cambridge University Press, 1999).

31. See Friedman, "Unraveling the Right of Return," 67.

32. Julie Peteet, "From Refugees to Minority: Palestinians in Post-War Lebanon" *Middle East Report* 26:3 (1996): 30.

33. Laleh Khalili, "Commemorating Contested Lands," in this volume, 1, 2, 36.

34. Quoted in Gorny, *Zionism and the Arabs*, 199.

35. Priscilla B. Hayner, *Unspeakable Truths: Confronting State Terror and Atrocity* (New York: Routledge, 2001), 14.

36. Ibid.

37. Ibid., 88.

38. Ernest Renan, "What Is a Nation?" in *Nation and Narration*, Homi Bhabha, ed. (London: Routledge, 1990), 8–22.

39. Benny Morris, *The Birth of the Palestinian Refugee Problem, 1947–1949* (Cambridge: Cambridge University Press, 1988).

40. The idea of a historical commission was first brought to my attention by Elazar Barkan.

41. This particular list was suggested by Bishara Doumani.

42. Sally Denton, *New York Times*, May 24, 2003.

43. John Torpey, "'Making Whole What Has Been Smashed': Reflections on Reparations," *The Journal of Modern History* 73:2 (June 2001): 338.

44. Ibid.

45. Ibid., 341.

46. Ibid., 348.

47. Walid Khalidi, ed., *All That Remains: The Palestinian Villages Occupied and Destroyed by Israel in 1948* (Washington D.C.: Institute for Palestine Studies, 1991), xxxiii.

48. Ibid., xxxii, xxxiii.

49. Ibid., xxxiv.

50. Tom Segev, *1949: The First Israelis* (New York: The Free Press, 1986).

51. Gershon Shafir and Yoav Peled, *Being Israeli: The Dynamics of Multiple Citizenship* (Cambridge: Cambridge University Press, 2002), 77.

52. Ibid., 320–23.

53. *Yediot Ahronot*, August 24, 2000.

54. Shafir and Peled, *Being Israeli*, 324–25.

55. Danny Rabinowitz, *Haaretz*, January 4, 2001.

56. Pierre Hassner, "Refugees: A Special Case for Cosmopolitan Citizenship?" in *Re-imagining Political Community: Studies in Cosmopolitan Democracy*, Daniele Archibugi, David Held, and Martin Kohler, eds. (Stanford, Calif.: Stanford University Press, 1998), 274.

57. Ibid., 281–83.

58. Ibid., 284.

Bibliography

Abdulaziz, A. Mahmud, Hallah Ghazzawi, Alain Joxe, Camille Mansour, and Elias Sanbar. *Palestine: Mémoire et territoires.* Cahiers D'Études Stratégiques no. 14. Paris: École des Hautes Études en Sciences Sociales, 1989.

Abed, George T. "The Palestinians and the Gulf Crisis." *Journal of Palestine Studies* 20:2 (winter 1991): 37.

Abu Hawash, Jabir. "Majmu'a Mahmud Dakwar turathiyya: Mathaf ithnugrafi lil-zakira al-Filastiniyya" (Mahmud Dakwar's heritage collection: An ethnographic museum commemorating Palestine." *Al-Jana* (The harvest: The journal of the Arab Resource Center for Political Arts [ARCPA]) 5 (1997): 14–18.

Abu Iyad with Eric Rouleau. *My Home, My Land: A Narrative of the Palestinian Struggle.* New York: Times Books, 1981.

Abu-Rabia, Aref. "The Bedouin Refugees in the Negev." *Refuge* 14:6 (November 1994).

Aburish, Said. *Arafat: From Defender to Dictator.* New York: Bloomsbury, 1998.

Abu Shakrah, Jan. "Deconstructing the Link: Palestinian Refugees and Jewish Immigrants from Arab Countries." In Naseer Aruri, ed., *Palestinian Refugees: The Right of Return*, 208–16. London: Pluto, 2001.

Abu-Sitta, Salman. *The End of the Palestinian-Israeli Conflict: From Refugees to Citizens at Home.* London: Palestinian Land Society and Palestinian Return Center, 2001.

———. "The Right of Return: Inalienable and Sacred." *Al-Ahram Weekly* 14–20 (August 2003).

———. "The Right of Return: Sacred, Legal and Possible." In Aruri, ed., Palestinian Refugees, 195–207. New York: Pluto, 2001.

Agamben, Giorgio. *Homo Sacer: Sovereign Power and Bare Life.* Stanford, Calif.: Stanford University Press, 1998.

Akenson, D.H. *God's Peoples: Covenant and Land in South Africa, Israel, and Ulster.* Ithaca, N.Y.: Cornell University Press, 1992.

Akram, Susan M. "Temporary Protection and Its Applicability to the Palestinian Refugee Case." Brief no. 4. Bethlehem: Badil, n.d.

Al-Ali, al-Hajj 'Abd al-Majid. *Kwaykat: Ahad sharayin Filastin* (Kwaykat: One of Palestine's arteries). Beirut: n.p., 2001.

Alessa, Shamlan V. *The Manpower Problem in Kuwait.* London: Kegan Paul International, 1981.

Allport, Gordon. *The Nature of Prejudice.* New York: Addison and Wesley, 1954.

Al-Najjar, Baquer Salman. "Population Policies in the Countries of the Gulf Co-operation Council." *Immigrants and Minorities* 12:2 (July 1993).

Alpher, J., and K. Shikaki. "Concept Paper: The Palestinian Refugee Problem and the Right of Return." *Middle East Policy* 6 (1999): 167–89.

Altbach, Philip. "Textbooks in Comparative Context." In R. Murray Thomas and

Victor N. Kobayashi, eds., *Educational Technology: Its Creation, Development and Cross-Cultural Transfer.* Oxford: Pergamon, 1987.

Amitzur, Ilan. *Bernadotte in Palestine, 1948: A Study in Contemporary Humanitarian Knight-Errantry.* London: Macmillan, 1989.

Amnesty International. *Nationality, Expulsion, Statelessness and the Right of Return.* New York: September 2000.

Anderson, Benedict. *Imagined Communities: Reflections on the Origin and Spread of Nationalism.* London: Verso, 1991.

Andrew, Ludanyi. "The Fate of Magyars in Yugoslavia: Genocide, Ethnocide or Ethnic Cleansing?" *Canadian Review of Studies in Nationalism* 28:1–2 (2001): 127–41.

Appadurai, Arjun. *Modernity at Large: Cultural Dimensions of Globalization.* Minneapolis: University of Minnesota Press, 1996.

Apple, Michael. *Ideology and Curriculum.* Boston: Routledge, 1979.

———. Official Knowledge: Democratic Education in a Conservative Age. New York: Routledge, 1993.

———. *The Politics of the Textbook.* London: Routledge, 1991.

Aptekman, David. "Jewish Emigration from the USSR, 1990–1992: Trends and Motivations." *Jews in Eastern Europe* 1:20 (summer 1993): 15–34.

———, Boris Biletsky, Leonid Goldman, and Alexandr Shraiber. *Ten Years of Big Aliya: Sociological Essays.* Jerusalem: Aliya Association, 1999.

Arab Resource Center for Popular Arts (ARCPA). "Bibliography." *Al-Jana* (2002): 67–74.

———. " 'This Illiterate Woman . . . She Talked to Us': Participants' Responses to ARCPA's 1948 Uprooting Oral History Project." *Al-Jana* (May 1998): 26–49.

Armanazi, Ghayth. "The Rights of the Palestinians: The International Definition." *Journal of Palestine Studies* 3:3 (1974): 88–96.

Aruri, Naseer, ed. *Palestinian Refugees: The Right of Return.* New York: Pluto, 2001.

Arzt, Donna E. *Refugees into Citizens: Palestinians and the End of the Arab-Israeli Conflict.* Syracuse, N.Y.: Syracuse University Press, 1997.

Ashayachat, Achara. "Three-Year Repatriation Goal Urged for Burmese Refugees." *Bangkok Post,* April 9, 2000.

Assiri, Abdul-Reda. *The Government and Politics of Kuwait.* Kuwait: n.p., 1996.

'Atiya, Ahmad and Hasan. *'Alma: Zaytuna bilad Safad* ('Alma: The olive tree of Safad province). Beirut: n.p., 1998.

Bader, Dahoud. "El-Ghabsiya: Remains Ever in the Heart." Association for the Defense of the Rights of the Displaced Persons in Israel, May 2002.

Badil. "Palestinian Refugees and the Right of Return: An International Law Analysis." *Palestine-Israel Journal* 9:2 (2002): 35–42.

Bar-Hillel, Moshe. *Change and Progress in Israel and the Nations in the Contemporary Age, 1870–1920.* Petah Tiqva: Lilach, 1998.

Bar-Tal, D., and Y. Teichman. *Stereotypes and Prejudice in Conflicts: Arab Representation in Israeli Society.* Cambridge: Cambridge University Press, in press.

Bar-Tal, Daniel. "Delegitimization: The Extreme Case of Stereotyping and Prejudice." In Daniel Bar-Tal et al., eds., *Stereotyping and Prejudice: Changing Conceptions.* New York: Springer, 1989.

Barghouti, Mourid. *I Saw Ramallah.* New York: Anchor, 2003.

Barkan, Elazar. *The Guilt of Nations: Restitution and Negotiating Historical Injustices.* New York: Norton, 2000.

———. "Repatriating Refugees and Crossing the Ethnic Divide: A Comparative Perspective." Unpublished paper, Haifa University, November 2003.

Barnai, Ya'akov. *Historiography and Nationalism: Trends in the Study of Israel and the Jewish Community, 634–1881* (Hebrew). Jerusalem: Magnes, 1995.

Barnavie, Elie, and Eyal Naveh. *Modern Times, 1920–2000.* History for high school. (Hebrew) Tel Aviv: Tel Aviv Books, 1999.

Barou, Noah. "Origin of the German Agreement." *Congress Weekly* 7 (1952): 19–24.

Barzily, Ronit, and Mustafa Kabha. *Refugees in Their Homeland: Internal Refugees in the State of Israel 1948–1996.* Givat Haviva: Institute for Peace Research, 1996.

Basch, L., Nina Glick Schiller, and Cristina Szanton Blanc. *Nations Unbound: Transnational Projects, Postcolonial Predicaments, and Deterritorialized Nation-States.* New York: Gordon and Breach, 1994.

Beilin, Yossi. "Solving the Palestinian Refugee Problem." 31 December 2001, http://bitterlemons.org/previous/b1311201ed5.html.

Being Citizens in Israel: Jewish and Democratic State. A civics textbook for high school in state and state-religious schools. Jerusalem: Ministry of Education, 2000.

Bell-Fialkoff, Andrew. *Ethnic Cleansing.* New York: St. Martin's, 1996.

Ben-Gurion, David. "The Imperatives of the Jewish Revolution." In Arthur Hertzberg, ed., *The Zionist Idea,* 606–19. Westport, Conn.: Greenwood, 1959.

Ben-Yehuda, Nachman. *The Masada Myth: Collective Memory and Mythmaking in Israel.* Madison: University of Wisconsin Press, 1995.

Benziman, Uzi, and Mansour Atallah. *Subtenants* (Hebrew). Jerusalem: Keter, 1992.

Berlovitz, Yaffah. *Inventing a Country, Inventing a People: The Literary and Cultural Infrastructure of the First Aliyah* (Hebrew). Tel Aviv: Hakibbutz Hameuhad, 1996.

Birch, J. "Ethnic Cleansing in the Caucusus." *Nationalism & Ethnic Politics* 1:4 (1996): 90–107.

Bligh, Alexander. "From UNRWA to Israel: The 1952 Transfer of Responsibilities for Refugees in Israel." *Refuge* 14:6 (November 1994): 7–10.

———. "Israel and the Refugee Problem: From Exodus to Resettlement, 1948–52." *Middle Eastern Studies* 43:1 (1998): 123–47.

Bocco, Riccardo, Blandine Detremau, and Jean Hannoyer, eds. *Palestine, palestiniens: Territoire national, espaces communautaires.* Amman: Centre d'Etudes et de Recherches sur le Moyen-Orient Contemporain (CERMOC), 1997.

Bonacich, Edna. "A Theory of Middleman Minorities." *American Sociological Review* 38 (1973): 583–94.

———, and John Modell. *The Economic Basis of Ethnic Solidarity: Small Business in the Japanese American Community.* Berkeley: University of California Press, 1980.

Boqae'e, Nihad. "Palestinian Internally Displaced Persons Inside Israel: Challenging the Solid Structures." Bethlehem: Badil, 2003.

Bovin, Alexander. *Piat' let sredi evreev i midovtsev* (Five years among Jews and foreign office officials). Moscow: Progress, 2000.

Boyarin, Jonathan. *Palestine and Jewish History: Criticism at the Borders of Ethnography.* Minneapolis: University of Minnesota Press, 1996.

Brand, Laurie. *Palestinians in the Arab World: A Cross-Cultural Analysis.* Albany: State University of New York Press, 1991.

———. *The Palestinians in the Arab World: Institution Building and the Search for a State.* New York: Columbia University Press, 1988.

Brecher, Michael. "Images, Process and Feedback in Foreign Policy: Israel's Decisions on German Reparations." *American Political Science Review* 67:1 (March 1973): 73–102.

Brophy, Jane, and Bruce van Sledright. *Teaching and Learning History.* New York: Teachers College Press, 1997.

Brown, Nathan. "Education as a Site of Contestation: Democracy, Nationalism and the Palestinian Curriculum." Ben-Gurion University conference, "Democracy in the Periphery," May 2000.

Brynen, Rex. "Imagining a Solution: Final Status Arrangements and Palestinian Refugees in Lebanon." *Journal of Palestine Studies* 26:2 (1997): 42–58.

———. *Sanctuary and Survival: The PLO in Lebanon.* Boulder, Colo.: Westview, 1990.

———. *A Very Political Economy: Peacebuilding and Foreign Aid in the West Bank and Gaza.* Washington, D.C.: United States Institute of Peace Press, 2000.

B'tselem and Ha'Moked. *Families Torn apart: Separation of Palestinian Families in the Occupied Territories.* Center for the Defense of the Individual, July 1999.

Caiman, Charles. "Ahri ha-asson: Ha-aravim bi midinat yisrael 1948–1950" (After the catastrophe: Arabs in Israel 1948–1950). *Annals of Research and Critique* 10 (1984).

Calhoun, C. "Ethiopia's Ethnic Cleansing." *Dissent* (winter 1999): 47–51.

Carmi, Shulamit, and Henry Rosenfeld. "When Most Israeli Cabinet Members Have Decided Not to Block the Option of Return of Palestinian Refugees" (Hebrew). *Medina ve Hevra* 2 (2002).

Central State Archive of Public Organizations of Ukraine (Tsentral'nyi Derzhavnyi Arkhiv Hromads'kykh Ob'ednan' Ukra'iny -TsDAHOU). F. 1, Op. 29, d. 494, 11.76–79.

———. "On the Desire of Some Individuals of Jewish Nationality to Leave for Permanent Residence in Israel and Reactions to Events in the Middle East." June 16, 1967, F. 1, Op. 24, d. 6289, 11.4–7.

———. "Report on the Work of the UkSSR Commissioner of the Council of the Affairs of Religious Cults for January-March 1949, Kiev, 18 May 1949." F. 1, O. 23, d. 5667.

Charalambos, Tsardanidis, and Asteris Huliaras. "Prospects for Absorption of Returning Refugees in the West Bank and the Gaza Strip." Unpublished report, Institute of International Economic Relations, December 1999.

Chervyakov, Valery, Zvi Gitelman, and Vladimir Shapiro. "The National Consciousness of Russian Jews." In Irit Keynan, ed., *Demographic Shifts in the Jewish World: Forecasts and Implications,* 39–52. Herzliya: Institute for Policy and Strategy, Lauder School of Government, December 2002.

Childers, Erskine. "The Other Exodus." *The Spectator,* May 12, 1961.

Christopher, Warren. Statement at the opening of the Balkan proximity peace talks (Nov. 1, 1995). In *In the Stream of History: Shaping Foreign Policy for a New Era* Stanford, Calif.: Stanford University Press, 1998.

Clifford, James. "On Ethnographic Allegory." In Clifford and Marcus, eds., *Writing Culture,* 98–121. Berkeley: University of California Press, 1986.

———, and George E. Marcus. *Writing Culture: The Poetics and Politics of Ethnography.* Berkeley: University of California Press, 1986.

Cohen, Adir. *The Ugly Face in the Mirror: The Arab-Israeli Conflict in Hebrew Children's Books* (Hebrew) Tel Aviv: Reshafim, 1985.

Cohen, Hillel. *The Present Absentees: The Palestinian Refugees in Israel since 1948.* Jerusalem: Institute for Israeli Arab Studies, 2000.

Cohen, Roberta, and Francis Deng. *Masses in Flight: The Global Crisis of Internal Displacement.* Washington D.C.: Brookings Institution, 1998.

———, eds. *The Forsaken People: Case Studies of the Internally Displaced.* Washington D.C.: Brookings Institution, 1998.

Council of Foreign Ministers. "The Protocol for Treatment of Palestinians in Arab States." Cited by Human Rights Watch, *Policy on the Right of Return.* New York, 2001. http://www.hrw.org/campaigns/israel/return/arab-rtr.htm.

Cox, Marcus. "The Right to Return Home: International Intervention and Ethnic Cleansing in Bosnia and Herzegovina." *International & Comparative Law Quarterly* 47 (1998): 599–611.

Crocker, D. A. "Reckoning with Past Wrongs: A Normative Framework." *Ethics & International Affairs* 13 (1999): 43–64.

———. "Transitional Justice and International Civil Society: Toward a Normative Framework." *Constellations* 5 (1998): 492–517.

Daiya, Kavita. "Migration, Gender, Refugees, and South Asia: On international Migration and Its Implications for the Study of Cultural Geographies." University of Chicago. http://regionalworlds.uchicago.edu/bibliographicessaysonmigrat.pdf.

Dallal, Shaw J. *Scattered Like Seeds.* Syracuse, N.Y.: Syracuse University Press, 1998.

Darraj, Faisal. "'An 'Alaqat al-Ardh wa al-Watan wa al-Zakira" (On the relations between land, homeland, and memory). *Al-Hadaf* 1183 (April 3, 1994): 8–9.

Dean, Elizabeth, Paul Hartmann, and May Katzen. *History in Black and White: An Analysis of South African School History Textbooks.* Paris: Unesco, 1983.

Deleuze, Gilles, and Félix Guattari. *A Thousand Plateaus: Capitalism and Schizophrenia.* Minneapolis: University of Minnesota Press, 1987.

Deutschkron, Inge. *Bonn and Jerusalem.* Philadelphia: Philadelphia Book Company, 1970.

Domke, Eliezer, ed. *The World and the Jews in Recent Generations, 1870–1920.* A textbook for high school (Hebrew). Jerusalem: Zalman Shazar Institute, 1998.

———. *The World and the Jews in Recent Generations, 1920–1970.* Vol. 2. (Hebrew) Jerusalem: Zalman Shazar Institute, 1999.

Dumper, Mick. "Comparative Perspectives on Repatriation and Resettlement of Palestinian Refugees: The Cases of Guatemala, Bosnia and Afghanistan." Unpublished paper.

———. "End of an Era." *Journal of Palestine Studies* 81 (autumn 1991).

al-Ebraheem, Hassan Ali. *Kuwait and the Gulf.* Washington, D.C.: Croon Helm, 1984.

The Economist Intelligence Unit. *Iraq Country Report* 1 (1991).

Eden, Shevach. "A Comparative Examination of History Textbooks in Israel and Germany" (Hebrew). *Kivunim* (1986).

Eldar, Akiva. "Akiva Eldar Interviews Yossi Beilin and Nabil Shaath." *Palestine-Israel Journal* 9 (2002): 12–23.

Epstein, Alek, and Nina Kheimets. "Immigrant Intelligentsia and Its Second Generation: Cultural Segregation as a Road to Social Integration?" *Journal of International Migration and Integration* 1:4 (2000): 461–76.

ESCWA (UN Economic and Social Commission for Western Asia). *Return Migration: Profiles, Impact and Absorption.* New York: United Nations, 1993.

Fafo. *UNRWA's Financial Crisis and Socioeconomic Conditions of Palestinian Refugees in Lebanon, Jordan, Syria, and the West Bank and Gaza.* Oslo: Royal Norwegian Ministry of Foreign Affairs, 2000; http://www.fafo.no.

Farah, Randa. "Reconstruction of Palestinian Identities in al-Baq'a Camp." In Bocco et al., eds., *Palestine, palestiniens: Territoire national, espaces communautaires.* Amman: Centre d'Etudes et de Recherches dur le Moyen-Orient Contemporain (CERMOC), 1997.

Feiler, Gil. "Palestinian Employment Prospects." *The Middle East Journal* 47:4 (autumn 1993).

Feldman, Eliezer. *Russkii Izrail: Mezhdu dvukh pol'usov* (The Russian Israel: Between two poles). (Moscow: Market DS, 2003).

Fergany, Nader. *Sa'yan wara' al rizq: Dirasa maydaniyya 'an hijret al masriyyin ll'amal fi al aqtar al arabiyya* (Striving for subsistence). Beirut: Centre d'Études de l'Unité Arabe, 1988.

Fischbach, Michael R. *Records of Dispossession: Palestinian Refugee Property and the Arab-Israeli Conflict.* New York: Columbia University Press, 2003.

Flapan, Simcha. *The Birth of Israel: Myth and Realities.* London: Croom Helm, 1979.

Fried, Shelly. "The Refugee Issue at the Peace Conferences, 1949–2000." *Palestine-Israel Journal* 9:2 (2002): 24–34.

Friedman, Adina. "Unraveling the Right of Return." *Refuge* 21:2 (February 2003): 62–69.

From Conservatism to Progress. History for eighth grade. Jerusalem: Ministry of Education, 1998.

Funkenstein, Amos. "Collective Memory and Historical Consciousness." *History and Memory* 1 (1989).

Gabbay, Rony. *A Political Study of the Arab-Jewish Conflict: The Arab Refugee Problem, a Case Study.* Genève: Librairie Droz, 1959.

Gat, Moshe. *A Jewish Community in Crisis: The Exodus from Iraq 1948–1951* (Hebrew). Jerusalem: Zalman Shazar Center, 1989.

Gazit, Shlomo. *The Palestinian Refugee Problem.* Final Status Issue no. 2. Jaffee Center for Strategic Studies, Tel Aviv University, 1995.

Geertz, Clifford. *Peddlers and Princes.* Chicago: University of Chicago Press, 1993.

The Geneva Accord (GA). *Journal of Palestine Studies* 33:2 (2004): 81–101.

Ghabra, Shafeeq N. "The Iraqi Occupation of Kuwait: An Eyewitness Account." *Journal of Palestine Studies* 78 (winter 1991): 112–25.

———. *Palestinians in Kuwait: The Family and the Politics of Survival.* Boulder, Colo.: Westview, 1987.

———. "Palestinians in Kuwait: Victims of Conflict." *Middle East International* 397 (April 5, 1991).

Ghazzawi, Hallah. "La Mémoire du village et la préservation de l'identité palestinienne." In Abdulaziz, A. Mahmud, Hallah Ghazzawi, Alaine Joxe, Camille Mansour, and Elias Sanbar, eds., *Palestine: Mémoire et territoires*, Cahiers D'Études Stratégiques no. 14. Paris: École des Hautes Études en Sciences Sociales, 1989.

Giacaman, Rita, and Penny Johnson. *Inside Palestinian Households: Initial Analysis of a Community-Based Household Survey.* Vol. 1. Birzeit: Birzeit University, 2002.

Gitelman, Zvi. *Immigration and Identity.* New York: David and Susan Wilstein Jewish Policy Study, 1995.

Gorny, Yosef. *Zionism and the Arabs.* Oxford, Clarendon, 1987.

Gorokhoff, Philippe. "Les Palestiniens au Kowëit." *Migrations et changements sociaux dans l'Orient arabe.* Beirut: CERMOC, 1985.

Granovetter, Marc, and Richard Swedberg. *The Sociology of Economic Life.* Boulder, Colo.: Westview, 1995.

Grillo, Ralph, Bruno Riccio, and Ruba Salih. Introduction to *Here or There? Contrasting Experiences of Transnationalism: Moroccans and Senegalese in Italy.* Sussex: University of Sussex Press, 2000.

Groiss, Arnon, ed. *Jews, Israel and Peace in Palestinian School Textbooks: A Survey of the Textbooks Published by the Palestinian National Authority in the Years 2000–2001.* Jerusalem: Center for Monitoring the Impact of Peace, 2001.

Groman, Shlomo, and Mark Kotlyarshi. "Aliya prodolzhayetsia—nesmotria ni na chto" (Aliyah is going on—in spite of everything). *Vesti,* May 12, 2002.

Grossman, Kurt R. "Germany's Moral Debt: The German-Israel Agreement." *Public Affairs Press* (1954): 10–14.

Gur-Ze'ev, Ilan, and Ilan Pappée. "Beyond the Destruction of the Other's Collective Memory: Blueprints for an Israeli-Palestinian Dialogue." *Theory, Culture and Society* 20:1 (February 2003): 93–108.

Hacohen, Dvora. *From Fantasy to Reality: Ben-Gurion's Plan for Mass Immigration, 1942–1945* (Hebrew). Tel Aviv: Ministry of Defense, 1994.

Hadawi, Sami. *Palestinian Rights and Losses.* London: Al-Saqi, 1985.

———. *Palestinian Rights and Losses in 1948: A Comprehensive Study.* London: Saqi Books, 1988.

Haddad, Reem. "Labor of Love Produces History of Lost Village." *Daily Star,* May 10, 2001.

Al-Haj, Majid. "Adjustment Patterns of the Arab Internal Refugees in Israel." *International Migration* 24:3 (September 1988): 651–74.

——. "Soviet Immigrants as Viewed by Jews and Arabs: Divided Attitudes in a Divided Country." In Elazar Leshem and Judith T. Shuval, eds., *Immigration to Israel: Sociological Perspective*, 211–28. New Brunswick, N.J.: Transaction, 1998.

Halevi, Ilan. "Another Transfer." Unpublished paper, Institute for Palestine Studies, 1995.

——. "The Status of the Palestinians within Israel under the Shadow of the Intifada." Keynote speech, Center for Strategic Studies (Jordan), August 27, 2002.

Hanafi, Sari. *Between Two Worlds: Palestinian Businessmen in the Diaspora and the Construction of a Palestinian Entity.* Cairo: CEDEJ (French), 1997; and Cairo: Dar al-Mostaqbal al-Arabi and Ramallah: Muwatin (Arabic), 1996.

——. *Business Directory of Palestinians in the Diaspora.* Jerusalem: Biladi, June 1998.

——. "Contribution de la diaspora palestinienne à l'économie des territoires investissement et philanthropie." *Maghreb-Machrek* 161 (November 1998).

——. *Hona wa honaq: Nahwa tahlil lil 'alaqa bin al-shatat al-falastini wa al markaz* (Here and there: Toward an analysis of the relationship between the Palestinian diaspora and the center). Ramallah: Muwatin; Jerusalem: Institute of Jerusalem Studies, 2001.

——. "Investment by the Palestinian Diaspora in the Manufacturing Sectors of the West Bank and Gaza Strip." In ESCWA, ed., *Proceedings of the Expert Group Meeting on the Impact of the Peace Process on Selected Sectors*, 201–26. Amman: ESCWA, 1999.

——. "Opening the Debate on the Right of Return." *Middle East Report* 222 (March 2002).

——. "Penser le raport diaspora, centre. La contribution de la diaspora palestinienne à l'économie des territoires." In Hachan Hassan-Yari, ed., *Le processus de paix au Moyen-Orient.* Paris: Harmattan, 2000.

——. "Rethinking the Palestinians Abroad as a Diaspora: The Relationships Between the Diaspora and the Palestinian Territories." In Andre Misho, ed., *Anthropology of the Diaspora.* Stanford, Calif.: Stanford University Press, 2003.

Harkabi, Yehoshafat. *Israel's Fateful Decisions.* London: I.B.Tauris, 1988.

Harvey, David. *The Condition of Postmodernity.* London: Blackwell, 1990.

Haskell, T.L. *Objectivity Is Not Neutrality: Explanatory Schemes in History.* Baltimore: Johns Hopkins University Press, 1998.

Hassner, Pierre. "Refugees: A Special Case for Cosmopolitan Citizenship?" In Daniele Archibugi, David Held, and Martin Kohler, eds., *Re-imagining Political Community: Studies in Cosmopolitan Democracy*, 273–86. Stanford, Calif.: Stanford University Press, 1998.

Al-Hayja, Muhammad Abu. "Ayn Hawd and the 'Unrecognized Villages.'" *Journal of Palestine Studies* 31:1 (autumn 2001): 39–49.

Hayner, Priscilla B. *Unspeakable Truths: Confronting State Terror and Atrocity.* New York: Routledge, 2001.

Heacock, Roger. *The Becoming of Returnee States: Palestine, Armenia, Bosnia.* Birzeit: Birzeit University, 1999.

Heiberg, Marianne, and Geir Ovensen. *Palestinian Society in Gaza, West Bank and Arab Jerusalem: A Survey of Living Conditions.* Fafo report 151. Oslo: Fafo, 1993.

Helton, Arthur. *The Price of Indifference: Refugees and Humanitarian Action in the New Century* New York: Oxford University Press, 2002.

Herf, Jeffrey. *Divided Memory: The Nazi Past in the Two Germanys.* Cambridge, Mass.: Harvard University Press, 1997.

Hertzberg, Arthur, ed. *The Zionist Idea.* Westport, Conn. and New York: Greenwood Press and Meridien Books, 1959.

Hilal, Jamil, Majdi Malki, et al. *Social Support Institutions in the West Bank and Gaza, Ramallah* (Arabic). Ramallah: MAS, 1997.

Hill, M. "Urban and Regional Planning in Israel." In Raphaella Bilsti, ed., *Can Planning Replace Politics? The Israeli Experience,* 259–82. The Hague: Martinus Nighoff, 1980.

Hirschon, Renee. *Heirs of the Greek Catastrophe.* Oxford: Oxford University Press, 1989.

Hofnung, Menachem. *Israel: Bitahun Aamidinah mul shilton hahok, 1948–1991.* Jerusalem: Magnes, 1991.

Holy, Ladislav. *Kinship, Honour and Solidarity: Cousin Marriage in the Middle East* Manchester: Manchester University Press, 1989.

Horowitz, Dan, and Moshe Lissak. *Trouble in Utopia: The Overburdened Polity of Israel.* Albany: State University of New York Press, 1989.

Horowitz, Tamar. "Ideology, Identity, Disappointment: Major Factors of Electoral Behavior of the FSU Immigrants." In Asher Arian and Mose Sami, eds., *Israeli Elections 1999.* Jerusalem: Israeli Democracy Institute, 1999.

———. "Integration Without Acculturation." Soviet Jewish Affairs 12:3 (1982): 19–23.

Al-Hout, Bayan. "Oral History: Continuous, Permanent Connection." *Al-Jana* (May 1998): 10–12.

Al-Hut, Shafiq. *'Ashrun 'aman fi Munazzamat al-Tahrir al-Filastiniyya 1964–1984* (Twenty years in the Palestine Liberation Organization 1964–1984). Beirut: Dar al-Istiqlal, 1986.

Hudson, Michael. "Palestinians and Lebanon: The Common Story." Paper presented at the Palestinians in Lebanon conference organized by the Centre for Lebanese Studies and the Refugee Studies Programme, Queen Elizabeth House, Oxford, 1996.

Human Rights Watch/Middle East (HRW). *A Victory Turned Sour.* New York: September 1991.

Hunt, Lynn. "The Paradoxical Origins of Human Rights." In Jeffrey N. Wasserstrom, Lynn Hunt, and Marilyn B. Young, eds., *Human Rights and Revolutions.* Lanham, Md.: Rowman and Littlefield, 2000.

ICBS. *Statistical Abstract of Israel.* Jerusalem: Central Bureau of Statistics, 2003.

Inbar, Shula. *Revival and State in Israel and the Nations in the New Age, 1945–1970.* (Hebrew) Petah Tikva: Lilach, 2000.

International Labor Organization (ILO). "Resolution concerning the Measurement of Underemployment and Inadequate Employment Situations." Sixteenth International Conference of Labor Statistics. Geneva: ILO, 1998.

Isotalo, Riina. "Gendering the Palestinian Return Migration: Migrants from the Gulf and Marriage as a Transnational Practise." Paper presented at the Third Mediterranean Social and Political Research Meeting, Mediterranean Programme, Robert Schuman Centre, European University Institute Florence, March 20–24, 2002.

———. "Yesterday's Outsiders, Today's Returnees: Transnational Processes and Cultural Encounters in the West Bank." In A. Linjakumpu and K. Virtanen, eds., *Under the Olive Tree: Reconsidering Mediterranean Politics and Culture.* Tampere: European Science Foundation and Tampere Peace Research Institute, 1997.

Israel. Supreme Court. HCJ 64/51. *Awni Sbeit et al. v. Government of Israel.* 1951.

———. *Daoud et al. v. Minister of Defence et al.* Supr. Cour. Rept. 5. 1117 (1951).

"Israel's Russian Community Divided over Putin Victory." *Newsroom,* Jerusalem: April 3, 2000.

Issa, Mahmud. "Abhath fi zakirat al-makan" (I search memories of the place). *Al-Jana* 7 (1999): 54–57.

Jaber, Hanna. "Le Camp de Wihdat à la croisée des territoires." In Riccardo Bocco, Blandine Destremau, and Jean Honnoyer, eds., *Palestine, palestiniens: Territoire national, espaces communautaires.* Beirut: CERMOC, 1997.

Jabotinsky, Vladimir. "O zhelezhoni stene" (On the iron wall). In *Razsviet.* Berlin: 1923.

Jacobmeyer, Wolfgang. *International Textbook Research.* Göteborg: Göteborg University Press, 1990.

Jacobsen, Laurie Blome, and Mary Deeb. "Social Network." In Ole Fr. Ugland, ed., *Difficult Past, Uncertain Future: Living Conditions Among Palestinian Refugees in Camps and Gatherings in Lebanon.* Fafo report 409 (www.fafo.no), 2003.

Jallul, Faisal. *Naqd al-silah al-Filastini; Burj al-Barajna: ahlan wa thawratan wa mukhayyaman* (Critique of Palestinian armed resistance; Burj al-Barajna: Its people, revolution and refugee camp). Beirut: Dar al-Jadid, 1994.

Jamal, Amal. "Ethnic Nationalism, Native Minorities and Politics: On the Dynamics of Constructing Inequality in Israel." *Iyunim Bitkomat Yisrael,* forthcoming.

Jaradat-Gassner, Ingrid. *The Public Campaign for the Defense of Palestinian Refugee Rights in Historical Palestine.* Bethlehem: Badil Resource Center, 2000.

Jarrar, Najeh. *Palestinian Refugee Camps in the West Bank: Attitudes Towards Repatriation and Integration.* Ramallah: Palestinian Diaspora and Refugee Center, Shaml, 2003.

Jayanth, V. "India: No Repatriation of Sri Lankan Refugees since March '95." *The Hindu,* June 24, 2000.

Jewish Education and National Identity of Russian-Speaking Jews of Israel and the Diaspora. Collection of papers from the inauguration conference of the Association for Jewish Education in Russian, Seminar Oranim, Qiryat Tivon, Israel, May 5–6, 1999.

Jiryis, Sabri. "Arab Lands in Israel." *Journal of Palestine Studies* 2:4 (summer 1973).

———. *The Arabs in Israel.* New York: Monthly Review Press, 1976.

Journey to the Israeli Democracy. Civics textbook for the state and state-religious Schools. Jerusalem: Ministry of Education, 1994.

Ju'beh, Nazmi. "The Palestinian Refugee Problem and the Final Status Negotiations. *Palestine-Israel Journal* 9:2 (2002): 5–11.

Kabha, Ziad Mohammed Daoud. *Barta'a: The Divided Heart.* Ramallah: Edition of Ziad Mohammed Daoud Kabha, 2003.

Kammen, Michael. *Mystic Chords of Memory: The Transformation of Tradition in American Culture.* New York: Knopf, 1991.

Kamusella, Tomasz D. I. "Ethnic Cleansing in Silesia 1950–89 and the Nationalizing Policies of Poland and Germany." *Patterns of Prejudice* 33:2 (1999): 51–73.

Kanafani, Ghassan. "The Child Discovers That the Key Looks Like an Axe." In *Palestine's Children: Returning to Haifa and Other Stories.* Boulder, Colo.: Lynne Rienner, 2000 (1967).

Kapiszewski, Andrzej. *Nationals and Expatriates.* Reading, U.K.: Ithaca, 2001.

Karmi, Ghada, and Eugene Cotran, eds. *The Palestinian Exodus 1948–1988.* London: Ithaca 1999.

Karsh, Efraim. *Fabricating Israeli History: The "New Historians."* 2d rev. ed. London: Frank Cass, 2000.

Kedar, Sandi. "Israeli Law and the Redemption of the Arab Land, 1948–1969." Dissertation, Harvard Law School, 1996.

———. "Zman rov, zman mi'ut: Karka', li'om ve-hukei ha-ba'alut bi-yisrael" (Majority time, minority time: Land, natonality and the laws of property in Israel). *Iyuni Mishpat* 21:3 (1998): 665–764.

Kedourie, Elie. "The Break between Muslims and Jews in Iraq." In Mark R. Cohen and Abraham L. Udobitch, eds., *Jews among Arabs: Contracts and Boundaries*, 21–63. Princeton: Darwin Press, 1989.

Kenningstei, Moshe. "Values and Stereotypes of 'Russian' Immigrants: An Ethnic Methodological Research." In Andrei Fedorchenko and Alek Epstein, eds., *Migration Processes and Their Influence on Israeli Society*. Moscow: Hebrew University of Jerusalem, Moscow Institute for Israeli and Middle Eastern Studies, and Open University of Israel, 2000.

Kernochan, Julia. "Land Confiscation and Police Brutality in Um El Fahem." *Adalah Review* (fall 1999): 49–53.

Khalidi, Rashid. "Attainable Justice: Elements of Solution to the Palestinian Refugee Issue." *International Journal* 53:2 (spring 1998): 233–52.

———. "Observations on the Palestinian Right of Return." In J. Boutwell, ed., *The Palestinian Right of Return: Two Views*. Emerging Issues, Occasional Paper Series of the Academy of Arts and Sciences 1–1. Cambridge, Mass.: American Academy of Sciences, 1990.

———. "The Palestinian Refugee Problem: A Possible Solution," *Palestine-Israel Journal* 2:4 (autumn 1995).

———. "Toward a Solution." In *Palestinian Refugees: Their Problem and Future*. Washington, D.C.: Center for Policy Analysis on Palestine, October 1994.

Al-Khalidi, Salah. "Al-Ardh al-Muqaddasa fi al-Qur'an" (The Holy Land in the Qur'an). *Filistin al-Muslima* (July 1993): 44–45.

Khalidi, Walid, ed. *All That Remains: The Palestinian Villages Occupied and Destroyed by Israel in 1948*. Washington D.C., Institute for Palestine Studies, 1991.

———. *Conflict and Violence in Lebanon: Confrontation in the Middle East*. Cambridge, Mass.: Center for International Affairs, Harvard University, 1979.

Khamaisi, Rassem. "Manganonei ha-shlita ba-karka' vi-yihud ha-meirhav bi-yisrael" (Mechanisms of land control and the Judaization of space in Israel). Unpublished paper, University of Haifa, 2003.

———. *Planning and Housing Among the Arabs in Israel*. Tel Aviv: International Center for Peace in the Middle East, 1990.

Khanin, Vladimir. "The Contemporary Ukrainian Jewish Community: Social, Demographic, and Political Changes." In Irit Keynan, ed., *Demographic Shifts in the Jewish World: Forecasts and Implications*, 29–37. Herzliya: Institute for Policy and Strategy, Lauder School of Government, December 2002.

———. *Documents on Ukrainian Jewish Identity and Emigration, 1944–1990*. London: Frank Cass, 2002.

———. "Israeli 'Russian' Parties and the New Immigrant Vote." *Israel Affairs* (London) 7:2 (2000).

———. "The New Russian Jewish Diaspora and 'Russian' Party Politics in Israel." *Nationalism & Ethnic Politics* 8:4 (December 2002).

———. "'Russian' Community and Immigrant Party Politics at the 2003 Elections." In Shmuel Sandler and Ben Mollow, eds., *Israel at the Polls, 2003*. London: Frank Cass, forthcoming.

———. *The "Russians" and Power in the State of Israel: Establishment of the USSR/CIS Immigrant Community and Its Impact on the Political Structure of the Country* (Russian). Moscow: Institute for Israel and Middle Eastern Studies, forthcoming.

———. "Social Consciousness and the Problem of Jewish Identity of Ukrainian Jewry." *Contemporary Jewry* (New York) 19 (1998): 120–50.

———. "The Ukrainian Exodus." *Oxford Journal of Opinion and International Affairs* (December 1991): 5–8.

Khawaja, Marwan. "Population." In Ole Fr. Ugland, ed., *Difficult Past, Uncertain Future: Living Conditions Among Palestinian Refugees in Camps and Gatherings in Lebanon*. Fafo report 409 (www.fafo.no), 2003.

————, and Åge A. Tiltnes, eds. *On the Margins: Migration and Living Conditions of Palestinian Camp Refugees in Jordan.* Oslo: Fafo, 2002.

Kimmerling, Baruch. "Academic History Caught in the Cross-Fire: The Case of Israeli-Jewish Historiography." *History and Memory* 6 (1995).

————. *Zionism and Territory.* Berkeley, Calif.: Institute of International Studies, 1983.

King, R. E. *Return Migration and Regional Economic Problems.* London: Croom Helm, 1984.

Kirzner, Israel M. *Discovery, Capitalism, and Distributive Justice.* Oxford: Basil Blackwell, 1989.

————. "Uncertainty, Discovery, and Human Action: A Study of the Entrepreneurial Profile in the Misesian System." In Israel Kirzner, ed., *Method, Process, and Austrian Economics: Essays in Honor of Ludwig von Mises*, 139–59. Lexington, Mass.: Lexington Books, 1982.

Klinov, Ruth. "Reparations and Rehabilitation of Palestinian Refugees." Paper presented at the Max Planck Institute's conference on Palestinian refugees, Heidelberg, July 11, 2003.

Kodmani-Darwish, Bassma. *La Diaspora palestinienne.* Paris: Presses Universitaires de France, 1997.

Korn, David A. *Exodus Within Borders: An Introduction to Crisis of Internal Displacement.* Washington D.C.: Brookings Institution, 1999.

Kozulin, Aleksei, and Alex Venger. "Immigration without Adaptation: The Psychological World of Russian Immigrants in Israel." *Mind, Culture and Activity* 1:4 (1994): 230–38.

Kraul, Chris. "Flood of Afghan Returnees Continues." *Los Angeles Times*, December 30, 2002.

Kretzmer, David. *The Legal Status of the Arabs in Israel.* Boulder, Colo.: Westview, 1990.

Kubursi, Atif A. "Palestinian Losses in 1948: Calculating Refugee Compensation." Centre for Policy Analysis on Palestine, Information Brief No. 81, 3. August 2001.

Kulischner, Eugene M. *Europe on the Move: War and Population Changes 1917–1947.* New York: Columbia University Press, 1948.

Kuttab, Daoud. "In the Aftermath of the War." *Journal of Palestine Studies* 80 (summer 1991).

Lamb, Christina. *Sunday Telegraph*, November 10, 2002.

Lapidoth, Ruth. "The Right of Return in International Law, with Special Reference to the Palestinian Refugees." *Israel Yearbook on Human Rights* 16 (1986): 103–25.

Lawyers Committee for Human Rights. *Laying the Foundations: Human Rights in Kuwait.* New York: 1993.

Lee, Luke T. "The Right to Compensation: Refugees and Countries of Asylum." *The American Journal International Law* 80:3 (July 1986): 532–67.

Lesch, Ann M. "Contrasting Reactions to the Persian Gulf Crisis." *The Middle East Journal* 45:1 (winter 1991).

————. "Palestinians in Kuwait." *Journal of Palestine Studies* 80 (summer 1991): 42–54.

Leshem, Eliezer. "The Israeli Public Attitudes Toward the New Immigrants of the 1990s." In Elazar Leshem and Judith T. Shuval, eds., *Immigration to Israel: Sociological Perspective*, 307–27. New Brunswick, N.J.: Transaction, 1998.

————. *Seker proyekt 'ha-zeut ha-yehudit' shlav alef ba-hama* (Study of the project "Jewish identity," stage A, in the CIS). Jerusalem: Jewish Agency for Israel, August 2002.

Lever-Tracy, Constance, David Ip, and Tracy Noel. *The Chinese Diaspora and Mainland China: An Emerging Economic Synergy.* London: Macmillan, 1996.

Levin, Itamar. "Confiscated Wealth: The Fate of Jewish Property in Arab Lands." *Policy Forum* 22 (Jerusalem: Institute of the World Jewish Congress, 2000).

————. *Locked Doors: The Seizure of Jewish Property in Arab Countries.* Westport, Conn.: Praeger, 2001.

Levy, Gideon. "Wombs in the Service of the State." *Haaretz* (English edition), September 9, 2002.

Lewis, Bernard. *History: Remembered, Recovered, Invented.* Princeton, N.J.: Princeton University Press, 1975.

Lisovski, Aharon. "The Present Absentees in Israel." *The New Orient* 10 (1960): 187–90.

Lithwick, Harvey. "An Urban Development Strategy for the Negev's Bedouin Community." www.bgu.ac.il/bedouin/monograph-Harvey.doc.

Little, D. "A Different Kind of Justice: Dealing with Human Rights Violations in Transitional Societies." *Ethics & International Affairs* 13 (1999): 65–80.

Longva, Anh Nga. "Keeping Migrant Workers in Check: The Kafala System in the Gulf." *Middle East Report* (summer 1999).

————. *Walls Built on Sand: Migration, Exclusion and Society in Kuwait.* Boulder, Colo.: Westview, 1997.

Lorch, Netanel, ed. *Major Knesset Debates, 1948–1981.* Lanham, Md.: University Press of America, 1993.

Lowenthal, David. *The Past Is a Foreign Country.* Cambridge: Cambridge University Press, 1985.

Lubani, Husayn Ali (al-Damuni). *Al-Damun: Qariya Filastiniyya fi al-bal* (Damun: A Palestinian village in the mind). Beirut: Dar al-Arabi, 1999.

Ludanyi, Andrew. "The Fate of Magyars in Yugoslavia: Genocide, Ethnocide or Ethnic Cleansing?" *Canadian Review of Studies in Nationalism* 28:1–2 (2001).

Lustick, Ian. *Arabs in the Jewish State: Israel's Control of a National Minority.* Austin: University of Texas Press, 1980.

————. "Israel as a Non-Arab State: The Political Implications of Mass Immigration of Non-Jews." *The Middle East Journal* 53:3 (1999): 417–33.

————. "To Build and to Be Built By: Israel and the Hidden Logic of the Iron Wall." *Israel Studies* 1:1 (summer 1996): 196–223.

Lyssak, Moshe, and Eliezer Leshem. "The Russian Intelligentsia in Israel: Between Ghettoization and Integration." *Israel Affairs* 2:2 (1995): 20–36.

Mac Curtain, Margaret. "Reconciliation of Memories." In Alan D. Falconer and Joseph Liechty eds., *Reconciling Memories,* 99–107. Dublin: Columba Press, 1998.

Machlis, Avi. "Compensation for Jews Who Fled Arab Countries." Jewish Telegraphic Agency, *Jewish News of Greater Phoenix* 52: 50 August 25, 2000, www.jewishaz.com/jewishnews/000825/fled.shtml.

Majodine, Zonke. "Dealing with Difficulties of Return to South Africa: The Role of Social Support and Coping." *Journal of Refugee Studies* 8:2 (1995): 210–27.

Malki, Majdi, and Yasser Shalabi. *Internal Migration and Palestinian Returnees in the West Bank and Gaza Strip* (in Arabic with English summary). Ramallah: MAS, 2000.

Malley, Robert, and Hussein Agha. "The Truth About Camp David." *New York Review of Books,* August 9, 2001.

Mansfield, Peter. *Kuwait.* London: Hutchinson, 1990.

Mantel, Hilary. "The Shape of Absence." *London Review of Books* 24:15 (2002).

Martin, Terry. "The Origins of Soviet Ethnic Cleansing." *Journal of Modern History* 70:4 (1998): 813–61.

Marx, Emanuel. "Palestinian Refugee Camps in the West Bank and the Gaza Strip." *Middle Eastern Studies* 28:2 (1992): 281–94.

———. "Refugee Compensation: Why the Parties Have Been Unable to Agree and Why It Is Important to Compensate Refugees for Losses." In J. Ginat and E. T. Perkins, eds., *The Palestinian Refugees*, 102–8. Norman: University of Oklahoma Press, 2001.

Masalha, Nur. "Debate on the 1948 Exodus." *Journal of Palestine Studies* 21:1 (autumn 1991): 90–97.

———. *Expulsion of the Palestinians: The Concept of "Transfer" in Zionist Political Thought, 1882–1948*. Washington, D.C.: Institute for Palestine Studies, 1992.

———. *Imperial Israel and the Palestinians: The Politics of Expansion*. London: Pluto 2000.

———. *The Palestinians in Israel: Is Israel the State of All Its Citizens and "Absentees"?* Haifa: Galilee Center for Social Research, 1993.

Mautner, Menachem. "Law as Culture: Towards a New Research Paradigm." In Menachem Mautner, Uri Sageh, and Ronen Shamir, eds., *Multiculturalism in a Jewish and Democratic State*, 545–87. Tel Aviv: Ramot, 1998.

McElroy, Damien. "Uighurs Warn of Return to Terror." *The Scotsman*, May 31, 2000.

Mehlinger, Howard. "International Textbook Revision: Examples from the United States." *Internationale Schulbuchforschung* 7 (1985).

Meir, Esther. "Conflicting Worlds: The Encounter between Zionist Emissaries and the Jews of Iraq during the 1940s and Early 1950s." In Dalia Ofer, ed., *Israel in the Great Wave of Immigration, 1948–1953* (Hebrew). Jerusalem: Yad Ben Zvi, 1996.

———. *The Zionist Movement and the Jews of Iraq 1941–1950* (Hebrew). Tel Aviv: Am Oved, 1993.

Meir, Yosef. *Beyond the Desert: Underground Activities in Iraq* (Hebrew). Tel Aviv: Ma'arakhot, 1973.

Meir-Glitzenstein, Esther. "The Riddle of the Mass Immigration from Iraq: Causes, Circumstances and Consequences" (Hebrew). *Pe'amim* 71 (1997): 25–53.

Meisels, Tamar. "Can Corrective Justice Ground Claims to Territory?" *The Journal of Political Philosophy* 11:1 (March 2003): 65–68.

Meron, Ya'akov. "The Expulsion of the Jews from Arab Countries: The Palestinians' Attitude toward It and Their Claims" In Malka Hillel Shulewitz, ed., *The Forgotten Millions: The Modern Jewish Exodus from Arab Lands*, 83–125. London: Cassell, 1999.

Ministry of Planning and International Cooperation (MOPIC), Aid Coordination Department. *MOPIC's 1997 Fourth Quarterly Monitoring Report of Donor Assistance*. Ramallah, 1998.

Mitsel, Michael. "Vystupaiut ochen' ot'iavlenno dersko sionistskie elementary (Shtrikhi k politicheskomu potretu P.E. Shelesta)." In Gelii Aronov et al., eds., *Jewish History and Jewish Culture in the Ukraine*, 3: 137–42. Kiev: Kiev Institute for Jewish Studies, 1996.

Morris, Benny. *The Birth of the Palestinian Refugee Problem, 1947–1949*. Cambridge: Cambridge University Press, 1987.

———. *The Birth of the Palestinian Refugee Problem Revisited*. Cambridge: Cambridge University Press, 2004.

———. "The Causes and Character of the Arab Exodus from Palestine: The Israeli Defense Forces Intelligence Branch Analysis of June 1948." *Middle Eastern Studies* 22 (1986): 5–19.

———. *Israel's Border Wars, 1949–1956: Arab Infiltration, Israeli Retaliation, and the Countdown to the Suez War*. Oxford: Clarendon, 1993.

———. *1948 and After: Israel and the Palestinians*. Oxford: Clarendon, 1990.

———. *Righteous Victims*. New York: Vintage, 1999.

———. "Yosef Weitz and the Transfer Committees, 1948–49." *Middle Eastern Studies* 22:4 (1986): 522–62.

Moubarak, Walid E. "Kuwait's Quest for Security, 1961–1973." Unpublished dissertation, Indiana University, 1979.

Moughrabi, Fouad. "Analysis Evaluation of the New Palestinian Curriculum." Israel/Palestine Center for Research and Information (IPCRI), March 2003.

———. "The Politics of Palestinian Textbooks." *Journal of Palestine Studies* 31:1 (autumn 2001).

Musa, Hassan. "The Geographical Distribution of the Arab Refugees in their Homeland: The Galilee Area 1948–1987." Unpublished master's thesis, Haifa University, 1988.

Nabulsi, Karma. "Right of Return." *The Guardian*, September 17, 2002.

Naimark, Norman M. *Fires of Hatred: Ethnic Cleansing in Twentieth-Century Europe.* Cambridge, Mass.: Harvard University Press, 2000.

Nakhleh, Khalil, and Elia Zureik, eds. *The Sociology of the Palestinians.* New York: St. Martin's Press, 1980.

Naqub, Fadl. "Absorption of the Palestinian Refugee: Economic Aspects." Unpublished paper, PRC, Ramallah, 2003.

National Committee for Defending Palestinian Human Rights in Kuwait. *Memorandum on the Situation of the Palestinians in Kuwait.* Kuwait: May 1991.

Al-Natour, Souheil. "The Legal Status of Palestinians in Lebanon." *Journal of Refugee Studies* 10:3 (1997).

Naveh, Eyal. *Teacher's Guide* (Hebrew). Tel Aviv: Tel Aviv Books, 1999.

———. *The Twentieth Century: On the Verge of Tomorrow.* History to ninth grade. (Hebrew) Tel Aviv: Tel Aviv Books, 1999.

Nazzal, Nafez. *The Palestinian Exodus from Galilee, 1948.* Beirut: Institute for Palestine Studies, 1978.

Nicholson, Frances, and Patrick Twomey, eds. *Refugee Rights and Realities: Evolving International Concepts and Regimes.* Cambridge: Cambridge University Press, 1999.

Nir, Ori. "We Can't Just Be Shoved Away." *Haaretz* (English edition), April 25, 2002.

Nudelman, Rafail. "Hanisayon lekhadesh hatsionut: Bein aliyat shnot hashiv'im laaliyat shnot hatish'im" (Attempts to renew Zionism: Between the aliyah of the 1970s and the 1990s). *Yehudei Brit Ha-Mo'etzot Ba-Ma'avar* 4:19 (2000): 67–84.

Oded, Yitzhak. "Land Losses Among Israel's Arab Villages." *New Outlook* 7:7 (September 1964): 19–25.

Olson, David R. "On the Language and Authority of Textbooks." In Suzanne De Castell, Allan Luke, and Carmen Luke, eds., *Language, Authority and Criticism: Readings on the School Textbook.* London: Falmer, 1989.

Ong, Ohayo. *Flexible Citizenship: The Cultural Logic of Transnationality.* Durham, N.C.: Duke University Press, 1999.

Oren, Michael. *Six Days of War: June 1967 and the Making of the Modern Middle East.* Oxford: Oxford University Press, 2002.

Osazki, Sarah. *Ikrit and Bir'am: The Full Story.* Givat Haviva: Institute for Peace Research, 1993.

Palestinian Centre for Policy and Survey Research (PCPSR). "Press Release on Refugee Views on the Settlement of the Refugee Issue, Ramallah, 18 July 2003." In documents and source material of *Journal of Palestine Studies* 33:1 (2003): 160–62.

Palestinian Human Rights Information Center. "A Bittersweet Coming Home: The Experience of Palestinians Returning from the Gulf." *From the Field* (October 1993).

Palumbo, Michael. *The Palestinian Catastrophe: The 1948 Expulsion of a People from Their Homeland.* London: Faber and Faber, 1987.

Pappé, Ilan. "Angst, Oferschaft, Selbst- und Frembilder." In Rafik Schami, ed., *Angst in eigenen Landen,* 65–77. Zurich: Nagel and Kimche, 2001.

————. "Breaking the Mirror: Oslo and After." In Haim Gordon, ed., *Looking Back at the June 1967 War*, 95–112. Westport, Conn.: Praeger, 1999.

————. "Fear, Victimhood, Self and Other." *MIT Electronic Journal of Middle East Studies* 1 (May 2001).

————. "Israeli Television Fiftieth Anniversary Series: Tekuma: A Post-Zionist Review?" *Journal of Palestine Studies* 27:4 (Summer 1998).

————. *The Making of the Arab-Israeli Conflict: 1947–1951.* London: I.B. Tauris, 1994.

————. "The Post-Territorial Dimensions of a Future Homeland in Israel and Palestine." Conference paper.

————. "Post-Zionist Critique: Part I: The Academic Debate." *Journal of Palestine Studies* 26:2 (winter 1997): 29–41.

————. "I Profughi Palestinesi tra Storia e Storiografia." In Marco Buttino, ed., *In Fuga: Guerre, Carestie e Migrazioni forzate nel Mondo Contemporaneo*, 81–106. Naples: L'Ancora, 2001.

————. "Were They Expelled?: The History, Historiography and Relevance of the Refugee Problem." In Ghada Karmi and Eugene Cotran, eds., *The Palestinian Exodus, 1948–1988*, 37–62. London: Ithaca, 1999.

Pearlman, Moshe. *Ben Gurion Looks Back.* New York: Simon and Schuster, 1965.

Pedersen, Jon, et al., ed. *Growing Fast: The Palestinian Population in the West Bank and Gaza Strip.* Oslow: Fafo, 2001.

Peled, Y., and N. N. Rouhana. "Transitional Justice and the Right of Return of the Palestinian Refugees." *Theoretical Inquiries in Law* (2004).

Peres, Yochanan. *Integration of New Repatriates from the CIS in Israel: The First Steps* (Hebrew). Tel Aviv: Tel Aviv University Press, 1992.

————, and Sabina Lissitsa. "Unity and Cleavages in Israeli Society: Initial Report—Immigrants from the Former Soviet Union and Veterans in Israel." *Israeli Sociology* 3:1 (March 2001).

Peretz, Don. *Israel and the Palestinian Arabs.* Washington, D.C.: Middle East Institute, 1958.

————. *Palestinians, Refugees, and the Middle East Peace Process.* Washington, D.C.: United States Institute of Peace, 1993.

Peteet, Julie. "From Refugees to Minority: Palestinians in Post-War Lebanon." *Middle East Report* 26:3 (1996): 27–30.

Phares, Walid. *Lebanese Christian Nationalism: The Rise and Fall of an Ethnic Resistance.* Boulder, Colo.: Lynne Rienner, 1995.

Phuong, Catherine. "'Freely to Return': Reversing Ethnic Cleansing in Bosnia-Herzegovina." *Journal of Refugee Studies* 13:2 (2000): 165–83.

Physicians for Human Rights. *Iraq-Occupied Kuwait: The Health Care Situation.* Somerville, Mass.: March 1991.

Pingel, Falk. *UNESCO Guidebook on Textbook Research and Textbook Revision.* Hannover: Verlag Hahnsche Buchhandlung, 1999.

Plascov, Avi. *The Palestinian Refugees in Jordan 1948–1957.* London: Frank Cass, 1981.

Podeh, Elie. *The Arab-Israeli Conflict in Israeli History Textbooks, 1948–2000.* Westport, Conn.: Bergin and Garvey, 2002.

————. "History and Memory in the Israeli Educational System: The Portrayal of the Arab-Israeli Conflict in History Textbooks (1948–2000)." *History and Memory* 12:1 (spring/summer 2000): 65–100.

Pohl, J. Otto. "The Exile and Repatriation of the Crimean Tatars." *Journal of Contemporary History* 37:3 (2002): 323–47.

Polanyi, Karl. "The Economy as Instituted Process." In *The Great Transformation*; reprint. Boston: Beacon, 1957.

Portes, Alejandro. *Latin Journey: Cuban and Mexican Immigrants to the U.S.* Berkeley: University of California Press, 1985.

————. "Social Capital: Its Origins and Applications in Contemporary Sociology." *Annual Review of Sociology* 24 (1998): 1–24.

Preece, Jennifer Jackson. "Ethnic Cleansing as an Instrument of Nation-State Creation: Changing State Practices and Evolving Legal Norms." *Human Rights Quarterly* 20:4 (1998).

Pribytkova, Irina. "Examination of the Citizenship Issue on the Return and Reintegration of the Formerly Deported Peoples of Crimea." In Natalia Panina et al., eds., *Sociology in Ukraine*, 244–305. Kiev: Institute of Sociology of the National Academy of Sciences of Ukraine, 2002.

Prilutsky, Alex. "Vek Russkoi alii" (The age of Russian aliyah). *Vesti,* January 2, 2000.

Quigley, John. "Displaced Palestinians and a Right of Return." *Harvard International Law Journal* 39 (Winter 1998): 171–229.

Quwaidar, Rashid. "Yawm al Ardh: Min tadmir al-mujtama' al-Filastini . . . ila i'ada bana' al-huwiyya al-wataniyya wa al-qawmiyya" (Land Day: From the destruction of Palestinian society . . . to the reestablishment of national and pan-Arab identity). *Al-Hurriyya* 801:1875 (April 9, 2000).

Rubinowitz, Dan, and Khawala Abu Baker. *Hador Hazakuf.* Tel Aviv: Keter, 2002.

Radi, Lamia. "Les Palestiniens due Koweit en Jordanie." *Maghreb-Machrek* 144 (April–June 1994): 55–66.

Rawls, John. "Justice as Fairness." *Philosophical Review* 67 (April 1958). pp. 164–194
————. *A Theory of Justice.* Cambridge, Mass.: Harvard University Press, 1971.

Raz, Joseph. *Ethics in the Public Domain: Essays in the Morality of Law and Politics.* Oxford: Clarendon, 1994.

Reiber, Alfred J. "Repressive Population Transfers in Central, Eastern and South-Eastern Europe: A Historical Overview." *Journal of Communist Studies and Transition Politics* 16:1–2 (2000): 1–27.

Reichman, Shalom. *From Foothold to Settled Territory* (Hebrew). Jerusalem: Yad Izhak Ben Zvi, 1979.

Renan, Ernest. "What Is a Nation?" In Homi K. Bhabha, ed., *Nation and Narration,* 8–22. London: Routledge, 1990.

Reynolds, Paul D., Michael Hay, and S. Michael Camp. *Global Entrepreneurship Monitor, 1999 Executive Report.* Babson College/Kauffman Center for Entrepreneurial Leadership/London Business School, 1999.

Riman, Aleksandr. " 'I ostalsia Yakov odin,' ili svideitel' obvinenia" ("And Ya'acov left alone," or the witness of the charge). *Vesti-2,* August 29, 2002, 9.

Al-Rimmawi, Hussein, and Hana Bukhari. *Population Characteristics of the Refugee Camps, Ramallah: PCBS and Dissemination and Analysis of Census Findings* (Arabic). Analytical Report Series no. 3, 2002.

Risse, Thomas, Stephan C. Ropp, and Kathryn Sikkink, eds. *The Power of Human Rights: International Norms and Domestic Change.* Cambridge: Cambridge University Press, 1999.

Roberts, Rebecca. *Bourj al-Barahneh: The Significance of Village Origin in a Palestinian Refugee Camp.* Master's thesis, University of Durham, 1999.

Rogers, James. "Why the Attacks Continue." BBC, 19 May, 2003. http://news.bbc.co.uk/1/hi/world/middle_east/3040543.stm.

Rosand, Eric. "The Right to Compensation in Bosnia: an Unfulfilled Promise and a Challenge to International Law." *Cornell International Law Journal* 33 (2000) 113–58.

Rotenberg, Vadim. "On Self-Determination of Jews from the Former Soviet Union Now Living in Israel" (Hebrew). *Yehudei Brit Ha-Moetzot Ba-Ma'avar* 4:19 (2000): 213–20.

————. "Samoindentificatsia rossiiskogo evreistva: Popytka analiza" (Self-identification of Russian Jewry: An attempt at analysis). http://www.machanaim.org.il.

Rothschild, Joseph. *Two World Wars: A History of East Central Europe.* Seattle: University of Washington Press, 1993.

Rouhana, Nadim. "Group Identity and Power Asymmetry in Reconciliation Processes: The Israeli-Palestinian Case." *Peace and Conflict: Journal of Peace Psychology* 10: 1 (2004): 33–52.

————. "Identity and Power in the Reconciliation of National Conflict." In A. H. Eagly, R. M. Baron, and V. L. Hamilton, eds., *The Social Psychology of Group Identity and Social Conflict: Theory, Application, and Practice.* Washington, D.C.: American Psychological Association, 2004.

————. *Palestinian Citizens in an Ethnic Jewish State: Identities in Conflict.* New Haven, Conn.: Yale University Press, 1997.

Rouhana, N. N., and H. C. Kelman. "Promoting Joint Thinking in International Conflicts: An Israeli-Palestinian Continuing Workshop." *Journal of Social Sciences* 50 (1994): 157–78.

Rouhana, Nadim N. and Nimer Sultany. "Redrawing the Boundaries of Citizenship: Israel's New Hegemony." *Journal of Palestine Studies* 33:1 (fall 2003): 5–22.

Roy, Sara. *The Gaza Strip: The Political Economy of De-development.* Washington, D.C.: Institute of Palestine Studies, 1995.

Rubenstein, Eliakim. "The Treatment of the Arab Question in Palestine in the Immediate Period after the 1929 Events and the Establishment of the Political Bureau: Political Aspect" (Hebrew). In Ilan Pappé, ed., *Jewish-Arab Relations in Mandatory Palestine: A New Approach to the Historical Research,* 65–102 Givat Haviva: Institute of Peace Research, 1995.

Rubinstein, Danny. *The People of Nowhere: The Palestinian Vision of Home.* New York: Times Books, 1991.

Russell, Sharon Stanton. "International Migration in Europe, Central Asia, the Middle East and North Africa." World Bank, Population and Human Resources Division, 1992.

————. "Politics and Ideology in Migration Policy Formulation: The Case of Kuwait." *International Migration Review* 23:1 (1989).

Ryvkina, Rozalina. *Russian Jews: Who Are They?* (Russian). Moscow: Opos, 2000.

Saad al Din, Ibrahim, and Mahmud Abdel Fadil. *Intiqal al 'amalah al 'arabiyya* (The movement of Arab labor). Beirut: Centre d'études de l'Unité Arabe, 1983.

Saban, Ilan. "The Impact of the Supreme Court on the Status of the Arabs in Israel" (Hebrew). *Mishpat Umimshal* 3:2 (July 1996): 541–70.

Sagi, Nana. *German Reparations: A History of the Negotiations.* Jerusalem: Magnes, 1980.

Said, Edward. *Peace and Its Discontents.* New York: Vintage, 1993.

————. *The Politics of Dispossession.* London: Chatto and Windus, 1994.

Said, Mahmud. "Adjustment Patterns and Living Conditions of the Internal Arab Refugees in the Arab Host Villages in the North, 1948–1986." Master's thesis, Hebrew University, 1991.

Salem, Walid. "Legitimization or Implementation?" *Palestine-Israel Journal* 9:4 (2002): 7–14.

Salih, Ruba. "Transnational Practices and Normative Constraints between Morocco and Italy: A Gendered Approach." Paper presented at the First Mediterranean Social and Political Research Meeting, Mediterranean Programme, Robert Schuman Centre, European University Institute, Florence, March 22–26, 2000.

Sanbar, Eli. "Remarks." *Palestine-Israel Journal* 2:4 (autumn 1995).

Sandel, Michael J. *Liberalism and the Limits of Justice.* Cambridge, Cambridge University Press, 1982.

Satloff, Robert. "The Times Tries to Rewrite History: Times Bomb." *The New Republic* (August 13, 2001).

Sayigh, Rosemary. "The History of Palestinian Oral History: Individual Vitality and Institutional Paralysis." *Al-Jana* (2002).

———. "Oral History for Palestinians: The Beginning of a Discipline." *Al-Jana* (May 1998): 4–9.

———. *Palestinians: From Peasants to Revolutionaries.* London: Zed, 1979.

———. "Palestinian Refugees in Lebanon: Implantation, Transfer or Return?" *Middle East Policy* 8:1 (2001): 95–105.

———. *Too Many Enemies: The Palestinian Experience in Lebanon.* London: Zed, 1994.

Sayigh, Yezid Y. *Armed Struggle and the Search for State: The Palestinian National Movement, 1949–1993.* Oxford: Oxford University Press, 1997.

Schaeffer, Robert K. *Severed States: Dilemmas of Democracy in a Divided World.* Lanham, Md.: Rowman and Littlefield, 1999.

———. *Warpaths: The Politics of Partition.* New York: Hill and Wang, 1990.

Schechla, Joseph. "The Invisible People Come to Light: Israel's 'Internally Displaced' and the 'Unrecognized Villages.'" *Journal of Palestine Studies* 31:1 (October 2001): 20–31.

Schechtman, Joseph. *The Arab Refugee Problem.* New York: Philosophical Library, 1952.

Schechtman, Joseph B. *Population Transfers in Asia.* New York: Hallsby Press, 1949.

———. *On Wings of Eagles: The Plight, Exodus, and Homecoming of Oriental Jews.* New York: Thomas Yoseloff, 1961.

Scheid, Kirsten. "'This Illiterate Woman . . . She Talked to Us': A Summary and Evaluation." *Al-Jana* (May 1998): 50–54.

Schenker, David. "Is a Jerusalem Deal Enough for Peace?" *New York Post,* July 24, 2000.

Schiff, Benjamin N. *Refugees unto the Third Generation: U.N. Aid to Palestinians.* Syracuse: Syracuse University Press, 1995.

Schissler, Hanna. "Limitations and Priorities for International Social Studies Textbook Research." *The International Journal of Social Education* 4 (1989–90).

———. "Perceptions of the Other and the Discovery of the Self." In Volker R. Berghahn and Hanna Schissler, eds., *Perceptions of History: International Textbook Research on Britain, Germany and the United States.* Oxford: Berg, 1987.

Schumpeter, J.A. *Capitalism, Socialism and Democracy.* New York: Harper, 1976.

Schwartz, Thomas Alan. *America's Germany: John J. McCloy and the Federal Republic of Germany.* Cambridge, Mass.: Harvard University Press, 1991.

Segev, Tom. *1949: The First Israelis.* New York: The Free Press, 1986.

———. *One Palestine Complete: Jews and Arabs Under the British Mandate.* New York: Metropolitan, 2000.

———. *The Seventh Million: The Israelis and the Holocaust.* New York: Hill and Wang, 1993.

Sen, Sumit. "Stateless Refugees and the Right to Return: the Bihari Refugees of South Asia," pt. 1. *International Journal of Refugee Law* 11:4 (1999): 625–45; pt. 2, 12:1 (2000): 41–70.

Sengupta, Somini. "Ivory Coast Haven Turns Hostile for Liberians." *New York Times,* January 21, 2003.

Shafir, Gershon. *The Citizenship Debates: A Reader.* Minneapolis: University of Minnesota Press, 1998.

———. "Ideological Politics or the Politics of Demography: The Aftermath of the Six Day War." In Ian S. Lustick and Barry Rubin, eds., *Critical Essays in Israeli Society, Politics, and Culture,* 41–61. Albany: State University of New York Press, 1991.

————, and Yoav Peled. *Being Israeli: The Dynamics of Multiple Citizenship.* Cambridge: Cambridge University Press, 2002.

Shahar, David. *The State of Israel.* Civics textbook for junior high. (Hebrew) Rehovot: Idan, 2002.

Shapira, Anita. *New Jews, Old Jews* (Hebrew). Tel Aviv: Am Oved, 1997.

Shenhav, Yehouda. *The Arab Jews: Nationalism, Religion, and Ethnicity* (Hebrew). Tel Aviv: Am Oved, 2003.

————. "Ethnicity and National Memory: World Organization of Jews from Arab Countries (WOJAC)." *British Journal of Middle Eastern Studies* 29 (2002): 25–55.

————. "The Jews of Iraq, Zionist Ideology, and the Property of the Palestinian Refugees of 1948: An Anomaly of National Accounting." *International Journal of Middle East Studies* 31:4 (November 1999): 605–30.

————. "Kehilot ve-mahozot shel zikaron mizrahi" (Communities and districts of Mizrahi memory). Unpublished paper, Van Leer Institute and Tel Aviv University, 2000.

————. "The Phenomenology of Colonialism and the Politics of 'Difference': European Zionist Emissaries and Arab-Jews in Colonial Abadan." *Social Identities* 8:4 (2002): 1–23.

Shiblak, Abbas. *The Lure of Zion: The Case of the Iraqi Jews.* London: Al Saqi Books, 1986.

————. *Reintegration of the Palestinian Returnees.* Monograph No. 6. Ramallah: Shaml, 1997.

————. "Residency Status and Civil Rights of Palestinian Refugees." *Journal of Palestine Studies* 99 (spring 1996).

Shikaki, Khalil. "Results of Palestinian Survey Research Unit's Refugees' Polls in the West Bank/Gaza Strip, Jordan and Lebanon on Refugees' Preferences and Behavior in a Palestinian-Israeli Permanent Refugee Agreement." Press release, July 18, 2003, http://www.pcpsr.org/survey/polls/2003/refugeesjune03.html#findings.

————. "The Right of Return." *Wall Street Journal.* July 30, 2003, A12.

Shlaim, Avi. *Collusion Across the Jordan: King Abdullah, the Zionist Movement, and the Partition of Palestine.* New York: Columbia University Press, 1988.

————. *The Iran Wall: Israel and the Arab World.* New York: Norton, 2000.

Shohat, Ella. "Sprache in Speil: Erinnerugsframente einner Arabisched Juden." In Rafik Schami, *Angst in Eigenen Landen,* 84–95. Zurich: Nagel and Kimche, 2001.

Short, Ramsay. "Struggling to Create a Future for Women." *Daily Star,* March 18, 2003.

Shulewitz, Malka Hillel, and Raphael Israeli. "Exchanges of Populations Worldwide: The First World War to the 1990s." In Malka Hillel Shulewitz, ed., *The Forgotten Millions: The Modern Jewish Exodus from Arab Lands,* 126–41. London: Cassell, 1999.

Shvarzword, Joseph, and Michael Tur Kaspa. "Preserved Threat and Social Dominance as Determination of Prejudice toward Russian and Ethiopian Immigrants in Israel" (Hebrew). *Megamot* 4 (December 1997): 504–27.

Simeon, Richard. "Citizen and Democracy in the Emerging Global Order." In Thomas J. Coutchen, ed., *The Nation State in a Global/Information Era: Policy Challenge* (Kingston, Ontario: John Deutsch Institute for the Study of Economic Policy, 1997.

Slater, John. "Methodologies of Textbook Analysis." In Alaric Dickinson et al., eds., *International Yearbook of History Education,* vol. 1 (London: Woburn, 1995).

Sletten, Pal, and Jon Pedersen. *Coping with Conflict: Palestinian Communities Two Years into the Intifada.* Oslo: Fafo, 2003 (also www.fafo.no).

Slyomovics, Susan. *The Objects of Memory: Arab and Jew Narrate the Palestinian Village.* Philadelphia: University of Pennsylvania Press, 1998.

Smith, Anthony. *The Ethnic Origins of Nations.* Oxford: Verso, 1987.

Smith, R. "Reflections on Migration, the State and the Construction, Durability and Newness of Transnational Life." In *Soziale Welt Transnationale Migration* 12. Baden-Baden: Nomos 1998.

Smooha, Sami. *The Orientation and Politicization of the Arab Minority in Israel.* Haifa: University of Haifa, 1984.

Snyder, Timothy. "'To Resolve the Ukranian Problem Once and for All': The Ethnic Cleansing of Ukranians in Poland, 1943–1947." *Journal of Cold War Studies* 1:2 (1999).

Sofer, Arnon. *Israeli Demographics 2000–2020: Dangers and Opportunities.* Haifa: The National Security Studies Center, 2002.

Stern, Frank. *The Whitewashing of the Yellow Badge: Antisemitism and Philosemitism in Postwar Germany.* Oxford: Pergamon, 1992.

Stillman, Norman. "Middle Eastern and North African Jewries Confront Modernity: Orientation, Disorientation, Reorientation." In Harvey Goldberg, ed., *Sephardi and Middle Eastern Jewries: History and Culture in the Modern Era.* Bloomington: Indiana University Press, 1996.

Suleiman, Jaber. "The Current Political, Organizational, and Security Situation in the Palestinian Refugee Camps of Lebanon." *Journal of Palestine Studies* 29:1 (1999): 66–80.

Sultany, Nimer. *Citizens without Citizenship—Mada's First Annual Political Monitoring Report: Israel and the Palestinian Minority 2000–2002.* Haifa: Mada—The Arab Center for Applied Social Research, 2003.

Swedenburg, Ted. *Memories of Revolt: The 1936–1939 Rebellion and the Palestinian National Past.* Minneapolis: University of Minnesota Press, 1995.

———. "The Palestinian Peasant as National Signifier." *Anthropological Quarterly* 63 (1990): 18–30.

Swirski, Shlomo. *Seeds of Inequality* (Hebrew). Tel Aviv: Breirot, 1995.

Symonides, Janusz, ed. *Human Rights: New Dimensions and Challenges.* Aldershot: Ashgate, 1998.

Tabibyan, K. *A Journey to the Past: From the Middle Ages to Modern Times.* (Hebrew) Jerusalem: Ministry of Education and Culture and the Center for Educational Technology, 1999.

———. *Journey to the Past: The Twentieth Century.* History to ninth grade for the secular school. (Hebrew) Jerusalem: Ministry of Education and Culture and the Center for Educational Technology, 1999.

Takkenberg, Lex. *The Status of Palestinian Refugees in International Law.* New York: Oxford University Press, 1998.

Tamari, Salim. *Palestinian Refugee Negotiations: From Madrid to Oslo.* Washington, D.C.: Institute for Palestine Studies, 1996.

Tchernin, Velvl. "Kak prekrasno eto derevo: Ramyshlenya o sovremennoi izrail'-skoii literatute" (What a beautiful tree is that: Thoughts about modern Israeli literature). *Ierusalimskie khoiniki* (Jerusalem chronicles), www.rjews.net/gazeta/chernin.html.

Tetreault, Mary Ann. "Kuwait: The Morning After." *Current History* 91:561 (January 1992): 6–10.

Teveth, Shabtai. "The Palestine Arab Refugee Problem and Its Origins." *Middle Eastern Studies* 26 (1990): 214–49.

Timmons, Jeffry A., Leonard E. Smollen, and Alexander L.M. Dingee, Jr. *New Venture Creation: Entrepreneurship in the 1990s.* Homewood, Ill.: Irwin, 1990.

Torpey, John. "'Making Whole What Has Been Smashed': Reflections on Reparations." *The Journal of Modern History* 73:2 (June 2001): 333–58.

Totary, Mary. "The Political Attitude in a Divided Village." In *The Case of Western Barta'a/Eastern Barta'a.* Haifa: Galilee Center for Social Research, 1999.

Towes, J. E. "Salvaging Truth and Ethical Obligations from the Historicist Tide: Thomas Haskell's Moderate Historicism." *History and Theory* 38 (1999): 348–64.

Troquer, Yann Le. "Du Kowëit à Jordanie: Le Retour suspendu des Palestinians." *Revue d'études palestiniennes* 14 (winter 1998): 54–70.

———, and Rozenn Hommery Al-Oudat. "From Kuwait to Jordan: The Palestinians' Third Exodus." *Journal of Palestine Studies* 111 (spring 1999).

Tsimhoni, Daphne. "The Diplomatic Background to the Operation of the Immigration of Iraq's Jews 1950–1951" (Hebrew). In Yitzhak Avishur, ed., *Studies in the History and Culture of Iraqi Jewry*, 89–113. Or Yehuda: Center for the Heritage of Babylonian Jewry, 1991.

Uehara, Edwina. "Dual Exchange Theory, Social Networks, and Informal Social Support." *American Journal of Sociology* 96 (1990): 521–57.

Ugland, Ole Fr., ed. *Difficult Past, Uncertain Future: Living Conditions Among Palestinian Refugees in Camps and Gatherings in Lebanon.* Fafo report 409 (www.fafo.no), 2003.

United Nations High Commissioner for Refugees (UNHCR). http:www.unhcr.ch/cgi-bin/texis/vtx/statistics.

———. *Les Réfugiés dans le monde: Cinquante ans d'action humanitaire.* Paris: Edition Autrement, 2000.

United Nations Relief and Works Agency (UNRWA). *Report of the Commissioner-General of the United Nations Relief and Works Agency for Palestine Refugees in the Near East.* New York: United Nations General Assembly Official Records, October 2, 2001.

Uthman, Ibrahim Khalil. *Dayr al-Qasi: Zanbaqa al-Jalil al-awsat al-gharbi* (Dayr al-Qassi: The lily of midwest Galilee). Beirut: n.p., 2000.

Van Hear, Nicholas. *New Diasporas: The Mass Exodus, Dispersal and Regrouping of Migrant Communities.* London: University College London Press, 1997.

———. *Reintegration of the Palestinian Refugees.* Monograph no. 6. Ramallah: Shaml Publications, 1996.

Vieira de Mello, Sergio. "Guiding Principles on Internal Displacement." http://www.reliefweb.int/ocha_ol/pub/idp_gp/idp.html.

Voronel, Alexander. "Sub'ektivnye zametki" (Subjective notes). *Vesti-Okna* (October 9, 2003), 14.

Wade, Rahima. "Content Analysis of Social Studies Textbooks: A Review of Ten Years of Research." *Theory and Research in Social Education* 21 (1993).

Wain, K. "Different Perspectives on Evaluating Textbooks." In Hilary Bourdillon, ed., *History and Social Studies: Methodologies of Textbook Analysis.* Amsterdam: Swets and Zeitlinger, 1992.

Wakim, Wakim. "The 'Internally Displaced: Seeking Return within One's Own Land." *Journal of Palestine Studies* 31:1 (autumn 2001): 32–38.

Waldron, Jeremy. "Redressing Historic Injustice." *University of Toronto Law Journal* (winter 2002), Lexis.

———. "Superseding Historic Injustice." *Ethics* 103 (1992): 4–28.

Warner, Daniel. "The Refugee State and State Protection." In Nicholson and Twomey, eds., *Refugee Rights and Realities: Evolving International Concepts and Regimes.* Cambridge: Cambridge University Press, 1999, 253–68.

———. "Voluntary Repatriation and the Meaning of Returning Home: A Critique of Liberal Mathematics." *Journal of Refugee Studies* 7:2–3 (1994): 160–74.

Werbner, Richard. "Smoke from the Barrel of a Gun: Postwars of the Dead, Memory and Reinscription in Zimbabwe." In Werbner, ed., 1998.

——, ed. *Memory and the Postcolony: African Anthropology and the Critique of Power.* London: Zed, 1998.

Weymar, Paul. *Konrad Adenauer: The Authorized Biography.* London: Andre Deutsch, 1957.

Williams, Brian Glyn. "The Hidden Ethnic Cleansing of Muslims in the Soviet Union: The Exile and Repatriation of the Crimean Tatars." *Journal of Contemporary History* 37:3 (2002).

Williams, Raymond. *The Country and the City.* London: Hogarth, 1985.

Wolgast, Elizabeth H. "Why Justice Isn't an Ideal." In Wolgast, *The Grammar of Justice* 125–46. Ithaca, N.Y.: Cornell University Press, 1987.

World Bank. *Fifteen Months—Intifada, Closure, and Palestinian Economy.* Jerusalem: World Bank, 2002.

Ya'akobi, Danny. *A World of Changes.* (Hebrew) Jerusalem: Ministry of Education and Culture, 1999.

Yevtuh, Vladimir. "The Dynamics of Interethnic Relations in Crimea." In Natalia Panina et al., eds., *Sociology in Ukraine*, 401–12. Kiev: Institute of Sociology of the National Academy of Sciences of Ukraine, 2002.

Yiftachel, Oren. "Binui uma vahalukat hamerhav ba'etnokratiya hiyisraelit: Karka'ot ufe'arim 'adatiyim" (Nation-building and the allocation of space in the Israeli ethnocracy: Lands and ethnic differentiation). *Iyuni Mishpat*, 21:3 (1998): 637–65.

——. *Guarding the Vineyard: Majd Al-Kurum as a Parable.* Beit Berl: Institute for Israeli Arab Studies, 1997.

——, and Sandi Kedar. "Al otzma va-adamah: Mishtar hamakarke'ei in hayisraeli" (On land and power: Israeli land regime). *Theory and Criticism* 16 (spring 2000): 67–100.

Yisrael b'Aliyah: Two Years on the Political Map. Jerusalem: Yisrael b'Aliyah, 1998.

Zacher, Mark W. "The Territorial Integrity Norm: International Boundaries and the Use of Force." *International Organization* 55:2 (spring 2001): 215–50.

Zakay, Dan, Yechiel Klar, and Keren Sharvit. "Jewish Israelis on the 'Right of Return': Growing Awareness of the Issue's Importance." *Palestine-Israel Journal* 9:2 (2002): 58–66.

Zehr, Howard. *Changing Lenses: A New Focus for Crime and Justice.* Scottdale, Pa.: Herald, 1990.

Zenner, Walter P. *Minorities in the Middle: A Cross-Cultural Analysis* (Albany: State University of New York Press, 1991.

Zerubavel, Eviatar. *Social Mindscapes: An Invitation to Cognitive Sociology.* Cambridge, Mass.: Harvard University Press, 1997.

Zerubavel, Yael. *Recovered Roots: Collective Memory and the Making of Israeli National Tradition.* Chicago: University of Chicago Press, 1995.

Zilberg, Narspi, and Eliezer Leshem. "Imagined and Real Community: Russian-Language Press and Renewal of Communal Life in Israel of Immigrants from the CIS." *Hevra Ve-revakha* 1 (1997): 9–27.

Zureik, Elia. *Palestinian Refugees: An Annotated Bibliography Based on Arabic, English and Hebrew Source 1995–1999.* Ottawa/Ramallah: IDRC and Department of Refugee Affairs, 2000.

——. "Palestinian Refugees and Peace." *Journal of Palestine Studies* 24:1 (1994); 5–17.

——. "Palestinian Refugees and the Peace Process." Washington, D.C.: Institute for Palestine Studies, 1996. http://www.ciaonet.org/wps/zue01/.

————. *The Palestinians in Israel: A Study in Internal Colonialism.* London: Routledge and Kegan Paul, 1979.

————. "The Trek Back Home: Palestinians Returning Home and Their Problem of Adaptation." In Are Hovdenak et al., *Constructing Order: Palestinian Adaptations to Refugee Life.* Oslo: Fafo Institute for Applied Social Science, 1997.

————, and Salim Tamari, eds. *Reinterpreting the Historical Record: The Uses of Palestinian Refugee Archives for Social Science and Policy Analysis.* Jerusalem: Institute of Jerusalem Studies, 2001.

Zweig, Ronald W. *German Reparations and the Jewish World: A History of the Claims Conference.* London: Frank Cass, 2001.

Archives

Adalah, the Legal Center for Arab Minority Rights in Israel, http://www.adalah .org/eng/backgroundhistory.php. Details of *Association for Civil Rights in Israel vs. The Government of Israel* available at http://216.239.41.104/custom?q = cache: Wlu8ylATCH4J:www.adalah.org/features/opts/2977petition-eng.doc + associa tion + for + civil + rights + in + israel + v + the + government + of + israel&hl = en &ie = UTF-8.

Archives of Israeli Government, Ministry of Welfare, 94/2146, "Summary on the Activities of the Coordination Agency with the International Aid Organizations," September 1949). Israel Ministry of Foreign Affairs website. Copyright State of Israel, 1999, www.mfa.gov.il/mfa/error_db.asp?MFAH0iaa0.

Institute for Social and Political Research (Tel Aviv) poll, http://www.ispr/al1.html.

Israeli Central Bureau of Statistics (ICBS), http://www.cbs.gov.il/israel_in_ figures.

Israeli Defense Forces, archives.

Palestinian Liberation Organization Affairs, http://www.nad-plo.org/permanent/ refugees.html.

Shaml, Palestinian Diaspora and Refugee Centre, http://www.shaml.org.

Tami Steinmetz Center for the Study of Peace, "Peace Index" (Tel Aviv University, December 2000).

United Nations Conciliation Commission for Palestine.

United Nations High Commissioner for Human Rights, http://www.unhchr.ch.

United Nations Office for the Coordination of Humanitarian Affairs, Online Guiding Principles on Internal Displacement, http://www.reliefweb.int/ocha_ol/.

United States Committee for Refugees, http://www.refugees.org.

United States Department of State, United States National Archives and Records Administration.

Periodicals

Agence France-Presse News Service
Haaretz
The Hindu
The Independent
International Herald Tribune
Jerusalem Post
Los Angeles Times
Maariv
Newsweek

New York Times
Russkii Zhurnal, www.russ.ru
Sunday Telegraph
Vesti
Yediot Ahronot

Contributors

Elazar Barkan is Professor of History and Cultural Studies at Claremont Graduate University in Los Angeles, California, and the Director of the Institute for Historical Justice and Reconciliation. He is the author of *The Guilt of Nations: Restitution and Negotiating Historical Injustices* (2000), *Claiming the Stones/Naming the Bones: Cultural Property and the Negotiation of National and Ethnic Identity* (edited with Ronald Bush, 2003), and *Taking Wrongs Seriously: Apologies and Reconciliation* (edited with Alexander Karn, forthcoming).

Michael R. Fischbach is Professor of History at Randolph-Macon College in Ashland, Virginia. He is author of *Records of Dispossession: Palestinian Refugee Property and the Arab Israeli Conflict* (2003) and *State, Society, and Land in Jordan* (2000), and was an associate editor of *The Encyclopedia of the Modern Middle East and North Africa*, 2nd edition (2004). His next project will focus on Mizrahi Jewish claims for property abandoned in Arab countries after 1948.

Sari Hanafi is a sociologist and Director of the Palestinian Refugee and Diaspora Centre, Shaml. He is the author of numerous journal articles and book chapters on economic sociology and network analysis of the Palestinian diaspora; relationships between diasporas and centers; and the sociology of new actors in international relations.

Amal Jamal is a Senior Lecturer in the Political Science Department at Tel Aviv University. He has published several articles on Palestinian and Israeli politics. His book on Palestinian elites and the politics of contention is forthcoming. Another book, on civil society, the media, and democracy in Palestine, is also forthcoming. His research interests are political and communication theory; state building and civil society; and minority politics and democratic theory.

Laleh Khalili, Lecturer in political studies at the School of Oriental and African Studies, is currently completing a manuscript on nationalist practices of commemoration among Palestinian refugees.

Ze'ev Khanin earned his Ph.D. from the Institute for African Studies, USSR Academy of Sciences, Moscow, and completed his postdoctoral studies at St. Anthony's College, University of Oxford. He currently lectures in political studies at Bar-Ilan University, Israel. His most recent publications include the books *Documents on Ukrainian Jewish Identity and Emigration, 1944–1990* (2003) and *The "Russians" and Power in the State of Israel* (2004), as well as articles in Israeli, East European, and Third World politics.

Ann M. Lesch is Dean of Humanities and Social Sciences at the American University in Cairo. She was previously Professor of Middle East Politics at Villanova University and US Director of the Palestinian American Research Center. She has published numerous books and articles on the politics of Palestine, Sudan, and Egypt and is on the advisory committee for Human Rights Watch/Middle East.

Ian S. Lustick is Professor of Political Science at the University of Pennsylvania, where he holds the Bess W. Heyman Chair. His previous books include *Unsettled States, Disputed Lands: Britain and Ireland, France and Algeria, Israel and the West Bank/Gaza* (1993) and *Right-sizing the State: The Politics of Moving Borders* (edited with Brendan O'Leary and Thomas Callaghy, 2001). He has published widely on Arab-Israeli affairs, with special focus on Jerusalem, non-Jewish Israelis, settlements, and American foreign policy, and has pioneered the use of agent-based modeling computer simulation techniques for the study of comparative and Middle Eastern politics.

Ilan Pappé is a Senior Lecturer in the Department of Political Science at Haifa University, Israel, and the chair of the Emil Touma Institute for Palestinian Studies in Haifa. He is the author of *The Making of the Arab-Israeli Conflict* (1994) and *A History of Modern Palestine* (2003). His *Middle East in the Twentieth Century* will come out in 2005.

Elie Podeh is Head of the Department of Islam and Middle East Studies at the Hebrew University of Jerusalem and editor of *The New East* (Hamizrah Hechadash), the Hebrew journal of the Israeli Oriental Society. He has published several books and articles on inter-Arab relations and the Arab-Israeli conflict, such as *The Arab-Israeli Conflict in the Israeli History Textbooks, 1948–2000* (2002) and *Rethinking Nasserism: Revolution and Historical Memory in Egypt* (edited with Onn Winckler, 2004).

Nadim N. Rouhana holds the Henry Hart Rice Chair of Conflict Resolution at the Institute for Conflict Analysis and Resolution at George Mason University. He is also the founding director of the Arab Center for Applied Social Research (MADA) and an associate of the Center for International Affairs at Harvard University. He is the author of numerous articles on political psychology and ethnic conflict, with specific reference to Israel and the Palestinians. He is the author of *Palestinian Citizens in an Ethnic Jewish State: Identities in Conflict* (1997).

Gershon Shafir is Professor of Sociology at the University of California, San Diego. He is the author of *Land, Labor, and the Origins of the Israeli-Palestinian Conflict, 1882–1914* (1989), the editor of *The Citizenship Debates* (1998), and coeditor with Alison Brysk of *People Out of Place: Globalization, Human Rights and the Citizenship Gap* (2004). His book coauthored with Yoav Peled, *Being Israeli: The Dynamics of Multiple Citizenship* (2002), won the Middle Eastern Studies Association's Albert Hourani Award for outstanding book in 2002.

Yehouda Shenhav is a professor in the Department of Sociology and Anthropology of Tel Aviv University, where he also served as department chair between 1995 and 1998. Shenhav is the Editor of *Theory & Criticism* and serves as Senior Editor of *Organization Studies*. Among his books are *Manufacturing Rationality* (1999, 2002), *The Organization Machine* (1995), *The Arab Jews: Nationalism, Religion and Ethnicity* (2003), and *Coloniality and the Postcolonial Condition* (2004).

Salim Tamari is Director of the Institute of Jerusalem Studies and Professor of Sociology at Birzeit University. He is currently Visiting Professor at the University of California at Berkeley (2005) and Editor of *Hawliyyat al Quds* and *Jerusalem Quarterly*. His recent publications include *Jerusalem 1948* (2001), *Mandate Jerusalem in the Memoirs of Wasif Jawahariyyeh* (with Issam Nassar, 2004), and *The Mountain against the Sea: Studies in Palestinian Urban Culture* (forthcoming).

Index

Page numbers in italics indicate tables in the text.